For more information:

www.gmathacks.com

Also by the author:

Total GMAT Verbal

GMAT 111: Tips, Tricks, and Tactics

Total GMAT Math

Total GMAT Math

Jeff Sackmann / GMAT HACKS

August 2010

Contents

CONTENTS

1   Introduction

Over the last ten years, I've taught dozens of classes and hundreds of students, all with the aim of helping people get the highest GMAT score they possibly can. During that time, I've worked with materials from large test-prep companies, questions published by the test-maker, and a variety of supplements that I've devised myself. But still, despite the proliferation of test-prep materials on the market, people still come to me asking if there's something else out there, a single resource that contains everything an aspiring MBA needs to know to ace the Quantitative portion of the GMAT.

Now there is. Total GMAT Math is that single comprehensive resource. In this book, you'll find tutorials on content and strategy, plus tidbits on time management and weeks worth of relevant practical material. You may well want to seek out additional material (and this book will tell you where to look), but you don't have to.

Unlike many other GMAT math books, this resource presumes almost no math knowledge. I start from the basics of manipulating fractions and simple algebraic equations, and steadily work up to the most complex content on the test. There may be times when you feel the need to read over a section three or four times (in fact, I encourage it!) but you'll never be forced to consult another book just to get through a section of this one.

My favorite part of this guide, especially when comparing it to the other options out there, is the combination of content and practice. For each of about forty sections, covering everything from mental math to simultaneous rate calculations to sequences, you'll have three different perspectives on the material:

First, an exposition. This explains the principles behind the content, the basic facts and techniques you need, and the ways in which the material will come up in test questions.

Second, a series of exercises. These questions are not in the GMAT format, but are designed to make sure that you understood the techniques that you read about in the first part.

Finally, a series of GMAT-like practice questions. There are between 5 and 10 practice items per section, totalling 300 problems. In most sections, some questions are identified as "Challenge" questions. These are more difficult and take you a step beyond the other practice questions. As you might expect, the easier content areas have no challenge questions, while the more difficult ones have almost all challenge questions.

The benefits of this structure, I think, are obvious. Unlike most books, in which you do a random sequence of questions every day, learning a technique then forgetting about it for a week, this one gives you test-like review for every single concept that the GMAT math section tests. Every one! While this book doesn't contain every single possible question that could arise on the GMAT, it does have a representative cross-section. When you finish each content area, you'll be well-equipped to take on those questions the next time you see them.

As you can probably tell, I'm very excited to release this book into the world. If it already existed, I would be using it with all of my students; heck, some of my students could probably have gotten by with only the book. With a well-structured, thorough resource like this one, you won't need to rely so much on classes or tutoring. Sticking to a steady preperation schedule is enough. For more on how to structure your study time, turn to the next section.

2   How to Use This Book

First, the basics. If you're just starting out, I recommend working through the book in order, starting with the first chapter. You don't need to do the chapters in order, but it's an effective approach.

If you've been studying for some time, you might find some of the chapters to be too elementary. I recommend reviewing them anyway, but feel free to skim until you find material that you are not as comfortable with. Working through the drill questions in every section is good way of determining where you need to focus your efforts.

Each content chapter is accompanied by several practice questions. The explanations are in the back of the book.

Next, let's discuss effective study techniques. The key to any successful GMAT training regimen, whether you're aiming for a 450 or a 750, is consistency. Too many students try to cram their studying into weekends, or the week before the test, or their occasional days off. Preparation of that sort is better than nothing, but it is far inferior to doing things the right way.

I've written extensively on my website about how to make the most of your study time. I won't recap all of that here; instead, I encourage you to browse gmathacks.com for more information. But I will review one simple concept: quality is more important than quantity. Too many students think their goal should be to do as many practice problems as possible, often numbering in the thousands. That is simply wrong.

Much better is to really learn from every practice problem you do. The GMAT not only tests your content knowledge, it tests how quickly you can recognize question types and deploy that knowledge. So, if you can't do a question correctly, or you can't complete it in two minutes or so, you might as well have gotten it wrong. Your preparation should reflect that. If you get a question right, but it takes you five minutes (even three!) you aren't done with that question. It should go on a list for review the next day.

In that vein, I often tell people that if they do (and understand, and can complete in two minutes) every question in The Official Guide to GMAT Review, they'll be ready for the test, and will likely score in the 90th percentile. I've rarely been wrong. 400 math questions is more than enough. Similarly, if you understand all the content, complete all the drills, and can comfortably and speedily complete the 300 practice questions in this book, you'll be nearly ready for the GMAT quantitative section.

Consistency is the name of the game. It's better to spend an hour a day for an entire week than to spend twelve hours on the weekend. With that in mind, do everything you can to carve out a bit of study time every single day (at worst, every other day). If you don't, you'll find yourself stressing out, spending a great deal of your study time catching up, and not making as much progress as you'd like. Trust me: I've watched it happen to too many people.

No matter how busy your life is, you can carve out a half-hour or an hour a day for the GMAT. If you can do that, your test preparation shouldn't take longer than two or three months. It may mean sneaking away from the office during lunch or setting the alarm thirty minutes earlier, but if you really care about getting into the business school of your choice, you can make that sacrifice. If you do that consistently, you will reach your goal.

And that, in a nutshell, is how to work through this book. Don't try to speed through it: read each section carefully, re-reading whenever you're not sure you understand something. Work through the examples on paper, actually writing down the steps as you read them. When you find a question that gives you trouble the first time around, mark it and return to it the following day. You can do a lot of work in an hour a day. In fact, I suspect that many of the sections of this book–including the content review, drill, and GMAT-like problems–can be completed in about an hour.

There's no magic bullet to GMAT success, but this book is designed to help you make your consistent study time that much more efficient.

3   GMAT Math Strategies

It's a little premature to start talking about strategies before getting to the content itself, but it's useful to have a framework in mind before learning rule after rule, technique after technique. Most of the strategies I'll discuss have more to do with knowing the test in general than dealing with specific questions.

In fact, many students preparing for the GMAT put far too much emphasis on "tricks." There's no substitute for learning the material; tricks are secondary, if they're necessary at all. I make something of an exception to that rule by focusing extensively on mental math, but it's better to think of that as a more efficient approach to arithmetic than some back-door strategy.

The first important GMAT math strategy, one that almost no one uses to its full potential, has to do with scratchwork. Remember that, while most of your practice will be with a book, the test itself will take place on a computer screen. That adds an extra layer of complexity: not only do you have to decipher the question, but you have to literally move it from the screen to your scratch paper. The strategy:

Write it down!

More specifically, actively take notes while you're reading the question. Most test-takers read the question, think about it for a few seconds, then read it again, then write down the important data. That's a huge waste of time. Instead, as the question gives you information (say, x is negative, or 22 of the members of a certain health club are men), write it down. That way, by the time you've read through the entire question, your notes are complete.

This is especially helpful on word problems. If you jot down all the data you're given in a word problem, by the time you're done, you can stop staring at the screen. You've got all the information on your scratch paper, and you may well have already reduced the problem to some simple algebra.

While this strategy applies to questions at all difficulty levels, it's all the more crucial on tough problems. Tough GMAT problems don't rely on some secret extra layer of content: they test the same stuff the easy and medium questions do, but with more complexity. Instead of one probability, there's three. Maybe the inequality has a lot of negative numbers. There are hundreds of ways problems can get more complex, but if you're writing down all the data along the way, you're much more likely to spot how to break the problem down into simpler component parts.

The second strategy is similar to the first. As I've said, difficult GMAT questions don't use some mysterious additional content. By the time you finish working through this book, you will know at least 99% of the underlying math the GMAT will ever test. Of course, that doesn't mean that every question you see from this point on will be easy, just that you will, at some level, know how to do it. That's at the heart of this strategy:

Look for what you know.

If a word problem appears to be completely foreign, do a quick scan through your knowledge of GMAT topics. Could it be a combinations problem? Maybe it has to do with a prime factorization? If it's a diagram, would it help to split the figure into two triangles, objects you know much more about? By the time you take the test, you will have that underlying knowledge: it's just a matter of matching the correct part of it to the question at hand.

Let's narrow our focus now to **Data Sufficiency (DS)**. DS scares a lot of people because of its unfamiliarity: one student of mine recently joked that he felt like he missed that day in school. For better or worse, everybody missed that day in school. To get ahead of the pack, your first DS-specific strategy is to internalize the details of the question type.

First, be absolutely clear on what each part of the question represents. To take an example:

Is x positive?
(1) $x^2 = 16$
(2) $x^2 - 6x + 8 = 0$

Every DS problem starts with a question: one that you can't answer without more information. Sometimes the question will give you a bit of information, like:

If x is an integer, is x positive?

Even with that additional background information, the question itself will never be enough. When you jot down the question, make sure to retain the question mark:

"$x > 0$?"

If you forget the question mark, you'll soon forget it should be there. Remember that you don't know whether x is positive: that's what you're trying to determine. Don't fall into the common trap of mixing up what you know with what you'd like to find out.

The statements ((1) and (2)) are, by contrast, things that you do know. When you're evaluating statement (1), for example, you should be asking yourself the following question:

"If $x^2 = 16$, is x positive?"

Note that the statement is assumed to be true: that's the way the question works. However, we jumped ahead a little bit. Before reaching that step, it's important to simplify the statement as much as possible. In this case, we can solve for x. If $x^2 = 16$, x is equal to 4 or -4. So, to rephrase our question:

"If $x = 4$ or $x = -4$, is x positive?"

Our answer: we don't know. Thus, (1) is insufficient.

Follow the same procedure for statement (2), ignoring for the time being the information you received from statement (1). Simplify the equation, which results in $x = 2$ or $x = 4$. Now our question is:

"If $x = 2$ or $x = 4$, is x positive?"

Our answer: yes. Since the answer is always "yes," (2) is sufficient. If the answer were "no," it would also be sufficient. On DS questions where we're looking for a "yes" or "no" answer, "always yes" or "always no" is sufficient, while "sometimes" or "I don't know" is insufficient.

We still don't have an answer choice. That's more information to internalize. The answer choices to every DS question are the same, and are as follows:

- (A) Statement (1) ALONE is sufficient, but statement (2) alone is not sufficient.
- (B) Statement (2) ALONE is sufficient, but statement (1) alone is not sufficient.
- (C) BOTH statements TOGETHER are sufficient, but NEITHER statement ALONE is sufficient.
- (D) EACH statement ALONE is sufficient.
- (E) Statements (1) and (2) TOGETHER are NOT sufficient.

[Note: in the body of this book, Data Sufficiency questions don't include the answer choices. You may want to print out this page for reference. On the test itself, these choices will be presented along with each Data Sufficiency item.]

In the previous example, our answer is (B). Note that two of the answers rely on combining the statements. If both statements are insufficient when taken individually, we combine them and see if together they are enough information. Consider a variant on the example we just looked at:

What is the value of x?

(1) $x^2 = 16$
(2) $x^2 + 6x + 8 = 0$

Statement (1) tells us that $x = 4$ or $x = -4$; we don't know which one is the value of x. The same applies to statement (2), in which x could be -2 or -4.

When we combine them, the only possible value of x is -4, since that's the only value of x that satisfies both equations. In this case, the correct choice is (C).

Eventually, you'll know those choices inside and out. An additional angle to consider is that, as soon as you evaluate one statement, you can eliminate choices:

If Statement (1) is sufficient, (B), (C), and (E) are eliminated.
If Statement (1) is insufficient, (A) and (D) are eliminated.
If Statement (2) is sufficient, (A), (C), and (E) are eliminated.
If Statement (2) is insufficient, (B) and (D) are eliminated.

Especially when you're first starting out, keep the answer choices, as well as these rules, handy. Each time you evaluate a statement, see which choices you can eliminate. Within a week or two of steady practice, you'll find you don't have to refer to them anymore.

Beyond the basics of knowing the test, the most valuable strategy you can use on Data Sufficiency is this:

Simplify the question.

In the examples we've looked at so far, that doesn't apply. There's nothing you can do to make "Is x negative?" simpler. But in many cases, breaking down the question is key to understanding the problem at all. Take this example, which is very similar to an actual GMAT question:

"Is $x - y + z > x + y - z$?"

That looks quite complicated, and appears to demand that you learn something about three variables. But, as you'll learn in one of the first chapters of the book, any time you have the same variable on both sides of an equation (or inequality, in this case), you can further simplify it.

For one thing, you can subtract x from both sides, leaving you with:

"Is $-y + z > y - z$?"

Next, you can add y to both sides:

"Is $z > 2y - z$?"

Further, add z to both sides:

"Is $2z > 2y$?"

Finally, divide by 2:

"Is $z > y$?"

Once we've simplified the question, we can completely forget about the original phrasing. x turned out to be completely irrelevant. We can pretend that the test itself asked the question "Is $z > y$?" because that question is precisely equivalent to the one the test asked, in the same way that $x = 4$ and $2x = 8$ are the same equation.

Finally, a word about time management. This book is more focused on mastering the content than on tweaking your approach to save a few seconds, but it's important to keep an eye on the clock from day one. The test gives you 37 math questions in a timed section of 75 minutes, allowing you about 2 minutes per question. Problem Solving questions (about $\frac{2}{3}$ of the total) take a bit longer than Data Sufficiency questions, so you'll want to aim for a bit more than 2 minutes for PS and less than 2 minutes for DS.

As you practice, keep a stopwatch handy. Early on, don't try to complete each question in 2 minutes, just track how long each item takes you. If a question takes three minutes or more, mark it for review. If you can't do it in 2 minutes or less, you don't understand the material well enough. As test day approaches, start trying to complete each question in 2 minutes the first time you see it, occasionally making educated guesses as necessary. It's better to miss a question here and there to save time than getting it right and taking 5 or 6 minutes–and thus jeopardizing questions later on the test–in the process.

4   Basic Facts and Definitions

Depending on whom you ask, there are anywhere from 10 to 100 or more formulas you should memorize to excel on the GMAT. I haven't undertaken a count, but I suspect that the underlying philosophy is flawed. What's a better use of your time: doing GMAT problems or sifting through a pile of flashcards for the 27th time? Of course, you will learn plenty of concepts that are new to you, and it's important that they stick.

What you should do, then, is maintain your own list of things you need to learn. Everyone has a few elementary formulas that they can never remember, perhaps a few holes in the multiplication table. Maybe you always forget that 1 isn't prime, or that 0 is an integer. Maybe you can't recall the difference between a factor and a multiple, or what the side ratio of a $45 : 45 : 90$ triangle is.

My point is simple: you need to make your own list. That way, you won't waste time on the things you do know, and you'll spend all of your memorization time on things you need to learn. Be sure to never stray far from actual practice questions: it's great to memorize details like pythagorean triplets and the work formula, but those facts are only as useful to you as the degree to which you can apply them. That's why every section of this book is accompanied by several realistic GMAT practice questions.

5 Mental Math

Given all of complicated math problems on the GMAT, it's a bit of a surprise where most people make their mistakes. Watching students do math problems, I see the most mistakes at a stage that they learned in elementary school: simple multiplication and division. Especially long division. Mistakes are even more common when decimals are involved.

In a way, that makes sense. For one thing, when you set up a two- or three-digit multiplication problem, you go through the steps automatically, one digit at a time. You aren't thinking about the numbers themselves, you're just doing each individual step by rote. So if you end up with an extra zero, or you carry a 2 instead of a 1, you don't ever notice the mistake. Long division invites even more of this type of problem.

There's a mental math technique for every one of these problems. Some of them save more time than others, and a few of them are particularly useful on the GMAT. There are plenty of books on the market about mental math, so I won't exhaustively cover every last detail. But I will focus on a few approaches that will pay dividends on the GMAT.

One note, before we get started. These techniques come with something of a learning curve. You won't immediately be much faster. In fact, you might slow down a little bit at first. That's to be expected. Remember, you've been doing multiplication and division the "old-fashioned way" for years, perhaps decades. Whatever the flaws of those methods, you've had plenty of practice. You won't need years to learn mental math strategies, but it will take more than a few hours. Most importantly, force yourself to use these techniques when practicing: that's the most effective way to incorporate them into your arsenal.

The first two strategies aren't so much about different ways to do math; instead, they are about avoiding math. First, whenever possible, approximate. Some GMAT test items even ask you to approximate. If you see the words "approximately" or "closest to" in the question, round up, round down, do whatever it takes to make the math easier. If you're not approximating in those cases, you're wasting your time.

But those aren't the only times you can approximate. When the test doesn't give you a key word like that, let the answer choices be your guide. If the choices are very close together, such as $48.00, $48.50, $49.00, etc., approximation isn't a very good idea. But if they are more dispersed, such as $40.00, $47.50, $54.00, etc., you can round off your numbers a bit.

One way you can get away with approximating more than usual is by keeping track of which way you've rounded. For instance, to take a grossly oversimplified example: if you're dividing 475 by 10, you may see that it's easier just to divide 500 by 10. If you do that, jot down a note that you've rounded up. Therefore, whatever number you end up with will be too high; the actual answer will be lower. So, when you get an answer of $50, and the closest choices are $47.50 and $54.00, you know the correct choice must be $47.50, not $54.00.

The other non-math math strategy involves putting off the calculations. To take a simple example, pulled straight from a question in the Official Guide, let's say you've interpreted the problem and set up the following equation:

$$\frac{15}{100} = \frac{x}{45}$$

You may immediately recognize that there's plenty of simplification you can do here. That's true, but we'll get to that strategy in a bit. For now, look at the next step:

$$15(45) = 100x$$

I guarantee you that the next step of a large percentage of GMAT test takers is to multiply 15 by 45. That's not the end of the world, but it's time consuming. Instead, isolate x:

$$x = \frac{15(45)}{100}$$

Now, rather than multiplying two two-digit numbers, you can start cancelling out common terms. I'm getting a bit ahead of myself, but you can break those terms down to some of their factors:

$$x = \frac{3(5)(5)(9)}{4(5)(5)} = \frac{3(9)}{4} = \frac{27}{4}$$

As it turns out, the most involved calculations you have to do are some factoring of common numbers and 3 times 9. Not bad, compared with 15 times 45.

Situations like this will arise more often than you expect. Not only that, but when you start looking for them, they come up even more. Like many of the techniques I'll describe in this chapter, it's up to you to try it out every time you think it might prove useful: in this case it's easy and risk-free. If you wait to do the math, the worst-case scenario is that you end up having to do the arithmetic you would've done in the first place.

As I suggested a moment ago, another way to avoid clumsy arithmetic is by aggressively simplifying fractions. For instance, when you set up the previous example like this:

$$\frac{15}{100} = \frac{x}{45}$$

you may recognize that $\frac{15}{100}$ is equivalent to $\frac{3}{20}$. That makes life a lot easier. Again, this is something that you'll get better at in direct proportion to how much you do it. You probably know off the top of your head that 15 and 100 are multiples of 5, but you may not instantly recognize, for instance, that 51 and 78 are multiples of 3. Factoids like the latter pair come in handy, too, and if you do enough GMAT questions with factoring and simplification in mind, you'll memorize those as well.

Percents are a great time to avoid math. Decimal arithmetic is especially error-prone, so it's important to have some tricks up your sleeve for those. You probably know how to quickly find 10% of something: just move the decimal point one digit to the left:

10% of 96 is 9.6

10% of 0.03 is 0.003

10% of 1.2 million is 120,000

Similarly, it's easy to find 1%: just find 10% of 10%, or move the decimal point two digits to the left:

1% of 96 is 0.96

1% of 0.03 is 0.0003

1% of 1.2 million is 12,000

Here's the good part: just about any percent you need to calculate on the GMAT can be easily deduced from some combination of 10s and 1s:

20%: double 10% of the number

5%: half of 10% of the number

15%: 10% plus 5%

30%: triple 10% of the number

You can even use this technique to find trickier percents:

16%: 10% plus 5% plus 1%

9%: 10% minus 1%

89%: the number minus 10% minus 1%

There's a limit to the effectiveness of this method, of course. I would never do something like this to find 77% of a number. On the other hand, it's rare that the GMAT will ask you to find 77%; 75%, 80%, and 90% are much more common. When the percents aren't round numbers, they tend to be small, like the examples given above.

I'll add a few more assorted tricks. Any time you need to multiply by 5, multiply by 10 and then divide by 2:

$$78(5) = 78(\tfrac{10}{2}) = \tfrac{780}{2} = 390$$

If you prefer, you can reverse the order: divide by 2 then multiply by 10:

$$78(5) = 78(\tfrac{10}{2}) = 39(10) = 390$$

A similar approach works for dividing by 5: divide by 10 and multiply by 2:

$$\tfrac{630}{5} = \tfrac{630(2)}{10} = 63(2) = 126$$

You can multiply by 9 using a variation of the percent method I explained above. Multiply the number by 10 and then subtract the number from the result:

$$17(9) = 17(10 - 1) = 170 - 17 = 153$$

While that technique is most useful with 9's, it's usable with just about any number. If you're multiplying by something cumbersome, see if you can break it up into two less cumbersome parts, such as:

$$12(21) = 12(20 + 1) = 240 + 12 = 252$$

or:

$$13(39.5) = 13(40 - 0.5) = 520 - 6.5 = 513.5$$

Finally, virtually any division can be done (or at least approximately closely) with a technique I call "nearest neighbor." It's especially useful when dividing large numbers by small, familiar ones, such as (just picking numbers at random) 252 by 7.

Here's how it works. If the denominator is a small number, you can probably come up with a slew of multiples. If the denominator is 3, you know that 30, 60, 120, 150, 210, 540, etc. are all multiples–you could come up with a nearly endless list. (If you can't, practice: it's an important skill.) So, find a number that's nearby, and count by multiples until you get close to the numerator.

That's easier explained in terms of an example. Say you want to figure out 162 divided by 3. You can use the divisibility rule for 3 (discussed in the factors chapter later in the book) to determine that 162 is in fact divisible by 3, but that doesn't give you an answer. So, you start by finding a nearby multiple that you know, such as 150, which is 3(50). 162 is 12 away from 150, so you need to add 4 more 3's ($4 \times 3 = 12$) to get to 162. Thus, 162 divided by 3 is $50+4 = 54$. If you don't know that 12 is 4 3's, you can count by 3's:

  150 (50), 153 (51), 156 (52), 159 (53), 162 (54)

The same approach works even if there's a remainder. If you were looking for 163 divided by 3, you would use the same steps to find that 162 is 54 times 3, and recognize that 163 is one greater. That's a remainder of one, or an added fraction of $\frac{1}{3}$.

Just like your nearest exit, which may be behind you, your nearest familiar multiple may be greater than the number. Say you want to divide 343 by 7. You could use 280 (40 times 7), but 350 (50 times 7) is much closer.   350 is exactly 7 greater than 343, so the answer is $50 - 1 = 49$.

As you may have noticed, there are many possible techniques for nearly every arithmetic problem you'll encounter. I've said it before, but it bears repeating: you're only going to learn them if you try them, and the learning curve may not be all that welcoming in the early stages. Expect to struggle a bit at first, and eventually you'll find yourself doing calculations like these in your head, with fewer errors, much faster than ever before.

6 Mental Math: Drill

1. Find the following percents using the mental math techniques described in this chapter:
    a. 10% of 196
    b. 5% of 120
    c. 20% of 95
    d. 15% of $42.00
    e. 16% of 2100

2. Simplify each of the following fractions without using long division:
    a. $\frac{180}{12}$
    b. $\frac{175}{25}$
    c. $\frac{(13)(24)}{(12)(52)}$
    d. $\frac{(210)(4)}{(28)(5)}$

3. Calculate each of the following using the techniques described in this chapter:
    a. 9.2×5
    b. 47×5
    c. $235 \div 5$
    d. $144 \div 5$
    e. 13×9
    f. 24×9

4. Divide each of the following using the "nearest neighbor" method:
    a. $147 \div 7$
    b. $252 \div 3$
    c. $242 \div 11$
    d. $595 \div 3$
    e. $400 \div 7$

(Answers and explanations for these questions are in the back of the book.)

7   Algebra: Fractions

Many of the things we'll discuss in this first section are elementary concepts; however, I've worked with many students who could use a lot of practice on them. While there aren't very many questions on the GMAT that focus 100% on fractions, the skills you use to work with fractions come into play on a broad range of questions. Perhaps more than any other single topic in this book, fractions are the backbone of the math on this test.

First, it's usually important to keep fractions in their most simplified form. For instance, it would be better to work with $\frac{1}{2}$ than $\frac{11}{22}$. They are the same number, but the first is much more straightforward. To simplify a fraction, look for common factors in the numerator (the top of the fraction) and the denominator (the bottom). For instance, if you were working with the fraction $\frac{11}{22}$, you may realize that both 11 and 22 are divisible by 11. So, rewrite each term of the fraction:

$$\frac{1(11)}{2(11)} =$$

Then "cancel out" the 11s on the top and bottom of the fraction. (We'll look more at the mechanics of cancelling when we get to multiplication and division of fractions.) We can do the same with fractions containing variables, such as $\frac{xy}{x}$. Both the numerator and denominator of that fraction are divisible by x, so the x cancels out:

$$\frac{xy}{x} = \frac{x(y)}{x(1)} = \frac{y}{1} = y$$

Things get more complicated when the numerator or the denominator contains addition or subtraction. Let's say you wanted to simplify the following fraction:

$$\frac{5x+7}{2x}$$

Since two terms in the fraction ($5x$ and $2x$) are divisible by x, you might be tempted to cancel out the x. You can't do that. When cancelling terms (dividing both the top and bottom by that term), you must divide the entire numerator or the entire denominator. By contrast, it is possible to simplify this fraction:

$$\frac{5x+7x}{2x} = \frac{x(5+7)}{x(2)} = \frac{5+7}{2} = \frac{12}{2} = \frac{2(6)}{2(1)} = \frac{6}{1} = 6$$

The key operation in that process is called "factoring:" factoring out an x from $5x$ and $7x$. That's covered in more detail below in the section on simplifying algebraic expressions.

A little more about simplifying fractions: most of the fractions we encounter in our daily lives have values of less than one, such as $\frac{1}{2}$, $\frac{3}{4}$, and $\frac{1}{10}$. However, it's perfectly acceptable for a fraction to have a value greater than one, as in $\frac{3}{2}$, $\frac{111}{5}$, or $6\frac{1}{6}$. The first two of those are called "improper fractions." They have only a numerator and a denominator, and the numerator is larger than the denominator, indicating that the number is greater than one. The last of the three is called a "mixed number," a mix of a whole number (6) and a fraction $\left(\frac{1}{6}\right)$.

When you're working with fractions, especially adding, subtracting, multiplying, or dividing, it's almost always better to work with an improper fraction than with a mixed number. With that in mind, let's see how to convert from one to the other. The mixed number $6\frac{1}{6}$ is really shorthand for $6 + \frac{1}{6}$. As we'll see in a moment when we discuss adding and subtracting fractions, you can only do so when there's a common denominator, meaning that we need to convert 6 to $\frac{36}{6}$. So:

$$6\frac{1}{6} = 6 + \frac{1}{6} = \frac{36}{6} + \frac{1}{6} = \frac{37}{6}$$

To reverse the process–to turn an improper fraction into a mixed number–start by dividing the denominator into the numerator. For instance, with the fraction $\frac{111}{5}$, 5 goes into 111 22 times, with a remainder of 1. So, the resulting mixed number is $22\frac{1}{5}$, where the whole number part is the quotient (the whole-number solution to the division problem), the numerator is the remainder, and the denominator is the original denominator. If there is no remainder, there should be no fractional part.

Adding and subtracting fractions works by the same method. Given two fractions, such as $\frac{1}{2}$ and $\frac{1}{3}$, you can't add or subtract them until you rewrite them in some way so that they share a common denominator. For instance, both 2 and 3 are divisible by 6, so rewrite each one to have a denominator of 6:

$$\frac{1}{2}\left(\frac{3}{3}\right) = \frac{3}{6}$$
$$\frac{1}{3}\left(\frac{2}{2}\right) = \frac{2}{6}$$

We'll discuss methods for multiplying fractions in a moment; for the time being, it's sufficient to recognize that $\frac{3}{6}$ and $\frac{2}{6}$ are equivalent to $\frac{1}{2}$ and $\frac{1}{3}$. Now, we can add the fractions by adding the numerators and keeping the denominator the same:

$$\frac{3}{6} + \frac{2}{6} = \frac{5}{6}$$

If $\frac{5}{6}$ could be simplified, we'd do that, but since it can't be, we're done. The same procedure works for subtracting fractions:

$$\frac{3}{6} - \frac{2}{6} = \frac{1}{6}$$

The key part of the process is finding a common denominator. I'll cover the concept of "least common multiple" in more detail in the chapter on multiples below, but in the meantime, it's sufficient to know that you can always find a common denominator by multiplying the two denominators.

Then, once you've determined the common denominator, multiply each fraction by 1 (in this case, $\frac{3}{3}$ or $\frac{2}{2}$) so that you're still working with the same fraction, but the denominator is different. Once the denominators are the same, add the numerators.

Multiplying fractions, as we've already seen, involves multiplying the numerators and multiplying the denominators. For instance, to multiply $\frac{1}{7}$ and $\frac{2}{5}$, multiply 1 and 2, multiply 7 and 5, and the first answer over the second answer:

$$\frac{1}{7} \times \frac{2}{5} = \frac{1 \times 2}{7 \times 5} = \frac{2}{35}$$

Again, if the solution could be simplified, we'd simplify it, but in this case, it's in its most basic form. As usual, we can do the same sort of thing with variables:

$\frac{a}{b} \times \frac{c}{d} = \frac{a \times c}{b \times d} = \frac{ac}{bd}$

Dividing fractions is almost exactly the same as multiplying them, with one twist. Dividing is the same as multiplying by the reciprocal of the second fraction. The "reciprocal" is just an upside-down version of the fraction. For instance, the reciprocal of $\frac{2}{3}$ is $\frac{3}{2}$, and the reciprocal of $\frac{x}{y}$ is $\frac{y}{x}$. So, let's see an example in action:

$\frac{5}{6} \div \frac{2}{3} = \frac{5}{6} \times \frac{3}{2} = \frac{5 \times 3}{6 \times 2} = \frac{15}{12} = \frac{3(5)}{3(4)} = \frac{5}{4}$

More commonly on the GMAT, you'll divide fractions when the problem is given to you in one giant fraction, like this:

$\frac{\frac{3}{8}}{\frac{1}{2}} = \frac{3}{8} \div \frac{1}{2} = \frac{3}{8} \times \frac{2}{1} = \frac{3 \times 2}{8 \times 1} = \frac{6}{8} = \frac{2(3)}{2(4)} = \frac{3}{4}$

Eventually, you'll recognize all sorts of shortcuts to get through problems like that in about half as many steps. But until you are completely comfortable with the mechanics of these processes, do all the steps. It's important both to ensure that you're doing them properly, and that you fully understand the way they work.

8 Algebra: Fractions: Drill

1.   Simplify the following fractions:
   - a. $\frac{3}{15}$
   - b. $\frac{8}{48}$
   - c. $\frac{17}{51}$
   - d. $\frac{9}{72}$
   - e. $\frac{(8)(7)}{21}$
   - f. $\frac{(6)(22)}{(11)(12)}$
   - g. $\frac{2x}{3x}$
   - h. $\frac{4x+x}{10}$
   - i. $\frac{xy}{xy^2}$

2.   Convert the following to mixed numbers:
   - a. $\frac{13}{4}$
   - b. $\frac{7}{3}$
   - c. $\frac{101}{5}$

3.   Convert the following to improper fractions:
   - a. $4\frac{1}{6}$
   - b. $2\frac{9}{10}$
   - c. $11\frac{1}{2}$

4.   Calculate the following:
   - a. $\frac{1}{5} + \frac{2}{5}$
   - b. $\frac{1}{3} + \frac{1}{6}$
   - c. $\frac{x}{3} + \frac{x}{4}$
   - d. $\frac{7}{3} - \frac{1}{12}$
   - e. $\frac{1}{3} - \frac{1}{4}$
   - f. $\frac{x}{2} - \frac{y}{3}$
   - g. $\frac{1}{6} \times \frac{5}{8}$
   - h. $\frac{2}{3} \times \frac{9}{4}$
   - i. $\frac{4}{5} \div 2$
   - j. $\frac{1}{2} \div \frac{1}{4}$

(Answers and explanations for these questions are in the back of the book.)

9 Algebra: Fractions: Practice

1. When $\frac{1}{10}$ of $\frac{1}{10}$ of 5,000 is subtracted from $\frac{1}{10}$ of 4,000, the difference is

    (A) 400
    (B) 350
    (C) 320
    (D) 40
    (E) 35

2. The number $2 - \frac{1}{3}$ is how many times the number $1 - \frac{1}{3}$?

    (A) 2
    (B) 2.5
    (C) 3
    (D) 3.5
    (E) 4

3. $\dfrac{50 - 5(24 \div 6)}{\frac{1}{3}} =$

    (A) 10
    (B) 30
    (C) 50
    (D) 70
    (E) 90

4. What is the value of $\frac{1}{m} + \frac{1}{n}$?

    (1) $m = 5$
    (2) $\frac{m+n}{mn} = \frac{7}{10}$

5. In the fraction $\frac{r}{s}$, where r and s are positive integers, what is the value of s ?

    (1) The least common denominator of $\frac{r}{s}$ and $\frac{1}{5}$ is 10.
    (2) $s < 10$

6. As z increases from 98 to 99, which of the following must increase?

    I. $4 - 3z$
    II. $4 - \frac{3}{z}$
    III. $\frac{4}{3 - z^2}$

    (A) I only
    (B) II only
    (C) I and II
    (D) I and III
    (E) II and III

7. $\left(\frac{1}{3}\right)^3 - \left(\frac{1}{3}\right)\left(\frac{1}{6}\right) =$
   (A) $-\frac{1}{27}$
   (B) $-\frac{1}{54}$
   (C) $\frac{1}{54}$
   (D) $\frac{1}{27}$
   (E) $\frac{1}{6}$

8. $2 + \dfrac{2}{2 + \dfrac{2}{2 + \frac{2}{3}}} =$
   (A) $\frac{8}{11}$
   (B) $\frac{3}{2}$
   (C) $\frac{30}{11}$
   (D) $\frac{22}{3}$
   (E) $\frac{15}{2}$

9. If $xy \neq 0$, is $\frac{1}{x} + \frac{1}{y} = 4$?
   (1) $4 - \frac{1}{y} = 2.5$
   (2) $5x = 2$

(Answers and explanations for these questions are in the back of the book.)

10   Algebra: Decimals

I don't much like working with decimals. There may be no other type of number that causes more people to make more careless calculation errors. Thus, one of the main focuses of this chapter is converting decimals to other types of numbers that are easier to work with.

First, you can always convert a decimal to a fraction. Sometimes this is more convenient than others, but you can always do it. Here are several common equivalencies that you should memorize, if you don't know them already:

$$\frac{1}{2} = 0.5$$
$$\frac{1}{3} = 0.\overline{33}$$
$$\frac{2}{3} = 0.\overline{66}$$
$$\frac{1}{4} = 0.25$$
$$\frac{3}{4} = 0.75$$
$$\frac{1}{5} = 0.2$$
$$\frac{2}{5} = 0.4$$
$$\frac{3}{5} = 0.6$$
$$\frac{4}{5} = 0.8$$
$$\frac{1}{6} = 0.1\overline{66}$$
$$\frac{5}{6} = 0.8\overline{33}$$
$$\frac{1}{7} \approx 0.14$$
$$\frac{1}{8} = 0.125$$
$$\frac{3}{8} = 0.375$$
$$\frac{5}{8} = 0.625$$
$$\frac{7}{8} = 0.875$$
$$\frac{1}{9} = 0.\overline{11}$$

If you need to convert a decimal that isn't on that list, remember that decimals are defined by 10s: that is, 0.01 is one-tenth of 0.1 which is one-tenth of 1. So, every time you move the decimal point one place to the right, multiply the denominator by 10. As an example:

$$0.0234 = \frac{0.234}{10} = \frac{2.34}{100} = \frac{23.4}{1000} = \frac{234}{10000}$$

Converting that particular decimal to a fraction doesn't make your life much easier, but with practice, you'll learn to quickly recognize when converting to a fraction will be an effective use of your time.

Another way you can make decimals into friendlier numbers is by using scientific notation. As with fraction conversions, it's based on the idea that decimals are, at their simplest, just a bunch of 10s. Scientific notation, if you don't recall it from high school science courses, is a way to express any number with the help of a term like this: 10^{-4}. Instead of comparing numbers like

0.0234 and 240,000, every number is converted into something between 1 and 10, then multiplied by 10 to some power.

Let's look again at 0.0234. If you move the decimal place four spaces to the right, the number becomes 234. Moving the decimal four spaces to the right is equivalent to multiplying by $10 \times 10 \times 10 \times 10$, or 10^4. So, if you wanted to get back from 234 to 0.0234, you'd divide by 10^4. So, as we saw when discussing fraction conversions:

$$0.0234 = \frac{234}{10000} = \frac{234}{10^4}$$

As you'll learn in the exponents chapter in a little while, dividing by a positive exponent is the same as multiplying by the same negative exponent, so:

$$\frac{234}{10^4} = 234 \times 10^{-4}$$

You can use the same method to make very large numbers simpler, as well. Let's say you're given the number 170 million. 170 million is the same as 170,000,000, so to change 170 million into 1.7, you have to move the decimal point eight times. Since you're moving it in the opposite direction of the 0.0234 example, the exponent will be positive, not negative:

$$170,000,000 = 1.7 \times 10^8$$

Note that it doesn't really matter exactly what number we convert to. We could just as easily convert 0.0234 into 23.4 or 170,000,000 into 17. Let the context of the question determine your end goal.

11 Algebra: Decimals: Drill

1. Convert each of the following to decimals:
   a. $\frac{6}{5}$
   b. $\frac{16}{25}$
   c. $\frac{38}{200}$
   d. $\frac{9}{30}$
   e. $\frac{125}{80}$

2. Convert each of the following to fractions:
   a. 0.12
   b. 0.95
   c. 0.48
   d. $2.8\overline{3}$
   e. 0.0032

3. Convert each of the following to scientific notation:
   a. 0.0102
   b. 0.00072
   c. 0.98
   d. 1.6 million
   e. 5,200,000,000

4. Convert each of the following to decimal format:
   a. 3.6×10^{-3}
   b. 6.0×10^{-6}
   c. 7.25×10^{8}
   d. 1.5×10^{6}
   e. 5.6×10^{-1}

(Answers and explanations for these questions are in the back of the book.)

12 Algebra: Decimals: Practice

11. $0.2 + 0.2^2 + 0.2^3 =$

   (A) 0.222
   (B) 0.2408
   (C) 0.248
   (D) 0.6
   (E) 1.4

12. Is the number x between 0.3 and 0.6 ?

   (1) $425x < 85$
   (2) $170x < 85$

13. Any decimal that has only a finite number of nonzero digits is a terminating decimal. For example, 16, 0.73, and 3.178 are three terminating decimals. If m and n are positive integers and the ratio $\frac{m}{n}$ is expressed as a decimal, is $\frac{m}{n}$ a terminating decimal?

   (1) $75 < m < 90$
   (2) $n = 8$

14. $\frac{32}{125} =$

   (A) 0.244
   (B) 0.256
   (C) 0.265
   (D) 0.312
   (E) 0.320

15. Is u less than 0.44?

   (1) u is less than $\frac{4}{11}$.
   (2) u is greater than $\frac{4}{13}$.

16. What is the 24th digit to the right of the decimal point in the decimal form of $\frac{8}{11}$?

   (A) 5
   (B) 4
   (C) 3
   (D) 2
   (E) 1

17. Of the following, which is greatest?

    (A)   0.5

    (B) $\frac{0.5}{5}$

    (C)   0.05

    (D) $(0.5)^2$

    (E) $\frac{1}{0.5}$

(Answers and explanations for these questions are in the back of the book.)

13 Algebra: Simplifying Expressions

Nearly every topic covered in the Algebra section of this book is about simplifying algebraic expressions in some way or other. However, before you can proceed to the more difficult topics, there are a few basics to cover first.

The fundamental concept behind simplification is the acronym PEMDAS. You may recall it from junior high or high school; it is a pneumonic device to remember the order of operations. Here's what the letters in PEMDAS stand for:

P:	Parentheses
E:	Exponents
M:	Multiplication
D:	Division
A:	Addition
S:	Subtraction

It really isn't quite as strict as all that: it doesn't matter whether you do multiplication before division or addition before subtraction. The key is that you follow that general order, evaluating what's inside any parentheses before moving on to exponents, which you must do before moving on to multiplication and division, which is followed by addition and subtraction.

Let's start with a simplistic example to see the order of operations in action:
$4(2 + 3)^2 - (4 - 2)$
First, evaluate what's inside the parentheses:
$4(5)^2 - (2)$
Now, calculate the exponent:
$4(25) - (2)$
Now, do the multiplication:
$100 - (2)$
Finally, subtract:
$100 - 2 = 98$
Of course, it will get much harder when variables are involved, and when there are exponents inside parentheses and parentheses themselves inside parentheses, but it's that basic process that you will use on everything from the very easiest to the most difficult algebra problems.

When you are working with variables, it is of the utmost importance to combine terms as much as possible. For instance, the following expression is not in the most convenient form:
$2(x - y) + 3x - 4y$
Since x and y both appear in multiple places, the expression can be further simplified. Start by multiplying:
$2(x - y) = 2x - 2y$ (we'll discuss the mechanics behind this in a moment)
$2x - 2y + 3x - 4y$

Since the order of terms doesn't matter when you're adding or subtracting them, you can rearrange the expression so that the x's and y's are grouped together. When you do so, be extra careful to retain the signs: don't think of the subtraction signs as subtraction, think of them as negative signs attached to the terms that follow them.

$2x + 3x - 2y - 4y$

Now you can add the x's and the y's:

$2x + 3x = 5x$

$-2y - 4y = -6y$

So, the most simplified version of the expression we started with is:

$5x - 6y$

One side note before going any further: you'll see a lot of references in this book to "expressions" and "equations." It may appear that the terms are being used interchangeably, but they aren't. An expression is a value (perhaps including variables, such as $4x - 6y$). An equation has an equals sign (such as $4x - 6y = 28$). An equation has two expressions, one on each side of the equals sign. When you start simplifying and solving equations, you'll be using many of these same skills, but with a few supplemental twists that allow you to work with both sides of an equation simultaneously.

One way to simplify expressions that comes up incessantly on the GMAT is what's known as the distributive law. In abstract terms, it looks like this:

$a(b + c) = ab + ac$

Basically, if you're multiplying two things together and one of them is in two parts (like the $b + c$ of the example above), you can simplify by multiplying the first term by each part of the second. That's what we did a couple of paragraphs ago in the following step:

$2(x - y) = 2x - 2y$

You'll do it a lot more, too.

A little trickier is the distributive law in reverse. Let's say that, instead of starting with $2(x - y)$, you started with $2x - 2y$. For whatever reason (perhaps it's part of equation and you want to isolate the value of $x - y$), you wanted it to look different. Since there's a 2 in both terms, you can factor it out, as follows:

$2x - 2y = 2(x) - 2(y) = 2(x - y)$

I haven't done a thorough study of the matter, but I suspect that you'll use that step even more often than you'll use the more straightforward application of the distributive law I explained in the previous paragraph. In general, if two terms are added or subtracted and they share a common term (such as 2, or x, or whatever), you want to consider factoring that term out. Here's a more complicated example:

$x^2y + y^2x$

Both terms have at least one x and at least one y in them. Reducing the exponents to multiplication turns the expression into the following:

$(x)(x)(y) + (y)(y)(x)$

Since it doesn't matter what order terms are in when you're multiplying them (just like addition, in this respect), you can rearrange them to more clearly see the common terms:

$(x)(y)(x) + (x)(y)(y)$

Both terms have an $(x)(y)$, so you can factor that out:

$(x)(y)(x + y)$

The more common way of writing that would look like this:

$xy(x + y)$

The GMAT rewards mental flexibility, so you'll want to keep in mind this possibility, but not blindly execute it every single time the occasion arises. Sometimes it's better to leave the expressions in the form you receive them; other times it's necessary to do all the factoring possible. The more practice problems you do (and fully understand), the more readily you'll recognize which is which.

14 Algebra: Simplifying Expressions: Drill

1. Evaluate each of the following expressions:
   a. $2 \times 3 + 4 \times 5$
   b. $4 - 6 \div 2 - 1$
   c. $3(5 - 2^2) + 4^2$
   d. $\frac{5 \times 3^2}{4^2 - 1}$

2. Distribute each of the following:
   a. $3(x - y)$
   b. $-(a + b)$
   c. $3m(n + 3m)$
   d. $-2x(y - z)$
   e. $a^2(a - a^2)$
   f. $n(n + 1)$

3. Factor each of the following:
   a. $4m + 4n$
   b. $xy + 2xz$
   c. $6a + 3b + 12c$
   d. $a^3 - 2a^2 - 8a$
   e. $8jkm - 12kmn$

4. Simplify each of the following expressions:
   a. $4x + 2(x - 1) - x$
   b. $10 - 3(x - y) + x(1 - y)$
   c. $a^2 + a(2 + a) - 2$
   d. $m(n + p) - p(m - n) - n(m + p)$
   e. $y^2 - 2y(y + 1) - 4y$

15   Algebra: Simplifying Expressions: Practice

21.   If $x > 1,000$, then the value of $\frac{2x+3}{3x+2}$ is closest to:

   (A) $\frac{2}{3}$
   (B) $\frac{3}{4}$
   (C) $\frac{5}{6}$
   (D) 1
   (E) $\frac{3}{2}$

22.   If $a = -6$ and $b = 6$, what is the value of $a - b + 2a^2$?

   (A)   -84
   (B)   -60
   (C)   60
   (D)   72
   (E)   84

$\left(\frac{x}{x-1}\right)^2$

23.   If $x \neq 1$, and if x is replaced by $-x$ everywhere in the expression above, then the resulting expression is equivalent to:

   (A) $\left(\frac{x}{x-1}\right)^2$
   (B) $\left(\frac{x}{1-x}\right)^2$
   (C) $\frac{x^2}{x^2-1}$
   (D) $\frac{x^2}{1-x^2}$
   (E) $\left(\frac{x}{x+1}\right)^2$

24.   Is $\frac{x}{p}(p^2 + q^2 + r^2) = xp + yq + zr$?

   (1) $q^2 = r^2$
   (2) $yq = zr$

25.   Is $ax + bx = 7$?

   (1) $x = 6$ and $a + b = 1$.
   (2) $24ab = x$

26.   What is the value of x ?

   (1) $2x + 4 = 2(2 + x)$
   (2) $2x + 3 = 3(2 + x)$

16   Algebra: Linear Equations

To solve linear equations, you'll use many of the techniques I outlined in the previous chapter on simplifying algebraic expressions. A linear equation is just two expressions separated by an equals sign, so working with the expressions themselves is at least half the battle.

Before we get any further, a bit of terminology. Most people are familiar with the term "linear equation" but don't know exactly what it means. A linear equation (as opposed to some other sort of equation, such as a quadratic equation, which you'll see later in the book) is an equation in which the variables aren't modified by exponents or roots. So, the following is a linear equation:

$3(y + 2) - 4y = 7$

While this not:

$2(y - 3) + y^2 = 4$

Here's why: when you graph an equation with no exponents or roots on the coordinate plane, the resulting graph is a line. When you graph an equation with roots or exponents, you get something with curves. One of the major implications of that is that, with no roots or exponents, there's only one possible value for a variable in a linear equation. In a non-linear equation, there may be two possible values for a variable, as in this example:

$y^2 = 4$

since y could be either 2 or -2.

For this chapter and the next, you don't have to worry about anything else: we'll be focusing solely on linear equations.

The fundamental concept behind solving linear equations (in fact, any kind of equation) is this: you can do anything you want to manipulate one side of the equation, so long as you do it to both sides. For instance, let's say you're working with the following example:

$4y + 3 = 3y$

and you want to solve for y. To do that, you need to combine all the y's together, and to get the y's together, you can't have y's on both sides of the equals sign. So, you can subtract $4y$ from both sides:

$$4y + 3 = 3y$$
$$-4y \qquad -4y$$
$$0 + 3 = -y$$

Now you have the much simpler equation $3 = -y$. You still don't have the value of y, though. To find that, you'll need to do something to both sides of the equation again. This time, subtraction or addition won't do the trick; you'll have to multiply. To turn $-y$ into y, you'll have to multiply $-y$ by -1. You can do that, but only if you multiply the other side of the equation by -1, as well:

$$3 = -y$$
$$-1(3) = -1(-y)$$

$-3 = y$

And you're done!

In that example, we got an early glimpse of the other important concept in solving linear equations: isolate the variable. If you're solving for x, you need to get all the x's on one side and everything else on the other side. That's what we did: there were terms with a y in them on both sides of the equation, but we manipulated it so that all the y's were on one side, leaving everything else on the other. Let's see one more:

$\frac{x}{2} + 3 = \frac{3}{2} + x$

This adds a new level of complexity: we haven't talked about simplifying or solving algebra with fractions yet. While it is a bit trickier, we use all of the same techniques. Since we'd rather have an x than an $\frac{x}{2}$, we can multiply the left side by 2. Of course, when we multiply the left side by two, we have to do the same to the right side:

$2(\frac{x}{2} + 3) = 2(\frac{3}{2} + x)$

Using the distributive law described in the previous chapter, multiply those out:

$2(\frac{x}{2}) + 2(3) = 2(\frac{3}{2}) + 2(x)$

$x + 6 = 3 + 2x$

Now, we need to isolate x. Let's get all the x's over to the right side:

$x + 6 = 3 + 2x$
$-x \qquad\qquad -x$
$6 = 3 + x$

Finally, let's get all the non-x terms on the left side:

$6 = 3 + x$
$-3 \quad -3$
$3 = x$

One way the GMAT will make these techniques more difficult is by requiring you to work with more than one variable at the same time. Let's say you're given an equation like this;

$x + y = x(y + z)$

and you're asked to solve for z. The way they'll phrase it is as follows: "Solve for z in terms of x and y." All that means is that your goal is to get z on one side of the equation and that, when you do so, x and y will be on the other. The method you'll use to solve for z is no different that the one we've used to solve for x and y in the previous examples:

$x + y = x(y + z)$

$x + y = xy + xz$ (multiply out the parentheses)

$x + y - xy = xz$ (move all the non-z terms to the left side)

$\frac{x+y-xy}{x} = \frac{xz}{x}$ (divide both sides by x)

$z = \frac{x+y-xy}{x}$ (complete the division)

Depending on the question, you might need to simplify the answer a bit more. Note that two of the terms in the numerator have x's in them. If you separate the fraction into three component parts, you can change the form and simplify quite a bit:

$$\frac{x+y-xy}{x} = \frac{x}{x} + \frac{y}{x} - \frac{xy}{x} = 1 + \frac{y}{x} - y$$

As I've said before, the GMAT rewards mental flexibility. It may not be necessary to take that last step, but if you get to an answer and it doesn't look anything like the answer choices, it may be that you need to simplify the answer, or change it to a different form.

One technique you'll find useful is called "cross-multiplication." It's really just a shortcut, a combination of a couple of the steps we've discussed so far. But because it comes up so often, it's important to mention it here. You can use it any time you're solving an equation in which both sides are fractions. It comes up most often when you're working with ratios. Here's an example:

$$\frac{x}{12} = \frac{8}{3}$$

Using the techniques above, you would isolate x by multiplying both sides by 12:

$$12\left(\frac{x}{12}\right) = 12\left(\frac{8}{3}\right)$$

$$x = \frac{12(8)}{3} = 32$$

In this example, cross-multiplication doesn't save you a lot of time, but it does avoid some of the messier work with fractions. To cross-multiply, multiply the numerator of each side by the denominator of the other side, and set the two products equal to each other. In this case, the result looks like this:

$$3x = 8(12)$$

Then, to solve, you would divide both sides by 3:

$$\frac{3x}{3} = \frac{8(12)}{3}$$

$$x = 32$$

Mathematically, the two methods are identical. But usually, cross-multiplying saves you a step, or at least lets you work with numbers in a slightly easier format. As with all the shortcuts I cover in this book, experiment with the shortcut and the more traditional approach; depending on context, either one could prove most efficient.

17 Algebra: Linear Equations: Drill

1. True or False? For each of the following, is this is a linear
    equation?
    a. $y = 2x + 7$
    b. $y^2 = 3 - 4x$
    c. $y = x^2 + x - 12$
    d. $y = x$
    e. $y = 4$

2. Solve for x:
    a. $9 = 2x + 5$
    b. $4 - x = x - 4$
    c. $\frac{x}{3} = \frac{2}{5}$
    d. $5 = \frac{x}{4} + \frac{1}{2}$
    e. $\frac{1}{4} = \frac{18}{x}$
    f. $3(2 - x) = 2(x - 3)$
    g. $\frac{x+2}{3} = 5x$
    h. $\frac{6}{1-x} = \frac{2}{x+3}$

3. Solve for k in terms of m:
    a. $m = 2k$
    b. $m - 3 = \frac{k}{4}$
    c. $km = 12$
    d. $k - 4 = km + 2$
    e. $m(2 + k) = k(5 - m)$
    f. $\frac{6}{11} = \frac{m}{2k}$
    g. $\frac{3m}{2k} = \frac{3-m}{1-k}$

18   Algebra: Linear Equations: Practice

31.   If -2 is 4 more than y, what is the value of $\frac{y}{2}$?

  (A)   -1
  (B)   -2
  (C)   -3
  (D)   -4
  (E)   -6

32.   If $x - y = y + 2x - 1$, what is the value of x?

  (1) $x = 1 - 2y$
  (2) $x = y + 1$

33.   If $\frac{5}{0.125+x} = 8$, then $x =$

  (A)   0.05
  (B)   0.5
  (C)   0.625
  (D)   1.25
  (E)   2.0

34.   If $\frac{3+x}{1-x} = x$, what is the value of x^2 ?

  (A)   -3
  (B)   -1
  (C)   0
  (D)   1
  (E)   3

35.   What is the value of y ?

  (1) $\frac{1}{y^2} = 4$
  (2) $4 - y = y + 3$

36.   If $n = 1$ and $\frac{m-n}{p} = 2$, which of the following is NOT a possible value of m ?

  (A)   -2
  (B)   -1
  (C)   0
  (D)   1
  (E)   2

$$y = mx - 5$$

37.   In the equation above, m is a constant. If $y = 16$ when $x = 7$,
        what is the value of y when $x = 16$?

     (A)   13
     (B)   23
     (C)   33
     (D)   43
     (E)   53

19   Algebra: Systems of Equations

When you have more than one variable, you generally need more than one equation to solve for those variables. The general rule is as follows:

If you have n variables, you need n linear equations to solve for those variables (a "system" of n equations)

Before we go any farther, a few definitions and exceptions: a "linear" equation is an equation without any exponents or variables in the denominator of fractions. For instance, $x = y - 4$ is a linear equation, while $x = y^2 - 4$ is not. However, if you are dealing with a word problem where there are no possible negative values (for instance, if y is the side of a triangle), then an equation with an exponent of 2 may still be solvable. Unfortunately, there's no hard and fast rule for this.

Finally, a linear equation does not need to have all of the variables in it: if your two variables are x and y and and your two equations are $x = 3$ and $y = -2$, that's enough information to solve for the two variables. (Obviously, in this case!)

There are two methods of solving systems: combination and substitution. Many of these questions show up in data sufficiency, so it is enough simply to recognize that you can solve; you don't have to go through the mechanics. It's important, however, that you've done enough examples so that you immediately recognize those cases where you could solve, even if you don't have to in that particular case.

Let's start by looking at combination. When you have multiple equations, you can add them. For instance:

$x - y = 4$
$2x + y = 8$

Add the equations just as you would add multiple-digit numbers:

$x + 2x = 3x$
$-y + y = 0$
$4 + 8 = 12$
$3x + 0 = 12$
$x = 4$

Note that, in this case, the y's cancelled out. That's the goal.

Usually it won't be that convenient; however, you can manipulate one of the equations so that they do cancel out. For instance:

$3x - 4y = 14$
$5x + 2y = 6$

In this case, if you double the second equation, you'll have a $4y$ in one and a $-4y$ in the other:

$2(5x + 2y) = 2(6)$

$10x + 4y = 12$

Now combine the two equations as you did above:

$3x + 10x = 13x$

$-4y + 4y = 0$

$14 + 12 = 26$

$13x = 26$

$x = 2$

You can always do this; however, you probably won't use this method on more than 20% of systems of equations. In general, if a question isn't set up for you to easily use this approach (i.e., you only need to do minimal adjustments, as in the two examples so far)), use substitution instead.

The other method for solving systems of equations is substitution. With substitution, you take one equation and substitute it into the other. In it's simplest form, it works like this:

$2x + y = 7$

$y = 3$

Substitute the second equation into the first:

$2x + (3) = 7$

$2x = 4$

$x = 2$

You can do the same steps even if the second equation has mutiple variables in it:

$3x + 2y = 13$

$x = 5 - y$

Again, plug in the value of x from the second equation into the first equation:

$3(5 - y) + 2y = 13$

$15 - 3y + 2y = 13$

$15 - y = 13$

$15 - 13 = y$

$y = 2$

Once you find one of the variables, you can plug it into either of the equations to find the other(s):

$x = 5 - y$

$y = 2$

$x = 5 - (2)$

$x = 3$

Usually, one of the equations will be simpler than the others; by all means, use that one!

Typically, the equations aren't laid out quite so nicely for you as the examples I've shown so far. First, you may have to rearrange one of the equations. For instance, let's say instead of $x = 5 - y$, you were given $x + y = 5$. You would recognize that you need at least one of the equations set equal to one of the variables. In other words: $x = $ something or $y = $ something. Rearrange $x + y = 5$ to be $x = 5 - y$, then it can be plugged in.

This next tip isn't something to obsess over, but it can save you some time: If you're solving for one variable, substitute the other variable. Notice that in the last example, we substituted the value of x into the other equation. When we solved, we ended up finding the value of y. If we had substituted the value of y into an equation, we would've ended up with a value of x. If time were not a constraint, it wouldn't matter: once you find one variable, you can find them all. However, time is a constraint, so you want to be as efficient as possible in getting to the variable you want.

You can use these same techniques with systems of three or more variables. You'll occasionally see one with three variables on the GMAT; you'll very very rarely encounter more than three. Technically, the rule from the beginning is as follows:

If you have n variables, you need n distinct linear equations to solve for those variables.

Obviously, having $x + y = 4$ and $x + y = 4$ isn't enough. Beware that, in data sufficiency, the GMAT will give you two equations that look different, but will be same. For example:

$x + y = 4$

$3y = 12 - 3x$

Divide the second equation by 3, and you have $y = 4 - x$. Move the x over, and it's $x + y = 4$. The same thing.

20 Algebra: Systems of Equations: Drill

1. Solve the following systems of equations using the combination method:

   a. $3x + 2y = 7$ and $x - 2y = 9$
   b. $5a - b = 6$ and $b = 4$
   c. $m + 2n = 13$ and $3m + 2n = 21$
   d. $\frac{y}{3} + z = 17$ and $y - 3z = -3$

2. Solve the following systems of equations using the substitution method:

   a. $x - 5y = 3$ and $3x - y = 37$
   b. $4x + 4y = 12$ and $3x + 5y = 13$
   c. $\frac{x}{2} - \frac{y}{3} = 2$ and $\frac{x}{3} + y = 13$
   d. $3a + 4b = 5$ and $18 + b = 2a$

3. Solve the following systems of equations using whichever method you prefer:

   a. $\frac{b}{4} = a + 1$ and $a = 1$
   b. $3(m + 2) = n$ and $2m + n = 6$
   c. $50x + 65y = 21,500$ and $x + y = 400$
   d. $\frac{x+y}{x-y} = -5$ and $\frac{5x}{2} = 3y - 4$

4. Solve the following three-variable systems of equations:

   a. $2x + y = 1$, $2y + z = 1$, and $z = -9$
   b. $x - y = 1$, $y - z = 3$, and $x + z = 4$
   c. $3a = b + 4$, $b = 11 - c$, and $c = 2a$
   d. $3q = m + p$, $\frac{m}{p} = \frac{q}{8}$, and $\frac{m}{2} = \frac{p}{3} + \frac{q}{4}$

5. True or False: For each of the following, are the equations equivalent?

   a. $x + y = 6$ and $y = 6 + x$
   b. $7 - 2z = -y$ and $y - 2z = 7$
   c. $\frac{a+b}{4} = 9$ and $a = 36 - b$
   d. $m = 4 - n$ and $3(m - n) = 12$

21 Algebra: Systems of Equations: Practice

41. If $2y + 4 = 0$ and $3y + 4z = -2$, what is the value of z ?

(A) -2
(B) -1
(C) 0
(D) 1
(E) 2

42. A certain floor mat is three times as long as it is wide. If its perimeter is 12 feet, then its dimensions in feet are

(A) $\frac{3}{2}$ and $\frac{9}{2}$
(B) $\frac{5}{3}$ and $\frac{10}{3}$
(C) 2 and 4
(D) 3 and 6
(E) $\frac{3}{4}$ and $\frac{9}{4}$

43. What is the value of $r - s$?

(1) $r - \frac{s}{3} = 13$
(2) $\frac{r}{3} - s = -1$

44. What is the value of $\frac{x}{3} + \frac{y}{3}$?

(1) $\frac{x-y}{2} = 6$
(2) $\frac{x+y}{2} = 9$

45. What is Walter's age now?

(1) Walter's brother Zachary is now twice as old as Walter was exactly five years ago.
(2) The positive difference between Walter's and Zachary's ages is less than three.

46. If Ferdinand, Quentin, and Zamir have a total of $28, how much money does Ferdinand have?

(1) Ferdinand has $3 less than Quentin, who has more money than Zamir does.
(2) Quentin has $5 more than Zamir, who has less money than Ferdinand does.

22 Algebra: Quadratic Equations

Quadratic equations are algebraic equations that look something like this:

$x^2 + 6x + 9$.

More generally speaking, they come in the following form:

$ax^2 + bx + c$, where a, b, and c are all constants.

However, you don't need to think about them this abstractly very often. Usually they'll look more like the first example than the second.

Making things easier still, almost all of the quadratic equations you'll see on the GMAT have no coefficient before the x^2. That is, in the first term, ax^2, a is usually one. It's much easier to work with an equation like this:

$x^2 + 4x + 3$

than an equation like this:

$3x^2 + 4x + 1$

Very occasionally, you will be given a quadratic where the value for a isn't 1, but we'll discuss those special cases below.

The key concept when it comes to working with quadratic equations is commonly known as the "FOIL" method. It (along with its reverse) is the most straightforward way to solve a quadratic equation. First, recognize the other form that quadratic equations appear in:

$x^2 + 6x + 9 = (x + 3)(x + 3)$

You can always rewrite a quadratic in the form of the right half of the equation. In fact, that's the only way to solve a quadratic. One thing I haven't touched on so far is that these are quadratic *equations*; that is, they equal something. In most cases, that something is zero. Consider the above example in equation form:

$x^2 + 6x + 9 = 0$

$(x + 3)(x + 3) = 0$

In the second form, there are two terms, the product of which is zero. The only way the product of two terms will be zero is if one of the terms itself is zero. Thus, either the first term $(x + 3)$ or the second term (also $x + 3$) must equal zero. In this example, there's only one possible outcome:

$x + 3 = 0$

$x = -3$

More frequently, there are two possible answers, as in this case:

$x^2 - 6x + 8 = 0$

$(x - 2)(x - 4) = 0$

$x - 2 = 0$ or $x - 4 = 0$

$x = 2$ or $x = 4$

Before we get into the mechanics of how to translate something like $x^2 - 6x + 8 = 0$ into $(x - 2)(x - 4) = 0$, we need to learn how to translate in the other direction. Take another example, $(x + 1)(x + 2)$. Using the distributive method, that simplifies to the following:

$(x + 1)(x) + (x + 1)(2)$

Distributing each of those two expressions results in the following:

$x^2 + x + 2x + 2$

which then simplifies further:

$x^2 + 3x + 2$

That's a slightly cumbersome approach, but it shows you the mathematics behind the FOIL method. FOIL is a pneumonic device designed to help you remember which combinations of terms need to be multiplied:

F: First

O: Outer

I: Inner

L: Last

In terms of the example above, $(x + 1)(x + 2)$, that means:

First: x times x: x^2

Outer: x times 2: $2x$

Inner: 1 times x: x

Last: 1 times 2: 2

Add those all together: $x^2 + 2x + x + 2 = x^2 + 3x + 2$, and you have the quadratic in a different form.

Most of the time on the GMAT, you don't need to translate in that direction. It's much more common to be given a quadratic in the form like that of $x^2 + 3x + 2$, and to have to "factor" it, or convert it into something like $(x+1)(x+2)$. The more comfortable you are with the FOIL method, the easier this will be.

Since you're usually working with a quadratic that begins with x^2 (not $3x^2$ or $5x^2$ or something), it's fairly simple. You know that, to end up with an x^2, the first term of each of the factors must be x. So, if you're factoring $x^2 + 6x + 5$, you know that the factors will look like this:

$(x+?)(x+?)$

Those two question marks are what will generate the $6x$ and the 5. To determine what those numbers are, you need the pair of numbers that add up to 6 and multiply to 5. In this case, those two numbers are 5 and 1: the sum is 6 and the product is 5. So, the factors of $x^2 + 6x + 5$ are $(x + 5)(x + 1)$. You can use the FOIL method to confirm your answer: multiply out $(x + 5)(x + 1)$:

$x^2 + 1x + 5x + 5 = x^2 + 6x + 5$

Since we ended up with the same equation we started with, we know we correctly factored the expression.

To save time, learn to recognize a few common quadratics. Rather than going through the factoring process, you will notice immediately that they are familiar. The most frequently encountered of these is often referred to as "the difference of squares":

$x^2 - y^2$

which can also include numbers instead of variables:

$x^2 - 9$

The first factors to $(x+y)(x-y)$, while the second factors to $(x+3)(x-3)$. If a quadratic has only two terms and one is subtracted from the other, the factorization will always follow this format.

The other common quadratics are also related to squares. Only here, they are squares of factors. For instance:

$(x+y)(x+y) = x^2 + 2xy + y^2$

Using an integer instead of y, it looks like this:

$(x+4)(x+4) = x^2 + 8x + 16$

It's a bit tougher to recognize something like $x^2 + 8x + 16$ as the square of a factor, but the fact that the constant (16) is itself a perfect square is a strong hint. If you change the $+8x$ to a $-8x$, you're looking at the square of a slightly different factor:

$x^2 - 8x + 16 = (x-4)(x-4)$

Or, in variable terms:

$x^2 - 2xy + y^2 = (x-y)(x-y)$

More so than almost any other topic on the GMAT, this is one to spend the time to master the mechanics. It's not all that conceptually difficult, but there will be problems that are very work-intensive, and if you're not comfortable with the techniques, you'll have a very hard time executing them in the limited time you're given on the test.

23   Algebra: Quadratic Equations: Drill

1.   FOIL each of the following:
   - a. $(x+2)(x+3)$
   - b. $(x-4)(x-1)$
   - c. $(x-3)(x+3)$
   - d. $(2x+1)(x-2)$
   - e. $(x+y)^2$

2.   Factor each of the following:
   - a. x^2-2x-8
   - b. x^2+x-6
   - c. x^2-y^2
   - d. a^2+6a+9
   - e. $z^2+9z+20$

3.   Solve for x:
   - a. $(x-1)(x+3)=0$
   - b. $(3x+2)(2x-3)=0$
   - c. $x^2-3x+2=0$
   - d. $x^2-6x=7$
   - e. $x^2+4x=-4$

4.   Factor each of the following:
   - a. y^2-x^2
   - b. $n^2-8n+16$
   - c. p^2-25
   - d. x^2+2x+1
   - e. z^2-4z+4

24   Algebra: Quadratic Equations: Practice

51.   If $(4 + \frac{a}{2})(3 - \frac{6}{a}) = 0$ and $a \neq 2$, then $a =$
   (A) -8
   (B) -4
   (C) 2
   (D) 4
   (E) 8

52.   Which of the following equations has a root in common with $x^2 - 6x + 5 = 0$?
   (A) $x^2 - 6x - 7 = 0$
   (B) $x^2 + 6x + 5 = 0$
   (C) $x^2 + 3x - 4 = 0$
   (D) $x^2 + 5x + 4 = 0$
   (E) $x^2 + 3x - 10 = 0$

53.   If $(r - 4)$ is a factor of $r^2 - kr - 36$, then $k =$
   (A) 16
   (B) 5
   (C) 0
   (D) -5
   (E) -16

54.   Is $c = 4$?
   (1) $c^2 - 2c - 8 = 0$
   (2) $c^4 = 16$

55.   If $y \neq 1$, does $\frac{x-1}{y-1} = 1$?
   (1) $x + y = 4$
   (2) $x = y$

56.   If $(x - 3)^2 = 225$, which of the following could be the value of $x + 3$?
   (A) -15
   (B) -12
   (C) -9
   (D) 15
   (E) 18

57.   What is the value of $a^2 - b^2$?
   (1) $b = 4 - a$
   (2) $b = a - 3$

58. What is the value of $4x^2 + 5x + 1$?

    (1) $4x + 1 = 7$
    (2) $x + 1 = 2.5$

59. If $\frac{3}{x} - 2 = x$, then x has how many possible values?

    (A) None
    (B) One
    (C) Two
    (D) A finite number greater than two
    (E) An infinite number

25 Algebra: Inequalities

Nearly everything you've learned so far about equations also applies to inequalities. There are four common inequality symbols that you should be familiar with:

$<$: less than. $x < y$ means "x is less than y"

$>$: greater than. $x > y$ means "x is greater than y"

$\leq$: less than or equal to: $x \leq y$ means "x is less than or equal to y"

$\geq$: greater than or equal to: $x \geq y$ means "x is greater than or equal to y"

As with equations, your goal is often to simplify an inequality as much as possible. So, if you're given the inequality $2x - 3 \geq 9$, you can simplify as follows:

$2x - 3 \geq 9$

$2x \geq 12$

$x \geq 6$

There's one exception to the rule that you can treat inequalities like equations. If you divide or multiply both sides of an inequality by a negative number, you must reverse the direction of the inequality sign. For instance, if you want to simplify the inequality $-x > 4$ by dividing by -1, you must turn the "greater than" sign into a "less than" sign:

$-x > 4$

$x < -4$

That's particularly important to remember when you're multiplying or dividing an inequality by a variable. Often, the question won't tell you whether a variable is a positive or negative number. For instance, consider simplifying the following:

$xy > xz$

At first glance, it's very straightforward: you divide both sides by x and the result is $y > z$. But, as we've just learned, that's only the case if x is a positive number. If x is negative, you can still divide both sides by x, but the result is $y < z$. So, the answer is very complicated:

If $x > 0$: $y > z$

If $x < 0$: $y < z$

In other words, y and z could have any relationship with each other at all, so long as they aren't equal. That's the sort of trick you can expect in a GMAT Data Sufficiency question, and unless you're told that x is positive or that x is negative, you wouldn't have enough information to determine the relationship between y and z.

The other way in which inequalities can get more complicated is when two inequalities are combined. Consider the following:

$10 < x < 50$

You can probably figure out what that means, even if you've never seen something like that before: x is greater than 10 and less than 50. It's a shorthand way of expressing two different inequalities: $x > 10$ and $x < 50$. When you're working with a three-part inequality like that, you can still operate on the terms the same way you would with an equation, only you have to do the same thing to all three parts of the inequality.

For instance, consider simplifying $10 < 3x + 1 < 40$:

$10 < 3x + 1 < 40$

$9 < 3x < 39$

$3 < x < 13$

In each step, we did something to all three parts of the inequality.

26   Algebra: Inequalities: Drill

1.   Simplify each of the following inequalities. Keep in mind that there may be more than one resulting inequality:

    a. $2y > 6 - y$

    b. $2a + b + 1 < a - b + 2$

    c. $n - 10 \leq 2 - n$

    d. $(x + 2)(x - 3) \geq x(x + 1)$

    e. $z^2 < 4$

    f. $-3c > -6$

    g. $\frac{5}{2} - m > -\frac{m}{4}$

    h. $-2w - 3 \geq -3w - 2$

    i. $17 < 4x + 3 < 29$

    j. $6 > -3y > -15$

27   Algebra: Inequalities: Practice

61.   If it is true that $z < 8$ and $2z > -4$, which of the following must be true?

     (A) $-8 < z < 4$
     (B) $z > 2$
     (C) $z > -8$
     (D) $z < 4$
     (E)   None of the above

62.   Is $x < y$?

     (1) $a < x < b$
     (2) $a < b < y$

63.   Is $xy > 9$?

     (1) $x \leq 4$ and $y \geq 2$
     (2) $x \geq 2$ and $y \leq 4$

64.   Are positive integers y and z both greater than x?

     (1) $y - z > x$
     (2) $z > x$

65.   If $k < g$, $h < j$, $g < j$, and $f < h$, which of the following must be true?

     I. $k < h$
     II. $f < g$
     III. $k < j$

     (A)   I only
     (B)   II only
     (C)   III only
     (D)   II and III
     (E)   I, II, and III

66.   Is $\frac{1}{x-y} < y - x$?

     (1) y is positive.
     (2) x is negative.

67.   Are positive integers m and n both greater than q?

     (1) $m > n$
     (2) $m > q$

28 Algebra: Inequalities: Challenge

68. If $xy < 4$, is $x < 2$?

    (1) $x > y$

    (2) y is positive.

69. If m and n are negative, is $\frac{m}{n}$ less than 1 ?

    (1) $mn < 1$

    (2) $m - n > n$

70. Is $x > y$?

    (1) $\frac{x}{2} = y - 3$

    (2) $y > 6$

29   Algebra: Absolute Value

In its simplest form, absolute value is just the "positive difference." Think of it this way: if you're measuring a length of string with a ruler, you may find that one end of the string is at the "2" mark on the ruler, and the other end of the string is on the "8" mark of the ruler. Thus, the length of the string is $8 - 2 = 6$. However, what if you reverse the numbers and find the length of the string is $2 - 8 = -6$? Sometimes, such as when you measure a physical distance, a negative value just doesn't make any sense. That's why there's absolute value.

More technically speaking, absolute value is denoted like this:
$|x|$
with two vertical lines on either side of an expression. The expression can be anything: a single variable, a single number, or something much more complicated. So, you might see any of the following:
$|-6|$
$|x - y|$
$|x^2 - 4x + 4|$
In any of those cases, if you needed to evaluate the expression, you'd first evaluate what was inside the absolute value signs, then turn it into a positive number. If the result was already a positive number, that means you don't have to do anything. If the result is a negative number, you just remove the negative sign. More precisely, if the result is a negative number, you multiply the result by -1.

Most of the time you encounter absolute value, you won't need any knowledge beyond the previous few paragraphs. However, as questions get more complicated, the concepts get trickier, too. Take, for instance, one of the examples above, only in an equation:
$z = |x - y|$
So, z equals the absolute value of the difference of x and y. Easy enough, except that you don't yet know anything about x or y, so you don't know whether $x - y$ will be positive or negative. As with inequalities in which you have to divide or multiply by a negative, this equation has two solutions.

First, let's say $x + y$ is greater than or equal to zero. In that case, the absolute value signs are redundant: they don't change anything about $x - y$. So,
If $x - y \geq 0$, $z = x - y$
But if the difference of x and y is negative, that means the result has to be multiplied by -1. So:
If $x - y < 0$, $z = -1(x - y) = -x + y = y - x$
If you have to evaluate an expression with variables inside absolute value signs, you may need to generate two solutions, as we did here. However, there are exceptions to that rule. For instance, the question may tell you that $x - y$ is

positive. (Or, the same but more complicated: x is positive and y is negative.) Also, you may see something like this:

$$\left| x^2 + 4 \right|$$

x^2 is always positive (any number squared is positive), and if you add 4 to a positive number, the result is always positive. Thus, the absolute value signs are always redundant for the expression $x^2 + 4$.

30   Algebra: Absolute Value: Drill

1.   Simplify each of the following:

      a. $|-5| =$

      b. $|-3| + 2 =$

      c. $|-3 + 2| =$

      d. $|11.5 - 2.91| - |2.91 - 11.5| =$

      e. $-\frac{|6|}{|-2|} =$

2.   For each of the following, find the possible values of x:

      a. $x = |y|$

      b. $x = |a - b|$

      c. $x = |m^2 + n^2|$

      d. $x > |z - 5|$

      e. $x \leq |y| + 3$

31   Algebra: Absolute Value: Practice

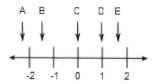

71.   Of the five coordinates associated with points A, B, C, D, and E on the number line above, which has the greatest absolute value?

(A) A
(B) B
(C) C
(D) D
(E) E

72.   Is $x < 0$?

(1) $|x| < 2$
(2) $3 - 2x > 0$

73.   Which of the following inequalities is an algebraic expression for the shaded part of the number line above?

(A) $|x| \le 2$
(B) $|x| \le 4$
(C) $|x - 2| \le 2$
(D) $|x - 1| \le 3$
(E) $|x + 1| \le 3$

74.   If n is an integer, then the least possible value of $|31 - 4n|$ is

(A)   0
(B)   1
(C)   2
(D)   3
(E)   4

32   Algebra: Absolute Value: Challenge

75.   Is $x = |y - z|$?

     (1) $x = y - z$

     (2) $y > z$

76.   Is $|x - z| = |y - z|$?

     (1) $x = y$

     (2) $|x| - z = |y| - z$

77.   If n and s are two numbers on a number line, what is the value of s?

     (1)   The distance between s and 0 is one half the distance between n and 0.

     (2)   -4 is halfway between n and s.

78.   What is the product of all the solutions of $x^2 - 4x + 6 = 3 - |x - 1|$?

     (A)   -8

     (B)   -4

     (C)   -2

     (D)   4

     (E)   8

79.   What is the value of $|x|$?

     (1) $|x + 3| = 4$

     (2) $|x| + 3 = 4$

33   Algebra: Exponents

More than nearly any other algebra concept on the GMAT, you need to memorize a whole bunch of rules in order to work with exponents. The GMAT will, quite literally, test these rules forward and backwards: in each case, be sure you understand how to work with the rule in both directions. Let's look at each one.

$\frac{1}{x^y} = x^{-y}$

An exponent in the denominator of a fraction can be converted into a negative exponent. The same can be done in reverse: it's often more convenient to have a positive exponent in the denominator of a fraction than to have a negative exponent. There's no hard-and-fast rule that determines which you should use; it's entirely reliant on context.

$\sqrt{x} = x^{\frac{1}{2}}$

If you're combining radicals and exponents, you need them all in the same form. It's much easier to convert a radical to exponent form than the other way around, so get in the habit of doing that. In more general terms, the fractional exponent is made up of two numbers:

$\sqrt[d]{x^n} = x^{\frac{n}{d}}$

Usually, $n = 1$, but if there's an exponent inside the radical, it becomes the numerator of the fraction. If there's no number outside the radical sign (where d is in this case), the denominator is 2. However, you'll occasionally see things like this:

$\sqrt[3]{x}$

We call that the "third root" of x. It's equivalent to $x^{\frac{1}{3}}$. It doesn't come up very often on the GMAT (and larger roots come up even less frequently), but you will have to be familiar with it.

$x^y x^z = x^{(y+z)}$

In practice, you'll usually see this with integers, not variables. For instance:
$2^3 2^5 = 2^{3+5} = 2^8$

or, some combination of integers are variables, like:
$y^4 y^3 = y^{4+3} = y^7$

The rule isn't limited to positive integers; you can combine fractional or negative exponents, as well.

This rule can be applied in reverse:
$x^{(y+z)} = x^y x^z$

In fact, as questions get harder, you'll end up using the rule in reverse as often as you use it the more straightforward way described above. When you have addition or subtraction in an exponent, this is only way to simplify:
$2^{x+1} = 2^x 2^1$

$\frac{x^y}{x^z} = x^{y-z}$

This is essentially the same rule as the one above. An exponent in the denominator of a fraction is equivalent to a negative exponent, so instead of adding a negative exponent, we just subtract the exponent in the denominator:

$\frac{2^3}{2^2} = 2^{3-2} = 2^1 = 2$

or:

$\frac{2^3}{2^2} = 2^3 2^{-2} = 2^1 = 2$

Again, be prepared to apply this rule in reverse:

$x^{y-z} = \frac{x^y}{x^z}$

It's less common to have to do this one in reverse as it is for the previous rule, but it does come up. To repeat: when you have addition or subtraction in an exponent, this is the only way to simplify.

$\left(x^y\right)^z = x^{yz}$

One more time: you'll end up applying this rule in reverse at least as often as you do in the traditional way described here. As an example:

$2^{3x} = (2^x)^3 = (2^3)^x$

Most commonly, you'll use this rule to change the base (2, in the previous example). For instance, let's say you're given the following expression, but you'd prefer to have a base of 2 instead of the base of 4:

$4^3 = (2^2)^3 = 2^6$

This arises if you're given an equation to solve like this one:

$4^{x+1} = 2^{3x}$

To answer it, you need to make the bases the same:

$4^{x+1} = (2^2)^{x+1} = 2^{2x+2}$

Then:

$2^{2x+2} = 2^{3x}$

When the bases on two sides of an equation are the same, they can be dropped, leaving only the exponents:

$2x + 2 = 3x$

To find x, you can solve that like you would any single-variable equation.

$(xy)^z = x^z y^z$

At it's simplest, this is how you'll evaluate expressions like:

$(3x)^2 = 3^2 x^2 = 9x^2$

Like all the others, this is something you can use in reverse:

$10^5 = (2 \times 5)^5 = 2^5 5^5$

This doesn't come up very often, but when it does, there's often no other way to solve the problem.

Exponents in Data Sufficiency

There is one specific, but oft-occurring question type that requires a bit more attention. Let's start with one example:

Is $x > 0$?

(1) $x < x^2$

(2) $x < x^3$

You've probably seen something like it. Usually, test-takers attack this type of question by trying out various numbers for x and seeing which ones work. Given the prevalence of this sort of question, you can learn a better way.

The two toughest parts of choosing values for x is knowing which numbers to pick, and when you're done

If it's possible to learn an approach that avoids picking numbers, it's to your advantage to do so. On questions that deal with exponents and have no coefficients, you can avoid those problems. Instead, you can focus on three numbers: -1, 0, and 1.

You're not going to try those exact numbers; you're going to try numbers in the "zones" defined by those numbers. For instance, you want to think about one value of x that's less than -1, one value that's between -1 and 0, one value between 0 and 1, and finally, one value greater than 1.

Consider how x, x^2, and x^3 behave in those four "zones:"

$x = -2$: $x^2 = 4$, $x^3 = -8$. Summary: $x^3 < x < x^2$
$x = -\frac{1}{2}$: $x^2 = \frac{1}{4}$, $x^3 = -\frac{1}{8}$. Summary: $x < x^3 < x^2$
$x = \frac{1}{2}$: $x^2 = \frac{1}{4}$, $x^3 = \frac{1}{8}$. Summary: $x^3 < x^2 < x$
$x = 2$: $x^3 = 4$, $x^3 = 8$. Summary: $x < x^2 < x^3$

It may not be an effective use of your time to memorize each and every one of these relationships, but if you're familiar with these "zones," you'll know exactly what numbers to test.

Let's look at the sample question one more time:

Is $x > 0$?
(1) $x < x^2$
(2) $x < x^3$

First, statement (1). x is almost always less than x^2, except when x is a positive number between 0 and 1. In other words, statement (1) says: "x is not between 0 and 1." In that case, it's insufficient: x could be positive or negative.

Statement (2) is a bit trickier. Referring to our summaries above, x is less than x^3 when x is between -1 and 0, and when x is greater than 1. Given that x could be in either one of those zones, (2) is also insufficient.

Taken together, the statements are still insufficient. (1) tells us that x could be anything less than 0 or larger than 1. (2) narrows that down somewhat: x could be between -1 and 0 or greater than 1. Thus, x could be positive or negative. Choice (E) is correct.

Anytime you see variables (without coefficients) in a question like this, you can use these zones. Note that we aggressively simplified each statement: after we evaluated statement (1), we ignored what it actually said, and focused on what we discovered: that x couldn't be between 0 and 1. Reducing complex expressions to simple statements makes questions like these much easier.

34   Algebra: Exponents: Drill

1.   Simplify each of the following:

       a. $a^5 a^3 =$

       b. $c^3 c^{-3} =$

       c. $j^{-2} j^3 =$

       d. $k^2 \sqrt{k} =$

       e. $\frac{1}{\sqrt{m}} =$

       f. $\frac{n^3}{n^2} =$

       g. $\frac{p^5}{p^7} =$

       h. $\left(t^3\right)^4 =$

       i. $(w^x)^x =$

       j. $\left(\frac{x^y}{x^z}\right)^{\frac{1}{z-y}} =$

2.   Solve for x:

       a. $2^{2x+1} = 2^{4x-3}$

       b. $2^{x+3} = 4^x$

       c. $9^{x+\frac{3}{2}} = 27^{x-1}$

35   Algebra: Exponents: Practice

81.   If $x = -\frac{1}{2}$, then $(x^4 + x^3 + x^2 + x) =$
   (A) $-\frac{15}{16}$
   (B) $-\frac{5}{16}$
   (C) 0
   (D) $\frac{5}{16}$
   (E) $\frac{15}{16}$

82.   If $(4^x)(8^y) = 32$ and $(5^x)(25^y) = 125$, then $(x, y) =$
   (A) $(1, 2)$
   (B) $(2, 1)$
   (C) $(1, 1)$
   (D) $(2, 2)$
   (E) $(1, 3)$

83.   Is $a = 4$?
   (1) $a^3 = 64$
   (2) $a^2 - 16 = 0$

84.   Is x^2 greater than x ?
   (1) x is less than -1.
   (2) x^2 is greater than 1.

85.   If y is an integer between 2 and 100 and if y is also the square of an integer, what is the value of y?
   (1) y is not a prime number.
   (2) y is evenly divisible by 3.

86.   If s and t are integers, what is the value of $s - t$?
   (1) $s^t = 1$
   (2) $s + t = 5$

36   Algebra: Exponents: Challenge

87.   If $x \neq 0$, what is the value of $\left(\frac{x^m}{x^n}\right)^5$?

    (1) $n - m = 2$

    (2) $x^2 = \frac{1}{4}$

88. $3^{x+1} + 3^{x-1} =$

    (A)   0

    (B) 3^x

    (C) 3^{2x}

    (D) $10(3^x)$

    (E) $10(3^{x-1})$

89.   If, for any integer n, $a^n = a^{n+4}$, what is the value of a?

    (1) $a^2 - 1 = 0$

    (2) $a^{n-4} = a^n$

90.   If k is a positive integer and $n = 1.7 \times 10^k$, what is the value of n ?

    (1) $n^2 = 2.89 \times 10^{10}$

    (2) $20,000 < n < 200,000$

37 Algebra: Roots

If you're jumping around in the book, make sure to read the previous chapter on exponents before starting in on this one. Not only does the exponents chapter cover a few roots-related topics, but the rules that pertain to exponents and roots are also very similar. That makes sense: exponents are roots are the mirror images of each other.

Before we get into those rules, let's start by seeing how simplify the square root of an integer. Take, for example, $\sqrt{20}$. Sometimes, the square root of an integer is already in its simplest form, but more often it is not. To find out, take the prime factorization of the integer. (For more on that, see the chapter on factors later on in the book; for now, just take my word for it.) $20 = (2)(2)(5)$, so $\sqrt{20} = \sqrt{(2)(2)(5)}$. Since there are two 2's under the radical sign, we can get rid of them and put one 2 outside the radical, like so:

$2\sqrt{5}$

Since 5 is a prime number, we're done. No matter how large or complicated a number is, you can find the square root by that process.

Some square roots are a lot easier to find when you know a few common perfect squares. If you don't already have them memorized, you should learn all the perfect squares up to 169, the square of 13. It isn't absolutely imperative that you memorize these, but it will save you a lot of time on test day if you do.

The underlying rule we used to find that square root is the first of a few we'll cover in this section. It goes like this:

$\sqrt{xy} = \sqrt{x}\sqrt{y}$

In plainer language: if two things are multiplied by each other under a square root sign, you can separate them into two different square roots. That's essentially what we did in the first example:

$\sqrt{20} = \sqrt{4(5)} = \sqrt{4}\sqrt{5} = 2\sqrt{5}$

As is often the case, the rule for division is similar to that of multiplication:

$\sqrt{\frac{x}{y}} = \frac{\sqrt{x}}{\sqrt{y}}$

So, to find the square root of $\frac{1}{4}$:

$\sqrt{\frac{1}{4}} = \frac{\sqrt{1}}{\sqrt{4}} = \frac{1}{2}$

As with exponents, you can't do much with addition. For instance:

$\sqrt{x+y} \neq \sqrt{x} + \sqrt{y}$

There will be questions that tempt you into taking that step, but remember not to.

Often, the trickiest part of a question involving roots isn't the mechanics, as discussed above, but getting the answer to match one of the choices. The most common cause is that the GMAT doesn't usually allow roots in the denominator of a fraction. (That's true in most math: it's generally good form to simplify expressions so that there are no roots in the denominator.)

So, what do you do if you find yourself with an expression like $\frac{1}{\sqrt{3}}$? As usual, when you need to simplify a fraction or just change how it looks, multiply it by 1. Specifically, multiply the denominator by itself. The process looks like this:

$$\frac{1}{\sqrt{3}} \left(\frac{\sqrt{3}}{\sqrt{3}} \right) = \frac{\sqrt{3}}{(\sqrt{3})(\sqrt{3})} = \frac{\sqrt{3}}{\sqrt{9}} = \frac{\sqrt{3}}{3}$$

One more concept you'll occasionally see is the "third root," or "cube root," which looks like this:

$$\sqrt[3]{x}$$

Just as the square root denotes the number which, when squared, equals x, the third root denotes the number which, when cubed, equals x. So, the cube root of 8 ($\sqrt[3]{8}$) is 2, since $2^3 = 8$. The GMAT doesn't expect you to memorize any cube roots except for 8, 64, and 125, so if a question appears to be testing your knowledge of a cube root any larger than that, there's some shortcut, or a way you can use the answer choices to determine which is correct.

38   Algebra: Roots: Drill

1.   Simplify each of the following:

      a. $\sqrt{32}$

      b. $\sqrt{48}$

      c. $\sqrt{50}$

      d. $\sqrt{6(12)}$

      e. $\sqrt{x^4}$

      f. $\sqrt[3]{a^6}$

      g. $\sqrt{12x^3}$

      h. $\frac{1}{\sqrt{2}}$

      i. $\sqrt{\frac{8}{12}}$

      j. $\frac{3}{\sqrt{z}}$

39 Algebra: Roots: Practice

91. $\sqrt{499}$ is between

(A)   21 and 22
(B)   22 and 23
(C)   23 and 24
(D)   24 and 25
(E)   25 and 26

92. The value of $\sqrt[3]{277}$ is

(A)   between 6 and 7
(B)   between 7 and 8
(C)   between 8 and 9
(D)   between 15 and 16
(E)   between 16 and 17

93. If $\sqrt{\frac{x}{y}} = n$, what is the value of x ?

(1) $n^2 y = 100$
(2) $n = 5$ and $y = 4$

94. $\sqrt{75} + \sqrt{108} =$

(A) $11\sqrt{3}$
(B) $30\sqrt{3}$
(C) $61\sqrt{3}$
(D) $\sqrt{183}$
(E)   90

40   Algebra: Roots: Challenge

95.   If z is a positive integer, is $\sqrt{z}$ an integer?

    (1) $\sqrt{xz}$ is an integer.

    (2) $x = z^3$

96.   If $x = 7$ and $y = 5$, what is the value of $(\sqrt{x} + \sqrt{y})(\sqrt{x} - \sqrt{y})$?

    (A)   2

    (B) $\sqrt{5}$

    (C) $\sqrt{7}$

    (D) $2\sqrt{6}$

    (E)   12

97.   If m and n are positive integers, is $3\sqrt{m} < \sqrt{m+n}$?

    (1) $m + n > 8m$

    (2) $n > 8m$

98.   If $x > 0$ and $y > 0$, which of the following is equal to $\frac{1}{\sqrt{x}+\sqrt{x+y}}$?

    (A) $\frac{1}{y}$

    (B) $\sqrt{2x+y}$

    (C) $\frac{\sqrt{x}}{\sqrt{x+y}}$

    (D) $\frac{\sqrt{x}-\sqrt{x+y}}{y}$

    (E) $\frac{\sqrt{x+y}-\sqrt{x}}{y}$

99.   If $\sqrt{3-x} = 1 - \sqrt{2x}$, then $9x^2 =$

    (A)   5

    (B)   8

    (C) $2 - 3x$

    (D) $12 - 4x$

    (E) $20x - 4$

41 Geometry: Lines and Angles

If you haven't done any geometry in years, your biggest challenge may simply be reacquainting yourself with the terminology. First, let's go over some of those terms along with definitions.

The word "line" denotes a straight line that extends both directions toward infinity. Usually they are shown on graphs with little arrows on either end to illustrate that they don't stop just because the graphic does.

A "line segment" is more realistic: it's a line with "endpoints." The line segment does not extend in either direction beyond the endpoints. The line segment shown below stops at endpoints A and B:

"Parallel" lines are multiple lines that will never meet. These will come in handy in a moment when we see some rules related to lines and angles.

"Perpendicular" lines are lines that intersect at a 90 degree angle. (A 90 degree angle is commonly referred to as a "right angle." In the illustration below, line l and line k are parallel, and line m is perpendicular to both line l and line k:

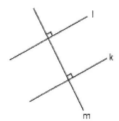

Note the little square at the intersection of the perpendicular lines. The GMAT uses that notation frequently to let you know that two lines are perpendicular.

You'll rarely see a GMAT question that explicitly tests any of those definitions. In fact, tidbits like parallel and perpendicular lines are almost always a secondary (but necessary!) part of a problem. But where they come in particularly handy is when you need to determine the measure of an angle.

The number of degrees on a line is 180; consider these two diagrams:

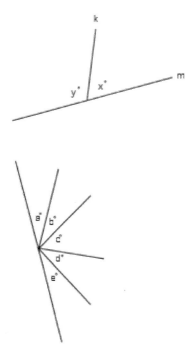

In the first, angles x and y sum to 180. In the second, angles a, b, c, d, and e sum to 180. No matter how to divide up the line, the sum of the angles will be 180.

This is useful when you consider the bottom of those lines. Consider the first diagram again, but extend line k below line m:

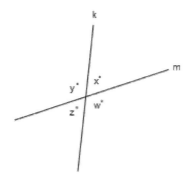

Still, x and y sum to 180. But notice now that y and z (as well as w and x) sum to 180 as well. The important point here is that "vertical angles" such as x and z or w and y are equal. The following diagram shows that more directly:

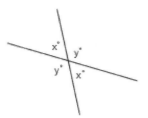

You can use parallel lines to help determine angle measures, as well. In the following diagram, m and n are equal:

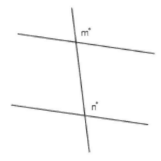

Note, also, that in each place where two lines intersect, you can use the rules just discussed to determine the measures of the other three angles.

Finally, a strategy note. All of these examples are drawn approximately to scale; the degree to which they are not accurate is only due to my ineptness with diagram creation. However, the GMAT is much more precise, for good reason.

On Problem Solving questions, diagrams are almost always drawn to scale. That's especially the case if an angle measure is given: if 45° appears in the diagram, the angle is probably exactly 45 degrees. There are some exceptions, notably when the test explicitly says "Note: not drawn to scale." Obviously, in that case, all bets are off. Be especially careful when you see that note, because it's included for a reason. Not only is the diagram not exactly correctly, it's often very misleading. As you discover the actual angle measures in the question, you may want to redraw the diagram so that you're not distracted by the one the test provided.

In a Data Sufficiency problem, you should assume that diagrams are not drawn to scale. Occasionally they are perfect, but because you are given so little information in the question of a DS problem, the diagrams follow suit. Assume nothing: a triangle that looks equilateral may not be; an angle that looks right may be anything from 10 degrees to 150.

42 Geometry: Lines and Angles: Drill

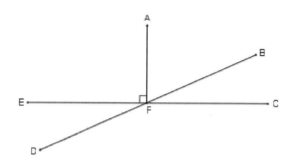

1.   The following questions refer to the diagram above:
   a.   Which of the line segments are perpendicular?
   b.   What is the degree measure of $\angle AFC$?
   c.   If the degree measure of $\angle BFC$ is 35°, what is the degree measure of $\angle AFB$?
   d.   If the degree measure of $\angle BFC$ is 30°, what is the degree measure of $\angle EFD$?
   e.   If the degree measure of $\angle AFB$ is 65°, what is the degree measure of $\angle DFC$?

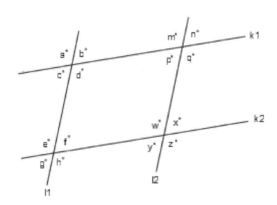

2.   The following questions refer to the diagram above, in which lines l_1 and l_2 are parallel, and lines k_1 and k_2 are parallel:
   a.   If $a = 120$, what is the value of d?
   b.   If $g = 70$, what is the value of h?
   c.   If $m = 112$, what is the value of w?
   d.   If $x = 75$, what is the value of h?
   e.   If $y = 72$, what is the value of b?

43   Geometry: Lines and Angles: Practice

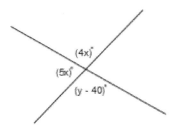

101.   In the figure above, the value of y is

(A)   120
(B)   100
(C)   80
(D)   60
(E)   40

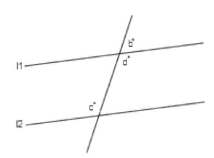

102.   In the figure above, if lines l_1 and l_2 are parallel, what is the value of c?

(1) $b = 98$
(2) $d = 82$

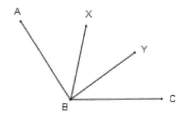

103.   In the figure above, what is the measure of $\angle ABC$?
       (1) $\angle ABY = 85$
       (2) $\angle XBC = 95$

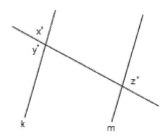

104.   In the figure above, if lines k and m are parallel, what is the value
       of x?
       (1) $z = 110$
       (2) $y = z$

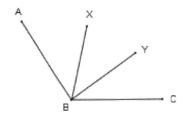

105.   In the figure above, what is the measure of $\angle ABC$?
       (1) BX bisects $\angle ABY$ and BY bisects $\angle ABC$.
       (2)   The measure of $\angle XBY$ is 35 degrees.

44   Geometry: Triangles

The makers of the GMAT simply love triangles. I would estimate that at least half of the questions you'll see on the test that involve geometry include triangles in some way or other. For better or worse, handling those questions involves a fair bit of memorization, so let's get right to it.

First of all, the GMAT favors various kinds of "special" triangles: figures with characteristics that set them apart from any random triangle you might doodle on your notepad. The three most important are as follows:

Equilateral: A triangle with three equal sides and three equal angles.

Isoceles: A triangle with at least two equal sides and at least two equal angles.

Right: A triangle with one right angle.

(The entire next chapter is devoted to right triangles, so we'll set them aside for the time being.)

To work with any triangle, it's crucial to know that the sum of the interior angles of a triangle is 180. For instance, in the following triangle:

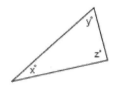

The angle measures of x, y, and z add up to 180. Thus, if triangle ABC were equilateral, x, y, and z would each be 60 degrees.

In isoceles triangles, the two equal sides "correspond" to the two equal angles. In the diagram above, angle x corresponds with side BC, angle y corresponds with side AB, and angle z corresponds with side AC. In other words, an angle corresponds to the side that it does not touch.

Thus, if triangle ABC were isoceles and angles x and y were equal, that would mean that sides AB and BC were equal, as well. Without further information, we wouldn't know anything about how those sides relate to the third side, AC.

Another recurring concept on triangle questions is that of area. The area of a triangle is determined by the following formula:

$\frac{1}{2}(base)(height)$

Where the base and the height are perpendicular to each other. In a right triangle, the base and height are easy to identify: they are both sides of the triangle, as in this example:

However, other triangles can be tricky. Consider any of the following:

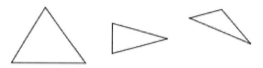

In each case, you can choose a side to be the base, but the height is not given. Usually the GMAT will help you out a little bit, but it's valuable to think through how you would find the area of these examples. Keep in mind that the base needn't be in any particular direction: all that matters is that the base and the height are perpendicular. It doesn't even matter if the height is "inside" the triangle. To illustrate, here are the heights of each of the examples above:

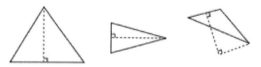

One more general concept before moving on to right triangles. Occasionally you'll see a question dealing with the length of sides in a triangle. There's a pair of rules for that, too:

> No side can be greater than or equal to the sum of the other two sides
> No side can be less than or equal to the difference of the other two sides

For example, say you're working with triangle XYZ, side XY has length 6 and side YZ has length 8. The third side, XZ, cannot be greater than 14 (the sum of 6 and 8) or smaller than 2 (the difference between 8 and 6). If XZ were greater than 14 or smaller than 2, it would be impossible to draw the triangle without leaving a gap somewhere between the lines.

That concept doesn't come up very often, but when it does, there's no other way to answer the question.

45 Geometry: Triangles: Drill

1. True or False:
    a. An equilateral triangle must be an isoceles triangle.
    b. An isoceles triangle can be a right triangle.
    c. An equilateral triangle can be a right triangle.

2. What is the area of a triangle with a base of 6 and a height of 2.5?

3. What is the height of a triangle with an area of 35 and a base of 14?

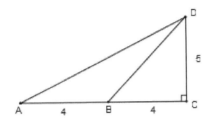

4. The next two questions refer to the diagram above:
    a. What is the area of triangle BCD?
    b. What is the area of triangle ABD?

5. If two sides of a triangle have lengths of 4 and 6, could the third side have a length of 10?

6. If two sides of a triangle have lengths of 8 and 2, could the third side have a length of 7?

7. If two sides of a triangle have lengths of 2 and 3, what is the range of possible lengths for the third side of the triangle?

46 Geometry: Triangles: Practice

111.   If 4 and 7 are the lengths of two sides of a triangular region,
which of the following can be the length of the third side?

I.   3
II.   4
III.   11

(A)   II only
(B)   III only
(C)   I and II only
(D)   II and III only
(E)   I, II, and III

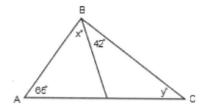

112.   In $\triangle ABC$ above, what is the value of $x + y$?

(A)   65
(B)   73
(C)   77
(D)   92
(E)   107

113.   In $\triangle MNP$, if $MN = x$, $NP = 2x$, and $MP = y$, which of
the three angles has the greatest degree measure?

(1) $\triangle MNP$ is a right triangle.
(2) $y < 2x$

47 Geometry: Triangles: Challenge

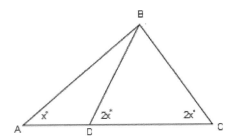

114.   In $\triangle ABC$ above, what is the measure of $\angle DAB$?

   (1) $\angle ABD = 36$

   (2) $\angle DBC = 36$

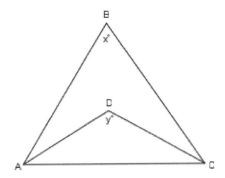

115.   In the figure above, if $\triangle ABC$ and $\triangle ADC$ are isosceles
   triangles, what is the value of x?

   (1) $y = 140$

   (2) $\angle DCA$ is one half the measure of $\angle BCA$.

116.   Is the perimeter of equilateral triangle T greater than the
   perimeter of square S?

   (1) The ratio of the area of T to the area of S is
     $\sqrt{3} : 1$.

   (2) The ratio of the length of a side of T to a side of S is
     $2 : 1$.

48   Geometry: Right Triangles

As I mentioned in the previous section, the GMAT loves triangles. It loves right triangles more than any other kind. To review, a right triangle is any triangle that includes one right angle. There are other definitions that go along with right triangles, too. Foremost, the side that corresponds to the right angle is called the "hypotenuse." The other two sides are (less frequently) referred to as the "legs."

The fundamental concept with right triangles is the Pythagorean theorem. You may recall it from younger days:

$$a^2 + b^2 = c^2$$

where a and b are the lengths of the legs and c is the length of the hypotenuse. So, if the legs have lengths 3 and 4, you can solve for the length of the hypotenuse:

$$3^2 + 4^2 = c^2$$
$$c^2 = 9 + 16 = 25$$
$$c = \sqrt{25} = 5$$

The Pythagorean theorem is the foundation of all that follows, but as it turns out, you don't use the formula itself all that often on the test. As you may have noticed, the GMAT prefers round numbers whenever possible. Naturally, then, you're not usually going to have to find the hypotenuse of a triangle with legs measuring 2.1 and 3.8 feet. Instead, the test relies heavily on those leg measurements that provide a round number for the hypotenuse as well.

You've already seen one of them: if the legs measure 3 and 4, the hypotenuse measures 5. We call these sets of values "Pythagorean triplets." More specifically, we refer to this particular triplet as a "3 : 4 : 5" right triangle, defining the figure by the ratio of its sides. Thinking of those measurements as a ratio is helpful: not only do the numbers work out nicely with legs of lengths 3 and 4; they also work out conveniently when the legs are any multiple of 3 and 4. For instance, if the legs measure 6 and 8, the hypotenuse is 10. If the legs measure 12 and 16, the hypotenuse is 20.

There are two other triples worth knowing:

$5 : 12 : 13$

$7 : 24 : 25$

In addition to these, all multiples of those triplets (such as $10 : 24 : 26$) work out as well. As you might imagine, as the numbers get larger, they appear less frequently on test questions, but these three fundamental triplets ($3 : 4 : 5$, $5 : 12 : 13$, and $7 : 24 : 25$) come up often enough that you should memorize them.

There are two more particular types of right triangles that arise often enough to learn. The first is a "45 : 45 : 90" right triangle, whose name refers to the ratio of its angles. Because the two non-right angles are equal, you may recognize that this is an isoceles triangle. (Alternatively, it is sometimes called an "isoceles right triangle.")

In a 45 : 45 : 90 triangle, the legs must be equal.   Using the Pythagorean theorem, if you call the length of each leg x, you can determine the length of the hypotenuse in terms of x:

$$x^2 + x^2 = c^2$$
$$c^2 = 2x^2$$
$$c = \sqrt{2x^2} = \sqrt{2}\sqrt{x^2} = x\sqrt{2}$$

So, the ratio of the side lengths of a 45 : 45 : 90 right triangle is $x : x : x\sqrt{2}$. Part of the reason this comes up as often as it does is that an isoceles right triangle results when you draw a diagonal through the middle of a square:

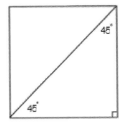

If you need to find the length of that diagonal, or if you are given the length of the diagonal and need to determine some other measurement of the square, knowing the 45 : 45 : 90 ratio will save you valuable time.

The other special right triangle is called a "30 : 60 : 90" right triangle. At this point, you can probably guess why: those are the measurements of its angles.   Just as a 45 : 45 : 90 is common because it results from splitting a square in two, a 30 : 60 : 90 is important because it is half of an equilateral triangle:

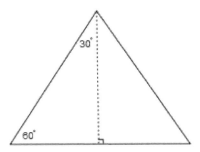

You may recognize that the height of the 30 : 60 : 90 triangle is also the height of the equilateral triangle, which gives a clue to the 30 : 60 : 90's importance. To find the area of an equilateral triangle, we need the height, and to get the measurement of the height, we need to use this right triangle.

The ratio of the sides of a 30 : 60 : 90 triangle is:

$$x : x\sqrt{3} : 2x$$

where the x side corresponds to the 30 degree angle, the $x\sqrt{3}$ corresponds to the 60 degree side, and the $2x$ side is the hypotenuse, as in this diagram:

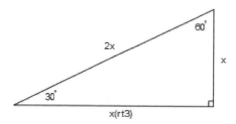

If you only memorize a handful of geometry-related facts, this section is the one to review. Right triangles, particularly "special triangles" like 45 : 45 : 90's, 30 : 60 : 90's, and Pythagorean triplets, will show up on test items again and again.

49 Geometry: Right Triangles: Drill

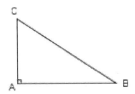

1. Each of the following refers to the diagram above:
   a. If $AB = 3$ and $AC = 4$, $BC =$
   b. If $AB = 8$ and $BC = 10$, $AC =$
   c. If $AB = 2$ and $AC = 5$, $BC =$
   d. If $AC = 5$ and $AB = 12$, $BC =$
   e. If $AC = 3$ and $BC = 3\sqrt{5}$, $AB =$

2. If each leg of isoceles right triangle XYZ has a length of 4, what is the perimeter of XYZ?

3. The shortest side of $30 : 60 : 90$ triangle MNP is $2\sqrt{3}$. What is the perimeter of MNP?

4. What is the length of the diagonal of a square with a side of 6?

5. What is the area of an equilateral triangle with a side length of 4?

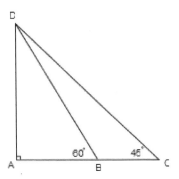

6. In the figure above, if $CD = 3\sqrt{6}$, what is the length of side BD?

50 Geometry: Right Triangles: Practice

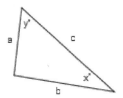

121.   In the triangle above, does $a^2 + b^2 = c^2$?
   (1) $b = c$
   (2) $y > x$

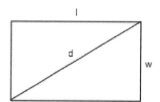

122.   What is the length of diagonal d in the rectangle above?
   (1)   The area of the rectangle is 24.
   (2) $2l = 3w$

123.   What is the perimeter of right triangle XYZ?
   (1) $XY = 11$
   (2) $XZ = 11$

51 Geometry: Right Triangles: Challenge

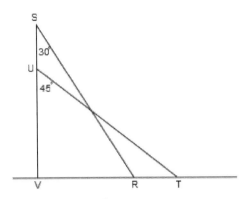

124. In the figure above, segments RS and TU represent two positions of the same support beam leaning against the side SV of a structure. The length TV is how much greater than the length RV ?

(1) The length of SU is $2\sqrt{2} - 4$ meters.

(2) The ratio of the length of VR to VT is $\sqrt{6} : 2$.

125. What is the perimeter of isoceles triangle TUV?

(1) $TU = UV = 18$

(2) $\angle U = 90$

126. Two of the interior angles in triangle XYZ measure 45 degrees. What is the perimeter, in centimeters, of the triangle?

(1) The area of the triangle is 18 square centimeters.

(2) The hypotenuse of the triangle is $6\sqrt{2}$ cm.

52 Geometry: Quadrilaterals

There are three main types of quadrilaterals that show up frequently on the GMAT: squares, rectangles, and trapezoids. The two main things the GMAT will test for all of those figures are perimeter and, more importantly, area.

For any of these figures, the perimeter is simply the sum of the four sides. In a square, the perimeter is $4s$; in a rectangle, it's $2l + 2w$, where l is one of the dimensions (length) and w is the other (width). A trapezoid may not have any equal sides, so there's no shortcut.

The area of a square is equally straightforward: it's the square of the length of a side: s^2. The area of a rectangle is the product of the two dimensions: length times width. Trapezoids (and other quadrilaterals that are not rectangles) are where things get interesting. The equation is as follows:

$$\frac{b_1+b_2}{2}(h)$$

where b_1 and b_2 are the two parallel sides of differing lengths. In other words, you are taking the average of the two parallel sides and multiplying them by the height. But, before we get ahead of ourselves, what is the height? As in a triangle, the height must be perpendicular to the base, so in many cases, the height is not a side of the trapezoid. See the diagram below for an example:

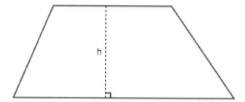

Finally, quadrilaterals (especially squares) will often be used in questions along with other geometrical figures. Most commonly, you'll see a square divided into two triangles. The most important thing to note in those cases is that the two resulting triangles are isoceles right triangles: the two sides they share with the square are equal (since every side of a square is equal), and the angle they share with the square must be equal as well. Thus, to determine the length of the diagonal (or use the length of the diagonal to find some measure of the square), you can use the ratio for a 45 : 45 : 90 triangle.

53   Geometry: Quadrilaterals: Drill

1. True or False:
   a.   A rectangle is a square.
   b.   A rectangle is a quadrilateral.
3. If a square has a side length of $5\sqrt{2}$, what is its area?
4. Rectangle $MNPQ$ has sides measuring 9 inches and 16 inches. What is the perimeter of $MNPQ$?
5. If square $ABCD$ has a perimeter of 18, what is its area?
6. Find the perimeter and area of each of the following:

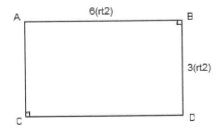

a.

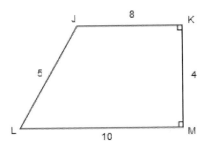

b.

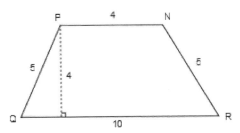

c.

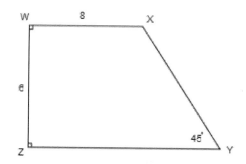

d.

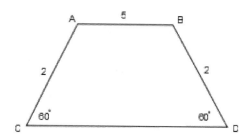

e.

54 Geometry: Quadrilaterals: Practice

131. Rectangular panel C has double the area of square panel D. If panel C is 8 inches wide and 9 inches long, what is the length of a side of D, in inches?

(A) 4
(B) 6
(C) 8
(D) 9
(E) 12

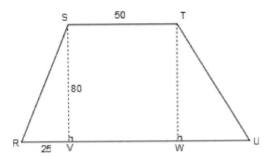

132. Quadrilateral $RSTU$ shown above is the outline for a planned city park in which side RU is parallel to side ST and RU is longer than ST. What is the area of the planned city park?

(1) $TW = 80$ meters
(2) $TU = 10\sqrt{17}$ meters

133. Two rectangular floors, A and B, have equal area. If floor A has a width of 9 feet and a length of 16 feet and floor B is 8 feet wide, what is the length of floor B, in feet?

(A) 17
(B) 18
(C) 19
(D) 21
(E) 24

134.   What is the combined area, in square inches, of the front and
        back of a rectangular trading card measuring $3\frac{1}{2}$ inches
        by 5 inches?

        (A)   17.5
        (B)   30.0
        (C)   35.0
        (D)   52.5
        (E)   70.0

135.   A square mirror has exactly half the area of the rectangular wall
        on which it is hung. If each side of the mirror is 42 inches and
        the width of the wall is 56 inches, what is the length of the
        wall, in inches?

        (A)   84
        (B)   72
        (C)   70
        (D)   63
        (E)   56

55 Geometry: Circles

The two fundamental concepts regarding circles on the GMAT are probably already familiar to you: circumference and area. To find either of those measurements for a given circle, first you need either the radius or the diameter. The radius is the length of any line starting at the exact center of the circle and ending on the circle itself. The diameter is the length of any line starting on the circle, ending on the circle, and passing through the exact center of the circle. Naturally, the diameter is twice the radius.

Every circle-related formula includes the greek letter π (pronounced "pie"), which is equal to about 3.14. You probably won't need to know that for the GMAT; if you do, it'll be sufficient to approximate π as about 3. The circumference of a circle–the length of the line going around the circle–is given by the following:

$2\pi r$, where r is the radius. This equation is the same as πd, where d is the diameter.

The area of the circle is given by this equation:

πr^2, where r, again, is the radius.

These two formulas will come up repeatedly: if you don't know them already, memorize them!

Things get more complicated when we start talking about arcs and sectors. Arcs and sectors are pieces of circumferences and areas, respectively. In the diagram below, the line between points X and Y is an arc, while the small region defined by OXY is a sector.

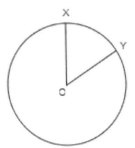

To find the length of an arc or the area of a sector, you use the same formulas as for circumference and area, with one twist. Since we aren't looking for the entire circumference or the entire area, we need to first determine what portion of the circle we are dealing with. To find that, we need the measure of the angle that defines the arc of sector. In the diagram, that angle is 60 degrees. Since an entire triangle contains 360 degrees around the center, we're working with $\frac{60}{360} = \frac{1}{6}$ of the circle. Thus, the length of an arc is:

$\frac{angle}{360}(2\pi r)$

Similarly, the area of a sector is:

$\frac{angle}{360}(\pi r^2)$

There are a few other terms you should be familiar with so that the GMAT doesn't surprise you. Occasionally, an arc will be referred to as a "minor arc." In the diagram above, there are technically two different arcs between the points X and Y: one is very long, one is much shorter. The short one is the minor arc while the longer one is called the major arc.

A "chord" is a line connecting two points on a circle, but is not necessarily the diameter of the circle. Knowing something about a chord (for instance, the length, or the degree at which it intersects a radius) is almost never useful information on a GMAT question.

A line is said to be "tangent" to a circle if it intersects the circle at exactly one point. That point, where the circle and the line intersect, is–naturally enough–termed the "point of tangency."

56 Geometry: Circles: Drill

1. If Circle O has a radius of 3, find the following:
   a. diameter
   b. perimeter
   c. area

2. If Circle O has an area of 9π, find the following:
   a. radius
   b. diameter
   c. perimeter

3. If Circle O has a perimeter of 6, find the following:
   a. radius
   b. diameter
   c. area

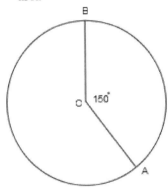

4. The following questions refer to the figure above. If the radius of circle O is 12,
   a. what fraction of the circle is made up by minor arc AOB?
   b. what is the area of the sector defined by minor arc AOB?
   c. what is the length of minor arc AB?

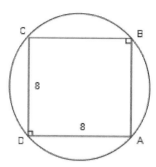

5.   The following questions refer to the figure above:
      a.   What is the diameter of the circle?
      b.   What is the area of the circle?
      c.   What is the difference between the area of the circle and
            the area of the square?

57 Geometry: Circles: Practice

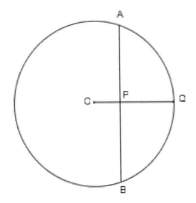

141.   What is the radius of circle O above?

   (1) P is the midpoint of chord AB.
   (2) $PQ = 2$

142.   Which of the following lists the number of points at which a circle can intersect two perpendicular line segments?

   (A)   1 and 2 only
   (B)   2 and 4 only
   (C)   1, 2, and 4 only
   (D)   2, 3, and 4 only
   (E)   1, 2, 3, and 4

143.   If M and N are points in a plane and M lies inside the circle C with center O and radius 5, does N lie inside circle C?

   (1)   The length of line segment ON is 4.
   (2)   The length of line segment OM is 4.

144.   The perimeter of the base of circular tank T is $\frac{1}{3}$ the length of the perimeter of the base of circular tank W. What is the area of the base of tank T?

   (A)   The area of W is 16π square inches.
   (B)   The perimeter of W is 8π inches.

145.   If O and P are each circular regions, what is radius of the smaller of these regions?

(1)   The radius of the larger region is equal to the diameter of the smaller region.

(2)   The difference between the area and the circumference of the smaller region is 24π.

58 Geometry: Circles: Challenge

146. Points A and B lie on a semicircle with a center at point O. What is the length of line segment AB?

   (1) The radius of semicircle O is 5.
   (2) The degree measure of angle AOB is 60.

147. A point on the rim of a circular tire that is rotating in a plane is 12 inches from the center of the rim. What is the distance traveled, in inches, by this point in 10 seconds when the tire turns at the rate of 250 revolutions per minute?

   (A) $36,000\pi$
   (B) $6,000\pi$
   (C) $1,000\pi$
   (D) 600π
   (E) 500π

59 Geometry: Solids

A solid is a three-dimensional figure. On the GMAT, you'll encounter two main types of solids: rectangular solids (including cubes) and cylinders. Test questions will generally be looking for one of two things: the volume of the solid (how much space is inside the thing) and the surface area of the solid (the area of all the faces, added together). The volume is much more common; it's unlikely that you'll see even one question on your test concerning surface area.

A rectangular solid is any three-dimensional figure with all right angles. As example, consider a shoebox, a six-sided die, or a skyscraper. The volume of a rectangular solid is given by this equation:

$(length) \times (width) \times (height)$

It doesn't particularly matter which side you assign to which name, so long as you account for all three dimensions. One way to think about calculating volume that applies to cylinders as well, is that you're finding the area of the base (in this case, length times width) and then multiplying it by the height. A cube is one type of rectangular solid: it just happens to have three equal dimensions. In the case of a cube, the volume can be expressed as $(side)^3$.

The surface area of a rectangular solid is the sum of its 6 faces. Note that only three of these faces are different: in the case of a shoebox, the top and bottom are equal, the left and right side are equal, and the front and back are equal. So, the equation for surface area is:

$2(lw) + 2(lh) + 2(wh)$

where l is length, w is width, and h is height. As with volume calculations, cubes are simpler: since all the dimensions of a cube are identical, the six faces are identical as well. Accordingly, the surface area of a cube is $6s^2$, where s stands for a side.

To visualize a cylinder (or cylindrical solid, as the GMAT often refers to them), think of a soup can, or perhaps a poster tube. As with rectangular solids, the volume is the product of the area of the base and the height. Specifically, the formula is:

$\pi r^2 h$

where r is the radius of the base and h is the height of the cylinder. The surface area of a cylinder is very rarely tested, but it's handy to think through at least once. The formula is:

$2\pi rh + 2\pi r^2$

The first term, $2\pi rh$ represents what would be the label of the soup can: everything but the top and bottom. Imagine removing the label from the can and flattening it out. You'd be left with a rectangle. The length of the rectangle used to be the circumference of a circle ($2\pi r$), while the height of the rectangle was the height of the cylinder. The second term, $2\pi r^2$, is double the area of the base: in other words, the surface area of the top and bottom.

Occasionally GMAT materials refer to figures such as cones and spheres. While those shapes do rarely appear on the GMAT, you will never need to know how to find the volume or surface area of those figures. Questions that concern cones and spheres are entirely spatial reasoning exercises, and you can solve them without knowing the first thing about calculating actual values.

60 Geometry: Solids: Drill

1. What is the volume of a cube with a side of 6?

2. If one face of a cube has an area of 20, what is the volume of the cube?

3. What is the surface area of a cube with a side of $\sqrt{2}$?

4. What is the volume of a rectangular solid with dimensions 3, 4, and 5?

5. What is the volume of a rectangular solid that has a square base with an area of 12 and a height of 9?

6. If a rectangular solid has a height of 5, a width of 6, and a length of 10, what is its surface area?

7. If one rectangular solid has a volume of 60, what is the volume of another rectangular solid with twice the width, twice the length, and half the height of the first?

8. What is the volume of a cylindrical solid with a radius of 4 and a height of 12?

9. If the base of a cylinder has an area of 16π and the height of the cylinder is 9, what is the volume of the cylinder?

10. What is the surface area of a cylinder with a diameter of 6 and a height of 12?

61 Geometry: Solids: Practice

151.   A storage company leases storage units in two different sizes. If Type A units have 72 cubic feet, while the Type B units have double the width, double the length, and double the height of Type A units, what would be the size, in cubic feet, of Type B units?

   (A)   144
   (B)   216
   (C)   288
   (D)   432
   (E)   576

152.   The volume of a rectangular solid is x. If the length and width are each increased by 50% and the height is increased by 300%, what is the volume of the solid?

   (A) x
   (B) $4x$
   (C) $6x$
   (D) $6.75x$
   (E) $9x$

153.   If a rectangular box has a volume of 32 cubic feet, what is the height of the box?

   (1)   The width of the box is $2\sqrt{2}$ feet.
   (2)   The box has a square base.

62 Geometry: Solids: Challenge

154. A rectangular steel container has three equal dimensions of 8 inches. If a cylindrical canister is to be placed inside the box so that it stands upright when the box rests on one of its six faces, what is the maximum possible volume, in cubic inches, of the canister?

 (A) 128
 (B) 64π
 (C) 128π
 (D) 512
 (E) 512π

155. What is the surface area of a certain cylindrical container?

 (1) The volume of the container is 45π cubic inches.
 (2) The diameter of the base of the container is 6 inches.

156. A cylindrical tank has a height of 10 feet and a base with a radius of 6 feet. If the thickness of the tank's sides is negligible, what is the volume, in cubic feet, of the largest rectangular solid that could be placed inside the tank?

 (A) 60
 (B) 360
 (C) $240\sqrt{3}$
 (D) $360\sqrt{2}$
 (E) 720

157. A cube has sides measuring 6 inches. What is the greatest possible (straight-line) distance, in inches, between any two points on the box?

 (A) $2\sqrt{6}$
 (B) $3\sqrt{6}$
 (C) $6\sqrt{2}$
 (D) $6\sqrt{3}$
 (E) 12

158. What is the volume of a certain rectangular solid?

 (1) The surface area of the solid is 148.
 (2) Each of two opposite faces of the solid has area 30.

63   Geometry: Coordinate Geometry

Like many topics in geometry, coordinate geometry isn't tested very often. But when it is, a few simple facts will come in handy. First, it's important that you have a working knowledge of the coordinate plane:

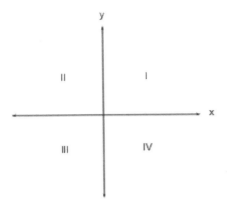

The two lines in the diagram are called "axes." More specifically, the one going from left to right is called the "x-axis" while the one going from top to bottom is called the "y-axis." The axes split the graph into quarters, which are commonly referred to as "quadrants." The roman numerals in the diagram are the conventional names for those quadrants: the upper right is quadrant I, etc.

The fundamental purpose of the coordinate plane is to plot points. (You'll also add lines and other figures to the plane, but it all comes down to plotting points.) Points are usually referred to in this form:

$(2,3)$

where the first number is the x-coordinate and the second is the y-coordinate. In other words, the first number indicates how far the point is to the left or right, and the second number tells you how far the point is to the top or bottom. In this case, $(2,3)$ is two spaces to the right of the center and three spaces above center. If you refer back to the diagram that labelled quadrants, you'll see that $(2,3)$ is in quadrant I.

For some reason, many GMAT test-takers seem to be confused by plotting points with negatives as coordinates. I don't really understand why that is; the rules are exactly the same, it's just a matter of going left instead of right and down instead of up.

Usually, the purpose of plotting points on a graph is to better understand something a little more complex than that. On the GMAT, it's usually about lines. A frequently occurring concept is that of "slope." You can think of the slope of a line as an approximate way of measuring its angle. For the purposes of the GMAT, you don't need to know a direct translation between certain slopes and certain angle measures, but it's useful to think of slope that way.

Before calculating the slope, consider a few common slopes. Line l below has a slope of 1:

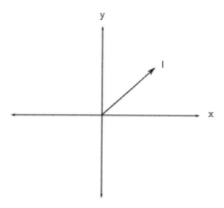

Note that the line progresses from lower left to upper right. Any line that moves in that general direction will have a positive slope. The next two lines show when the slope gets bigger or smaller:

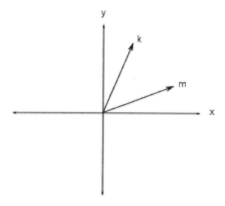

Both line k and line m have positive slopes, but are very different. Because line k has a sharper angle than line l, it's slope is greater than 1. Line m, because it is flatter than line l, has a slope less than 1.

We can extend the same reasoning to lines with negative slopes–that is, lines that move from upper left to lower right. Consider lines p, q, and r in the diagram below:

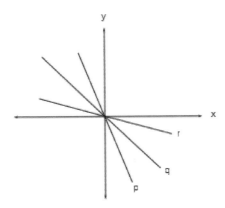

Line q is very similar to line l; it relates to the axes at exactly a 45 degree angle. Thus, its slope is -1. Line p, because it has the "sharper" angle that line k also exhibited, has a slope less than -1, such as -3. Line r has a slope between 0 and -1.

The only remaining consideration is the slope of each axis. First, consider the slope of the x-axis, a flat line moving from left to right. Since slopes get smaller as they move downward from line l, it stands to reason that the x-axis has a slope of 0. And since slopes get larger as they move up from line l, the y-axis, a line that goes straight up and down, has a slope of infinity.

As you may have figured out by now, slope is a measure of steepness. The flatter the line, the closer the slope is to 0. The steeper the line, the closer to infinity. To calculate the slope, then, we measure the "rise" over the "run," that is, the change in the y-coordinates over the change in the x-coordinates:

$$\frac{y_2 - y_1}{x_2 - x_1}$$

To find the slope, then, we need two points on the line. Consider the diagram below, in which a line runs through points $(-1, -1)$ and $(4, 2)$. Based on the discussion above, you can probably deduce at a glance that the slope is positive and a bit less than 1:

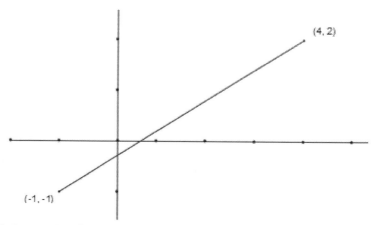

To find the precise slope, you'll need to call one of the points (x_1, y_1) and the other (x_2, y_2). It doesn't matter which is which. So, say that $(-1, -1)$ is (x_1, y_1), meaning that, for the purposes of the slope equation:

$x_1 = -1$
$x_2 = 4$
$y_1 = -1$
$y_2 = 2$
$\frac{y_2 - y_1}{x_2 - x_1} = \frac{2 - (-1)}{4 - (-1)} = \frac{3}{5}$

As we predicted, the slope is positive and less than one.

The slope is an important component of the final concept in coordinate geometry, the equation of a line. You may recall the format of that equation:

$y = mx + b$

In that equation, m is the slope and b is the y-intercept. x and y remain as variables, so an equation of a line looks like this:

$y = \frac{3}{5}x - 4$

The y-intercept refers to the point at which the line intersects the y-axis. That is, it's the point where the x-coordinate is equal to zero. So, if $b = -4$, the line with the equation $y = \frac{3}{5}x - 4$ goes through the point $(0, -4)$.

In less abstract terms, the equation of a line tells you two things: the steepness of the line (the slope) and how much higher or lower it is than the x-axis (the y-intercept). To see this in action, consider the following diagram, with several lines and their equations. Note that each one has the same slope and differs only by their y-intercepts:

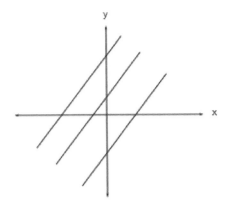

As a side note, it's useful to be familiar with the x-intercept as well. Instead of indicating the point at which the line intersects the x-axis, it tells you where the line intersects the y-axis. So, a line with an x-intercept of 5 goes through the point $(5, 0)$.

Now you know how to interpret the equation of a line. Somewhat more challenging is generating the equation of a line yourself. Let's say that you're given two points, $(-3, -2)$ and $(1, 4)$, and you need to find the equation of a line that runs through those two points. The first step is to find the slope:

$$\frac{4-(-2)}{1-(-3)} = \frac{6}{4} = \frac{3}{2}$$

Given the slope, you know that the equation of a line will look like this:

$$y = \frac{3}{2}x + b$$

To find the y-intercept, plug in either of the two points into the equation and solve for b:

$$x = 1, \ y = 4$$
$$4 = \frac{3}{2}(1) + b$$
$$4 = \frac{3}{2} + b$$
$$b = 4 - \frac{3}{2} = \frac{5}{2}$$

Now that you know the y-intercept, you have the equation of the line:

$$y = \frac{3}{2}x + \frac{5}{2}$$

Going through that process provides a hint as to how the equation of a line can be useful. Let's say you were given that equation, $y = \frac{3}{2}x + \frac{5}{2}$, and you were asked to find the x-intercept. In other words, when the value of y is 0, what is the value of x?

To answer that question, just plug in 0 for y and solve:

$$0 = \frac{3}{2}x + \frac{5}{2}$$
$$-\frac{5}{2} = \frac{3}{2}x$$
$$-5 = 3x$$
$$x = -\frac{5}{3}$$

Similarly, let's say you needed to check whether the line ran through the point $(2,6)$. Using the equation of a line, you can take the x-coordinate, 2, and determine what the y-coordinate should be:

$$y = \tfrac{3}{2}(2) + \tfrac{5}{2}$$
$$y = 3 + \tfrac{5}{2} = \tfrac{11}{2}$$

When the x-coordinate is 2, the y-coordinate is $\tfrac{11}{2}$. Since there is only one point at which the x-coordinate is 2, $(2,6)$ is not on the line.

Everything up to this point has been concerned with the direction of the line. However, you'll occasionally see questions that ask about the length of a specific line segment. In middle school or high school, you may have learned something called the "distance formula," but you don't need it now. Finding the distance of a line segment on the coordinate plane is almost as simple as finding the hypotenuse of a right triangle–in fact, the concept is identical.

Here's an example. This diagram shows the coordinate axes with a line segment extending from $(0,2)$ to $(2,0)$:

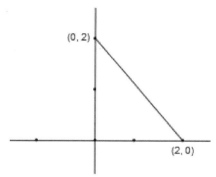

You may notice that the line segment forms a right triangle with the x-axis and the y-axis. Each of the legs has a length of 2 and the hypotenuse is the line segment. If we want to find the length of the line segment, we can use the length of the legs in the pythagorean theorem:

$$a^2 + b^2 = c^2$$
$$2^2 + 2^2 = c^2$$
$$8 = c^2$$
$$c = \sqrt{8} = 2\sqrt{2}$$

That's it. The important thing here is to realize that finding the distance of a line on the coordinate plane is the same type of problem as finding the hypotenuse of a right triangle, and can be handled exactly the same way.

That type of question is a little more difficult when the line segment doesn't end at each axis. Say, for example, that you need to find the distance between the points $(3,1)$ and $(7,4)$. If that was a GMAT question, it might not give you a diagram at all. When you draw it on your scratch paper, you should not only plot those points and draw the line segment that connects them, but also draw a right triangle that has two legs parallel to the two axes, like this:

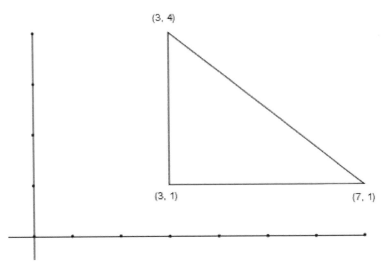

That third point will have one coordinate equal to the one of the coordinates of each of the two other points. In this case, the third point, $(7, 1)$, draws the coordinate 7 from the point $(7, 4)$ and the coordinate 1 from the point $(3, 1)$. We could also use the opposite coordinates and get a third point of $(3, 4)$: that would result in a different (but equally-sized) right triangle.

Now that we've drawn the triangle, we can find the length of the two legs. The leg from $(3, 1)$ to $(7, 1)$ has a length of 4, and the length of the leg from $(7, 4)$ to $(7, 1)$ has a length of 3. That's a right triangle with legs of 3 and 4, so we know the hypotenuse–the line segment we're interested in–must be 5. We had to draw a couple of extra lines, but we don't need to learn any additional formulas.

64 Geometry: Coordinate Geometry: Drill

1. For each of the following, find the slope of the line that runs through the two given points:
   a. $(5, 5)$ and $(0, 0)$
   b. $(3, 2)$ and $(2, 3)$
   c. $(4, -7)$ and $(-5, 1)$

2. For each of the following, find the equation of the line that runs through the two given points:
   a. $(-4, 0)$ and $(0, 10)$
   b. $(\frac{3}{2}, \frac{1}{2})$ and $(-\frac{3}{2}, \frac{1}{2})$
   c. $(0, -1)$ and $(7, 4)$

3. If line k has a slope of $\frac{1}{2}$ and the point $(-5, -5)$ lies on line k, what is the equation of line k?

4. If the point $(-6, 2)$ lies on line m and line m has a slope of $-\frac{4}{3}$, what is the equation of line m?

5. Is the point $(10, 6\frac{1}{3})$ on the line defined by the equation $y = \frac{2}{3}x - \frac{1}{2}$?

6. Is the point $(\frac{10}{9}, \frac{1}{9})$ on the line defined by the equation $x = 1 - \frac{y}{3}$?

65   Geometry: Coordinate Geometry: Practice

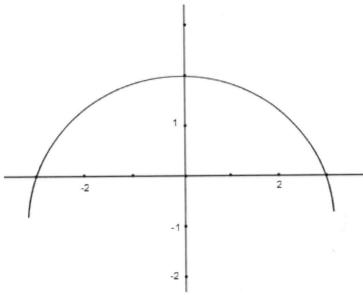

161.   On the graph above, when $x = -3$, $y = -3.25$; and when $x = -2$,
        $y = 1.25$. The graph is symmetric with respect to the y axis.
        According to the graph, when $x = 2$, $y =$

   (A) -1.5
   (B) -1.25
   (C) 0
   (D) 1.25
   (E) 1.5

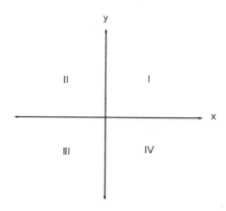

162. Point (x, y) lies in which quadrant of the rectangular coordinate system shown above?

(1) $x + y < 0$
(2) $y = 7$

163. In the xy-plane, does the point $(3, 9)$ lie on line k ?

(1) The point $(1, 2)$ lies on line k.
(2) The point $(-2, -8)$ lies on line k.

164. In the xy-plane, point P has coordinates (m, n) and point Q has coordinates (n, m). What is the distance between P and Q?

(1) $m - n = 2$
(2) $m + n = 5$

66   Geometry: Coordinate Geometry: Challenge

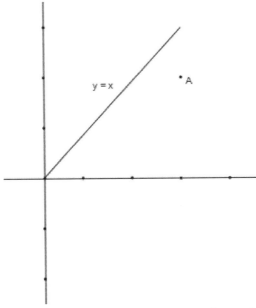

165.   In the rectangular coordinate system above, the line $y = x$ is the perpendicular bisector of segment AB (not shown), and the y-axis is the perpendicular bisector of segment BC (not shown). If the coordinates of point A are $(3, 2)$, what are the coordinates of point C?

    (A) $(-3, -2)$
    (B) $(-2, 3)$
    (C) $(3, -2)$
    (D) $(2, -3)$
    (E) $(2, 3)$

166.   In the xy-plane, if line k has negative slope and passes through the point $(s, -2)$, is the x-intercept of line k positive?

    (1) $s = 0$
    (2)   The y-intercept of line k is negative.

167.   The endpoints of line segment MN have coordinates $(-3, 2)$ and $(5, -2)$. Which of the following points is NOT located on line segment MN?

(A) $(-1, 1)$

(B) $(0, \frac{1}{2})$

(C) $(1, 0)$

(D) $(2, -\frac{1}{2})$

(E) $(4, -1)$

168.   In the xy-plane, region A consists of all the points (x, y) such that $1 - x < 2y$. Is the point (a, b) in region A?

(1) $a > 2b$

(2) $b = 1$

169.   If line l in the xy-plane has equation $y = mx + 5$, where m is a constant, what is the slope of l?

(1) l is parallel to the line with equation $y = (m^2)x + 6$.

(2) l intersects the line with equation $y = -2x - 4$ at the point $(-3, 2)$.

67   Geometry: Polygons

Polygons come up so rarely on the GMAT that I debated whether to include this chapter. If you don't have a lot of time to prepare for the exam, you're better off spending your time and energy elsewhere. However, the concepts (really, only one concept) the GMAT tests regarding polygons are simple.

First, you'll occasionally encounter the phrase "regular polygon." "Regular," in this context, indicates that all the interior angles of the polygon are equal. So, if the sum of the interior angles in a pentagon is 540, each interior angle of a regular pentagon is $\frac{540}{5} = 108$.

The main concept, though, is determining the sum of those interior angles in the first place. For that, we have a formula:

$180(n-2)$

where n is the number of sides in the polygon. So, in the case of a pentagon (five sides), the sum of the interior angles is:

$180(5-2) = 180(3) = 540$

The reason why this works is that any polygon can be divided into some number of triangles. For instance, if you draw the diagonal of a square, you have two triangles. Since a square is a four-sided polygon, the interior angles of a square sum to $180(4-2) = 180(2)$, equivalent to two triangles. You can do the same with, for example, a hexagon:

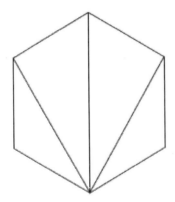

While triangles and quadrilaterals are polygons (and adhere to the formula shown above), the GMAT will never refer to them as such. The only three other polygons you are remotely likely to see on the test are:

Pentagon (five sides)

Hexagon (six sides)

Octagon (eight sides)

68 Geometry: Polygons: Drill

1. How many non-overlapping triangles can be created by drawing lines connecting the vertices of a(n)
   a.   pentagon?
   b.   octagon?
   c.   hexagon?
   d.   quadrilateral?
2. What is the sum of the interior angles of a(n)
   a.   hexagon?
   b.   pentagon?
   c.   octagon?
3. What is the measure of a single interior angle in a regular
   a.   octagon?
   b.   pentagon?
   c.   hexagon?

69 Word Problems: Ratios

A ratio is nothing more than a relationship between numbers, just like a fraction, a decimal, or a percent. A ratio is often represented with a colon (":"), as in the ratio 3 : 2, but that ratio is equivalent to several other numbers you may be more comfortable working with. For example, 3 : 2 is equivalent to the fraction $\frac{3}{2}$. A ratio can also be expressed as a percent: 1 : 4 is equivalent to $\frac{1}{4}$, which equals 25%. Finally, a ratio can also be expressed as a decimal. First, you would convert to a fraction or percent, then convert to a decimal. (That will rarely be useful, however.)

One of the most common types of ratios you'll encounter is the "part-to-part" ratio. When the two parts of a ratio do not overlap, they are a part to part ratio. For example: if the ratio of boys to girls in the first grade is 4 : 5, there's no overlap between boys and girls; each one of those segments represents a part of the whole class.

Further, there can be more than two parts in a part to part ratio. On the GMAT, however, you'll only occasionally see a ratio with more than three parts. An example of a three-part ratio would go like this: "The ratio of Stockholder A's holdings to Stockholder B's holdings to Stockholder C's holdings is 5 : 2 : 1." Again, there's no overlap between any of the individual holdings.

The other common type of ratio is a "part-to-whole" ratio. A part to whole ratio is more like a fraction. You can usually think of fractions as "part over whole," so a ratio expressing the relationship between a part and a whole is very similar to that. Here's what that might look like:

"The relationship between the number of teenage members of a club and the number of total members is expressed by the ratio 2 : 5."

In this case, the number of teenage members is a subset of the total number of members.

Everything we've discussed so far is very elementary. GMAT questions start getting trickier when you have to convert from one type of ratio to another. Whenever you have a part to part ratio, you can convert it into a part to whole ratio.

Consider the first example above: "The ratio of boys to girls in the first grade is 4 : 5." If, for every 4 boys, there are 5 girls, then for every 4 boys , there are a total of 9 children. Thus, the ratio of boys to girls generates two more ratios:

> boys to total: 4 : 9
> girls to total: 5 : 9

Similarly, if you have a part to whole ratio, you can convert it into a part to part ratio. Again, to use an example from above: "The relationship between the number of teenage members of a club and the number of total members is expressed by the ratio 2 : 5."

If, for every 5 members, 2 are teenagers, that means 3 are not teenagers. Thus, this part to whole ratio generates two other ratios:

non-teenagers to total: $3 : 5$

non-teenagers to teenagers: $3 : 2$

One last thing: note that any of these ratios could be reversed: to say that the ratio of non-teenagers to teenagers is $3 : 2$ is equivalent to saying that the ratio of teenagers to non-teenagers is $2 : 3$.

Still, we haven't quite gotten to where GMAT questions will expect you to be. It's a rare question that asks explicitly for a ratio; more commonly, you'll be required to use a ratio to find a number.

In order to find a number from a ratio, you need some other number. If I just tell you the relationship between two quantities, you can never find the actual amount of one of the quantities without further information. If, for instance, the ratio of native Spanish speakers to native English speakers in a certain group is $3 : 2$, the group could consist of 3 Spanish speakers and 2 English speakers or 300 Spanish speakers and 200 English speakers. (Or an infinite number of other possibilities!)

Thus, the important piece of data in such a question is an actual number. Given the ratio above, let's say you're told that there are 50 people in the group and you need to determine the number of native English speakers. If you're given the total and need one part, you'll need a part to whole ratio to answer the question.

The equation you'll set to answer such a question will almost always look like this:

$$\frac{part(ratio)}{whole(ratio)} = \frac{part(actual)}{whole(actual)}$$

In this case, the ratio of English speakers (part) to total group members (whole) is $2 : 5$, so the left side of the equation is $\frac{2}{5}$. The actual number of group members is 50 and the number of English speakers is our unknown, so the right side of the equation is $\frac{x}{50}$. Put it all together, and the equation looks like this:

$$\frac{2}{5} = \frac{x}{50}$$

To solve, cross-multiply and isolate x:

$$2(50) = 5x$$

$$x = \frac{100}{5} = 20$$

There is one thing worth accentuating about that process. It doesn't matter what type of ratio you're given. In this case, we started with a part to part ratio. What matters is the actual numbers we're given and the one we need. Since we were provided the number of total group members and we needed the number of English speakers, the ratio we needed was the one between those two quantities.

Most of the time, when ratios arise in GMAT problems, you'll do something like what we've discussed so far. But sometimes, you'll be asked to manipulate a ratio. In the simplest form, a question will tell you that a ratio "doubles" or "halves." In those cases, it's easier to think of the ratio as a fraction. So, if the ratio of boys to girls is initially $2:3$, and then it doubles, just multiply the ratio/fraction by two:

$$\frac{2}{3}(2) = \frac{4}{3} = 4:3$$

It's more complicated when you're asked to add to or subtract from a ratio. Let's say, again, that the ratio of boys to girls is $2:3$. If two more boys are added, what is the resulting ratio? The short answer is that we don't know. In order to know the effect of two boys, we need to know how many children were there in the first place, and a ratio doesn't give us that.

However, we can express the result algebraically. If the ratio is $2:3$, we typically write is as a fraction like so:

$$\frac{2}{3}$$

But, if we want to represent the actual number of boys and girls, we can add a variable. You might think of it as a multiplier:

$$\frac{2x}{3x}$$

The relationship is the same: the x's cancel out. But now, each part of the ratio represents an actual number. If there are 20 boys, $x = 10$ and $\frac{2x}{3x}$ is the same as $\frac{20}{30}$. If there are 6 boys, $x = 3$ and $\frac{2x}{3x} = \frac{6}{9}$. No matter what the multiplier is (how many children there actually are), $\frac{2x}{3x}$ represents that number.

So, if you want to add two boys to the group, add it to the fraction that represents the original number (not just the ratio) of children:

$$\frac{2x+2}{3x}$$

It may not be very satisfying right away, but it comes in handy. If this were an actual GMAT question, it would give you the original ratio of boys to girls, tell you that two more boys were added, and then tell you that the resulting ratio was, say, $4:5$. Thus, you know that the ratio you came up with, $\frac{2x+2}{3x}$, is equal to $\frac{4}{5}$, and you can solve for the value of x. Once you have x, you can determine the the the original number of boys, the original number of girls, or any number of other things.

70   Word Problems: Ratios: Drill

1.   Simplify each of the following ratios:
   a. $20 : 8$
   b. $54 : 36$
   c. $15 : 25$

2.   If the ratio of green marbles to blue marbles in a bag is $5 : 3$ and every marble is either green or blue, what is the ratio of green marbles to total marbles?

3.   If the ratio of the number of men on a certain committee to the number of women on the committee is $4 : 3$, what is the ratio of the number of women on the committee to the total number of committee members?

4.   For every student at a certain university under the age of 21, there are 3 students who are at least 21 years of age. What percent of students at the university are at least 21 years of age?

5.   A solution contains only alcohol and water. If the ratio of ounces of solution to ounces of alcohol is $5 : 2$, what is the ratio of ounces of water to ounces of alcohol?

6.   If $\frac{1}{4}$ of the employees in a certain company are managers, what is the ratio of managers to non-managers in the company?

7.   In a certain class, 30% of the students have blonde hair. What is the ratio of students who do not have blonde hair to those who have blonde hair?

8.   An estate is to be divided among heirs A, B, and C according to the ratio $5 : 3 : 2$, respectively. What is the ratio of the amount of the estate granted to heir A to the total amount of the estate?

9.   A family divides their monthly budget among rent, food, and other according to the ratio $3 : 4 : 9$. What fraction of the family's monthly budget is allocated to food?

10.   Each diner at a banquet has a choice of steak, chicken, or fish. If, for every diner who chooses steak, 2 choose chicken and 5 choose fish, what percent of the diners choose chicken?

11.   The student to teacher ratio at a certain school is $15 : 1$. If there are 300 students at the school, how many teachers are at the school?

12.   Of the families in a certain neighborhood, the ratio of those who have children to those who don't have children is $3 : 2$. If there are 65 families in the neighborhood, how many of the families don't have children?

13.   An investor's portfolio contains one utilities stock for every five total stocks. If the portfolio contains 7 utilities stocks, how many non-utilities stocks does it contain?

14.   What is the result if the ratio $7 : 2$ is doubled?

15.   What is the result if the ratio $3 : 4$ is halved?

16. What is the result if the ratio 1 : 6 is tripled?

17. The ratio of seniors to juniors on a certain swimming team is 5 : 4. If 2 more juniors are added, what is the resulting ratio?

18. The ratio of federal taxes to local taxes paid by a certain corporation is 7 : 5. If the corporation is levied an additional $10,000 in federal taxes, what is the resulting ratio?

71 Word Problems: Ratios: Practice

181.   The ratio $\frac{3}{4}$ to $\frac{1}{8}$ is equal to the ratio

    (A)   6 to 1
    (B)   3 to 1
    (C)   2 to 3
    (D)   1 to 3
    (E)   1 to 6

182.   What is the ratio of x to y?

    (1) x is 3 more than half of y.
    (2) x and y are integers.

183.   What is the ratio of $x : y : z$?

    (1) $xy = 14$
    (2) $yz = 21$

184.   The infant mortality rate for children under the age of one in
    Country X is 0.082 per thousand. If two million children
    were born in Country X in 1992, how many of those died
    before reaching one year of age?

    (A)   41
    (B)   82
    (C)   164
    (D)   420
    (E)   1640

185.   Of the students on a high school football team, $\frac{1}{6}$ are freshmen,
    $\frac{1}{4}$ are sophomores, $\frac{1}{3}$ are juniors, and the remaining 9 are
    seniors. What is the number of students on the football team?

    (A)   11
    (B)   18
    (C)   24
    (D)   36
    (E)   72

72 Word Problems: Ratios: Challenge

186. In a certain department, the ratio of the number of college graduates to the number of non-college graduates is 5 to 36. If 4 additional non-college graduates were to be transferred to the department, the ratio of the number of college graduates to non-college graduates would be 5 to 38. How many non-college graduates does the department have?

  (A) 36
  (B) 38
  (C) 72
  (D) 76
  (E) 152

187. The ratio, by volume, of salt to pepper to oregano in a certain recipe is $3 : 30 : 6$. The recipe will be altered so that the ratio of salt to pepper is doubled while the ratio of salt to oregano is halved. If the altered recipe will contain $2\frac{1}{2}$ teaspoons of pepper, how many teaspoons of oregano will it contain?

  (A) $\frac{1}{2}$
  (B) 1
  (C) $1\frac{1}{2}$
  (D) 2
  (E) $2\frac{1}{2}$

188. At a certain school, the ratio of the number of English majors to the number of Sociology majors is 5 to 2, and the ratio of the number of Psychology majors to the number of Sociology majors is 3 to 4. If the ratio of the number of History majors to the number of English majors is 5 to 3, what is the ratio of the number of Psychology majors to the number of History majors?

  (A) 25 to 3
  (B) 10 to 9
  (C) 9 to 50
  (D) 6 to 25
  (E) 3 to 10

189.   If t_1 and t_2 are the numbers of teachers and s_1 and s_2 are the numbers of students in District 1 and District 2, respecitvely, the ratio of the number of students to the number of teachers is greater for which of the two districts?

(1) $s_1 > s_2$

(2) $t_1 > t_2$

73 Word Problems: Percents

As I mentioned in the previous section, ratios are just relationships between numbers—the same as fractions, decimals, or percents. Naturally, the same applies here.

A percent is equivalent to a fraction or decimal, just one hundred times greater. For instance:

$1 = 100\%$

$0.25 = 25\%$

$\frac{2}{5} = 40\%$

While it is natural to convert percents into decimals, it's often easier on the GMAT to work with fractions. Especially when you are multiplying, it's less cumbersome to use a fraction such as $\frac{4}{5}$ than a decimal such as 0.8. There's no hard-and-fast rule for when to use one instead of the other, but most people would benefit from using fractions more and decimals less.

In that vein, a handy way to think about percents is that any percent is the numerator of a fraction over 100:

$\frac{2}{5} = \frac{x}{100}$

In this case, x is the percent. Solve, and $x = 40$.

There are a variety of ways the GMAT explicitly and implicitly tests your knowledge of percents. Let's go through each one.

First, you'll often see the phrase "percent of." In context, you'll need to find what percent one quantity is of another. For instance:

"If 30 of the 75 students in a class are female, what percent of the class is female?"

Keeping in mind that the word "of" indicates multiplication and the word "is" indicates an equals sign, you can convert that into an equation:

$(percent) \times (total) = female$

Since 30 students are female and the total is 75, that is:

$(percent) \times 75 = 30$

$(percent) = \frac{30}{75} = \frac{2}{5} = 40\%$

Even if you're working with variables, you can set up an equation like this one. For instance:

"What percent of p is q?"

Keeping in mind that a percent is a fraction over 100, that looks like:

$(percent) \times (total) = (part)$

$\frac{x}{100} \times p = q$ (here, x is the percent we're looking for)

If you want to find the percent (x) in terms of p and q, solve the equation for x.

Especially in word problems, you'll frequently see the phrases "percent greater" and "percent less." They also appear in the guises of "percent increase," "percent decrease" and "percent discount."

When you're working with numbers, this is often quite straightforward: if you need to find what is 20% less than 80, you do the math as follows:

$$80 - 20\%(80) = 80 - 16 = 64$$

Whether you're working with simple numbers, complicated numbers, or variables, you can always set up these problems that way.

However, there's a more elegant approach. For instance, if something has been decreased (discounted) by 20%, the new price is 80% of the old price. Taking the example from above:

$$80 - 20\%(80)$$
$$(100\%)80 - 20\%(80)$$
$$(80\%)80$$
$$(0.8)80 \qquad (\text{or } \tfrac{4}{5}(80))$$

Translating "20% less" to "80% of" should become automatic. It reduces three steps to one, and that one step is often no more difficult than any of the three steps in the original approach.

When you're increasing a total, it's even easier: the result of an increase of 30% is the same as 130% of the original amount:

$$x + (30\%)x$$
$$(100\%)x + (30\%)x$$
$$(130\%)x$$
$$1.3x$$

Again, it reduces three steps to one, and it should become automatic.

In the examples above, you were given the percent change and asked to find the corresponding amount. The questions are a bit trickier when they are the other way around. In these cases, you're given an original number and a new number and are asked to find the percent change. Think of it like a sale where you know the retail and discounted prices, but you want to know the percent off for each item.

The formula for percent change is $\frac{difference}{original}$, where difference is the change from the original price to the new amount. It will always be positive, regardless of whether the amount goes up or down. (As far as the GMAT is concerned, you'll never work with negative percents.)

Let's look at an example:

"Last week, John worked 24 hours. This week, John worked 30 hours. By what percent did his number of hours increase?"

The original is last week's total: 24. The difference is $30 - 24 = 6$ hours. The percent change, then, is:

$$\tfrac{6}{24} = \tfrac{1}{4} = 25\%$$

Sometimes it may be confusing to determine which of the two numbers is the original. Use this rule of thumb: if you're looking for a percent increase, the original is the smaller number. If you need the decrease, use the larger number. If you're simply asked for the "percent change," you'll have to deduce which is which, but usually you can apply common sense to the situation and determine whether the amount is going up or down.

Note that even if the numbers are the same, the percent increase and percent decrease won't be the same. For instance, if we alter the above example:

"Last week, John worked 30 hours. This week, John worked 24 hours. By what percent did his number of hours decrease?"

Now, the original is 30, the difference is 6, and the change is:

$$\frac{6}{30} = \frac{1}{5} = 20\%$$

The absolute change stays the same (in both cases, it's a difference of six hours), but the denominator changes. Because of that, the percent changes as well. Remember this tidbit: the GMAT loves to test it.

74   Word Problems: Percents: Drill

1.   Convert each of the following to the equivalent percent:
     a.   0.56
     b.   0.001
     c. $\frac{4}{5}$
     d. $\frac{3}{20}$
     e. $\frac{16}{25}$

2.   Given the following values of x of y, what percent of x is y?
     a. $x = 50$, $y = 32$
     b. $x = 6$, $y = 1$
     c. $x = 1.2$ million, $y = 30,000$
     d. $x = 25$, $y = 400$
     e. $x = 72$, $y = 90$

3.   What number is 25% greater than 40?
4.   What number is 6% greater than 200?
5.   What number is 150% greater than 3?
6.   What number is 15% less than 150?
7.   What number is 90% less than 180?
8.   What is the percent increase from 100 to 125?
9.   What is the percent decrease from 125 to 100?
10.   What is the percent increase from 24 to 30?
11.   What is the percent decrease from 144 to 36?
12.   What is the percent increase from 21 to 84?

75   Word Problems: Percents: Practice

191.   150 is what percent of 3?

   (A)   2%
   (B)   5%
   (C)   500%
   (D)   2,000%
   (E)   5,000%

192.   A certain tax rate is $5.20 per $100.00. What is this rate, expressed as a percent?

   (A)   52%
   (B)   5.2%
   (C)   0.52%
   (D)   0.052%
   (E)   0.0052%

193.   How much is 70 percent of a certain number?

   (1)   25 percent of twice the number is equal to half the number.
   (2)   50 percent of the number is 10 less than the number.

194.   What percent of the technology stocks on a certain exchange increased in price yesterday?

   (1)   Exactly 150 of the 500 stocks on the exchange increased in price yesterday.
   (2)   Exactly 27 of the 90 technology stocks on the exchange increased in price yesterday.

195.   Twenty percent of incoming freshmen at a certain university have taken a calculus course. Among the incoming freshmen who have not taken a calculus course, 148 have taken a pre-calculus course and 44 have not taken a pre-calculus course. How many incoming freshmen are there at the university?

   (A)   200
   (B)   240
   (C)   280
   (D)   320
   (E)   360

196.   What percent of $\frac{1}{10}$ of 4,000 is $\frac{1}{4}$ of 1,000?

      (A)   10
      (B) $16\frac{2}{3}$
      (C)   25
      (D) $62\frac{1}{2}$
      (E)   100

197.   A company accountant estimates that next year cars purchased for the company fleet will increase in price by 10 percent and that vans purchased for the company fleet will increase in price by 30 percent. This year thte total cost of cars purchased for the company fleet was $49,000 and the total cost of vans purchased for the company fleet was $27,000. According to the accountant's estimate, if the same number of vehicles are purchased for the company fleet next year as this year, how much will be spent on vehicles for the company fleet?

      (A) $83,600
      (B) $89,000
      (C) $90,000
      (D) $93,400
      (E) $98,800

198.   By what percent did the infant mortality rate in Country X decrease from 1972 to 1976?

      (1)   On average, the infant mortality rate in Country X decreased by 10% per year from 1972 to 1976.
      (2)   On average, the infant mortality rate in Country X decreased by 8% per year from 1970 to 1980.

76 Word Problems: Percents: Challenge

199. If $p > 0$ and x is p percent of y, then, in terms of x and y, what is the value of p?

    (A) $\frac{x}{y}$

    (B) $\frac{y}{x}$

    (C) $\frac{100x}{y}$

    (D) $\frac{100y}{x}$

    (E) $\frac{x}{100y}$

200. A corporation paid $7 million in federal taxes on its first $50 million of gross profits and then $30 million in federal taxes on the next $150 million in gross profits. By approximately what percent did the ratio of federal taxes to gross profits increase from the first $50 million in profits to the next $150 million in profits?

    (A)   6%

    (B)   14%

    (C)   20%

    (D)   23%

    (E)   43%

77 Word Problems: Rate

Like ratios, it's useful to think of rates as fractions. In fact, rates are essentially the same as ratios, with one key difference. Ratios express the relationship between two like things: if the ratio of men to women is $3 : 4$, we may separate people into two segments, but they are all people. Rates, on the other hand, express the relationship between two unlike things.

The most common type of rate is speed. You've probably heard the phrase "miles per hour" or "kilometers per hour" so many times in your life you've long since stopped thinking about it as a relationship between two different quantities. But a relationship is, in fact, what it is. When you say you're traveling at 60 miles per hour, you're expressing a relationship between the number of miles you're traveling and the number of hours you're traveling:

$$\frac{60 \text{ miles}}{1 \text{ hour}}$$

You can handle many of the rate problems you'll see on the GMAT if you treat them just like the ratios you saw a few chapters ago. Just as with ratios, you'll be given a relationship ("60 miles per hour") and one actual number (say, 180 miles). With those, you can set up a ratio:

$$\frac{60 \text{ miles}}{1 \text{ hour}} = \frac{180 \text{ miles}}{x \text{ hours}}$$

Since the units are the same on both sides of the equation, you can forget about them. Then, cross-multiply and solve for x:

$$60x = 180(1)$$
$$x = \frac{180}{60} = 3$$

Rate problems need not be speed-related, though. You will see plenty of rates that express some form of speed, such as:

> miles per hour
>
> widgets per day
>
> dollars per month

However, a rate can consist of any relationship of two unlike things. Here are some examples of rates you might come across on GMAT questions:

> sales per customer
>
> GDP per capita
>
> shares of stock per portfolio

While you may be most comfortable with speed-related rates, it's important to understand rates at a more abstract level, one that allows you to accomodate these other types of rates with ease. To reach that level, force yourself to express every single rate you see as a fraction, consciously using the word "per" as a signal. Just as "miles per hour" means you'll have some number of miles divided by some number of hours, "GDP per capita" means you'll have some amount of GDP divided by some number of people.

In most such cases, the problem isn't much more complicated than anything you'd see on a ratio question. The techniques discussed in that section work just as well here.

GMAT rate questions get tricky when the test combines multiple rates. In fact, one type of question, sometimes called "work" or "simultaneous rate," merits the entire next chapter. Before getting to work problems, we'll take a look at a couple of others way in which the GMAT will combine rates.

The first type of problem is "average rate" or "average speed." An example might go like this:

> "Karen drove 100 miles at a speed of 40 miles per hour, then
> another 100 miles at a speed of 50 miles per hour. What was
> her average speed for the entire 200-mile trip?"

Most people, upon initial exposure to this type of question, have a reflex answer: 45 miles per hour. Accordingly, most people are wrong. To discover why, we'll need to walk through the problem, step by step.

The formula for average speed is just like that for any other type of rate. If we're looking for miles per hour, we need to find the total miles over the total number of hours. Total miles in this case is easy: 200 miles. Total hours takes more effort. 100 miles at 40 miles per hour takes 2.5 hours, while 100 miles at 50 miles per hour takes 2 hours. Thus, total hours is 4.5, and the average speed is:

$$\frac{200}{4.5} = 44\frac{4}{9}$$

Why do we get such a counter-intuitive answer? The key is the times that we solved for. Karen spent more time driving at the slower speed, so her average speed was closer to 40 than 50. The average speed is weighted by amounts of time, so the fact that the distances were the same doesn't mean the weights are equal. (For more on weighted averages, consult the chapter specifically covering that topic.)

It's great if you understand exactly why the intuitive answer is wrong. But most importantly, you need to remember that to solve for an average speed, you must calculate total distance and total time, as we did working through this example.

The other type of combined rate problem involves two objects moving toward each other. (Or, in another variation, one catching up with the other.) The stereotypical example goes something like this:

> "Stations A and B are 100 miles apart. If Train X leaves Station A
> moving at 20 miles per hour and Train Y leaves Station B at the
> same time moving at 30 miles per hour along a parallel track, how
> long will the trains travel before they meet?"

The key concept needed to solve a problem like this is that the trains move toward each other at the sum of their rates. After one hour, Train X will have traveled 20 miles, and Train Y will have traveled 30 miles. So after that first hour, the trains are 50 miles closer to each other than they were when they started. Another way to put that is to say that the trains are converging at 50 miles per hour.

The math involved is very simple. In fact, it's the same math you'd need to figure out how long it takes you to drive 100 miles at a speed of 50 miles per hour. It's 2 hours. If the question asked, instead, how far Train Y traveled before the trains meet, you would begin the problem the same way. Once you discovered that it took 2 hours before they met, you'd use Train Y's speed (30 miles per hour) to determine how far Train Y traveled in 2 hours: 60 miles.

The variation–one object catching up with another–is very similar. Here's an example of the basic framework that these questions follow:

"Ron and Sara are driving along the same road. Sara is driving at a constant rate of 30 miles per hour, while Ron is driving at a constant rate of 40 miles per hour. If Ron is currently 5 miles behind Sara, at what point will Ron catch up with Sara?"

Much like the converging trains of the previous example, the first step here is to distill the two rates into a single number. We don't particularly care how far Ron or Sara get, or how fast they do so. What matters is how fast Ron catches up. We can find that by subtracting Sara's rate from Ron's rate, for a "catch-up rate" of 10 miles per hour. In an hour, Ron drives 10 more miles than Sara does, so that's the number of miles Ron gains on Sara.

The final step is identical to that of the train example above. We want to know when Ron will make up 5 miles, and he makes up 10 miles per hour. Given that information, Ron will catch up in a half hour.

78 Word Problems: Rate: Drill

1. In 8 hours, a factory produces 176,000 wing nuts. How many wing nuts does the factory produce per hour?

2. An airplane travels a 1,200 mile route in 4 hours. What is the airplane's average speed for the trip?

3. A certain insect can crawl 900 feet in 12 hours. What is the insect's average distance per hour over that time?

4. The national income of Country X is $1,800,000,000. If Country X has a population of 3 million, what is its per capita national income?

5. If Charles drives at an average speed of 55 miles per hour, how long would it take him to drive 275 miles?

6. A certain hose fills a tank at a rate of 16 gallons per minute. If the tank has a capacity of 960 gallons, how long would it take the hose to fill the tank?

7. How long would it take someone walking at a rate of 4 miles per hour to cover a distance of 27 miles?

8. If Oscar can build 24 feet of fencing per day, how many days would it take Oscar to build a 144 foot long fence?

9. A train travels at an average rate of 35 miles per hour for 2.5 hours. What distance does it cover in that time?

10. A certain university graduates 120 students per year. How many students does it graduate in an 8-year period?

11. A pool drains at a rate of 600 gallons of water per hour. How many gallons of water will be drained from the pool in $1\frac{1}{4}$ hours?

12. How many meters will a satellite travel in 1 minute if it travels at an average speed of 18 meters per second?

13. If Eileen drives at an average speed of 50 miles per hour for 3 hours and an average speed of 60 miles per hour for the next 2 hours, what is her average speed for the entire trip?

14. A train travels at a speed of 60 miles per hour for the first 180 miles of its trip, then it travels at a speed of 45 miles per hour for the remaining 180 miles of its trip. What is the train's average speed for the entire trip?

15. A factory produces 220 engines per week for six weeks. Following the installation of new equipment, the factory produces 320 engines per week for next eight weeks. What is the average number of engines produced per week over the 14-week period?

16. If a truck driver travels 455 miles at an average speed of 70 miles per hour, then takes a one-hour break, then travels another 315 miles at the same speed, what is his average speed for the entire 770-mile trip, including the break?

17.   Ana and Bradley are 12 miles away from each other on opposite ends of a straight path. If Ana walks toward Bradley at a rate of 4 miles per hour and Bradley walks toward Ana at a rate of 5 miles per hour, how long will it take before they meet?

18.   Xavier and Yoelle are proofreading a 144-page manuscript. Xavier starts at the first page and works at a rate of 20 pages per hour and Yoelle starts at the last page and works at a rate of 16 pages per hour. When Xavier and Yoelle have read the entire manuscript between them, how many pages will Xavier have read?

19.   Frankie and Georgia are driving along the same road. If Frankie is driving at a speed of 52 miles per hour and Georgia is 30 miles behind him, driving at a speed of 58 miles per hour, how long will it take before Georgia catches up with Frankie?

20.   Janelle and Karl both sell insurance. This year, Janelle has sold $60,000 less than Karl has. If Janelle sells $3,200 per day and Karl sells $2,000 per day, how many days will it take before Janelle catches up with Karl and moves $12,000 ahead?

79   Word Problems: Rate: Practice

201.   How long did it take Fiona to drive the 240 miles nonstop from her home to Columbus, Ohio?

(1)   Fiona's average speed over the first 180 miles was 50 miles per hour.

(2)   Fiona's average speed over the final 60 miles was 45 miles per hour.

202.   Train X and train Y traveled the same 100-mile route. If train X took 2.5 hours and train Y traveled at an average speed that was 25 percent faster than the average speed of train X, how many hours did it take train Y to travel the route?

(A)   1

(B) $1\frac{3}{4}$

(C) $1\frac{7}{8}$

(D)   2

(E) $3\frac{1}{8}$

203.   When flying between Chicago and New York, did a certain airplane ever exceed 400 miles per hour?

(1)   By the route the airplane took, the distance between Chicago and New York is 750 miles.

(2)   The total time the airplane spent in the air was 2 hours.

204.   A rectangular swimming pool with uniform depth is full to capacity with water. If water is pumped out of the pool at a constant rate, how long will it take to empty the pool?

(1)   40 minutes after water begins to be pumped out of the pool, the pool will be $\frac{5}{6}$ full.

(2)   2 hours after water beings to be pumped out of the pool, $\frac{1}{2}$ of the water will have been removed.

205.   Factory A fulfills 100 orders twice as fast as factory B does. Factory B fulfills 100 orders in 30 minutes. If each factory fulfills orders at a constant rate, how many orders does factory A fulfill in 9 minutes?

(A)   15
(B)   30
(C)   60
(D)   90
(E)   100

206. A computer printer manufacturer produces 500 units of a certain model each month at a cost to the manufacturer of $65 per unit and all of the produced units are sold each month. What is the minimum selling price per unit that will ensure that the monthly profit (revenue from sales minus the manufacturer's cost to produce) on the sales of these units will be at least $35,000?

  (A) $70
  (B) $85
  (C) $105
  (D) $115
  (E) $135

207. How long, in minutes, did it take a bicycle wheel to roll along a flat, straight 300-meter path?

  (1)   The diameter of the bicycle wheel was 0.6 meter.
  (2)   The wheel made one full 360-degree rotation every 0.6π meters.

208. A phone company charges $\frac{3}{4}$ of its regular per-minute rate for long-distance calls for each minute in excess of 1000 per month, excluding calls made on Sundays, and $\frac{1}{2}$ of its regular per-minute rate for all long-distance calls made on Sundays. How much did the phone company charge Victoria last month?

  (A)   Last month, Victoria made a total of 1500 minutes worth of long-distance calls, including 200 minutes worth on Sundays.
  (B)   The regular rate for long-distance calls is $0.10 per minute.

80 Word Problems: Rates: Challenge

209.   A shipping company currently charges the same price for each
package that it ships. If the current price of each package
were to be increased by $1, 6 fewer of the packages could
be shipped for $120, excluding sales tax. What is the current
price of shipping each package?

(A) $2
(B) $3
(C) $4
(D) $5
(E) $6

210.   At the rate of f feet per s seconds, how many feet does a
pedestrian travel in m minutes?

(A) $\frac{sm}{f}$
(B) $\frac{fm}{s}$
(C) $\frac{60f}{ms}$
(D) $\frac{60fm}{s}$
(E) $\frac{60fs}{m}$

81 Word Problems: Work

Work problems, also known as "combined work" or "simultaneous rate" problems, are very similar to the combined rate questions discussed at the end of the previous chapter. In fact, they are combined rate problems; it's just easier to look at them as a different type of problem.

In the Rate chapter, we discovered that if two objects are moving toward each other, they are converging at the sum of their respective rates. We can think about that in more general terms: if two things are both working to achieve the same goal at the same time, their combined rate is the sum of their respective rates. As an equation, we can write it like this:

$$r_a + r_b = r_t$$

That doesn't move us much further than the previous chapter did, but the next step will. Often, on GMAT questions, you won't be given rates for the individual components. Instead, you'll find out the time it takes for each item (perhaps a machine producing widgets, or a person building a fence) to complete an entire job. It would be more useful, then, to express the equation in terms of time, not rate.

To recall, rate is equal to amount divided by time. So, if it takes 6 hours to do the entire job, the rate is:

$$r = \frac{amount}{time} = \frac{1}{6}$$

Putting it all together, if the information you're given is in terms of the time it takes to complete an entire job (or travel an entire distance), you can use a variation of that initial equation:

$$\frac{1}{t_a} + \frac{1}{t_b} = \frac{1}{t_t}$$

In a moment, we'll discuss a shortcut to use in these situations that will help you avoid all of those fractions. (Trust me, it can get messy sometimes.) But the advantage of this approach is twofold. First, it's very flexible: while the example above shows what to do if you know that 1 job takes, say, 6 hours, you could easily change it to accomodate a question in which 3 jobs take 18 hours, or some other simple variation. Second, it can be expanded for more rates. If three or more machines are working together, for instance, you can just add another term to the left side of the equation:

$$\frac{1}{t_a} + \frac{1}{t_b} + \frac{1}{t_c} = \frac{1}{t_t}$$

It's rare that the GMAT will require you to do this, but when it does, this equation will allow you to handle it.

As promised, there's a shortcut for the most straightforward cases. Let's work with a common example:

"Working alone, it would take John 3 hours to paint a certain room. Working alone, it would take Kevin 4 hours to paint the same room. Working together at their respective rates, how long would it take John and Kevin to paint the room?"

This is a classic case for the equation we just learned:

$$\frac{1}{t_a} + \frac{1}{t_b} = \frac{1}{t_t}$$

$$\frac{1}{3} + \frac{1}{4} = \frac{1}{t}$$
$$\frac{7}{12} = \frac{1}{t}$$
$$t = \frac{12}{7}$$

Especially when the numbers aren't so simple, the fractions can get unwieldy. So, when you're given amounts of time and you're looking for an amount of time, use this alternative equation. (I'm using A instead of t_a, etc., by convention.)

$$\frac{AB}{A+B} = T$$

You may notice that this equation is mathematically identical to the first one:

$$\frac{1}{A} + \frac{1}{B} = \frac{1}{T}$$
$$\frac{B}{AB} + \frac{A}{AB} = \frac{1}{T}$$
$$\frac{A+B}{AB} = \frac{1}{T}$$
$$\frac{AB}{A+B} = T$$

In practice, familiarity with that algebra isn't the important thing. What's useful is being able to recognize when this shortcut will save you time. The example above is certainly one of those cases:

$$\frac{AB}{A+B} = T$$
$$\frac{3(4)}{3+4} = T$$
$$\frac{12}{7} = T$$

In general, if the question gives you amounts of time, use the shortcut. If it gives you rates, or you have to do some preliminary work to determine rates or times, use the original equation. As usual, it's valuable to occasionally experiment with both methods to learn for yourself when each approach will be most useful.

82 Word Problems: Work: Drill

1. If it takes Machine A 12 hours to complete a job and Machine B 8 hours to complete the same job, how long would it take the two machines to complete the job working together?

2. Hose H can fill a pool with water in 15 minutes. If Hose J can fill the pool with water in 20 minutes, how long would it take the hoses to fill the pool with water if they filled the pool simultaneously?

3. Camille can paint a room in 2 hours. If David can paint an identical room in 3 hours, how long would it take the two of them to paint two such rooms, working simultaneously?

4. Pump X can replenish the air in a 1000 cubic foot space in 40 minutes, while Pump Y can replenish the air in a 1000 cubic foot space in one hour. How long would it take Pumps X and Y to replenish the air in a 1000 cubic foot space if they both operated at the same time?

5. Drain N can remove the water from a 500 gallon tank in 3 hours, and Drain P can remove the water from a 500 gallon tank in 3.5 hours. If Drains P and N operated simultaneously, how long would it take them to remove the water from a 2,000 gallon tank?

6. If Victor can construct 20 feet of fencing in 6 hours and Wanda can do the same in 8 hours, how long would it take Victor and Wanda, working together, to construct 50 feet of fencing?

7. If Adam can assemble 2 parts per hour and Brianne can assemble 5 parts per hour, how long will it take the two of them, working simultaneously, to assemble 105 parts?

8. Pump O can extract 150 gallons of oil per hour, and Pump P can extract 200 gallons of oil per hour. How long would it take the two pumps, working simultaneously, to extract 70 gallons of oil?

9. Machine A can fill an order in 20 hours, and Machine B can do the job twice as fast. If the two machines work simultaneously, how long would it take them to fill 5 such orders?

10. Randy can paint 60 square feet of a ceiling in an hour, and Samir can paint the same amount of ceiling in one-third the time. If Randy and Samir both paint the same ceiling for 3 hours, how many square feet can they finish in that time?

83 Word Problems: Work: Practice

211. Krista repairs electrical components at a uniform rate of 25 per day, and Lawrence repairs electrical components at a uniform rate of 15 per half-day. If Krista and Lawrence work simultaneously, how many days will it take for them to repair a total of 330 electrical components?

    (A) $4\frac{1}{8}$
    (B) 5
    (C) 6
    (D) $8\frac{1}{4}$
    (E) $13\frac{1}{5}$

212. One pipe fills an empty pool in 4 hours. A second pipe fills the same pool in 3 hours. If both pipes are used together, how long will it take, in hours, to fill $\frac{1}{2}$ the pool?

    (A) $\frac{1}{12}$
    (B) $\frac{7}{12}$
    (C) $\frac{6}{7}$
    (D) $\frac{7}{6}$
    (E) $\frac{12}{7}$

213. Machines X and Y run simultaneously at their respective constant rates. If machine X produces 120 boxtops in 30 minutes, how many boxtops do machines X and Y produce per hour?

    (1) Machine Y produces as many boxtops in 20 minutes as machine X produces in 30 minutes.
    (2) Working simultaneously, machines X and Y produce more than twice as many boxtops per hour as machine X does.

214. An empty swimming pool with a capacity of 40,000 liters is to be filled by hoses X and Y simultaneously. If the amount of water flowing from each hose is independent of the amount flowing from the other hose, how long, in hours, will it take to fill the pool?

    (1) It would take 22 hours for hose X alone to fill the pool.
    (2) It would take 20 hours for hose Y alone to fill the pool.

215.   If machine X ran continuously at a uniform rate to fill a
        production order beginning at 9:30 a.m., at what time did
        the machine finish filling the order?

    (1)   If machine Y had begun filling the order at 9:30 a.m.,
           it would have finished filling the order at 12:30 p.m.

    (2)   If machine X and machine Y, working simultaneously,
           had begun filling the order at 9:30 a.m., the order
           would have been filled by 10:42 a.m.

84 Word Problems: Work: Challenge

216. Carolina stuffs envelopes at a rate of 8 per minute. When Carolina works with David, the two of them, working simultaneously at their respective constant rates, they stuff 1,080 envelopes per hour. How many envelopes does David stuff per minute?

    (A) 6
    (B) 8
    (C) 9
    (D) 10
    (E) 12

217. Machines C and D produced identical computer chips at different constant rates. After Machine C operated alone for 3 hours and Machine D operated alone for 5 hours, the two machines produced a total of 2,100 chips. How many hours would it have taken Machine D operating alone to produce all 2,100 chips?

    (1) Machine D produces 50% more chips per hour than Machine C does.
    (2) Machine C produces 200 chips per hour.

218. Rhonda, Sam, and Tara, working simultaneously and independently at their respective constant rates, can complete a certain task in 144 minutes. How long does it take Tara, working alone at her constant rate, to complete the task?

    (1) Rhonda, working alone at her constant rate, can complete the task in 372 minutes.
    (2) Sam, working alone at his constant rate, can complete the task in 285 minutes.

85 Word Problems: Measurement

Of all the topics with individual chapters in this book, this is one least likely to represent an entire question. That doesn't mean it won't be tested. Think of it like dividing fractions: You'll need this skill to handle a whole range of problems, but it'll never be the sole focus of a single one.

For the purposes of the GMAT, what "measurement" means is converting from one unit of measure to another. For instance, you're given a quantity in gallons and you have to convert it to ounces. Or you're given a length in inches and you have to convert it to yards. Or, even harder, you're given a rate in meters per second and you have to convert it to kilometers per hour. Most people can figure these things out, but they don't have a concrete understanding of the math behind it.

Whenever you're working with a number that represents something (millimeters, liters, whatever), it's useful to keep those units in the math itself. For instance, when you're told that a car is traveling at 40 miles per hour, you probably jot that down on your scratch paper as "40 mph." Maybe just as "40." Sometimes that's good enough, but if you have to convert from one unit of measure to another, it will be confusing. Any time you are given a rate (usually represented in the units as the word "per"), you can write it as a fraction with the units intact. Using that method, you'd write down 40 miles per hour as:

$$\frac{40 \text{ miles}}{1 \text{ hour}}$$

It requires a little more writing, and sometimes it won't end up doing you any good, but as we'll see in a moment, it's crucial to executing unit conversions.

Before we convert rates, let's start with something simpler. Let's say you need to convert 15 yards to the equivalent number of feet. 3 feet is equal to 1 yard, so we'll calculate as follows:

$$15 \text{ yards} \times \frac{3 \text{ feet}}{1 \text{ yard}}$$

Notice that the fraction is equal to one: 3 feet is the same as 1 yard, so we're not altering 15 yards in any way, we're just changing the way we represent it. Units can be cancelled out in the same way that numbers are, so the result looks like this:

$$\frac{15 \text{ yards}}{1} \times \frac{3 \text{ feet}}{1 \text{ yard}} = \frac{45 \text{ feet}}{1} = 45 \text{ feet}$$

It may be obvious to you that 15 yards is equal to 45 feet; indeed, many of the conversions the GMAT asks you to execute are that simple. However, for the times when they are not that simple, you need a foolproof method to convert from one unit to another. There are several more examples like this among the drill questions.

More complicated are conversions of rates. They are also more common; these are less likely to be intuitive to you, so it's all the more important that you learn the mechanics behind converting one rate to another.

Let's try another example. If a jogger runs at the rate of k miles per hour, what is her rate in terms of miles per minute?

As we discussed above, we should write our rate in terms of a fraction, retaining all of the units:

$\frac{k \text{ miles}}{1 \text{ hour}}$

We want to translate this to miles per minute, which means the miles will stay the same, but the hours will somehow change into minutes. In other words, we want our final fraction to have miles in the numerator and minutes in the denominator. To do this, we'll use a similar fraction to what we used to convert from feet to yards. 1 hour equals 60 minutes, so we could multiply our rate by the fraction $\frac{1 \text{ hour}}{60 \text{ minutes}}$, or by the fraction $\frac{60 \text{ minutes}}{1 \text{ hour}}$ without changing the rate. Since we want our final rate to have minutes in the denominator, we'll use the first fraction, like so:

$\frac{k \text{ miles}}{1 \text{ hour}} \times \frac{1 \text{ hour}}{60 \text{ minutes}} = \frac{k \text{ miles}}{60 \text{ minutes}} = \frac{k}{60}$ miles per minute.

One final note: for the most part, the GMAT does not expect you to know conversion rates. However, you should know that there are 60 seconds in a minute, 60 minutes in an hour, 12 inches in a foot, and 1,000 meters in a kilometer. When the test asks you to convert using other ratios, it will give you the ratio by adding a note at the end of the question such as (3 feet = 1 yard). You have quite enough to do to prepare for the test without unnecessarily memorizing conversation ratios.

86   Word Problems: Measurement: Drill

1.   288 inches is equal to how many feet?
2.   27.5 kilometers is equal to how many meters?
3. $6\frac{1}{2}$ hours is equal to how many seconds?
4.   55 miles per hour is equal to how many miles per minute?
5.   0.75 meters per second is equal to how many meters per minute?
6.   0.5 miles per second is equal to how many miles per hour?
7.   16 feet per second is equal to how many inches per second?
8.   24 feet per second is equal to how many yards per minute?
9.   90 kilometers per hour is equal to how many meters per second?
10.   32 feet per second is equal to how many miles per hour? (1 mile = 5,280 feet)

87   Word Problems: Measurement: Practice

221.   If 1 mile is approximately 1.61 kilometers, which of the following best approximates the number of miles in 5 kilometers?

   (A)   2.9
   (B)   3.1
   (C)   6.1
   (D)   7.9
   (E)   8.1

222.   The speed of light is approximately 1.86×10^5 miles per second. This approximate speed is how many miles per hour?

   (A) 1.11×10^7
   (B) 6.70×10^7
   (C) 1.11×10^8
   (D) 1.86×10^8
   (E) 6.70×10^8

223.   If Lino had an appointment on a certain day, was the appointment on a Friday?

   (1)   Exactly 80 hours before the appointment, it was Tuesday.
   (2)   The appointment was between 9:00 a.m. and 12:00 a.m.

224.   At Narendra's grocery store, Brand X soda is sold by the liter and Brand Y milk is sold by the quart. Excluding sales tax, what is the total cost for 1 gallon of Brand X soda and 1 gallon of Brand Y milk?

   (1)   Excluding sales tax, the total cost for 10 liters of Brand X soda and 6 quarts of Brand Y milk is $27.00. (There is no quantity discount.)
   (2)   Excluding sales tax, the total cost for 4 liters of Brand X soda and 12 quarts of Brand Y milk is $25.20. (There is no quantity discount.)

88 Word Problems: Mixture

Mixture problems are not common on the GMAT. There are only a handful of examples among the hundreds of questions in The Official Guide, but on the off chance you encounter one on the test, it's worth outlining an approach to these questions.

That approach is very similar to what you'll do with weighted average problems, which are still a few chapters away. In fact, mixtures *are* weighted averages: in both cases, you're trying to determine the results of combining different amounts of separate quantities. With weighted averages, you're usually looking for the end result, say, the average salary of five employees. With mixtures, on the other hand, it's more common that you'd be looking for the number of employees at a certain salary that would result in that average salary.

Enough generalities. Here's a sample mixture problem:

"Solution A consists of 50% chlorine. Solution B consists of 75% chlorine. If 12 ounces of solution A are poured into a container, how many ounces of solution B must be added so that the resulting solution consists of 60% chlorine?"

First, some basics. Obviously, no matter much much solution A or solution B you use, the chlorine level will never be less than 50% or greater than 75%. Further, the closer the chlorine level is to 50%, the larger portion of the resulting solution must be solution A. And vice versa: the closer the chlorine level is to 75%, the larger portion of the resulting solution must be solution B.

Here's how you'd set up the equation to solve the problem:

$$\frac{0.5(12) + 0.75(x)}{12 + x} = 0.6$$

As you'll see in a few chapters, that's exactly like a weighted average problem. In the meantime, let's look at it in terms of the question we're dealing with now. The numerator of the fraction gives us the total amount of chlorine. If there are 12 ounces of a 50% chlorine solution, there are 6 ounces of chlorine. We don't know how many ounces there are of the 75% chlorine solution, but that's the quantity we're looking for, so we'll call it x. Thus, the addition amount of chlorine is $0.75x$.

The denominator of the fraction is the total quantity of the two solutions. The fraction as a whole, then, is the amount of chlorine over the amount of combined solution. That ratio, we know, is 0.6, our target chlorine level. To solve:

$$0.5(12) + 0.75(x) = 0.6(12 + x)$$
$$6 + 0.75x = 7.2 + 0.6x$$
$$0.15x = 1.2$$
$$x = \frac{1.2}{0.15} = \frac{120}{15} = 8$$

There's one additional step the GMAT may ask you to take. In the example above, they gave you an amount for one of the solutions. However, the question could be rephrased without any quantities, to ask for a ratio instead:

"Solution A consists of 50% chlorine. Solution B consists of 75%
chlorine. If the two solutions are combined so that the resulting
solution consists of 60% chlorine, what fraction of the resulting
solution is solution A?"

Going back to the equation we set up for the previous example, it looks like
we now have two variables:

$$\frac{0.5(x)+0.75(y)}{x+y} = 0.6$$

However, we're looking for a ratio, not actual quantities. The fraction of the
solution that started life as solution A and the fraction that began as solution
B adds up to 1–that is, everything that is in the resulting solution came from
one of those two places. Therefore:

$$x + y = 1$$

or:

$$y = 1 - x$$

So we can reduce the equation to something with only one variable:

$$\frac{0.5(x)+0.75(1-x)}{1} = 0.6$$

Now we have something we can solve:

$$0.5(x) + 0.75(1 - x) = 0.6$$

$$0.5x + 0.75 - 0.75x = 0.6$$

$$-0.25x = -0.15$$

$$25x = 15$$

$$x = \frac{15}{25} = \frac{3}{5}$$

Of course, that fraction is the same as that represented by the quantities
we solved for the first time around. In that example, we were told that the
resulting solution consisted of 12 ounces of solution A, and then discovered than
it contained 8 ounces of solution B. Therefore, the fraction consisting of solution
A was

$$\frac{12}{12+8} = \frac{12}{20} = \frac{3}{5}$$

89 Word Problems: Mixture: Drill

1. A 100-gallon solution consisting of water and alcohol consists of 80 percent water. If 20 gallons of water evaporate, what percent of the remaining solution is alcohol?

2. 60 ounces of a certain solution consists of 75% water. How much water must evaporate in order for water to represent 50% of the remaining solution?

3. Mixture A consists of water and chlorine in a 4 : 1 ratio. Mixture B consists of water and fluoride in a 9 : 1 ratio. If a solution includes 2 pints each of Mixture A and Mixture B, what fraction of the solution is water?

4. Solution X consists of 60% water and 40% ammonia. Solution Y consists of 70% water and 30% ammonia. If equal amounts of Solution X and Solution Y are combined, what percent of the resulting solution is ammonia?

5. A certain solution is 60% methanol. How many ounces of methanol must be added to 80 ounces of the original solution so that the resulting solution is 75% methanol?

6. Mixture M consists of 65% water and 35% ethanol. Mixture N consists of 80% water and 20% ethanol. If 200 gallons of Mixture M is combined with 100 gallons of Mixture N, what percent of the resulting solution is ethanol?

7. Solution R contains water and fluoride in a 3 : 1 ratio, and Solution S contains water and fluoride in a 3 : 2 ratio. If 20 ounces of Solution R is to be combined with x ounces of Solution S to create a solution that contains water and fluoride in a 7 : 3ratio, what is the value of x?

8. An 80-gallon solution contains 90% water and 10% glycerol. If 20 gallons of a solution containing equal parts water and glycerol is added, what percent of the resulting solution is glycerol?

9. Mixture X contains 60% water and 40% chloride. If 120 gallons of Mixture Y is to be added to 80 gallons of Mixture X in order to produce a solution that contains 75% water and 25% chloride, how many gallons of water must Mixture Y contain?

10. Solution A contains 18 ounces of alcohol and 32 ounces of water. Solution B contains 72 ounces of water and 8 ounces of alcohol. What percent of Solution B must be added to Solution A so that the resulting mixture contains $\frac{5}{7}$ water?

90 Word Problems: Mixture: Practice

231.   A bag of marbles contains 13 red marbles and 22 green marbles. How many green marbles must be removed from the bag so that 65 percent of the marbles will be red?

(A)   2
(B)   7
(C)   15
(D)   17
(E)   20

232.   A chlorine solution contains 3 ounces of chlorine per 20 cubic centimeters of solution. If 7 cubic centimeters of the solution were poured into an empty container, how many ounces of chlorine would be in the container?

(A)   0.35
(B)   0.95
(C)   1.05
(D)   1.35
(E)   1.50

233.   A tank contains 5,000 gallons of a solution that is 1 percent red dye by volume. If 2,000 gallons of water evaporate from the tank, the remaining solution will be approximately what percent red dye?

(A)   0.71%
(B)   1.00%
(C)   1.67%
(D)   2.50%
(E)   5.00%

234.   Company A's workforce consists of 10 percent managers and
        90 percent software engineers. Company B's workforce
        consists of 30 percent managers, 10 percent software
        engineers, and 60 percent support staff. The two companies
        merge, every employee stays with the resulting company, and
        no new employees are added. If the resulting company's
        workforce consists of 25 percent managers, what percent of
        the workforce originated from Company A?

        (A)   10%
        (B)   20%
        (C)   25%
        (D)   50%
        (E)   75%

235.   After winning 50 percent of the first x games it played, Team
        A won the remaining 10 games it played. What is the
        value of x?

        (1)   Team A won $\frac{5}{8}$ of all the games it played.
        (2)   The total number of games Team A won is equal to
               $\frac{x}{2} + 10$.

91 Word Problems: Interest

Interest is one of the many topics on the GMAT that is not as hard as it seems. You don't have to look for long before you'll find "the interest formula," a tremendously useful tool for calculating returns on certain interest rates...just not on the GMAT. Remember, of course, that you don't have a calculator, and the people who write the GMAT are just as aware of that as you are. Thus, when a question involves interest, there will be a simple way to solve it, without a complicated exponential expression.

It is important to know the difference between simple interest and compound interest. For the most part, compound interest is what we encounter in our daily lives. Compound interest generates greater returns than simple interest because the interest for each period is based on the principal accumulated up to that period. In case that definition is opaque, let's look at an example:

> If Kelly invests $10,000 at 10% annual simple interest for two years, how much will she have at the end of the two years?

The calculation for the first year is the same whether we're doing simple interest or compound interest. At 10% per year, the interest gained in the first year is 10% of $10,000, or $1000. Thus, at the end of a year, Kelly has $11,000. The second year is where things start to change. With simple interest, interest is always based off of the initial amount, so in the second year, the interest is once again 10% of $10,000: $1000.

If it were compound interest, the second year's interest would be more: instead of 10% of the original amount of $10,000, Kelly would make 10% of the sum at the end of the first year, $11,000. So, the second year's interest would be 10% of $11,000, $1,100. With simple interest, the answer to the question is $12,000. With compound interest, the answer would be $12,100. The difference is slight, but as long as interest is accured over more than one period, compound interest will be greater than an equal rate of simple interest.

You may note that, working through the two variations of that example, I didn't use a single formula. That's by design. For the purposes of the GMAT, interest problems are no more than percent problems. Once you understand the few definitions related to interest, they require very simple math. I've never seen a compound interest problem that involved compounding more than twice, so any problem of this sort can be done the same way you'd handle any other percent problem.

One more set of definitions is important for handling compound interest. You'll often see the phrases "compounded monthly," compounded quarterly," or "compounded semi-annually." In the example above, interest compounded annually: at the end of the first year, the first year's interest was added to the principal, and then the second year's interest was calculated based on the new amount of principal.

However, if the question specified that the interest compounded semi-annually (twice per year), we'd have to calculate it differently. The frequency of compounding (semi-annually, quarterly, etc.) determines how frequently interest is added to the principal. So, in the example above, if interest were compounded semi-annually, there would be four periods (two per year) rather than two. The first six-month period would generate interest of 5% (half of the annual interest rate), $500. Thus, the principal after the first six months would be $10,500, and the 5% interest for the next six-month period would be based on the new principal level of $10,500.

There are two important things to remember when compounding more frequently than once per year. First, the interest rate for each period is less than the annual interest rate. (If the annual interest rate is 12%, the interest rate per month is 1%.) Second, the more frequent the compounding, the more interest there will be. In the example above, 5% of $10,500 is $525, so the principal at the end of the first year is $11,025. That's $25 more than Kelly earned on a single year of 10% interest. It would be a rare question that would ask you to figure out semi-annual compounding over a period of two years, but it's easy to imagine a Data Sufficiency question testing a concept such as the frequency of compounding.

92 Word Problems: Interest: Drill

1. If $20,000 is invested at 6% simple annual interest, how much interest is earned over 3 years?

2. If $5,000 is invested in an account that returns 8% simple annual interest and no additional funds are added to the account, how much money is in the account after 10 years?

3. If $12,000 is invested at x% simple annual interest and $3,000 is earned in interest over 5 years, what is the value of x?

4. If $50,000 is invested at 8% interest, compounded annually, what is the total of the investment, including principal, after 2 years?

5. If $6,000 is invested at 20% interest, compounded annually, what is the total of the investment, including principal, after 3 years?

6. If $25,000 is invested at 5% interest, compounded annually, what is the total of the investment, including principal, after 2 years?

7. Both Account A and Account B start with $10,000. If Account A is invested at 10% interest, compounded annually, and Account B is invested at 10% simple annual interest, how much more money is in Account A at the end of 3 years?

8. If $20,000 is invested at 10% interest, compounded semi-annually, what is the total of the investment, including principal, after one year?

9. If $40,000 is invested at 8% interest, compounded quarterly, what is the total of the investment, including principal, after six months?

10. If $100,000 is invested at 6% interest, compounded monthly, what is the total of the investment, including principal, after two months?

93 Word Problems: Interest: Practice

241.   Kevin deposited $20,000 to open a new savings account that
earned 8 percent annual interest, compounded quarterly.
If there were no other transactions in the account, what the
amount of money in Kevin's account 6 months after the
account was opened?

   (A) $20,400
   (B) $20,404
   (C) $20,800
   (D) $20,808
   (E) $21,600

242.   If $10,000 invested for one year at y percent simple annual
interest yields $700, what amount must be invested at z
percent simple annual interest for one year to yield the
same number of dollars?

   (1) $y = 7$
   (2) $y = 0.7z$

243.   Orlando deposited $5,000 to open a new savings account that
earned four percent annual interest, compounded semi-
annually. If Orlando deposited an additional $1,000 into the
account six months after it was opened, what was the
amount of money in his account one year after the account
was opened?

   (A) $6,200
   (B) $6,202
   (C) $6,222
   (D) $6,240
   (E) $6,262

244.   If $10,000 was invested at an annual interest rate of 6.5 percent
compounded annually, which of the following represents the
amount the investment was worth after 4 years?

   (A) $10,000(1.065)(4)$
   (B) $10,000(4 + 1.065)$
   (C) $10,000[1 + 4(0.065)]$
   (D) $10,000[1 + (0.065)^4]$
   (E) $10,000(1.065)^4$

94   Number Properties: Primes

A prime number is any (positive) number that is divisible only by 1 and itself. For reasons that aren't worth spending time on, 1 is NOT prime. Additionally, by convention, negative numbers are not prime. There will be questions on the GMAT that hinge on you knowing that. It's very useful to memorize primes up to 30 or so: 2, 3, 5, 7, 11, 13, 17, 19, 23, and 29. You'll occasionally have to determine whether a larger number (say, 67) is prime, but the testmaker assumes that figuring it out will take you some time.

Note that 2 is the only even prime. It's obvious once you think about it, but keep it in mind: it will come up on GMAT problems, and it may not be obvious when it arises.

A prime number is, by definition, the only type of number that has exactly two factors: 1 and itself. By extension, the only numbers that have exactly three factors are squares of primes. A square of a prime (for instance, 9) is divisible by 1, itself, and its square root. In the case of 9, those numbers are 1, 3, and 9.

Once you've done a few dozens GMAT Number Properties problems, you'll have a good sense of which numbers are prime. However, you'll occasionally come across a number that is unfamiliar. Take, for instance, 67.

To determine whether a large number is prime, first approximate its square root. If you're working with 67, you know the square root is between 8 and 9 (the square of 8 is 64, less than 67, and the square of 9 is 81, greater than 67). That means that, if the number is NOT prime, 67 must be divisible by at least one number that is less than 9. So, try each of the prime numbers less than 9: 2, 3, 5, and 7. (To do this, use the divisibility rules discussed in the chapter on factors, as well as the mental math tricks covered in that section.) It turns out that 67 isn't divisible by 2, 3, 5, or 7, so 67 must be prime.

This is a short section: primes are really just building blocks for other topics, such as factors and multiples. Before moving on, make sure you understand exactly what makes a number prime, which number is the smallest prime, and how to determine whether a number is prime. Those skills, along with your knowledge of the first several primes, will be useful repeatedly in the next several chapters.

95   Number Properties: Primes: Drill

True or False: Is the number prime?

1. 31
2. 9
3. 23
4. 71
5. 27
6. 51
7. 111
8. 19
9. 87
10. 2

96 Number Properties: Primes: Practice

251.   The sum of prime numbers that are greater than 80 but less
than 90 is

      (A)   259
      (B)   172
      (C)   170
      (D)   89
      (E)   87

252.   Is the prime number p equal to 3 ?

      (1) $p = n + 1$, where n is a prime number.
      (2) p is divisible by 3.

253.   Is $xy < 5$?

      (1) x is prime and y is the reciprocal of a prime.
      (2) $7 > x > y > 0$

254.   Can the positive integer p be expressed as the product of two
integers, each of which is greater than 1?

      (1) p is odd.
      (2) $41 < p < 49$

97 Number Properties: Primes: Challenge

255. Cousin primes are defined as prime numbers that can be
expressed as p and $(p + 4)$, and any number p that is a
member of such a pair is considered to "have" a cousin.
For example, 3 and 7 are cousin primes, and 3 has a
cousin. Which of the following prime numbers has a
cousin?

(A) 5
(B) 19
(C) 29
(D) 31
(E) 53

256. Is the prime number q equal to 23 ?

(1) $r = 2p + 1$, where p is prime.
(2) $r = 3q + 2$, where q is prime.

257. The "prime total" of an integer n greater than 1 is the number
of distinct prime numbers by which n is evenly divisible.
For example, the prime total of 12 is 2, since
$2 \times 2 \times 3 = 12$ and 2 and 3 are the only distinct prime
numbers by which 12 is evenly divisible. For which of the
following integers is the prime total greatest?

(A) 80
(B) 82
(C) 84
(D) 86
(E) 88

98 Number Properties: Factors

While factors and multiples are are complicated concepts and arise on some of the toughest GMAT problems (especially Data Sufficiency!), many people get stuck on a very early part of the process: recognizing which is which.

It may take a bit of memorization and self-browbeating, but it's worth it: a factor is less than or equal to a number, while a multiple is greater than or equal to a number. There's more to the definitions than that, but when it comes to telling the two apart, that's all you need to remember.

Now for the actual definition. x is a factor of y if y is divisible by x. "Divisible" in this case means that there's no remainder. In more formal terms, x is a factor of y if:

$\frac{y}{x} = $ integer

Note that this is always the case if $x = 1$, and it is always the case when $y = x$. So, as you discovered in the previous chapter, every number has at least two factors, 1 and itself. Prime numbers are unique in that those two factors are their only factors. Non-primes often have many more factors. For instance, if b is a factor of 24, then: $\frac{24}{b} = $ integer. b could be 1, 2, 3, 4, 6, 8, 12, or 24.

A GMAT problem will never explicitly require you to generate an exhaustive list of all of a number's factors, but it occasionally comes in handy to do so. To come up with that list, follow these steps:

1. start with 1:   1 is always a factor, as is the number itself
2. try each successive number, using the divisibility rules shown above.
3. if a number turns out to be a factor of x, find $\frac{x}{number}$. Think of that number as it's "match." If you find that 4 is a factor of 24, $\frac{24}{4} = 6$ is also a factor of 24.
4. once you reach the square root of x, stop.

In the case of 24, the steps will look like this:

1 is a factor, as is 24
2 is a factor, as is 12
3 is a factor, as is 8
4 is a factor, as is 6

We're done, because the square root of 24 is less than 5.

You'll also sometimes need to find the prime factors of a number. In that case, you can skip some of the steps of the above: you're just looking for primes. More complicated is a "prime factorization," another technique that will never be explicitly tested, but one that will often prove useful.

A prime factorization is not only a list of all the prime factors of a number, it includes the number of times each prime factor occurs. For instance:

$24 = (2)(2)(2)(3) = 2^3 3$

While 24's prime factors are 2 and 3, the prime factorization contains the additional information that, to multiply 2's and 3's to get to 24, you need 3 2's. Many numbers have prime factors of only 2 and 3 (for instance, 6, 12, and 18, among an infinite number or others), but only one number has a certain prime factorization.

To find a prime factorization, you'll do something called a "factor tree." To use a factor tree, start by finding the easiest pair of numbers you can that multiplies to the number itself.

If either one of the numbers is prime, don't break that one down any further. (Some people like to circle prime numbers to remind themselves that they don't need to go any further in that direction.) However, keep breaking down each number until there's nothing but primes.

For instance, 2 is prime. But 12 is not:

The process continues: 2 is prime, but 6 is not:

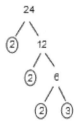

Finally, now that all of the numbers have "branched out" to prime factors, you have the prime factorization of the number.

Note that if you're looking at a number with many factors, there's no right or wrong way to start: it would have been equally valid to start by saying that 24 = 4(6), or 24 = 3(8). In practice, "right" is the same as "fast," and that's dependent on whatever you're most comfortable with. (Or sometimes, on whatever pops into your head first.)

All of the techniques I've described in this chapter (along with many simple arithmetic calculations) are simpler if you memorize some divisibility rules. If you want to find the prime factorization of, say, 576, you don't want to spend all day doing long division, figuring out which of a slew of numbers are factors of 576. Here are the rules:

2:   If a number is even (you can check just by looking at the last digit), it's divisible by 2.

3:   Add the digits of the number. If the result is a multiple of 3, the number is, too.

4.   If the last two digits are a multiple of 4, the number is a multiple of 4. (e.g., the last two digits of 524 are 24, which is a multiple of 4, so 524 is a multiple of four.)

5.   If the last digit is 5 or 0, the number is a multiple of 5.

6.   If a number is divisible by 2 and 3, it's divisible by 6.

7.   There's no easy rule. To quickly determine whether a number is divisible by 7, it's best to use the "nearest neighbor" method I described in the Mental Math chapter.

8.   No good rule. Just keep dividing by 2. If you can divide the number by 2, then divide the result by 2, and the result is still an even number, you've got a multiple of 8.

9.   Similar rule to that of 3: if the sum of the digits is a multiple of 9, the number is a multiple of 9.

Numbers With Three Factors

The only positive integers with exactly three factors are the squares of primes. For instance, the factors of 9 are 1, 3, and 9, and the factors of 49 are 1, 7, and 49.

Here's why. If you find all of the factors of a non-square, you can "pair off" the factors. For instance, the factors of 12 are 1, 2, 3, 4, 6, and 12. You can split those six factors into three pairs, each of which multiplies to 12:

   1 and 12
   2 and 6
   3 and 4

However, if you try the same thing with a square, you end up with a duplicate. The factors of 16 are 1, 2, 4, 8, and 16, some of which pair off:

   1 and 16
   2 and 8
   4 and ... itself

Any time you are finding the factors of a square, the final step will involve the square root, like 4 above. That square root only counts once–4 is only one factor, not two. So 16, like 9 and 49, has an odd number of factors.

We can generalize this and state the rule in a couple of different ways. First, if an integer has an odd number of factors, it is a perfect square. The reverse is also true: if a number is a perfect square, it has an odd number of factors.

The Number of Factors of a Large Integer

Sometimes you'll be asked to find the number of factors of an integer large enough to make the techniques I've describe so far seem inadequate. The method I'm about to show you isn't for the math-averse; it introduces permutations into a question type that doesn't need them, so unless you're comfortable with the idea of factors and you aren't confused by permutations, you should probably stick with what we've already discussed in this chapter.

The concept behind this method is that the prime factorization of a number determines all of its factors. If a number is divisible by 2, for instance, 2 will be a factor of many of the number's factors. In fact, each factor of a number is built up of one or more of the number's other factors.

Take 18, for instance. The prime factors of 18 are 2 and 3; the prime factorization is 2 times 3 times 3, or $(2^1)(3^2)$.

Consider each of 18's factors in terms of its own prime factorization:

$1 = (2^0)(3^0)$
$2 = (2^1)(3^0)$
$3 = (2^0)(3^1)$
$6 = (2^1)(3^1)$
$9 = (2^0)(3^2)$
$18 = (2^1)(3^2)$

If you look at all of those numbers in terms of their factorizations, you'll see every possible arrangement of 2 to the 0 or 1 power with 3 to the 0, 1, or 2 power. That's no accident.

To generalize that method, here's your approach:

1.   Find the prime factorization of a number (each one of the number's prime factors raised to the appropriate power).
2.   List all of the exponents.
3.   Add one to each of the exponents. (Remember, it's possible to raise the prime factor to the zero power.)
4.   Multiply the resulting numbers.

Let's try those steps with the type of number the GMAT would give you: 196.

1.   The prime factorization: $196 = (2^2)(7^2)$
2.   The powers: 2 and 2
3.   Add one to the powers: 3 and 3
4.   Multiply the results: $(3)(3) = 9$

There are 9 factors of 196. To see what those are, work through the permutations of the exponents 0, 1, and 2 for the prime factors 2 and 7:

$(2^0)(7^0) = 1$
$(2^1)(7^0) = 2$
$(2^2)(7^0) = 4$
$(2^0)(7^1) = 7$
$(2^1)(7^1) = 14$

$(2^2)(7^1) = 28$
$(2^0)(7^2) = 49$
$(2^1)(7^2) = 98$
$(2^2)(7^2) = 196$

I can't imagine a GMAT question on which you'll *need* to figure out what all the factors are, but it's nice to see that the method works. This is the sort of technique that should be very far down your list: It's just not that high of a priority. But if you are attempting to add 20 or 30 points to an already high score, it's a handy time-saving method.

99 Number Properties: Factors: Drill

1.   For each of the following numbers, find all of its factors. Then,
        find the prime factorization:
        a.   110
        b.   96
        c.   84
        d.   60
        e.   144
        f.   147
        g.   180
        h.   182
        i.   205
        j.   225

2.   For each of the following, is x a factor of y ?
        a. $x = 15, y = 15$
        b. $x = 9, y = 336$
        c. $x = 3, y = 51$
        d. $x = 8, y = 98$
        e. $x = 4, y = 154$

3.   Which of the following numbers are factors of 144?
        a.   24
        b.   9
        c.   16

4.   Which of the following numbers are factors of 96?
        a.   18
        b.   12

100   Number Properties: Factors: Practice

261.   If $n = 6p$, where p is a prime number greater than 3, how many different positive even divisors does n have, including n ?

      (A)   Two
      (B)   Three
      (C)   Four
      (D)   Six
      (E)   Eight

262.   Is the integer s divisible by 32?

      (1) s is divisible by 16.
      (2) s is divisible by 4.

263.   If q is a member of the set $\{21, 22, 24, 25, 26, 27\}$, what is the value of q?

      (1) q has exactly one prime factor.
      (2) q is divisible by 3.

264.   If n is an integer, is $\frac{50-n}{n}$ an integer?

      (1) $n > 4$
      (2) $n^2 = 25$

265.   If n is an integer, then n is divisible by how many positive integers?

      (1) $n = 2^x + 1$, where x is an integer.
      (2) $x < 5$

101 Number Properties: Factors: Challenge

266. If p is a positive integer less than 75 and $\frac{3p}{84}$ is an integer, then p has how many different positive prime factors?

   (A) One
   (B) Two
   (C) Three
   (D) Four
   (E) Five

267. How many different positive integers are factors of 625 ?

   (A) 1
   (B) 3
   (C) 5
   (D) 6
   (E) 7

268. If k is the product of the integers from 1 to 12, inclusive, what is the greatest integer n for which 3^n is a factor of k ?

   (A) 3
   (B) 4
   (C) 5
   (D) 6
   (E) 7

269. How many prime numbers between 1 and 100 are factors of 2,730?

   (A) Two
   (B) Three
   (C) Four
   (D) Five
   (E) Six

270. If k is the smallest positive integer such that $2,940k$ is the square of an integer, then k must be

   (A) 3
   (B) 5
   (C) 6
   (D) 15
   (E) 21

102   Number Properties: Multiples

Factors and multiples are mirror images of each other. If y is a factor of x, x is a multiple of y. To repeat my important rule of thumb from the previous chapter: a multiple of x is greater than or equal to x, while a factor is less than or equal to x. Note, in those definitions, that if x and y are equal to each other, each one is both a factor and a multiple of the other.

A more traditional definition of a multiple is this: if x is divisible by y, x is a multiple of y. For example, some multiples of 9 are 18, 45, 72, and 999. (Not to mention 9 itself and an infinite number of others.)

Finally, here's a technical definition: if x is a multiple of y, $\frac{x}{y} = $ integer .

There's no need to memorize each of these ways of thinking about multiples; I include them all to give you a few different angles to approach the concept. While the final, technical one will prove useful on a handful of difficult GMAT problems, you'll do fine most of the time if you've internalized one of the first two.

As a side note: Questions will appear to use the phrasing "multiple of", "factor of", and "divisible by" interchangeably. They mean very similar things, but there's one key difference. Factors and multiples are always positive. The factors of 24 are the positive numbers listed above, for instance. However, 24 is divisible by several negative numbers; $\frac{24}{-6} = $ integer, so 24 is divisible by -6. It's not something to wrack your brain trying to understand too thoroughly; it just is.

One additional concept regarding multiples is that of the "least common multiple." Like many number properties techniques, it will never be explicitly tested on the GMAT, but you will benefit greatly if you're able to apply the skill.

The least common multiple (LCM) of two numbers is exactly what it sounds like: the smallest number that is a multiple (is divisible by) of the two numbers. For instance, the LCM of 2 and 3 is 6, and the LCM of 4 and 8 is 8. As it turns out, to calculate an LCM, you need to apply more knowledge of factors than multiples.

To find the LCM of two numbers, you first need the prime factorization of each one. Let's try 12 and 27. The prime factorizations are as follows:

$12 = (2^2)(3)$
$27 = 3^3$

You'll end up writing the LCM in the same form: prime numbers raised to certain powers. Start by finding every unique prime number in either factorization. There's a 3 in both, and 2 in one of them, so both of those primes are part of the LCM. No other prime is in the factorization of either number.

$LCM = (2^x)(3^y)$

For each prime, the exponent you need is the largest exponent associated with that prime. So, since 12 contains 2^2 and 27 doesn't contain any twos, the

exponent for 2 in the LCM is 2. Since 27 contains 3^3 and 12 contains 3^1, the exponent for 3 in the LCM is the larger of the two, 3. The LCM, then, is:
$$LCM = (2^2)(3^3) = (4)(27) = 108$$

As I've said, the GMAT will never explicitly ask you to do that. However, you can think of LCMs a little more abstractly. In addition to finding the LCM of two numbers, you can use the technique to find the LCM of two multiples. For instance, if x is a multiple of 12 and a multiple of 27, x must be a multiple of ...you guessed it, 108. It doesn't mean that x is 108, but it must be a multiple of 108. That concept arises quite a bit on roman numeral questions and Data Sufficiency questions.

103   Number Properties: Multiples: Drill

1.   For each of the following, is x a multiple of y ?
   - a. $x = 12, y = 1$
   - b. $x = 96, y = 3$
   - c. $x = 15, y = 30$
   - d. $x = 24, y = 8$
   - e. $x = 180, y = 8$
   - f. $x = 108, y = 9$
   - g. $x = 51, y = 17$
   - h. $x = 100, y = 16$
   - i. $x = 36, y = 36$
   - j. $x = 147, y = 7$

2.   For each of the following, find the least common multiple (LCM) of x and y:
   - a. $x = 6, y = 7$
   - b. $x = 3, y = 18$
   - c. $x = 8, y = 12$
   - d. $x = 70, y = 4$
   - e. $x = 56, y = 5$
   - f. $x = 12, y = 9$
   - g. $x = 48, y = 16$
   - h. $x = 18, y = 24$
   - i. $x = 6, y = 27$
   - j. $x = 37, y = 1$

104   Number Properties: Multiples: Practice

271.   What is the least positive integer that is divisible by each of the odd integers between 1 and 9, inclusive?

    (A)   105
    (B)   210
    (C)   315
    (D)   630
    (E)   945

272.   If y is an integer, is y^3 divisible by 9?

    (1) y^2 is divisible by 9.
    (2) y^4 is divisible by 9.

273.   The number N is $4,3G5$, the ten's digit being represented by G. What is the value of G?

    (1) N is divisible by 9.
    (2) N is divisible by 5.

274.   If r and s are integers, is rs divisible by 5 ?

    (1) r is divisible by 10.
    (2) s is a factor of 5.

275.   If the two-digit integers P and Q are positive and have the same digits, but in reverse order, which of the following could be the difference between P and Q?

    (A)   23
    (B)   24
    (C)   25
    (D)   26
    (E)   27

276.   If the positive integers p and q are each a multiple of 6, then pq must be a multiple of which of the following?

   I. 6
   II. 12
   III. 18

   (A)   I only
   (B)   III only
   (C)   I and II only
   (D)   I and III only
   (E)   I, II, and III

277.   If $\frac{1}{2} + \frac{1}{4} + \frac{1}{6} = \frac{11}{x}$, which of the following must be an integer?

   I. $\frac{x}{8}$
   II. $\frac{x}{12}$
   III $\frac{x}{24}$

   (A)   I only
   (B)   II only
   (C)   I and III only
   (D)   II and III only
   (E)   I, II, and III

278.   Is the positive integer p a multiple of 18?

   (1) p is a multiple of 24.
   (2) p is a multiple of 27.

105   Number Properties: Multiples: Challenge

279.   Which of the following could be the least common multiple of two distinct positive integers x and y, where $x > y$?

     (A)   1
     (B) $x - y$
     (C) x
     (D) $y - x$
     (E) y

280.   The "spin" of any two-digit number is defined as double the amount of the tens digit of the number. For instance, the "spin" of 54 is 10. Is the "spin" of x divisible by 4?

     (1)   The sum of the digits of x is 9.
     (2) $x > 50$

106   Number Properties: Evens/Odds

For such a superficially elementary concept, even and odd numbers come up quite a bit on the GMAT, even on difficult questions. First, let's go over the basics.

Evens are numbers that are divisible by 2, such as 0, 2, 4, 26, and -38. Odds are integers that are not divisible by 2: 1, 3, 5, 99, -41. Note that negative numbers are even or odd, and that zero is an even number.

More abstractly, an even number can be written as $2i$, where i is an integer. (Put another way, an even number is a multiple of 2.) Similarly, an odd number can be expressed as $2i - 1$, where i is an integer. (An odd is NOT a multiple of 2.)

There are several addition and multiplication identities for evens and odds:

$even + even = even$
$even + odd = odd$
$odd + odd = even$
$even \times even = even$
$even \times odd = even$
$odd \times odd = odd$

(The rules for addition are also true for subtraction.)

I don't recommend that you memorize those rules; simply know that they exist; it's much easier to try a pair of even numbers than to try to keep all of those rules straight. For instance, if you want to know the product of an odd and an even variable, figure out the product of 2 and 3. It's 6, so the product of the two variables must be even, as well.

107   Number Properties: Evens/Odds: Drill

1.   If x is even and y is odd, determine whether each of the following is even, odd, or undetermined:
   a. $xy + x$
   b. $xy + y$
   c. $y - x$
   d. $x - y$
   e. $x^2 - y^2$

2.   If both x and y are even, determine whether each of the following is even, odd, or undetermined:
   a. $xy - x$
   b. $\frac{xy}{2}$
   c. $3x - y$
   d. $y^2 - 1$
   e. $\frac{xy}{4}$

3.   If both x and y are odd, determine whether each of the following is even, odd, or undetermined:
   a. $xy - y$
   b. $x^2 + y^2$
   c. $2(x - y)$
   d. $3x + 2y$
   e. $x + y + xy$

4.   If x is even and y is an integer, determine whether each of the following is even, odd, or undetermined:
   a. $2(x + y)$
   b. $3(x - y)$
   c. $x^2 + 2y^2$
   d. $3x - 2y$
   e. $2x - 3y$

108 Number Properties: Evens/Odds: Practice

281.   How many positive integers less than 20 are either a multiple of 2, an odd multiple of 7, or the sum of a positive multiple of 2 and a positive multiple of 7 ?

    (A)   19
    (B)   18
    (C)   17
    (D)   16
    (E)   15

282.   Is r an even integer?

    (1) r^2 is an even integer.
    (2) $\sqrt{r}$ is an even integer.

283.   If p and q are consecutive positive integers, is p odd?

    (1) pq is even.
    (2) q^2 is even.

284.   If s is an integer, is s odd?

    (1) $\frac{s}{2}$ is an even integer.
    (2) $2s - 3$ is an odd integer.

285.   If r is an integer, is r odd?

    (1) $r - 2$ is prime.
    (2) $r + 2$ is prime.

286.   If m and x are greater than zero, is $\frac{m}{x}$ an integer?

    (1) x is an even integer.
    (2) m is an odd integer.

287.   When a player in a certain game rolled a six-sided die a number
of times, 6 more even numbers than odd numbers resulted.
An even or an odd number resulted each time the player
rolled the die. How many times did an even number result?

    (1)   The player rolled the die 18 times.

    (2)   The player received 2 points each time an even
number resulted and 1 point each time an odd
number resulted, for a total of 30 points.

288.   The product of the digits of the integer x, where $100 \leq x \leq 999$,
is 70. What is the value of x?

    (1) $x > 600$

    (2) x is even.

289.   If k is an integer greater than 3, which of the following must be an
even integer?

    (A) $k(k-2)$

    (B) $k(k+4)$

    (C) $(k-1)(k+3)$

    (D) $k(k-1)(k+4)$

    (E) $(k-3)(k-1)(k+3)$

109   Number Properties: Consecutive Numbers

Consecutive numbers are numbers that are equally spaced.   The sequence
$\{1, 2, 3, 4, 5\}$ consists of consecutive numbers, as does the sequence $\{107, 114, 121, 128\}$.
However, the most common types of consecutive numbers covered on the GMAT
are consecutive integers. Consecutive integers are numbers that are one apart,
such as $\{9, 10, 11, 12, 13\}$. They can be written as follows: x, $x+1$, $x+2$, $x+3$,
etc, where x is the smallest of the consecutive numbers.

The same logic and techniques extend to more complicated ideas, such as
"consecutive odds" or "consecutive multiples of 5." Consecutive odds are spaced
by two, so they are written as x, $x+2$, $x+4$, etc. Consecutive evens are also
spaced by two, so such a sequence could be represented in the same way. The
only difference, of course, is that x must be even. Consecutive multiples operate
in the same way: consecutive multiples of 5 are spaced by 5 (of course), so they
are written as x, $x+5$, $x+10$, etc.

Consecutive (evenly spaced) numbers come up occasionally in the context
of statistics questions. In a series of consecutive numbers, the average and the
median are the same. Take, for example, the series $\{3, 6, 9, 12, 15\}$. The average
is $\frac{3+6+9+12+15}{5} = \frac{45}{5} = 9$, and the median (middle number) is also 9. Since the
numbers are equally spaced, the average is right in the middle–the numbers on
either side of the middle have equal weight. So, the average (arithmetic mean)
will always be the middle number.

The other advanced topic that repeatedly arises along with consecutive numbers relates to divisibility. In any sequence of consecutive numbers, multiples of
prime numbers will arise in roughly the same order that they do among integers.
Look at the series of consecutive evens:

   2
   4 (multiple of 4)
   6 (multiple of 3, multiple of 6)
   8 (multiple of 4)
   10 (multiple of 5)
   12 (multiple of 3, multiple of 4, multiple of 6)
   14 (multiple of 7)

Of course there are more multiples of 4 here than there would be in a random
sampling of numbers, because an even number is more likely to be a multiple of
4. The more important concept is to notice the frequency that multiples of 3
arise: every 3 numbers. Multiples of 5 appear every 5 numbers, and multiples
of 7 appear every 7 numbers. These things won't always be obvious, but if
you're working on a question that involves consecutive numbers and divisibility,
it's worth writing out the first few terms in the sequence to see if you recognize
any patterns.

This will be tested in a wide variety of ways. It's handy to know that the
product of any two consecutive integers is even. No matter which numbers you

pick, one of them will be even and one will be odd, so the product will be even. The underlying concept is that, in a sequence of consecutive integers, every other number will be even.   Similarly, in nearly every consecutive sequence, every third number will be a multiple of 3, every fifth number will be a multiple of 5, and so on.

110   Number Properties: Consecutive Numbers: Drill

1. True or False: For each of the following, are the numbers in the sequence consecutive?

     a. $\{1, 2, 4, 8, 16, 32, 64\}$

     b. $\{-25, -20, -15, -10, -5\}$

     c. $\{0, 1, 4, 9, 16, 25, 36\}$

     d. $\{101, 102, 103, 104, 105\}$

     e. $\{x, x + 3, x + 6, x + 9, x + 12\}$

2. What is the average (arithmetic mean) of each of the following sets?

     a. $\{60, 62, 64, 66, 68, 70, 72\}$

     b. $\{-12, -8, -4, 0, 4, 8\}$

     c. $\{y, y + 1, y + 2, y + 3, y + 4\}$

3. In a sequence of consecutive even integers, what fraction of the integers are multiples of 4?

4. In a sequence of consecutive multiples of 5, what fraction of the terms are multiples of 7?

111   Number Properties: Consecutive Numbers: Practice

291.   If x is equal to the sum of the even integers from 50 to 70, inclusive, and y is the number of odd integers from 50 to 70, inclusive, what is the value of $x + y$?

    (A)   610
    (B)   611
    (C)   660
    (D)   670
    (E)   671

292.   If the sum of n consecutive integers is 2, which of the following must be true?

    I. n is an even number
    II. n is an odd number
    III.   The median of the n integers is equal to the average (arithmetic mean).

    (A)   I only
    (B)   II only
    (C)   III only
    (D)   I and III
    (E)   II and III

293.   If r, s, and t are three integers, are they consecutive integers?

    (1)   None of the three integers are multiples of 4.
    (2) $19 < r < s < t < 25$

294.   If r and s are consecutive odd integers, is r greater than s ?

    (1) r and s are prime.
    (2) $5 < r < 11$

295.   What is the the sum of the numbers in a list of m even integers?

    (1)   The largest integer on the list is 12.
    (2)   The list consists of 6 consecutive multiples of 4.

112   Number Properties: Remainders

The basic arithmetic principle behind remainders is simple.   On the GMAT, though, remainder questions can be very difficult.

Remainders are closely related to multiples.   One way of seeing this is by recognizing that, by definition, if x is a multiple of y (that is, x is evenly divisible by y), there is no remainder when x is divided by y.   Since 21 is a multiple of 3, there is no remainder when 21 is divided by 3.   Another way of discovering the same fact is by doing the arithmetic.   When you divide 21 by 3, the result is 7. There's no fractional part to the answer, so there is no remainder.   When there is a fractional part, there is a remainder.   For instance, when 22 is divided by 3, the result is $7\frac{1}{3}$.   Another of putting it: 7, remainder 1.   Thus, when 22 is divided by 3, the "quotient" (whole number result) is 7 and the remainder is 1.

As you might expect, the GMAT tests remainders in more complex ways. Try thinking about that last example in a different way.   Instead of finding the remainder when 22 is divided by 3, think about the possible numbers that, when divided by 3, have a remainder of 1.   We know that 22 has that property, but what else?   4 works, since 4 divided by 3 is $1\frac{1}{3}$, or 1 remainder 1.   7 and 10 fit the description as well, as they are 2 remainder 1 and 3 remainder 1, respectively.

The common thread you might notice is that all such numbers are one greater than a multiple of 3.   4 is one greater than 3, 7 is one greater than 6, and 22 is one greater than 21.   Thankfully, there's a handy way to express this algebraically. Recall from the chapter on multiples that, if x is divisible by y, then:

$\frac{x}{y}$ = integer

Another way of putting that is, by multiplying both sides by y:

$x = y(integer)$

In more concrete terms, we're saying that, if x is a multiple of 3, x is always the product of 3 and some integer.

To extend the reasoning to remainders, remember that anything with a remainder of 1 is one greater than a multiple.   Thus, we just add one to the right side of the equation:

$x = y(integer) + 1$

Or, in the example we've been discussing, if we're looking for numbers that, when divided by 3, have a remainder of 1, the equation looks like this:

$x = 3(integer) + 1$

From there, we can generate infinitely many values of x that, when divided by 3, have a remainder of 1.

Now that we've established the basic principle behind remainders and started to think about them in algebraic terms, let's go all the way.   When dividing two numbers, the result is a quotient (the whole number result) and a remainder.

For instance, when dividing 13 by 5, the quotient is 2 and the remainder is 3. Here's one way of writing that as an equation:

$$\frac{13}{5} = 2 + \frac{3}{5}$$

Note that, in fractional form, the remainder is part of a fraction. It's the numerator, above the denominator of the original fraction.

We can extrapolate a general statement from this form. When dividing x by y, the quotient is q and the remainder is r:

$$\frac{x}{y} = q + \frac{r}{y}$$

From there, you can solve for x:

$$x = qy + r \quad \text{(that's the general form of } x = 3(\text{integer}) + 1)$$

Or the quotient:

$$q = \frac{x-r}{y}$$

Or, even, the remainder itself:

$$r = x - qy$$

Aside from the way we used one of those forms to generate numbers that, when divided by 3, have a remainder of 1, you'll rarely use these equations on the GMAT. However, there are a handful of questions that ask you to come up with some question very much like this one. If the GMAT tells you that, when n is divided by 7, the quotient is q and the remainder is r, you'll be able to express the value of any of the variables in terms of the other variables. It's an important skill to have.

Assorted Remainder Facts

As we saw in the list of numbers that, when divided by 3, have a remainder of 1, those numbers are spaced apart by 3. Just as multiples of 3 are spaced 3 apart (6, 9, 12, 15, etc.), numbers with a remainder of 1 are spaced by 3's as well: 4, 7, 10, 13, etc. Imagine these numbers on the number line–they are the same sequence as the multiples of 3, only displaced by 1. By the same principle, numbers that, when divided by 5 have a remainder of 2 are separated by 5's–7, 12, 17, 22, etc.

As noted in the Consecutive Numbers chapter, even numbers are multiples of 2. Odd numbers, then, when divided by 2, have a remainder of 1. They can be expressed as 2i + 1, where i is an integer.

Some remainders give you hints about units digits. Think of the numbers that, when divided by 10, have remainders of 3: 13, 23, 33, 43, etc. See the pattern? The units digit is always 3. Same goes for any remainder, when divided by 10. It also applies when divided by any multiple of 10. All of the numbers that, when divided by 70, have a remainder of 6 also have a units digit of 6.

Something similar applies when dividing by 5. Consider the numbers that, when divided by 5, have a remainder of 4: 9, 14, 19, 24, 29, etc. It's not as predictable as the pattern with 10, but it's close. The units digit always alternates between two different numbers.

Finally, let's look at how to convert decimals to remainders. Let's say that, when a is divided by b, the result is 5.6. What's the remainder when a is divided by b? Remember that remainders are based on fractions, so the first step is to convert 5.2 into a fraction:

$$5 + \frac{6}{10} = 5 + \frac{3}{5}$$

The fractional part of 5.6, then, is $\frac{3}{5}$. Does that mean that the remainder when a is divided by b, is 3? Not quite. It could be 3, but only if $b = 5$. As we saw when setting up a generic formula for remainders, the denominator underneath the remainder is the same as the denominator on the left side of the equation. In other words, the denominator underneath the remainder, in this question, is equal to b.

Thus, if we don't know the value of the denominator, we don't know the remainder. Sometimes, though, we can narrow things down. We're usually talking about integers, so the fractional part must consist only of integers. It could be $\frac{3}{5}$, or it could be some other form of the same fraction, like $\frac{6}{10}$ or $\frac{15}{25}$. There are an infinite number of possibilities, but all of the possible remainders are multiples of 3. No matter what, 2 could not be the remainder if, when a is divided by b, the result is 5.6.

Questions along these lines will always follow the same pattern. Without additional information, you won't be able to find the exact remainder, but you will be able to convert a decimal part into a most simplified fraction (like $\frac{3}{5}$) and then figure out the rule all possible remainders must follow.

113   Number Properties: Remainders: Drill

1.   What is the remainder when...
    a.   13 is divided by 2?
    b.   21 is divided by 4?
    c.   3 is divided by 7?
    d.   37 is divided by 10?

2.   If x is less than 40, what are the possible values of x if...
    a.   when x is divided by 5, the remainder is 2?
    b.   when x is divided by 9, the remainder is 8?
    c.   when x is divided by 7, the remainder is 1?
    d.   when x is divided by 17, the remainder is 3?

3.   When 31 is divided by d, the remainder is 1. What are the possible values of d?

4.   If $\frac{m}{n} = 7.12$ and m and n are integers, what are the three smallest possible remainders when m is divided by n?

114   Number Properties: Remainders: Practice

296.   When the positive integer n is divided by 15, the remainder is 4.
        What is the value of n?

     (1)   When n is divided by 10, the remainder is 9

     (2) $n < 50$

297.   Is z odd?

     (1)   When z is divided by 7, the remainder is odd.

     (2)   When z is divided by 8, the remainder is odd.

115   Number Properties: Remainders: Challenge

298.   If m and n are positive integers, what is the remainder when m is divided by n?

     (1) $\frac{m}{n} = 12.64$

     (2) $n < 50$

299.   When positive integer a is divided by 5, the remainder is 3. What is the value of a?

     (1)   When a is divided by 6, the remainder is 1.

     (2)   When a is divided by 4, the remainder is 1.

300.   Are x, y, and z consecutive integers?

     (1)   The remainder when $x + y + z$ is divided by 3 is 2.

     (2)   The remainder when xyz is divided by 3 is 1.

116   Sets: Average

It's important to start with some definitions. The GMAT will usually refer to average by saying "average (arithmetic mean)." In other contexts, "average," "mean," and "arithmetic mean" are synonymous.   There are other ways to measure the "middle" of a set of numbers such as median and mode, but we won't look at those for another couple of chapters.

Average is given by a straightforward equation:
$$\text{average} = \frac{\text{sum of terms}}{\text{number of terms}}$$
Every average question you'll ever see boils down to that three-part equation. Even weighted average questions, which merit their own chapter right after this one, use that equation as a framework. Let's look at a basic example:

> "Joe bowled three games, scoring 180, 190, and 212. What was the average (arithmetic mean) or Joe's three bowling scores?"

The "terms" in this case are Joe's bowling scores. So the "sum of terms" is $180 + 190 + 212$. Since there are three bowling scores, the "number of terms" is 3:
$$\text{average} = \frac{180+190+212}{3} = \frac{582}{3} = 194$$
In the next chapter, on weighted averages, I'll show you a shortcut for handling averages with large or unwieldy numbers. Dividing 582 by 3 isn't the end of the world, but if you'd like a way to find this average and avoid the math, come back and try this question again after learning that shortcut.

More commonly, the GMAT will make average problems more difficult. Instead of giving you the convention inputs (sum of terms, number of terms) and asking for the conventional output (average), these questions will give you the average and ask for one of the terms.   Consider this twist on the previous question:

> "Joe bowled three games with an average score of 194. If his first two scores were 180 and 212, what was his third score?"

As you probably noticed, the numbers are all the same.   The difference is the variable. To set it up, use the same equation, just put an x in a new place:
$$194 = \frac{180+212+x}{3}$$
$$194(3) = 392 + x$$
$$x = 190$$
The equation will never change; it's just a matter of assigning the data you're given to the correct places in the formula.

Finally, an additional complication is the average-within-an-average.   This is best seen within an example, again based on the previous one:

> "Joe bowled three games with an average score of 194. If the average of his first two scores was 196, what was his third score?"

In this case, we don't have any of the individual terms. But, if you notice the steps we took solving the last example, you'll see that the exact terms (180 and 212) were meaningless. What mattered was that the sum of those terms was 392. The results would be the same if those two terms were 0 and 392 or 100 and 292. So, what we really need is the information to fill out this equation:

$$\text{average} = \frac{(\text{sum of first two terms}) + x}{\text{number of terms}}$$

We know the average (194) and the number of terms (3). Using the average formula itself, we can find the sum of the first two terms:

$$196 = \frac{\text{sum of first two terms}}{2}$$

$$sum = 196(2) = 392$$

Now we can plug in all of our data to the initial equation:

$$194 = \frac{392 + x}{3}$$

From here, the math is the same as that of the previous example. The key thing to take away from this version of the question is that, given the average of some terms and the number of terms, you can find the sum. And that's enough to find some new average, or a missing term that figures into a new average.

117   Sets: Average: Drill

1.   Find the average (arithmetic mean) of each of the following sets:
    a. $\{200, 208, 234\}$
    b. $\{4, 6, 10, 11, 14\}$
    c. $\{96, 82, 86, 90, 86\}$
    d. $\{3, 5, 7, 9, 11, 13, 15\}$
    e. $\{50, 60, 70, 80\}$

2.   Find the sum of the terms in each of the following sets:
    a.   Set A contains 6 terms and has an average of 92.
    b.   Set B has an average of 6.5 and contains 12 terms.
    c.   There are 3 terms in Set C, which has an average of 180.
    d.   The 5 terms in Set D have an average of 9.6.
    e.   The arithmetic mean of the 4 terms in Set E is $15\frac{3}{4}$.

3.   A set containing three terms has an average of 140. If one of the terms is 160, what is the sum of the remaining terms?

4.   A set containing five terms has an average of 7.6. If one of the terms is 8, what is the average of the remaining terms?

5.   The following questions refer to Set Z, which has six terms and a mean of 32:
    a.   If one of the terms in Set Z is 32, what is the average of the remaining five terms?
    b.   If one of the terms in Set Z is 22, what is the average of the remaining five terms?
    c.   If two of the terms in Set Z have an average of 36, what is the average of the remaining four terms?
    d.   If three of the terms in Set Z have an average of 21, what is the average of the remaining terms?
    e.   If five of the terms in Set Z sum to 165, what is the other term?
    f.   If five of the terms in Set Z have an average of 30, what is the remaining term?
    g.   If a seventh term, 25, is added to Set Z, what is the average of the new set?
    h.   If six new terms with an average of 39 are added to Set Z, what is the average of the new set?

118   Sets: Average: Practice

301.   If the average (arithmetic mean) of 6 numbers is 75, how many
of the numbers are greater than 75?

(1)   Four of the numbers are equal to 75.
(2)   One of the numbers is less than 75.

302.   If Juan's average (arithmetic mean) score for three games
of pinball was 57, what was his highest score?

(1)   The sum of Juan's two lowest scores was 107.
(2)   The sum of Juan's three scores was 171.

303.   What is the average (arithmetic mean) of p and q ?

(1)   The average (arithmetic mean) of $3p$ and $2q$ is 12.
(2)   The average (arithmetic mean) of p^2 and q^2 is 26.

304.   What is the average (arithmetic mean) of x, y, and z ?

(1) $x + z = 6$ and $y + z = 8$.
(2) $z = 0$

305.   If the average (arithmetic mean) of a and b is 40 and the
average (arithmetic mean) of b and c is 56, what is the
value of $c - a$?

(A)   46
(B)   32
(C)   16
(D)   8
(E)   It cannot be determined from the information given.

$$\{y, y + 3, y + 4, y + 6, y + 7\}$$

306.   In the set of positive integers above, the mean is how much
greater than the median?

(A)   0
(B)   1
(C) $y + 1$
(D) $y + 2$
(E) $y + 3$

119   Sets: Weighted Average

The last example in the previous chapter is an intermediate step between averages and weighted averages. As I mentioned in that section, a weighted average is really just an average; the reason for an entire chapter is that there are more sophisticated techniques for solving weighted average problems.

In a weighted average problem, there are averages within averages: say, two bowling scores of 190 and three scores of 210. You can solve for the average of the five scores using the traditional average formula:

$$\frac{190+190+210+210+210}{5} = \frac{1010}{5} = 202$$

But it's simpler to combine the terms:

$$\frac{190(2)+210(3)}{5}$$

Using the condensed form of the equation for weighted averages is especially handy when you're solving for, say, the average score of the final three games. If you're told that the overall average was 202 and the average of the first two games was 190, the equation would look like this:

$$\frac{190(2)+3x}{5} = 202$$

As a side note, if you've already worked through the mixture chapter, this should all look very familiar. Mixtures are just one form of weighted averages, so the shortcut that follows applies just as well to mixture problems as any other form of weighted averages.

As it turns out, weighted average problems are some of the easiest to make educated guesses on. Take the example above. If you've bowled two games of 190 and three games of 210, what might you guess about the average? If you bowled an equal number of games of 190 and 210, the average would be the average of those two numbers: 200. But you didn't: you bowled more 210 games than 190 games, so the weighted average will be closer to 210. But the difference isn't that great, just 3 games to 2. Thus, the weighted average should be just a bit greater than 200. Depending on the answer choices, that might be enough information to answer the question.

To think about that in slightly more abstract terms, imagine a weighted average as a tug-of-war between the two (or more) quantities. In this case, the two quantities are 190 and 210. If there are equal numbers of 190 games and 210 games, the two sides are equally weighted, so the average will end up precisely in the middle:

But, if one side is more heavily weighted than the other (as in the example we've been using), the average will move further in the direction of the heavier weight:

190 •————————————•————————• 210

The trick that will help you do weighted average problems much faster is that the weights matter, but the numbers themselves don't. Compare this to the image above:

0 •————————————•————————• 20

In effect, you can subtract 190 from every single number in the problem above and it still works out the same way. (Just remember to add that 190 back in before clicking an answer!) To see this technique in action, let's turn to a new example:

"If Jason purchased two suits for $179 each and three suits for $189 each, what is the average price Jason paid for each suit?"

The traditional setup for this problem is:

$$\frac{2(179)+3(189)}{5} =$$

That would work just fine, but I don't want to spend all the time it would take to multiply 3 by 189, or divide the numerator by 5. Instead, recognize that a problem with quantities of 179 and 189 is the same as one with quantities of 0 and 10, just like in the diagrams above:

$$\frac{2(0)+3(10)}{5} = \frac{30}{5} = 6$$

What that answer tells you is that the weighted average is 6 greater than the lowest number in the problem. Since we began by subtracting 179 from everything, add that 179 back to the resulting 6 and you have your answer: 185.

This technique will work on more complicated problems, as well. Let's try a variation of the suit question:

"If Jason paid an average price of $185 for five suits, and the average price of three of the suits was $189, what was the average price of the remaining suits?"

Again, let's look at the traditional setup:

$$\frac{189(3)+x(2)}{5} = 185$$

That equation will lead us through some time-consuming arithmetic. In this case, the smallest quantity is 185, so subtract 185 from each of the dollar amounts, leaving x as is:

$$\frac{4(3)+2x}{5} = 0$$
$$12 + 2x = 0$$
$$2x = -12$$
$$x = -6$$

Our answer, then, is 185 greater than our result of -6. The average price of the remaining suits is 179.

120 Sets: Weighted Average: Drill

1. Six test scores included 4 scores of 86 and 2 scores of 92. What was the average of the six scores?

2. Of seven employees, 3 are paid an annual salary of $14,000, 2 are paid an annual salary of $16,000, and 2 are paid an annual salary of $19,000. What is the average annual salary paid to these employees?

3. A researcher measured the time a certain procedure took 8 times. 5 times, the procedure took 9.2 seconds, while the other 3 times, the procedure took 8.4 seconds. What was the average of the 8 times?

4. Kevin purchased 10 shirts at an average cost of $31.20 per shirt. If he paid $28 each for 6 of the shirts, what was the average price he paid for the other 4 shirts?

5. Of a group of 5 packages to be mailed, 3 of the packages weigh $7\frac{1}{4}$ ounces. If the average weight of the 5 packages is $8\frac{1}{4}$ ounces, what is the average weight of the other 2 packages?

6. 10 pieces of music have an average length of 61 minutes. If 3 of the pieces are 72 minutes long and 5 of the pieces are 52 minutes long, what is the average length of the other 2 pieces?

7. At a weightlifting competition, the participants lift an average of 465 pounds in a certain round. If 5 of the participants average 480 pounds and the rest of the participants average 440 pounds, what is the total number of participants?

8. Jocelyn purchased several books at an average cost of $26. If 2 of the books cost $18, 4 of the books cost $26 each, and the rest of the books cost $30 each, how many books did she purchase at $30 each?

9. In a certain office, some of the employees live 12 miles away from the office and the rest of the employees live 15 miles away from the office. If the average distance that each employee lives from the office is 13 miles, what is the ratio of employees who live 15 miles away to those who live 12 miles away?

10. The average of a certain set of measurements was 0.4 inches. If some of the measurements were 0.2 inches and the remainder were 0.56 inches, what was the ratio of 0.2 inch measurements to 0.56 measurements?

121 Sets: Weighted Average: Practice

311. An office supply store has 150 boxes of paper clips in stock. If 125 of these boxes each contain 200 paper clips and the rest each contain 500 paper clips, what is the average number of paper clips per box?

    (A) 250
    (B) 300
    (C) 350
    (D) 400
    (E) 450

312. A certain factory employs six managers. It pays annual salaries of \$21,000 to 2 of the managers, \$22,000 to 1 of the managers, and \$24,000 to each of the remaining 3 managers. The average (arithmetic mean) annual salary of the six managers is closest to which of the following?

    (A) \$22,000
    (B) \$22,400
    (C) \$22,700
    (D) \$23,000
    (E) \$23,200

313. A taxicab driver worked exactly 18 shifts in a month. He used an average of $10\frac{1}{4}$ gallons of gasoline for each of the first 10 shifts, and an average of $12\frac{1}{8}$ gallons of gasoline for each of the rest of his shifts. What is the average amount of gasoline, in gallons, that the taxicab driver used per shift?

    (A) 11
    (B) $11\frac{1}{12}$
    (C) $11\frac{3}{16}$
    (D) $11\frac{1}{6}$
    (E) $11\frac{7}{24}$

314. If a, b, and c are numbers, is $c = 15$?

    (1) The average (arithmetic mean) of a, b, and c is 10.
    (2) The average (arithmetic mean) of a and b is 7.5.

122   Sets: Weighted Average: Challenge

315.   If a football team scores an average (arithmetic mean) of x points per game for m games and then scores y points per game for its next p games, what is the team's average score for the $m + p$ games?

   (A) $mx + py$
   (B) $\frac{x}{m} + \frac{p}{y}$
   (C) $\frac{x+y}{m+p}$
   (D) $\frac{mx+py}{m+p}$
   (E) $\frac{mx+py}{x+y}$

316.   When Company A and Company B merge, the resulting corporation retains all employees of the two companies and does not hire any additional employees. Before the merger, did Company A have more employees than Company B?

   (1)   Before the merger, the average (arithmetic mean) salary of the employees of Company A was $41,200 and the average salary of the employees of Company B was $44,700.
   (2)   Before the merger, the average (arithmetic mean) salary of the employees of the two companies was $43,600.

$$x = 8\left(\frac{a}{c}\right) + 16\left(\frac{b}{c}\right)$$

317.   In the formula above, a, b, c, and d are positive numbers. If $c = a + b$ and $b > a$, which of the following could be the value of x?

   (A)   8
   (B)   10
   (C)   12
   (D)   15
   (E)   21

318.   On six consecutive vocabulary quizzes, Kelvin's lowest score was 70. Was his average (arithmetic mean) quiz score for the six quizzes less than 80?

   (1)   The average of Kelvin's three lowest quiz scores was 72.
   (2)   The average of Kelvin's three highest quiz scores was 92.

123   Sets: Statistics

Average is the most common measurement of a set on the GMAT, but there are several others you need to be familiar with. This section largely focuses on defining those terms; when they arise on GMAT items, recognizing the terms themselves is often enough.

Along with mean (average), median is a frequently-used measure of centrality. In any set of numbers, the median is the middle term. So, if you line up the numbers in a set in ascending order,
$$\{1, 2, 5, 8, 9, 11, 32\}$$
the median is the number in the middle. Since three numbers are greater than 8 and threee numbers are less than 8, 8 is the median. It's only a little bit more complicated when the set has an even number of terms:
$$\{1, 2, 5, 8, 9, 11, 32, 33\}$$
In that case, the median is the mean of the middle two numbers. The middle two in this set are 8 and 9, so the median is $\frac{8+9}{2} = \frac{17}{2}$.

One trick that will come in handy is that, when the terms of a set are consecutive, the mean and the median are equal. It doesn't matter whether they are consecutive integers, consecutive odds, or consecutive multiples of 7–as long as the numbers are equally spaced, the mean and median are identical. Usually that's most useful when you're looking for the mean of a set of large numbers: it doesn't require very much arithmetic to find the median, so if you can find the median instead of solve for the mean, you've probably saved some time.

Yet another measure of centrality is "mode." Mode is much less common on the GMAT than mean or median. The mode of a set is the most frequently-occuring term, so in this example,
$$\{1, 1, 1, 2, 2, 3, 4, 4\}$$
1 is the mode. If we change the set a little bit,
$$\{1, 1, 1, 2, 2, 3, 4, 4, 4\}$$
the set is now "bi-modal" or "multi-modal." Both 1 and 4 are considered modes.

The GMAT also expects you to be conversant with the concept of "range." The range of a set is the difference between the largest term and the smallest term, and as such is always a positive number. As with median, when you're solving for range, it's useful to first put the set in ascending or descending order. So, if you're given this:
$$\{7, 3, 2, 9, 4, 11\}$$
First rearrange it:
$$\{2, 3, 4, 7, 9, 11\}$$
Then subtract the smallest term from the largest term to find the range:
$$11 - 2 = 9$$

Finally, an increasing number of GMAT test items include standard deviation and, less often, variance. The two are very similar, and the distinction isn't all that important. While some GMAT books teach you how to solve for standard deviation, that will never be tested on the test itself. Instead, you need to understand what standard deviation measures, and how to use it.

Standard deviation is a measure of "variability." In other words, it indicates how spread out the numbers in a set are. Compare sets A and B:

A = $\{1, 2, 3, 4, 5, 6, 7\}$

B = $\{1, 5, 9, 13, 17, 21, 25\}$

The mean of A is 4, while the mean of B is 13. The numbers in A are, on average, closer to the mean of their set than the numbers in B are to theirs. Thus, the standard deviation of A is smaller than the standard deviation of B.

While you don't need to memorize the technique to calculate standard deviation, it may be useful to see it. Using A as an example, start by finding the mean, as we did: 4. Next, for each number in the set, find the square of the difference between that number and the mean:

$(4 - 1)^2 = 9$

$(4 - 2)^2 = 4$

$(4 - 3)^2 = 1$

etc.

Compute the average of all of those squares and take the square root of the result:

$$\sqrt{\frac{9+4+1+0+1+4+9}{7}} = \sqrt{4} = 2$$

Variance is nearly identical; you compute it the same way, but don't take the square root of the result.

As I've said, you don't need to memorize that process. I show it only because it's useful to have seen it in action, because you may need to eyeball a few sets and determine which has the largest or smallest standard deviation. (Don't worry, they'll be like A and B above: the differences won't be subtle.)

Occasionally, a test item will give you the mean and standard deviation of a set and ask, for instance, which of a series of choices is more than 2 standard deviations from the mean. The terminology may be a bit unfamiliar. If the mean of a set is 4 and the standard deviation is 2, a number exactly 1 standard deviation from the mean is expressed by:

4 ± 2

In other words, both 2 and 6 are 1 standard deviation from the mean. In set A above, there are two numbers (1 and 7) that are more than 1 standard deviation from the mean. A number exactly 2 standard deviations from the mean is expressed by:

$4 \pm 2(2)$

Calculated, that's 0 or 8. Thus, any number less than zero or greater than 8 would be more than two standard deviations away from the mean. No numbers in set A are two or more standard deviations from the mean.

Advanced Standard Deviation Principles

Of course, the GMAT has plenty of ways to make questions a little harder, even based on those principles. Here are some tips to handle those questions:

The actual numbers don't matter. For standard deviation, it's all about how far each term is from the mean. For instance, the set {10, 20, 30} has the same standard deviation as {150, 160, 170}. In other words, if you add or subtract the same amount from every term in the set, the standard deviation doesn't change.

If you multiply or divide every term in the set by the same number, the standard deviation will change. For instance, if you multiply {10, 20, 30} by 2, you get {20, 40, 60}. Those numbers, on average, are further away from the mean.

When you multiply or divide every term in a set by the same number, the standard deviation changes by that same number. In the example I just gave, the standard deviation of {20, 40, 60} is exactly double that of the standard deviation of {10, 20, 30}. (The same is true of range, incidentally.)

124   Sets: Statistics: Drill

1.   Find the median and range of each of the following sets. If any
numbers appear more than once in a set, find the mode as well:
   a. $\{-4, 6, 3, 1, -7, 2, 3\}$
   b. $\{12, 12, 18\}$
   c. $\{1, 2, 3, 4, 5, 6, 7, 8, 9\}$
   d. $\{15, 16\}$
   e. $\{-10, 6, 11, -2, \frac{3}{2}, -15\}$

2.   Rank the following sets from greatest standard deviation to
least standard deviation:
   a. $\{1, 2, 3, 4, 5\}$
   b. $\{2, 3, 3, 3, 5\}$
   c. $\{-5, 0, 5, 10, 15\}$
   d. $\{3, 3, 3, 3, 3\}$
   e. $\{-5, -5, 0, 15, 15\}$

3.   Find the value of x:
   a.   Set S has a mean of 15 and a standard deviation of 2.5.
      x is two standard deviations above the mean.
   b. x is one standard deviation below the mean of Set S,
      which has a mean of 12 and a standard deviation of $\frac{5}{3}$.
   c.   Set S has a mean of -5 and a standard deviation of 1.5.
      x is 1.5 standard deviations above the mean.
   d. x is two standard deviations below the mean of Set S,
      which has a standard deviation of 3.5 and a mean of m.
   e.   Set S has a mean of m and a standard deviation of s. x
      is k standard deviations below the mean.

125 Sets: Statistics: Practice

321. The prices of one pair of Brand X shoes recorded on June 12th
at department shoes in a certain township were $70, $60,
$75, $72, $54, and $65. What is the median of these prices?
    - (A) $73.50
    - (B) $70.00
    - (C) $67.50
    - (D) $66.00
    - (E) $65.00

322. The arithmetic mean and standard deviation of a certain
normal distribution are 13.0 and 1.75, respectively. What
value is exactly 3 standard deviations less than the mean?
    - (A) 6.75
    - (B) 7.25
    - (C) 7.75
    - (D) 8.25
    - (E) 8.75

323. If S $=\{18, 7, 11, 3, 15, 0\}$, what is the positive difference between
the median of the numbers in S and the mean of the numbers
in S?
    - (A) 2.0
    - (B) 1.5
    - (C) 1.0
    - (D) 0.5
    - (E) 0.0

324. If set S consists of the numbers w, x, y, and z, is the range of
the numbers in S greater than 5 ?
    - (1) The range of any three numbers in set S is greater
than 5.
    - (2) The positive difference between any two numbers in set
S is greater than 3.

325. Is the range of the integers 4, 7, x, 6, 5, y greater than 9 ?
    - (1) $y > x^2$
    - (2) $3 < x < y$

326. For a certain set of n numbers, where $n > 2$, is the average
(arithmetic mean) equal to the median?
    - (1) The n numbers are positive, consecutive integers.
    - (2) The smallest integer in the set is odd.

126   Sets: Statistics: Challenge

327.   The arithmetic mean and standard deviation of a certain normal
distribution are m and d, respectively. Which of the following
expressions represents a value one standard deviation below
the mean?

(A) $d - m$
(B) $d - 2m$
(C) $m + d$
(D) $m - d$
(E) $d - m$

328.   If the range of the set containing the numbers x, y, and z is 8,
what is the value of the smallest number in the set?

(1)   The average of the set containing the numbers x, y, z,
and 8 is 12.5.

(2)   The mean and the median of the set containing the
numbers x, y, and z are equal.

329.   A certain automobile dealership sells only cars and trucks.
The retail price of the most expensive car at the dealership
is \$22,000 and the retail price of the least expensive truck
at the dealership is \$27,500. What is the median retail price
of all the automobiles at the dealership?

(1)   The average (arithmetic mean) retail price of all the
automobiles at the dealership is \$23,750.

(2)   There are 5 more trucks than cars at the dealership.

127   Sets: Overlapping Sets

At its most basic level, an overlapping sets question involves dividing a group up multiple ways. If you have a group of people, you can split it into men and women, children and adults, college graduates and non-graduates, or any number of other pairs of characteristics. Overlapping sets requires you to track what happens when a set is split up in multiple ways.

Say, for instance, that a group consists of 50 people. Every member of the group is either a man (M) or a woman (W), and every member of the group is a child (C) or an adult (A). Using the notation X&Y to denote the subgroup consisting of people who are both X and Y, the following equation represents the resulting subgroups:

50 = M&C + M&A + W&C + W&A

In other words, the sum of 50 people is equivalent to the sum of male children, male adults, female children, and female adults. We can also write an equation using only M and A, with the addition of the word "not." "notM" is the same as W, since anyone who is not male must be female:

50 = M&A + M&notA + notM&A + notM&notA

The first term, M&A, we'll later refer to as "both," as it's the intersection of both of the sets we're looking at, men and adults. The last term, notM&notA, we'll refer to as "neither." Visually, you can picture those four subgroups as the parts of a Venn Diagram:

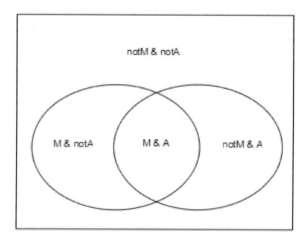

Unfortunately, the GMAT rarely feeds us the data that we can plug straight into that equation. Take this example, for instance:

"Of the 200 members of a certain gym, 110 have been members for at least a year and 40 have attended a fitness class. If 25 members of the gym have been members for at least a year and have attended a fitness class, how many have not been members for at least a year and have not attended a fitness class?"

Some of the quantities in this example may look familiar after the preceding section. For instance, 25 members have both been members for a year and have attended a fitness class. That's equivalent to the subgroup of male adults: "both." Similarly, the quantity we're looking for: those who haven't been members for at least a year and haven't attended a fitness class are similar to non-male non-adults (female children), "neither."

However, the other two quantities, the number who have been members for at least a year and the number who have attended a fitness class, don't have a direct analogue. They are each the sum of two subgroups. To make that clearer, let's look at the four distinct subgroups in the example, where Y = members for at least a year, and F = attended a fitness class.

$$200 = Y\&F + Y\&notF + notY\&F + notY\&notF$$

As I've already pointed out, $Y\&F = 25$, and $notY\&notF$ is what we're looking for. The 110 who have been members for a least a year is the sum of two subgroups: $Y\&F + Y\&notF$. Similarly, the 40 who have attended a fitness class are also the sum of two subgroups: $Y\&F + notY\&F$. That's where the "overlapping" in overlapping sets came from: both of those numbers include $Y\&F$. That's the space where the two ovals overlap in a Venn Diagram, labeled "M&A" in the diagram above.

So, we need a better equation to use numbers like those in the example above. This will do the trick:

Total = Group 1 + Group 2 - Both + Neither

Total is the total number of people. Group 1 is the number of one of the groups (such as those who have been members for at least a year, or men). Group 2 is the other group (such as those who have attended a fitness class, or adults). Both is the intersection of the two groups: those who have attended a fitness class and have been members for at least a year, or $Y\&F$. Neither is the subgroup that isn't represented by either of the groups: $notY\&notF$.

In a Venn Diagram, Group 1 is the left oval. Group 2 is the right oval. Both is the intersection of the ovals, and neither is the area outside of the ovals.

Most of the time, this last equation will be all you need. At other times, the initial equation, representing the four subgroups, will work. You may prefer to use the Venn Diagram; I don't care for it myself, but it works for some people, as it visually represents the mathematics in the last equation. You may also consider a fourth approach, which is even more comprehensive that those we've gone through so far.

For this method, construct a table, as shown:

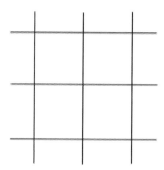

Label the rows and columns as follows. Make sure that the rows are labelled with the same type of thing: male and female, not male and adult. Same thing applies to the columns. Once labelled, the table will look like this:

	>1 yr	<1 yr	Total
Yoga			
No yoga			
Total			

Each of the empty boxes is the intersection of its row and column. For instance, the upper left is Y&F: those who have been members for at least a year and have attended a fitness class. The Total column on the right and the Total row at the bottom allow you to sum numbers across and down: for instance the upper right empty box is the total number of members who have attended a fitness class, and the bottom right is the total of all members.

The next step is to fill in the numbers you are given. From the example question we're working with:

	>1 yr	<1 yr	Total
Yoga	25		40
No yoga		x	
Total	110		200

x represents the number we're looking for.

Notice that there are four boxes we can fill in. For one, the box in the top row between 25 and 40. 25 plus the amount in the empty box adds up to 40, so we can fill in a 15 there, representing the number of members who have attended a fitness class but have not been members for at least a year. Follow the same process for the remaining three empty boxes:

	>1 yr	<1 yr	Total
Yoga	25	15	40
No yoga	85	x	160
Total	110	90	200

Finally, you can use x's row or column to find its value. To use the column:

$$90 = 15 + x$$
$$x = 75$$

As with all types of questions that have multiple possible approaches, it's important that you experiment with each one. The two I use most often are the last equation and the table. The equation is fastest, but it doesn't work every time: some questions don't give you the pieces of information to plug directly in for those variables. The table will work every time, but isn't always the most efficient. Another valuable consideration, of course, is what you are most comfortable with. It's up to you to find out.

Three Overlapping Sets

Questions with more than two sets aren't common on the GMAT, but at the same time, they don't require much more thinking that do the two-set questions.

Here's what one of those might look like:

> Of the shoe stores in City X, 30 carry Brand A shoes, 40 carry Brand B shoes, and 25 carry Brand C shoes. If each store carries at least one of the brands, 32 of the stores carry two of the three shoe brands, and none of the stores carry all three, how many shoe stores are there in City X?

We can't use a table for this, because it would have to be three-dimensional. A Venn Diagram is a possibility, but there's no place to put 32. We'll have to look at an expansion of the formula. Here what such an expansion would look like:

$Total = Group1 + Group2 + Group3 - (sum of 2 - group overlaps) - 2 * (all three) + Neither$

This looks more complicated, but the concept is the same as the two-set formula. $G1 + G2 + G3$ is the sum of all the stores that carry these brands, only we've double-counted some of them. Since 32 of the stores carry two brands, we've double-counted exactly 32, so we subtract 32, the "sum of 2-group overlaps."

The tricky part is the second-to-last term: "2*(all three)." It doesn't come up very often, as when it does, it's almost always on Data Sufficiency questions. However, it's worth thinking about.

If one of the stores in City X carried all three shoe brands, that store is being counted three times–once in the 30 A's, once in the 40 B's, and once in the 25 C's. But it's still only one store. Thus, if it's represented three times, we need to subtract it twice. In this case, the question tells us that the "all three" term is equal to zero.

So, to solve this example:

$Total = 30 + 40 + 25 - 32 - 2 * 0 + 0 = 63$

("Neither" equals 0 because every shoe store in City X carries at least one of the brands.)

Problems with three overlapping sets can be daunting, but like two-set questions, they can generally be handled with the same approach you use when practicing.

128 Sets: Overlapping Sets: Drill

1. Of the books in a certain bookstore, 250 are fiction and 600 are hardcover. If 150 of the books are both hardcover and fiction and 200 are neither hardcover nor fiction, what is the total number of books in the bookstore?

2. In a certain class, 20 of the students were male and 12 of the students received an "A." If 5 of the male students received an "A" and 11 of the female students did not receive an "A," what was the total number of students in the class?

3. Company X has 180 employees. 35 of the employees are managers, 50 of the employees have advanced degrees, and 125 of the employees are not managers and do not have advanced degrees. How many of the employees are managers who have advanced degrees?

4. Of the 80 stamps in Lawrence's collection, 54 are European and 20 date from the 19th century. If 22 of the stamps are neither European nor date from the 19th century, how many are European and date from the 19th century?

5. There are 36 athletes on a certain team, 21 of whom are at least 6 feet tall and 25 of whom weigh at least 200 pounds. If 15 of the athletes are at least 6 feet tall and weigh at least 200 pounds, how many are not at least 6 feet tall and do not weigh at least 200 pounds?

6. A certain used car lot has 65 sedans and 40 vehicles with four-wheel drive. If the lot has a total of 96 vehicles and 18 of them are sedans with four-wheel drive, how many of the cars are not sedans and do not have four-wheel drive?

7. Of the 32 reporters at a certain newspaper, 20 cover local news. If 4 reporters cover both local and national news and no reporters cover neither local nor national news, how many reporters cover national news?

8. There are 75 restaurants in City X. 20 of those restaurants serve Chinese food, and 15 of the restaurants that serve Chinese food advertise in the local newspaper. If 13 of the restaurants in City X neither serve Chinese food nor advertise in the local paper, how many restaurants in City X advertise in the local paper?

9. 45 of the students at a certain school study one or more of the languages French, Spanish, or Japanese. If 22 of the students study French, 20 of the students study Spanish, 15 of the students study Japanese, and none of the students study all three, how many students study two lanaguges?

10. Of the intelligence agents assigned to a certain region, 40 are assigned to Country X, 35 are assigned to Country Y, and 36 are assigned to Country Z. If 9 are assigned to Country X and

Country Y, 12 are assigned to Country X and Country Z, 6 are assigned to Country Y and Country Z, and no agents are assigned to all three countries, what is the total number of agents assigned to the region?

129   Sets: Overlapping Sets: Practice

331.   Of the members of a certain health club, 30 percent are women at least 40 years of age. What percent of the members are men under 40 years of age?

    (1)   Of the female members of the health club, half are at least 40 years of age.

    (2)   Of the members of the health club at least 40 years of age, half are men.

332.   Of the blue-chip stocks analyzed in a recent study, 30 percent both returned a dividend last year and increased in value at least 5% last year. What percent of the blue-chip stocks analyzed neither returned a dividend or increased in value at least 5% last year?

    (1)   Of the blue-chip stocks analyzed, 70 percent returned a dividend last year.

    (2)   Of the blue-chip stocks analyzed, 12 percent increased in value at least 10% last year.

333.   If 60 percent of the towels available at a certain store retail for $9.99 or more, 30 percent of the towels are discounted, and 40 percent of the towels retail for less than $9.99 and are not discounted, what percent of the towels retail for $9.99 or more and are discounted?

    (A)   10
    (B)   20
    (C)   30
    (D)   40
    (E)   60

334.   Of the members of a tour group, twenty five percent speak Japanese. Among the members who do not speak Japanese, 11 speak Spanish and 19 do not speak Spanish. How many members of the tour group speak Japanese?

    (A)   4
    (B)   6
    (C)   8
    (D)   10
    (E)   12

335.   Yesterday, 72 percent of the entrees served at a certain restaurant were fish entrees (including salmon), and 54 percent of the entrees served were salmon entrees. What percent of the fish entrees served at the restaurant yesterday were not salmon entrees?

　　(A)   16%
　　(B)   25%
　　(C)   32%
　　(D)   40%
　　(E)   52%

130   Sets: Overlapping Sets: Challenge

336.   In 1997, N people graduated from college. If $\frac{1}{3}$ of them received a degree in the applied sciences, and, of those, $\frac{1}{4}$ graduated from a school in one of six northeastern states, which of the following expressions represents the number of people who graduated from college in 1997 who did not both receive a degree in the applied sciences and graduate from a school in one of six northeastern states?

   (A) $\frac{11N}{12}$

   (B) $\frac{7N}{12}$

   (C) $\frac{5N}{12}$

   (D) $\frac{6N}{7}$

   (E) $\frac{N}{7}$

337.   Of the 250 students in a certain class, each student who majors in mathematics also majors in computer science, and 90 of the students major only in biology. If no student majors in all three subjects, how many of the students major in two of the three subjects?

   (1)   50 of the students major only in computer science.

   (2)   40 of the students do not major in any of the three subjects.

338.   Of the 174 shirts available at a certain retail store, 116 of the shirts are long-sleeved, 110 are on sale, and 75 percent of the long-sleeved shirts are on sale. If a shirt is to be randomly selected from those available, what is the probability that the shirt is long-sleeved and is not on sale?

   (A) $\frac{1}{8}$

   (B) $\frac{1}{6}$

   (C) $\frac{1}{4}$

   (D) $\frac{1}{3}$

   (E) $\frac{2}{3}$

339.   At Company X, is the number of employees who work part-time greater than the number of employees who have worked for the company for at least five years?

    (1)   Of the employees who work part-time, 60 percent have not worked for the company for at least five years.

    (2)   Of the employees who have worked for the company for at least five years, 70 percent do not work part-time.

Basketball: 20
Soccer: 25
Tennis: 12

340.   The table above shows the number of students in three sports teams at Eckerd School. No student is on all three teams, but 6 students participate in Basketball and Soccer, 5 students participate in Basketball and Tennis, and 3 students participate in Soccer and Tennis. How many different students are on the three teams?

    (A)   29
    (B)   43
    (C)   47
    (D)   53
    (E)   57

131   Advanced Topics: Probability

If there's one thing that worries GMAT test-takers more than anything else, it's probability. It's as if there's a big warning sign on the inside cover of every GMAT prep book ever printed telling students that they won't get the score they want until they spent 50 hours studying probability.

Let me tell you: it isn't true.

In fact, there are exactly four fundamental concepts you need to nail all but the very hardest of GMAT probability questions. That's it. Naturally, this section will cover each of them.

The basic formula for probability is:

$$p = \frac{\text{number of desired outcomes}}{\text{number of possible outcomes}}$$

Let's say there are 8 marbles in a bag and 3 of them are blue. The probability that a randomly selected marble from that bag will be blue is:

$$p = \frac{3}{8}$$

Most questions involve more complexity than that, but every probability question starts there.

Often, that additional complexity comes in the form of multiple probabilities to be combined in some way. The most common is the word "and." (Usually it's explicit; occasionally it's implicit.) For instance:

> "There is a 25% chance that Krista will be assigned to a 9 a.m. calculus class. There is a 40% chance Krista will be assigned to an 11 a.m. physics class. If the likelihood that Krista is assigned to either class is independent of the other, what is the probability that Krista will be assigned to both the 9 a.m. calculus class and the 11 a.m. physics class?"

In this example, each probability is given; we just have to translate them into the corresponding fractions, $\frac{1}{4}$ and $\frac{2}{5}$. When we want the probability that two things both happen, we multiply the individual probabilities:

$$P_{both} = \left(\frac{1}{4}\right)\left(\frac{2}{5}\right) = \frac{2}{20} = \frac{1}{10}$$

Don't be distracted by the phrase, "if the likelihood ...is independent of the other." It's just the way the question closes all the loopholes. It's possible to imagine a scenario in which, if Krista is assigned to the 9 a.m. calculus class, her chances of getting the 11 a.m. physics class would change. The GMAT doesn't want you to be distracted by that sort of digression.

As you see, the words "and" and "both" are fairly straightforward. The word "or" is trickier. Consider two examples:

1.   "A bag contains 25 marbles. 11 of the marbles are green, 10 of the marbles are red, and the remainder are blue. What is the probability that a randomly selected marble will be green or blue?"

> 2.   "A fair coin is flipped twice. What is the probability that the coin lands showing heads on the first flip, the second flip, or both?"

The key difference between these two examples is that, in the second case, the separate probabilities are "discrete." The result of the first flip has nothing to do with the result of the second flip. By contrast, if in 1., a green marble is selected, a blue marble cannot be selected. The probabilities are dependent on each other.

When the probabilities are dependent, as in 1., the word "or" signals addition. Find the probability of each of the desired outcomes and add them together:

$$p_{\text{green or blue}} = \frac{11}{25} + \frac{4}{25} = \frac{15}{25} = \frac{3}{5}$$

The approach to the second example is more involved. If we add the probabilities of getting a head on the first flip and getting a head on the second flip, it doesn't make sense:

$$p_{\text{head on first or head on second}} = \frac{1}{2} + \frac{1}{2} = 1$$

If you've ever flipped a coin twice, you probably know that the probability of getting at least one head isn't 100%. Something's wrong.

Since the probabilities are discrete, we can't add them. Instead, we have to convert the question into one with an "and"–something we can multiply. In such a case, your task is to figure out what the opposite of the desired probability is. If the desired outcome is a head on the first flip, a head on the second flip, or both, the opposite is no heads at all: a tail on both flips.

That's something we can attack using multiplication. The probability of getting a tail on any given flip is $\frac{1}{2}$, so the likelihood that each flip will be tails is:

$$p_{\text{two tails}} = \left(\frac{1}{2}\right)\left(\frac{1}{2}\right) = \frac{1}{4}$$

That isn't what we're looking for, but it's close. Once we find the opposite of the probability we seek, we subtract it from one:

$$p_{\text{head on first or head on second}} = 1 - \frac{1}{4} = \frac{3}{4}$$

The more general form of this rule is:

$$p_{\text{desired outcome}} + p_{\text{opposite of desired outcome}} = 1$$

One handy approach that I haven't discussed is brute force. On any GMAT probability question, you can use the techniques I've described so far. But sometimes you may not know how, or you may decide that it's faster just to generate all the possibilities and count them up. For instance, in the previous example, you might recognize that there are only four possible outcomes:

H H
H T
T H
T T

Of those four outcomes, three of them contain at least one head. Therefore, using the rule we learned at the beginning of the chapter, the probability is $\frac{desired}{possible} = \frac{3}{4}$. As you might imagine, this approach loses effectiveness quickly as the numbers get larger, but in some cases it works just fine. Keep it in mind when the numbers are manageable.

132   Advanced Topics: Probability: Drill

1.   If a fair coin is flipped three times, what is the probability that it comes up heads all three times?

2.   If a standard six-sided die is rolled twice, what is the probability that the result on the first roll is even and the result on the second roll is odd?

3.   A bag contains 27 marbles: 4 green, 5 red, 10 blue, and 8 white. If a marble is to be randomly selected from the bag, what is the probability that it will be either green or white?

4.   A group of 20 people includes 8 with blonde hair, 5 with red hair, and 7 with dark hair. What is the probability that a randomly selected member of the group has either blonde or dark hair?

5.   6 of the 24 numbers in set S are prime. What is the probability that a randomly selected number from set S would not be prime?

6.   Each member of a board of directors is on exactly one of three committees: planning, acquisitions, or budget. If $\frac{3}{4}$ of the members of the board are on the planning or acquisitions committee, what is the probability that a randomly selected member of the board is on the budget committee?

7.   The probability that an odd number is selected from set A is $\frac{1}{3}$ and the probability that an odd number is selected from set B is $\frac{1}{2}$. If a number is to be randomly selected from each of the two sets, what is the probability that at least one of the numbers is odd?

8.   If two standard six-sided dice are rolled, what is the probability that at least one of the rolls results in a prime number?

9.   If 6 of the 10 members of a certain class are boys, what is the probability that two members, selected at random without replacement, are both boys?

10.   Paula and Quentin are two members of an eight-member committee. If the committee selects its president and secretary at random, and the same member cannot hold both positions, what is the probability that Paula is selected as president and Quentin is selected as secretary?

133   Advanced Topics: Probability: Practice

341.   The probability is $\frac{1}{2}$ that a certain coin will turn up heads on any given toss. If the coin is to be tossed three times, what is the probability that on at least one of the tosses the coin will turn up heads?

    (A) $\frac{1}{8}$
    (B) $\frac{1}{2}$
    (C) $\frac{3}{4}$
    (D) $\frac{7}{8}$
    (E) $\frac{15}{16}$

342.   What is the probability that a random number selected from the set of integers 101 through 250, inclusive, has a tens digit of 1?

    (A) $\frac{1}{15}$
    (B) $\frac{2}{15}$
    (C) $\frac{2}{25}$
    (D) $\frac{3}{25}$
    (E) $\frac{20}{149}$

343.   If a number between $\frac{1}{2}$ and 1 is selected at random, which of the following will the number most likely be between?

    (A) $\frac{1}{2}$ and $\frac{13}{20}$
    (B) $\frac{13}{20}$ and $\frac{7}{10}$
    (C) $\frac{7}{10}$ and $\frac{3}{4}$
    (D) $\frac{3}{4}$ and $\frac{4}{5}$
    (E) $\frac{4}{5}$ and 1

344.   Forty percent of the residents of Town T are men, and 15 percent of those men are over the age of 60. If one resident of the town is to be selected at random, what is the probability that the resident selected is a man over the age of 60?

    (A)   0.02
    (B)   0.06
    (C)   0.11
    (D)   0.20
    (E)   0.55

134   Advanced Topics: Probability: Challenge

345.   If x is to be chosen at random from the set $\{1, 2, 3\}$ and y is to
be chosen at random from the set $\{4, 5, 6, 7\}$, what is the
probability that xy will be even?

   (A) $\frac{1}{6}$
   (B) $\frac{1}{3}$
   (C) $\frac{1}{2}$
   (D) $\frac{2}{3}$
   (E) $\frac{5}{6}$

346.   One bag contains 100 marbles, numbered consecutively from 0
to 99, inclusive. Another bag contains 60 marbles, numbered
consecutively from 90 to 149, inclusive. If a marble is
randomly drawn from each bag, what is the probability that
the two marbles have the same number?

   (A) $\frac{1}{10}$
   (B) $\frac{1}{60}$
   (C) $\frac{1}{100}$
   (D) $\frac{1}{600}$
   (E) $\frac{1}{6000}$

347.   From a group of 3 sophomores and 3 juniors, 4 students
are to be randomly selected. What is the probability that
more juniors than sophomores will be selected?

   (A) $\frac{1}{10}$
   (B) $\frac{1}{6}$
   (C) $\frac{1}{5}$
   (D) $\frac{1}{4}$
   (E) $\frac{1}{3}$

348.   If 2 different members are to be selected at random from a
group of 8 people and if p is the probability that both
members selected will be older than 35 years old, is
$p > \frac{1}{3}$?

   (1)   More than half of the group members are older than
35 years old.
   (2)   The probability that both members selected will be 35
years old or younger is greater than $\frac{1}{10}$.

349.   Company X has 800 employees and Company Y has 600
employees. Among these employees, there are 50
married couples, each consisting of an employee from
Company X and an employee from Company Y. If 1
employee is to be selected at random from each company,
what is the probability that the 2 employees selected will
be a married couple?

(A) $\frac{1}{480,000}$

(B) $\frac{1}{9,600}$

(C) $\frac{7}{2,400}$

(D) $\frac{1}{192}$

(E) $\frac{7}{48}$

350.   Nora will enter a ticket lottery every day until she wins the lottery,
after which she will no longer enter. If the probability that
she wins the ticket lottery is 0.1 on each of the first three
days, what is the probability that she wins on the third day?

(A)   0.001

(B)   0.009

(C)   0.081

(D)   0.729

(E)   0.900

135   Advanced Topics: Combinations

Like probability, combinations and permutations are topics that strike fear into the mind of GMAT test takers. There are two reasons it doesn't have to be that way: first, they don't come up on the GMAT that often, and they aren't all that hard. I've heard all the rumors out there, including the story that you can't get a 700 unless you see at least one difficult combinations problem...it's just that, a rumor. Your task is to learn the material. Leave the rumors to those with all that extra time on their hands.

Both combinations and permutations have to do with selecting the number of possible subsets or arrangements from a group. The most challenging aspect of these two topics is telling them apart. The key difference is:

If order doesn't matter, it's a combination problem. If order does matter, it's a permutation.

So we'll be starting with combinations, questions in which the order of the subset doesn't matter. I'll save most of my discussion of permutations for that chapter, but for now, here are two examples to illustrate the difference between combinations and permutations:

1.   "A board of directors has six members. If a three-person subcommittee is to be selected from the members of the board of directors, how many possible subcommittees could result?"

2.   "A board of directors has six members. If the board is to elect a president, vice president, and secretary from among its members, how many arrangements of president, vice president, and secretary could be elected?"

The first example is a combinations problem, while the second is a permutations question.

To understand why, let's start by naming the six members: A, B, C, D, E, and F. In 1., the first subcommittee I can think of is:

A B C

It doesn't matter what order those three are selected; the subcommittee is the same as long as those three people are in it. By contrast, there are several different ways that A, B, and C could be elected to the three positions. In order of president, vice president, and secretary:

A B C
A C B
B A C
B C A
C A B
C B A

For every one combination of three members, there are six permutations. As the definition stated, the second example is a permutations question because order matters.

For the remainder of the chapter, we're going to set permutations aside and focus on how to calculate the answer to a combinations problem once you've identified it.

For that, we'll turn to the combinations formula:

$$c = \frac{n!}{k!(n-k)!}$$

where n is the size of the group (the board of directors in the previous example) and k is the size of the desired subgroup (the subcommittee). You may have been exposed to this before with different terminology: "n choose k." Regardless of what you call it, this is your formula for every combinations question.

Once again, let's look at example 1:

> "A board of directors has six members. If a three-person subcommittee is to be selected from the members of the board of directors, how many possible subcommittees could result?"

The size of the group is 6 and the size of the subgroup is 3. Thus, $n = 6$ and $k = 3$:

$$c = \frac{n!}{k!(n-k)!} = \frac{6!}{3!(6-3)!} = \frac{6!}{3!3!} = \frac{6\times5\times4\times3\times2\times1}{3\times2\times1\times3\times2\times1}$$

Before finishing off the math, allow me to point out a very easy shortcut that many students miss. In a rush to solve for a number, it's easy to multiply all the numbers on top and then multiply all the numbers on the bottom:

$$\frac{6\times5\times4\times3\times2\times1}{3\times2\times1\times3\times2\times1} = \frac{720}{36}$$

But that approach usually gives you a somewhat large denominator and, thus, an unfriendly long division problem. Instead, look for ways to cancel out some of the terms:

$$\frac{6\times5\times4\times3\times2\times1}{3\times2\times1\times3\times2\times1} = \frac{6\times5\times4}{3\times2\times1} = \frac{5\times4}{1} = 20$$

That's much easier, and much less error-prone.

One way combinations questions get more difficult is by including multiple combinations in the same problem. Consider this example:

> "A five-person research team is to consist of 2 members of Group A and 3 members of Group B. If Group A has 6 members and Group B has 5 members, how many possible research teams could be constructed?"

From what we've done so far, we know how to determine the number of possible subgroups of selected members from Group A and Group B:

$$c_A = \frac{6!}{2!(6-2)!} = \frac{6!}{2!4!} = \frac{6\times5\times4\times3\times2\times1}{2\times1\times4\times3\times2\times1} = \frac{6\times5}{2\times1} = 15$$

$$c_B = \frac{5!}{3!(5-3)!} = \frac{5!}{3!2!} = \frac{5\times4\times3\times2\times1}{3\times2\times1\times2\times1} = \frac{5\times4}{2\times1} = 10$$

When you're combining combinations, simply multiply the results. You could pair any one of the 15 subgroups of Group A members with any one of the 10 subgroups of Group B members, so the number of possible five-person research teams is:

$$c_{\text{a and b}} = 15(10) = 150$$

Here's another twist that I call "backwards combinations." There are a handful of questions that leave the size of the group unknown, and provide the number of combinations.

Take a look at an example:

> Two members of a certain club are selected to speak at the next club meeting. If there are 36 different possible selections of the 2 club members, how many members does the club have?

In this case, we have the subset of 2 members, and we have the total number of combinations.

On other types of questions, this would be a trivial change. In a rate question, it doesn't matter whether we are given rate and time, distance and time, or rate and distance: Given any pair of values, we can find the third. Since the combinations formula includes factorials, though, that makes things more difficult.

To solve, start with the combinations formula:

$C = \frac{n!}{k!(n-k)!}$

We know that $C = 36$, $k = 2$, and we're solving for n. That gives us:

$36 = \frac{n!}{2!(n-2)!}$

Without some college math under your belt, you've probably never encountered anything like this before.

The factorial notation, $n!$, represents something more specific:

$n! = n(n-1)(n-2)...(1)$

We just don't know the value of n, so we don't know how many terms there are. However, we can simplify it a number of intermediate ways:

$n! = n(n-1)!$ (n times the factorial of $n-1$)

$n! = n(n-1)(n-2)!$ (n, times $n-1$, times the factorial of $n-2$)

$n! = n(n-1)(n-2)(n-3)!$ ...etc.

In this case, we know what we're trying to simplify, with a $(n-2)!$ in the denominator. So substitute the second of those options for $n!$:

$36 = \frac{n(n-1)(n-2)!}{2(n-2)!}$

Now cancel out the $(n-2)!$:

$36 = \frac{n(n-1)}{2}$

This solves as follows:

$72 = n^2 - n$

$n^2 - n - 72 = 0$

$(n-9)(n+8) = 0$

$n = 9$ or $n = -8$

Combinations refer to actual quantities of people and things, so only the positive answer is relevant.

This type of math can get very complicated, and that's a signal that the GMAT (which knows you probably don't have a math degree) won't take it much farther. In fact, I've never seen a question like this that had a value of k other than 2.

By learning to tinker with the combinations formula this way, you also pick up a shortcut for a substantial number of more basic combinations problems. Any time $k = 2$, the combinations formula simplifies to the following:

$C = \frac{n(n-1)}{2}$

So, if there are 8 tennis players in a league and we want to know how many possible pairings there are, we multiply 8 times 7 and divide by 2. (Try it with the original combinations formula: you'll see that it simplies to exactly that.)

Intuitively, that makes sense. In the tennis example, every one of the eight players has seven possible opponents. That makes 56 (8 times 7) possible pairings, but each pairing has been counted twice. (Joe playing Keith is the same as Keith playing Joe.) So we divide by 2.

If you know that, you don't have to do nearly as much work to get to the answer of the example we started with. Knowing that $k = 2$, you could plug in the value for C:

$36 = \frac{n(n-1)}{2}$

It's worth remembering this. A disproportionate number of "typical" combinations problems have $k = 2$, and the "backwards" combination problem will almost always have $k = 2$. If you understand it intuitively, that's even better.

That's as difficult as combinations are likely to get. The only additional twist is that, occasionally, a GMAT question will combine combinations and permutations or combinations and probability. While those problems can be mind-benders, it's just a matter of applying a couple of different skills at once. You don't need any additional formulas, just a bit of discipline to take apart the question into its component parts, each of which you should have the skills to solve.

136   Advanced Topics: Combinations: Drill

1.   For each of the following, determine whether it is a combinations problem or a permutations problem:
   a.   How many different ways can five dancers be arranged in a row?
   b.   How many different three-person subgroups can be selected from a group of ten people?
   c.   How many different two-person teams can be chosen from a committee of twelve people?
   d.   How many different arrangements of President, Vice President, and Secretary can be chosen from a committee of seven people?

2.   For each of the following, find the number of combinations given the size of the group n and the size of the subgroup k:
   a. $n = 6$, $k = 3$
   b. $n = 8$, $k = 5$
   c. $n = 5$, $k = 4$

3.   A child is allowed to choose three toys from a group of eight toys. How many different groups of three toys could the child select?

4.   The leader of a six-piece band is to select two members of the band to play a duet. How many possible pairs of band members could she select?

5.   A committee is to be made up of 3 employees of Company X and 2 employees of Company Y. If the Company X employees are to be chosen from among 5 possibilities and the Company Y employees are to be chosen from among 8 possibilities, how many possible 5-member committees could result?

137   Advanced Topics: Combinations: Practice

351.   A circus puts two lions on display during each performance. If it has five lions to choose from, how many different pairs of lions could the circus select for a performance?

   (A)   40
   (B)   20
   (C)   10
   (D)   5
   (E)   4

352.   There are six players in a certain chess tournament. If each of the players are to play each one of the other players exactly once, how many total matches will be played?

   (A)   15
   (B)   18
   (C)   24
   (D)   30
   (E)   36

353.   Mari is going to take two non-fiction books and one fiction book with her on vacation. If she is to choose between 7 non-fiction books and 10 fiction books, how many different groups of books could she take with her on vacation?

   (A)   31
   (B)   42
   (C)   105
   (D)   210
   (E)   420

354.   Of the 10 beads in a bag, no two beads are the same color. If 4 beads are to be selected at from the bag, how many different groups of 4 beads could be selected?

   (A)   40
   (B)   80
   (C)   120
   (D)   210
   (E)   420

138   Advanced Topics: Combinations: Challenge

355.   How many distinct triangles could be drawn using as their
vertices three of the vertices of a regular hexagon?

(A)   6
(B)   12
(C)   15
(D)   20
(E)   30

356.   A secretary differentiates files by a variety of color
combinations. If she uses 4 different colors, and marks
each file with 1, 2, or 3 of the colors, how many different
color combinations can she generate?

(A)   4
(B)   12
(C)   14
(D)   15
(E)   24

357.   From a group of 18 athletes that include 10 people with
professional experience, a 3-person team is to be
selected so that exactly 1 person on the team has
professional experience. How many different teams of
this type are possible?

(A)   280
(B)   360
(C)   504
(D)   560
(E)   816

358.   A certain musical piece is to be played by an equal number
of violinists and cellists. If there are 6 violinists and 2 cellists
available to play the piece, how many different groups of
musicians could be selected to play the piece?

(A)   12
(B)   15
(C)   27
(D)   28
(E)   70

139   Advanced Topics: Permutations

If you're skipping around in the book (which is okay!), you should go back and read the chapter on combinations before working through this one. It provides an overview of the difference between combinations and permuations and how to recognize it.

To recall, permutations questions ask you for the number of possible arrangements of a group or subgroup. As I put it in the combinations chapter: order matters. For example:

> "There are 12 students in a certain classroom. If there are four rows of three desks each in the classroom, how many different arrangements of students can be assigned to the desks in the front row, from left to right?"

First, the word "arrangements" signals that this is a permutations question. If that wasn't clear enough, the final phrase, "from left to right," emphasizes the fact that order matters. If you labelled the twelve students using the letters of the alphabet, you could probably think up several possible arrangements off the top of your head:

A B C
C D E
E D C
etc.

Of course, there's a better way to solve the problem than to write out the (many!) different arrangements on your scratch paper. In fact, there are two methods!

The first is closely related to the equation for combinations. The permutations equation is the same, except there's no "$k!$" in the denominator:

$$perm = \frac{n!}{(n-k)!}$$

n and k stand for the same things as in the combinations formula: the size of the overall group and the size of the desired subgroup. In this example, $n = 12$ and $k = 3$, so the answer is:

$$perm = \frac{12!}{(12-3)!} = \frac{12!}{9!} = \frac{12 \times 11 \times 10 \times 9 \times 8 \times 7 \times 6 \times 5 \times 4 \times 3 \times 2 \times 1}{9 \times 8 \times 7 \times 6 \times 5 \times 4 \times 3 \times 2 \times 1} = 12 \times 11 \times 10 =$$
1320

One of the dangers of relying on the permutations formula is that it offers you another way in which to confuse combinations and permutations. Whenever possible, it's always better to use a method that relies on the logic of the problem itself, and that's how the other approach works.

First, depict the problem visually. If there are three desks in the front row, draw three lines to show them:

Let's start on the left. If we are to assign one of the students to the leftmost desk, we have 12 choices. So, write in a 12 in that spot:

$$\frac{12}{1} \quad \frac{}{2} \quad \frac{}{3}$$

Moving over to the middle: we've assigned a student to the leftmost desk, leaving us with 11 choices for the middle seat. Write an 11 there. Then move to the right. We've assigned two students to desks, leaving us with 10 choices. Write a 10 in that spot:

$$\frac{12}{1} \quad \frac{11}{2} \quad \frac{10}{3}$$

To find the answer, multiply those numbers. Note that this step is the same as the final step in the method we used before trying this one:

$$12 \times 11 \times 10 = 1320$$

The latter, visual method is particularly useful when there are constraints on the arrangements. Let's alter our example a bit to make it a harder question:

"There are 12 students in a certain classroom, 6 boys and 6 girls. If there are four rows of three desks each in the classroom, how many different arrangements of students can be assigned to the desks in the front row, from left to right, if a boy must be in the middle desk?"

Doing this question with the equation is a tall order: we'd have to split it up into multiple different permutation problems. That's a lot of work, so let's try it visually.

The main constraint is the fact that one of the 6 boys must be in the middle desk. Let's start there, by depicting the fact that there are 6 choices for that place in the front row:

$$\frac{}{L} \quad \frac{6}{M} \quad \frac{}{R}$$

Now we can fill in the rest. Since we've assigned one student to the middle desk, we have 11 left. There are no constraints on the left or right desk, so we can put an 11 on the left (there are 11 students who could sit there) and a 10 on the right (there are now 10 remaining students once we've assigned two to the other desks). The diagram looks like this:

$$\frac{11}{L} \quad \frac{6}{M} \quad \frac{10}{R}$$

Just as in the previous case, we get our answer by multiplying the numbers:

$$11 \times 6 \times 10 = 660$$

In the examples we've looked at so far, we've been asked for an arrangement of a subset. That is, we only cared about 3 of the 12 students. As it turns out, it's an easier question when we are arranging the entire set. Let's say we wanted to know how many ways we could arrange the 12 students in the 12 desks, with no constraints. We could use the formula, where $n = 12$ and $k = 12$:

$$\frac{12!}{(12-12)!} = \frac{12!}{0!} = 12!$$

It's not important to understand why, but $0! = 1$. Also, $12!$ is a gigantic number, one that would never arise in this sort of context on the GMAT. If the test did ask this question, the answer choice would almost certainly be in the form $12!$ rather than 479,001,600.

As you probably noticed, using the formula in this case is a bit redundant. There's no need to solve for the denominator when the denominator turns out to be one. Instead, when the set and the subset are the same size, you can again turn to the visual approach. Instead of stopping at 12 times 11 times 10, keep going down to 1:

$$12 \times 11 \times 10 \times 9 \times 8 \times 7 \times 6 \times 5 \times 4 \times 3 \times 2 \times 1$$

Multiply all those numbers, and you've got $12!$.

Note that in all of the diagrams, I labelled each blank space, either with a number (1, 2, 3, etc.) or something else (L(eft), M(iddle), etc.). That's completely optional, and after you practice a few of these questions, you'll probably find it superfluous. But as with most extra steps, they only take an additional second or two of work, and they can help clarify the steps ahead of you.

As with combinations, if you have a problem with multiple permutations, solve for each individual permutation then find the product of the results. And to reiterate what I said in the previous chapter, permutations only get harder in conjunction with other topics. The task is not to learn a slew of new strategies, it's to focus on how to break apart the question into component parts. Each of those parts is something that you'll learn over the course of this book, usually something you can attack with a straightforward formula.

Permutations In a Circle

One common variation of permutation problems occurs when items are arranged in a circle.

Here's an example:

> In a garden, seven flowers are to be arranged around a circular walk. Two arrangements of the flowers are considered different only when the positions of the flowers are different relative to each other. What is the total number of different possible arrangements of the flowers?

Even if you've never seen a problem like this before, you might suspect that something is different that your typical permutation problem. All that verbiage about "different relative to each other" doesn't come up in other settings.

If the seven flowers were to be arranged in a row, this would be a relatively simple question. There would be seven flowers to choose from in the first position (say, on the left-hand side), then six for the next, then five, and so on. The answer would be 7!, or 5,040.

It's a safe bet, then, that the circular scenario differs. Consider the following two "rows" of seven flowers, in which each different flower is labeled with a different letter:

   * A B C D E F G
   * B C D E F G A

In a "row" question, those are two different permutations. However, if you arrange them in a circle, the pattern–A B C D E F G–is the same. The positions of the flowers are not different relative to each other.   In this case, there are seven different rows that end up being the same circular arrangement:

   * A B C D E F G
   * B C D E F G A
   * C D E F G A B
   * D E F G A B C
   * E F G A B C D
   * F G A B C D E
   * G A B C D E F

For any "row" arrangement you can think of, there are six other row arrangements that result in the same circular arrangement. Thus, each circular arrangement represents seven different rows.

Putting that into practice, you can start by finding the number of row arrangements: 7!. Since that is 7 times the correct answer, divide it by 7:

$\frac{7!}{7} = 6! = 840$

Just as "row" permutations (at least, problems without further wrinkles) can be solved by finding n!, circular permutations are $(n-1)!$

That doesn't mean I've just given you a simple fact to memorize. Few GMAT questions will be this simple. It's important to understand all the underlying steps discussed here, so that if an additional twist is added to a circular permutations question, you know how to apply this technique, even if it isn't as simple as $(n-1)!$.

140   Advanced Topics: Permutations: Drill

1.   If three people are to be awarded a gold, silver, and bronze medal, respectively, how many different ways could the medals be assigned to different people?

2.   A building has six offices. How many different ways could six different companies be arranged in those offices?

3.   Five people enter a footrace, and all five finish it, with no ties. How many different ways could the five competitors be ranked in order of finish?

4.   A judge is to select and schedule 3 cases to be heard on Monday morning. If there are 12 cases to choose from, how many different schedules are possible?

5.   Of the ten members in a certain theatre group, three are to be chosen to play lead roles A, B, and C. How many different ways could members of the theatre group be selected for those lead roles?

6.   A coffee shop has four different shifts throughout the day, and a different manager is on duty for each one of the shifts. If 7 managers work at the coffee shop, how many different orders of four managers could work the four shifts on a single day?

7.   A choreographer is arranging five dancers, V, W, X, Y, and Z, in a row. If dancer X must be in the middle, how many different ways can the dancers be arranged?

8.   An executive is planning his morning schedule, which will include five meetings, three of which are with Human Resources. If none of the meetings with Human Resources are to be consecutive, how many different ways can he arrange the five meetings?

9.   A six-member class of three men and three women is to be seated in a classroom consisting of a front row with three desks and a back row with three desks. If all the men are to be seated in the back row, in how many different arrangements can the six people be seated?

10.   In a race C, seedings are determined as follows: seeds 1, 2, and 3 are given to the top three finishers in race A, while seeds 4, 5, and 6 are given to the top three finishers in race B. If race A and race B both consist of six entrants, how many possible arrangements of seeds are there for race C?

141   Advanced Topics: Permutations: Practice

361.   Francie is planning a trip from City A to City D, during which
she will pass through both City B and City C. If there are two
possible routes she could take from A to B, three possible
routes she could take from B to C, and two possible routes
she could take from C to D, how many possible routes could
she take from A to D?

(A)   6
(B)   7
(C)   12
(D)   14
(E)   36

142   Advanced Topics: Permutation: Challenge

364.   In how many arrangements can a teacher seat 3 girls and 4 boys in a row of 7 seats if the girls are to have the second, fourth, and sixth seats?

     (A)   12
     (B)   36
     (C)   144
     (D)   288
     (E)   5,040

365.   How many different three-digit integers have exactly three different digits?

     (A)   504
     (B)   648
     (C)   720
     (D)   891
     (E)   1,000

366.   A sequential three-letter code consists of the letters A, B, C, D, E, and F, any of which may be repeated. If a three-letter code is randomly selected, what is the probability that it matches the correct code?

     (A) $\frac{1}{18}$
     (B) $\frac{1}{20}$
     (C) $\frac{1}{120}$
     (D) $\frac{1}{180}$
     (E) $\frac{1}{216}$

367.   How many four-digit odd numbers do not use any digit more than once?

     (A)   1728
     (B)   2160
     (C)   2240
     (D)   2268
     (E)   2520

368.   How many distinct six-letter sequences are there that consist of 2 X's, 2 Y's, and 2 Z's?

     (A)   6
     (B)   45
     (C)   90
     (D)   240
     (E)   720

143   Advanced Topics: Symbolism

Throughout this book, I've said multiple times that a topic is perceived as difficult, but really isn't. I hope that, after reading my explanations, you've begun to agree. I bring that up now because no topic has a larger perceived-actual difficulty disconnect than symbolism.

Symbolism is really just algebra. The first example I'm going to offer isn't a symbolism question, but it's only one small step removed:

"If $x = 4$ and $y = -3$, what is the value of $\frac{x+y}{x-y}$?"

I hope that, by now, you don't have to think twice before attacking that question. I'd even understand if you started laughing that I included such a question in my "Advanced Topics" section. To answer it, of course, you plug in the given values of x and y and simplify:

$\frac{x+y}{x-y} = \frac{4+(-3)}{4-(-3)} = \frac{1}{7}$

By now, you're probably wondering when I'm going to get to the symbolism. Here's the same question, looking quite a bit more daunting to the novice:

"If $x \neq y$, $x \rightarrow y$ is equal to $\frac{x+y}{x-y}$. What is the value of $4 \rightarrow (-3)$?"

Identical problem, new clothes. The question gives you a rule:

$x \rightarrow y = \frac{x+y}{x-y}$

Then it asks you to apply it. $4 \rightarrow (-3)$ implies that $x = 4$ and $y = -3$, so:

$4 \rightarrow (-3) = \frac{4+(-3)}{4-(-3)} = \frac{1}{7}$

It doesn't matter whether the symbol in question is an arrow, an inverted triangle, or an ampersand; it all boils down to algebra that you learned in the first few chapters of this book. (And, probably, in middle school.)

One way symbolism questions can get more involved is by asking you to apply the rule multiple times. Consider this sample question:

"When n is positive, $m \nabla n = \frac{m^2}{\sqrt{n}}$. What is the value of $(-2 \nabla 4) \nabla (10 \nabla 16)$?"

When you are to apply the rule more than once–as in this case, with three ∇ signs–use the same order of operations you would use with a more traditional algebra problem. In other words, work your way out of the parentheses.

$(-2 \nabla 4) = \frac{(-2)^2}{\sqrt{4}} = \frac{4}{2} = 2$

$(10 \nabla 16) = \frac{10^2}{\sqrt{16}} = \frac{100}{4} = 25$

Now that you've evaluated the contents of each of the parentheses, you're left with a single problem:

$(2 \nabla 25)$

Once again, apply the rule:

$(2 \nabla 25) = \frac{2^2}{\sqrt{25}} = \frac{4}{5}$

Finally, a variant on symbolism problems involves using a symbol to stand for a more traditional operator, such as addition, subtraction, multiplication, or division.   This usually arises in Data Sufficiency, when the question will read like this:

> "The symbol $\lozenge$ represents one of the following operations: addition, subtraction, multiplication, or division. What is the value of $4\lozenge 1$?"

In this case, all that matters is that we determine which of the operations the symbol stands for.   The trap to watch out for is that a statement will often appear to provide enough information, but really leave multiple options.   For instance, consider this statement, paired with the question above:

> "(1) $2\lozenge 2 = 4$"

The symbol could stand for addition: $2 + 2 = 4$.   If so, $4\lozenge 1 = 5$.   However, the symbol could also signify multiplication: $2 \times 2 = 4$.   In that case, $4\lozenge 1 = 4$. The statement is not sufficient on its own.

Don't worry too much about distinguishing between the different types of symbolism questions.   If it's a problem where the symbol stands for one of the common operators, as in this example, the question will tell you.   If the symbol refers to some new rule, the question will tell you that.   Just follow the instructions, and do the algebra.

144   Advanced Topics: Symbolism: Drill

All of the following exercises refer to one or more of the following:

    a.   If $y \neq 0$, $x \Leftrightarrow y = \frac{x^2}{y}$

    b. $a \spadesuit b = (a - b)(a + b)$

    c. $p \oplus q = |2p - q|$

1. $4 \spadesuit 5$
2. $1 \oplus 3$
3. $2 \Leftrightarrow 6$
4. $\left(-\frac{3}{2}\right) \oplus \frac{1}{2}$
5. $(-2) \spadesuit (-4)$
6. $(-3) \Leftrightarrow \frac{1}{3}$
7. $(1 \oplus 2) \oplus 3$
8. $(\sqrt{2} \Leftrightarrow \sqrt{2}) \Leftrightarrow (2 \Leftrightarrow 2)$
9. $(-1) \spadesuit (3 \spadesuit 6)$
10. $(0 \Leftrightarrow 0.5) \spadesuit (0.5 \oplus 0)$

145   Advanced Topics: Symbolism: Practice

371.   If $m@n = (m+n)(m-n)$ for all integers m and n, then $2@(-4) =$

     (A) -12
     (B) -4
     (C) 0
     (D) 4
     (E) 12

372.   The symbol ▶ represents one of the following operations: addition, subtraction, multiplication, or division. What is the value of $2 ▶ 3$?

     (1) $2 ▶ 3 = 3 ▶ 2$
     (2) $2 ▶ 3 > 4$

373.   If $a * b = ab + a(2 - b)$ for all integers a and b, then $3 * (-2) =$

     (A)   -18
     (B)   -6
     (C)   -4
     (D)   6
     (E)   18

146   Advanced Topics: Symbolism: Challenge

374.   For all numbers p and q, the operation $\hat{}\hat{}$ is defined by
$p\hat{}\hat{}q = (p+q)(p-q)$. If $x\hat{}\hat{}4 = 9$, which of the following
could be the value of x?

    (A)   4
    (B) $\frac{4}{3}$
    (C) $\frac{1}{4}$
    (D) -3
    (E) -5

375.   If the operation $*$ is defined for all m and n by the equation
$m * n = \frac{m^2}{n}$, then $6 * (-3 * -2) =$

    (A) -72
    (B) -8
    (C) $-\frac{9}{2}$
    (D)   8
    (E)   81

376.   If the operation $\Diamond$ is defined for all positive integers y and t by
$y \Diamond t = \frac{y}{t^2}$, then $(5 \Diamond 2) \Diamond 5 =$

    (A)   25
    (B)   10
    (C) $\frac{1}{4}$
    (D) $\frac{1}{5}$
    (E) $\frac{1}{20}$

147   Advanced Topics: Functions

Functions are even more feared than symbolism, but are really just a subset of that topic. Best of all, they appear very rarely on the test. If there's any section of the book you can feel free to skip entirely, it's this one.

"Function notation" looks like this:

$$f(x) = x^2 - 1$$

"$f(x)$" is pronounced "f of x" and is really just a common, specialized form of symbolism with only one variable. (In mathematics, functions can have infinite numbers of variables, but on the GMAT, they'll only have one.) Also be aware that functions may not always use the letters f and x; you may see something like $h(x)$ or $g(a)$. They are the same thing. The example above is no different than this sort of symbol definition:

$$x\sharp = x^2 - 1$$

Just as, in a symbol question, the problem would ask for the value of, say, $7\sharp$, a function question would ask for $f(7)$. Here's what the solution should look like:

$$f(7) = 7^2 - 1 = 49 - 1 = 48$$

So $f(7) = 48$.

Of course, function questions are not always so straightforward, though they do always rely on the exact technique just described. One variation involves substituting an expression instead of a number. Take this example:

"If $f(x) = x^2 + 4x + 4$, what is the value of $f(x + 2)$?"

Instead of plugging in a 7 for x, as we did in the previous example, here we'll plug in $x + 2$ for x:

$$f(x+2) = (x+2)^2 + 4(x+2) + 4 = x^2 + 4x + 4 + 4x + 8 + 4 = x^2 + 8x + 16$$

The technique is the same, it's just one more step removed from the comfort zone of most test-takers. Here's another example along the same lines, in which you're looking for the function itself, not the result of a function:

For which of the following functions is $f(x) = f(-x)$?

     (A) $f(x) = x^3 + 3x$
     (B) $f(x) = x^3$
     (C) $f(x) = x^2 - 2x$
     (D) $f(x) = (x - 3)^2$
     (E) $f(x) = (x + 2)(x - 2)$

In each of the answer choices, we're given the value of $f(x)$. To determine which one results in an equal value of $f(-x)$, we need to substitute $-x$ for x in each of the five choices:

     (A) $f(-x) = (-x)^3 + 3(-x) = -x^3 - 3x$
     (B) $f(-x) = (-x)^3 = -x^3$
     (C) $f(x) = (-x)^2 - 2(-x) = x^2 + 2x$
     (D) $f(x) = (-x - 3)^2 = x^2 + 6x + 9$
     (E) $f(x) = (-x + 2)(-x - 2) = x^2 - 4$

Only (E) is the same in both cases. $[(x+2)(x-2) = x^2 - 4]$ Note that the techniques we're using are still nearly identical to what we applied on basic symbolism questions.

Finally, functions can be combined and embedded in each other. A question could ask for $f(f(x))$, or even use multiple functions, as in this example:

"If $f(x) = \sqrt{x+3}$ and $g(y) = \frac{6}{y}$, what is the value of $f(g(1))$?"

As in symbolism questions with multiple symbols, work your way out of the parentheses. That means starting with the $g(1)$:

$g(1) = \frac{6}{1} = 6$

Thus, our final step is solving for $f(6)$:

$f(2) = \sqrt{6+3} = \sqrt{9} = 3$

As with nearly any type of question on the GMAT, the testmaker can add plenty of levels of complexity, but can't add more basic content. Any tricky function question you see on the test will contain these rules. If you don't see how, keep looking: it's your best chance of solving the problem.

148   Advanced Topics: Functions: Drill

1.   Evaluate each of the following for the function $f(x) = \frac{x+1}{x-1}$:
   a. $f(3)$
   b. $f(\frac{1}{2})$
   c. $f(f(2))$
   d. $f(x+2)$

2.   Evaluate each of the following for the function $f(x) = 2^{-x}$:
   a. $f(4)$
   b. $f(-\frac{1}{2})$
   c. $f(f(0))$

3.   For which of the following functions is $f(0) = 1$?
   a. $f(x) = (x-1)^2$
   b. $f(x) = x^x$
   c. $f(x) = x(x-1)(x+1)$

149   Advanced Topics: Functions: Challenge

381.   For which of the following functions is $f(0) = f(1)$?

     (A) $f(x) = x + 1$
     (B) $f(x) = x^x$
     (C) $f(x) = x^2 - 1$
     (D) $f(x) = \frac{x-1}{x+1}$
     (E) $f(x) = (x + 1)^2$

382.   If $f(x) = (x + 1)(x - 1)$, what is the value of $f(7) - f(3)$?

     (A)   4
     (B)   10
     (C)   21
     (D)   36
     (E)   40

383. $f(f(3)) = 3$ for all of the following functions EXCEPT

     (A) $f(x) = \frac{x+1}{x-1}$
     (B) $f(x) = -x$
     (C) $f(x) = \frac{1}{x}$
     (D) $f(x) = x - 1$
     (E) $f(x) = 3$

384.   For any numbers p and q, maxint(p, q) denotes the the largest integer between p and q, inclusive. For example, maxint$(1.7, 4.7) = 4$ and maxint$(3, 2.3) = 3$. For the number k, what is the value of maxint$(7, k)$?

     (1) $k < 6$
     (2) $k < 8$

385.   For any positive integer n, the sum of the first n positive integers equals $\frac{n(n+1)}{2}$. What is the sum of all the integers between 250 and 350, inclusive?

     (A)   100
     (B)   6,600
     (C)   20,200
     (D)   30,300
     (E)   55,000

150   Advanced Topics: Sequences

While I haven't used the word "sequence" more than a couple of times in the book up to this point, we've actually looked at quite a few. In fact, you can think of sequences and functions as very similar: a sequence is a set of numbers generated by a function. But I'm getting ahead of myself. Let's start with the technical details.

Usually a sequence will be written like this:

$$S_1 = 2, S_2 = 4, S_3 = 6, \ldots, S_k = 2k$$

The subscript numbers are sometimes referred to as the "index numbers," though I've never seen that terminology on the GMAT itself. Often, the test will give you three of the numbers in the sequence (as it does in this case) and then provides the rule. It doesn't need to do that, though: in cases like this, if it just gave you the rule, you could figure out all the members of the sequence that you wanted.

That's what I meant when I said that a sequence is a set of numbers generated by a function. That last term is essentially the same as saying $f(k) = 2k$. For any index k, you use that rule to determine the value at that point.

As you probably figured out, the sequence above consists of all even numbers. I can't imagine the GMAT would ever give you something so obvious, but it's important to look at a sequence with the intent to figure it out, even if deciphering the method behind the madness isn't strictly necessary. That way, if the question asks about some characteristic of the set (are the members multiples of four? are they perfect squares?) you won't have to spend valuable time testing a slew of numbers.

Sequences get more difficult when each term relies on the term (or terms) that preceded it, like in this case:

$$S_1 = 1, S_2 = 1, S_3 = 2, S_4 = 3, \ldots, S_k = S_{k-1} + S_{k-2}$$

The big step here is the abstract definition of the final term. In less mathematical language, it's saying that any term after the fourth term (S_k) is the sum of the term that precedes it (S_{k-1}) plus the term that precedes it by two places (S_{k-2}). So, if you needed to find the value of S_6, you'd first need the value of both S_5 and S_4. S_4 you know, but in order to find S_5, you need to go through the process one more time with the values of S_3 and S_4.

If you were to solve for S_6, your scratchwork should look something like this:

$$S_6 = S_4 + S_5$$
$$S_4 = 3$$
$$S_5 = S_3 + S_4 = 2 + 3 = 5$$
$$S_6 = S_4 + S_5 = 3 + 5 = 8$$

Occasionally, a sequence will be disguised in a word problem. In the real world, compound interest at a consistent rate is a sequence: each term is a certain percent greater than the previous term. More commonly on the GMAT, you'll see something like this:

"The population of Country X doubles approximately every 15
years. If this rate of growth continues, what percent greater
will the population of Country X be in 2080 than in 2035?"

You may not need to write this sequence in the notation we've been discussing, but if you're so inclined, it should look like this:

$$S_k = 2(S_{k-1})$$

More practically, you may want to assign a number to the population in 2035, and create a table of some kind to track how the population will grow:

2035	1,000
2050	2,000
2065	4,000
2080	8,000

While we chose 1,000 virtually at random, it doesn't matter what number we choose: the 2080 population will always be 8 times the 2035 population. To find the percent growth, use the percent change formula:

$$\frac{change}{original} = \frac{7,000}{1,000} = 7 = 700\%$$

The GMAT question pool contains far more slightly tricky word problems than it does abstract "Advanced Topics" problems. While it's important to understand the underlying mathematics of subjects like sequences, probability, and the others, it's more important to be able to apply those basics to word problems: that's what you'll have to do on test day.

151   Advanced Topics: Sequences: Drill

1.   For each of the following, find S_1 through S_5 in the given sequence S:

     a. $S_k = 2k - 1$

     b. $S_k = 1 - \frac{1}{2^k}$

     c. $S_k = \frac{1-k}{k+1}$

     d. $S_k = (-1)^k - (-2)^k$

2.   For each of the following, find S_3 through S_5 in the given sequence S:

     a. $S_1 = 2,\ S_2 = 3,\ \dots\ ,\ S_k = S_{k-1} - S_{k-2}$

     b. $S_1 = 1,\ S_2 = 4,\ \dots\ ,\ S_k = (S_{k-1})(S_{k-2})$

     c. $S_1 = 5,\ S_2 = 10,\ \dots\ ,\ S_k = S_{k-2}$

3.   For each of the following, find the rule that governs the sequence S:

     a. $S_1 = 144,\ S_2 = 72,\ S_3 = 36,\ S_4 = 18,\ S_5 = 9$

     b. $S_1 = 0,\ S_2 = 3,\ S_3 = 8,\ S_4 = 15,\ S_5 = 24$

     c. $S_1 = -7,\ S_2 = -4,\ S_3 = -1,\ S_4 = 2,\ S_5 = 5$

152   Advanced Topics: Sequences: Practice

270, 90, 30, 10, ...

391.   If 270 is the first term in the sequence above, how many terms
in the sequence are greater than 1?

(A)   2
(B)   4
(C)   6
(D)   7
(E)   8

392.   If sequence S has 100 terms, what is the 83rd term of S?

(1)   Each term of S after the first term is 4 greater than the
preceding term.

(2)   The 84th term of S is twice the 82nd term of S.

153   Advanced Topics: Sequences: Challenge

394.   The sequence s_1, s_2, s_3, ..., s_n, is such that $s_n = (s_{n-1})(s_{n-2})$ for all $n \geq 3$. If $s_3 = 2$ and $s_5 = 8$, what is the value of s_6?

    (A)   2
    (B)   4
    (C)   8
    (D)   16
    (E)   32

$$p, r, s, t, u$$

395.   An arithmetic sequence is a sequence in which each term after the first is equal to the sum of the preceding term and a constant k. If the list of numbers shown above is an arithmetic sequence, for which of the following sequences is the value of k greatest?

    (A) p, r, s, t, u
    (B) $\frac{p}{2}, \frac{r}{2}, \frac{s}{2}, \frac{t}{2}, \frac{u}{2}$
    (C) $p + 4, r + 4, s + 4, t + 4, u + 4$
    (D) $2p + 3, 2r + 3, 2s + 3, 2t + 3, 2u + 3$
    (E) $3p + 2, 3r + 2, 3s + 2, 3t + 2, 3u + 2$

396.   A geometric progression is a sequence in which the quotient of any two successive numbers of the sequence is a constant. For example, {1, 2, 4, 8} is a geometric progression in which the quotient of any two successive numbers is 2. Is the infinite sequence S a geometric progression?

    (1)   Any subset of 3 consecutive terms selected from S forms a geometric progression.

    (2)   If each term in S were divided by π, the resulting sequence would form a geometric progression.

397.   If T is the infinite sequence $T_1 = 6$, $T_2 = 66$, $T_3 = 666$, . . . , $T_k = 6(10^k) + T_{k-1}$, . . . , is every term in T divisible by the prime number p ?

    (1) p is greater than 3.

    (2)   At least one term in sequence T is divisible by p.

398.   The values of p and q vary with the value of x so that each additive increase of 1 in the value of x corresponds to the value of p decreasing by a factor of 4 and the value of q decreasing by a factor of 2. If p and q are positive for each $x > 0$, what is the value of $\frac{p}{q}$ when $x = 8$?

(1)   When $x = 6$, $p = q + 2$.
(2)   When $x = 7$, $p = 3q$.

399.   The sequence $a_1, a_2, a_3, ..., a_n$ is such that $a_n = 2^{10-n} - n$ for all positive integer values of n. For how many terms in the sequence is $a_n > 0$?

(A)   6
(B)   7
(C)   8
(D)   9
(E)   10

154   Further Resources

For realistic, supplemental practice, you can't do better than The Official Guide to GMAT Review, which is published by the testmakers themselves.   You can buy it at many major bookstores, mba.com, or online booksellers such as Amazon.com.   There are actually three such books: the main book has an orange cover, and has several hundred math and verbal practice items.   There is also a supplemental book for math (with a green cover) and for verbal (with a purple cover).

In addition, you may find my own "Guides to the Official Guide" helpful. The explanations in the Official Guide are thorough, but they often don't show you the best, most strategic way.   I've written my own explanation to every math question in the orange book and the green book.   You can read more about those and purchase them here:

http://www.officialguidegmat.com

If you need more focused practice, I can recommend more resources of mine. I've published eighteen different sets of 100 questions each in every subject area that GMAT Math covers, including sets that focus on Algebra, Geometry, Number Properties, and Word Problems.   There are also sets that include a broad range of topics, but include only Data Sufficiency or Problem Solving questions.   You can read more about those and order them at this webpage:

http://www.gmatproblems.com

For more general advice, I've written several dozen tips at my website, www.gmathacks.com.   You'll find strategies for math (many of which are included in this book) as well as approaches to verbal items and overall test-taking tips that apply to all aspects of the test.

Good luck, and study hard!

155   Explanations: Mental Math: Drill

1.   Find the following percents using the mental math techniques described in this chapter:
   a.   10% of 196 = 19.6
   b.   5% of 120 = $\frac{12}{2}$ = 6
   c.   20% of 95 = 9.5(2) = 19
   d.   15% of \$42.00 = 4.2 + $\frac{4.2}{2}$ = 4.2 + 2.1 = 6.3
   e.   16% of 2100 = 210 + $\frac{210}{2}$ + 21 = 210 + 105 + 21 = 336

2.   Simplify each of the following fractions without using long division:
   a. $\frac{180}{12} = \frac{12(15)}{12} = 15$
   b. $\frac{175}{25} = \frac{25(7)}{25} = 7$
   c. $\frac{(13)(24)}{(12)(52)} = \frac{(1)(24)}{(12)(4)} = \frac{(1)(2)}{(1)(4)} = \frac{1}{2}$
   d. $\frac{(210)(4)}{(28)(5)} = \frac{(5)(42)(4)}{(4)(7)(5)} = \frac{42}{7} = 6$

3.   Calculate each of the following using the techniques described in this chapter:
   a. $9.2 \times 5 = 9.2(\frac{10}{2}) = \frac{92}{2} = 46$
   b. $47 \times 5 = 47(\frac{10}{2}) = \frac{470}{2} = 235$
   c. $235 \div 5 = 235(\frac{2}{10}) = \frac{470}{10} = 47$
   d. $144 \div 5 = 144(\frac{2}{10}) = 14.4(2) = 28.8$
   e. $13 \times 9 = 13(10 - 1) = 130 - 13 = 117$
   f. $24 \times 9 = 24(10 - 1) = 240 - 24 = 216$

4.   Divide each of the following using the "nearest neighbor" method:
   a. $147 \div 7$
      $147 = 140 + 7 = 7(20) + 7(1)$
      $147 \div 7 = 21$
   b. $252 \div 3$
      $252 = 240 + 12 = 3(80) + 3(4)$
      $252 \div 3 = 80 + 4 = 84$
   c. $242 \div 11$
      $242 = 220 + 22 = 20(11) + 2(11)$
      $242 \div 11 = 20 + 2 = 22$
   d. $595 \div 3$
      $595 = 600 - 6 + 1 = 3(200) - 3(2) + 1$
      $595 \div 3 = 200 - 2 + \frac{1}{3} = 198\frac{1}{3}$
   e. $400 \div 7$
      $400 = 350 + 49 + 1 = 7(50) + 7(7) + 1$
      $400 \div 7 = 50 + 7 + \frac{1}{7} = 57\frac{1}{7}$

156   Explanations: Fractions: Drill

1.   Simplify the following fractions:
    a. $\frac{3}{15} = \frac{1}{5}$

    b. $\frac{8}{48} = \frac{1}{6}$

    c. $\frac{17}{51} = \frac{1}{3}$

    d. $\frac{9}{72} = \frac{1}{8}$

    e. $\frac{(8)(7)}{21} = \frac{(8)(1)}{3} = \frac{8}{3}$

    f. $\frac{(6)(22)}{(11)(12)} = \frac{(1)(22)}{(11)(2)} = \frac{(1)(2)}{(1)(2)} = 1$

    g. $\frac{2x}{3x} = \frac{2}{3}$

    h. $\frac{4x+x}{10} = \frac{5x}{10} = \frac{x}{2}$

    i. $\frac{xy}{xy^2} = \frac{xy}{xy(y)} = \frac{1}{y}$

2.   Convert the following to mixed numbers:
    a. $\frac{13}{4} = 3\frac{1}{4}$

    b. $\frac{7}{3} = 2\frac{1}{3}$

    c. $\frac{101}{5} = 20\frac{1}{5}$

3.   Convert the following to improper fractions:
    a. $4\frac{1}{6} = \frac{25}{6}$

    b. $2\frac{9}{10} = \frac{29}{10}$

    c. $11\frac{1}{2} = \frac{23}{2}$

4.   Calculate the following:
    a. $\frac{1}{5} + \frac{2}{5} = \frac{3}{5}$

    b. $\frac{1}{3} + \frac{1}{6} = \frac{2}{6} + \frac{1}{6} = \frac{3}{6} = \frac{1}{2}$

    c. $\frac{x}{3} + \frac{x}{4} = \frac{4x}{12} + \frac{3x}{12} = \frac{7x}{12}$

    d. $\frac{7}{3} - \frac{1}{12} = \frac{28}{12} - \frac{1}{12} = \frac{27}{12}$

    e. $\frac{1}{3} - \frac{1}{4} = \frac{4}{12} - \frac{3}{12} = \frac{1}{12}$

    f. $\frac{x}{2} - \frac{y}{3} = \frac{3x}{6} - \frac{2y}{6} = \frac{3x-2y}{6}$

    g. $\frac{1}{6} \times \frac{5}{8} = \frac{(1)(5)}{(6)(8)} = \frac{5}{48}$

    h. $\frac{2}{3} \times \frac{9}{4} = \frac{(2)(9)}{(3)(4)} = \frac{(1)(9)}{(3)(2)} = \frac{(1)(3)}{(1)(2)} = \frac{3}{2}$

    i. $\frac{4}{5} \div 2 = \frac{4}{5} \div \frac{2}{1} = \frac{4}{5} \times \frac{1}{2} = \frac{4}{10} = \frac{2}{5}$

    j. $\frac{1}{2} \div \frac{1}{4} = \frac{1}{2} \times \frac{4}{1} = \frac{4}{2} = 2$

157   Explanations: Fractions: Practice

1.   **B**
   EXPL: $\frac{1}{10}$ of 5000 is $(\frac{1}{10})(5000) = 500$, so $\frac{1}{10}$ of $\frac{1}{10}$ of 5000 is $(\frac{1}{10})(500) = 50$. $\frac{1}{10}$ of 4000 is $(\frac{1}{10})(4000) = 400$. We can then reduce to the question to: "when 50 is subtracted from 400, the difference is:"
   $400 - 50 = 350$, choice (B)

2.   **B**
   EXPL $2 - \frac{1}{3} = 1\frac{2}{3}$. $1 - \frac{1}{3} = \frac{2}{3}$. The question is then asking, "$1\frac{2}{3}$ is how many times $\frac{2}{3}$?" We can set that up as a fraction, in which it's easier to work with the improper fraction $\frac{5}{3}$ instead of the mixed number $1\frac{2}{3}$:
   $(\frac{\frac{5}{3}}{\frac{2}{3}}) = (\frac{5}{3} \times \frac{3}{2}) = \frac{5}{2} = 2.5$, choice (B).

3.   **E**
   EXPL: $\frac{50-5(24\div6)}{\frac{1}{3}} = \frac{50-5(4)}{\frac{1}{3}} = \frac{50-20}{\frac{1}{3}} = \frac{30}{\frac{1}{3}} = 30 \times \frac{3}{1} = 90$, choice (E).

4.   **B**
   EXPL: First, see if you can simplify the question stem. To combine $\frac{1}{m} + \frac{1}{n}$ into one fraction, find a common denominator:
   $\frac{1}{m} + \frac{1}{n} = \frac{n}{mn} + \frac{m}{mn} = \frac{m+n}{mn}$.
   Statement (1) is insufficient: without the value of n, it isn't enough. Statement (2) is sufficient: as we discovered when simplifying the question, $\frac{m+n}{mn}$ is equivalent to $\frac{1}{m} + \frac{1}{n}$. If we know one, we know the other, so the correct choice is (B).

5.   **C**
   EXPL: Start with (1). If the LCD of the two fractions is 10, each denominator can be no larger than 10. s could be 10: the LCD of 5 and 10 is 10. However, s could also be 2, since the LCD of 2 and 5 is 10. Insufficient. Statement (2) is also insufficient on its own: s could be any integer between 1 and 9, inclusive.
   Taken together, the statements are sufficient. If s must be 2 or 10, and it must be less than 10, s must equal 2. Choice (C) is correct.

6.   **E**
   Explanation: Look at each roman numeral in turn:
   I.   If z gets bigger, $3z$ gets bigger. Since $3z$ is subtracted, as $3z$ gets bigger, $4 - 3z$ gets smaller. This one isn't right, so eliminate A, C, and D.
   II.   If z gets bigger, $\frac{3}{z}$ gets smaller, since z is in the denominator. Since $\frac{3}{z}$ is subtracted, $4 - \frac{3}{z}$ gets bigger. II is right, which we already knew, since the two remaining choices–B and E–both include it.
   III.   If z gets bigger, so does z^2. Since z^2 is subtracted, $3 - z^2$ gets smaller. But since $3 - z^2$ is in the denominator, as it gets smaller, the fraction gets bigger. Thus, III is correct, so the answer is (E).

7.   B

Explanation: $\left(\frac{1}{3}\right)^3 = \left(\frac{1}{3}\right)\left(\frac{1}{3}\right)\left(\frac{1}{3}\right) = \frac{1}{27}$, and $\left(\frac{1}{3}\right)\left(\frac{1}{6}\right) = \frac{1}{18}$. $\frac{1}{27} - \frac{1}{18} =$ $\frac{2}{54} - \frac{3}{54} = -\frac{1}{54}$, choice (B). In terms of conceptual difficulty, this question isn't very hard, but it's the sort of thing that many test-takers get wrong, because they rush through the calculations and make careless errors.

8.   C

Explanation: Start by simplifying the innermost denominator $(2+\frac{2}{3})$ and work your way out:

$2 + \frac{2}{3} = \frac{6}{3} + \frac{2}{3} = \frac{8}{3}$

That leaves us with $2 + \frac{2}{2+\frac{2}{\frac{8}{3}}}$

$\frac{2}{\frac{8}{3}} = 2(\frac{3}{8}) = \frac{6}{8} = \frac{3}{4}$

Now we have $2 + \frac{2}{2+\frac{3}{4}}$

$2 + \frac{3}{4} = \frac{8}{4} + \frac{3}{4} = \frac{11}{4}$

That gives us $2 + \frac{2}{\frac{11}{4}}$

$\frac{2}{\frac{11}{4}} = 2(\frac{4}{11}) = \frac{8}{11}$

Now it's simplified to $2 + \frac{8}{11}$

$2 + \frac{8}{11} = \frac{22}{11} + \frac{8}{11} = \frac{30}{11}$, choice (C).

9.   C

EXPL: Statement (1) is insufficient: to answer the question you need to know something about both x and y, and while this statement allows you to solve for y, it tells you nothing about x.

Statement (2) is insufficient for a similar reason: you can solve for the value of x, but you discover nothing about the value of y.

Taken together, the statements are sufficient. From (1), you can find the value of y; from (2), you can find the value of x. Regardless of whether $\frac{1}{x} + \frac{1}{y} = 4$, you have enough information to answer the question.

158 Explanations: Decimals: Drill

1. Convert each of the following to decimals:
    a. $\frac{6}{5} = 1 + \frac{1}{5} = 1 + 0.2 = 1.2$
    b. $\frac{16}{25} \times \frac{4}{4} = \frac{64}{100} = 0.64$
    c. $\frac{38}{200} = \frac{19}{100} = 0.19$
    d. $\frac{9}{30} = \frac{3}{10} = 0.3$
    e. $\frac{125}{80} = \frac{25}{16} = \frac{6.25}{4} \times \frac{25}{25} = \frac{1.5625}{100} = 1.5625$

2. Convert each of the following to fractions:
    a. $0.12 = \frac{12}{100} = \frac{3}{25}$
    b. $0.95 = \frac{95}{100} = \frac{19}{20}$
    c. $0.48 = \frac{48}{100} = \frac{12}{25}$
    d. $2.8\overline{3} = 2 + \frac{5}{6} = 2\frac{5}{6}$
    e. $0.0032 = \frac{32}{10,000} = \frac{16}{5,000} = \frac{8}{2,500} = \frac{4}{1,250} = \frac{2}{625}$

3. Convert each of the following to scientific notation:
    a. $0.0102 = 1.02 \times 10^{-2}$
    b. $0.00072 = 7.2 \times 10^{-4}$
    c. $0.98 = 9.8 \times 10^{-1}$
    d. 1.6 million $= 1.6 \times 10^{6}$
    e. $5,200,000,000 = 5.2 \times 10^{9}$

4. Convert each of the following to decimal format:
    a. $3.6 \times 10^{-3} = 0.0036$
    b. $6.0 \times 10^{-6} = 0.000006$
    c. $7.25 \times 10^{8} = 725,000,000$
    d. $1.5 \times 10^{6} = 1,500,000$
    e. $5.6 \times 10^{-1} = 0.56$

159 Explanations: Decimals: Practice

11.   C

EXPL: As is so often the case, it may be easier to do this question by converting each of the decimals into fractions. Because you're eventually going to have to convert them back into decimals, you don't need to simplify: keep 10's, 100's, and the like in the denominator for easy conversion.

$0.2 = \frac{2}{10}$, so the problem is equivalent to:

$\frac{2}{10} + (\frac{2}{10})^2 + (\frac{2}{10})^3 = \frac{2}{10} + \frac{4}{100} + \frac{8}{1000} = \frac{200}{1000} + \frac{40}{1000} + \frac{8}{1000} = \frac{248}{1000} = 0.248$, choice (C).

12.   A

EXPL: To determine the range of values for x, simplify each of the statements. In (1), divide both sides by 425:

$x < \frac{85}{425}$

Using the mental math tricks described in that section, count by 85's to determine that $425 = 85(5)$, so the inequality is the same as

$x < \frac{85}{85(5)} = \frac{1}{5} = 0.2$

If x is less than 0.2, it cannot be between 0.3 and 0.6, so (1) is sufficient.

Use the same methodology for (2):

$x < \frac{85}{170} = \frac{1}{2} = 0.5$

If x is less than 0.5,. it could be between 0.3 and 0.6, but it might be less than 0.3. Insufficient. Choice (A) is correct.

13.   B

EXPL: The most important factor in determining whether a ratio converts to a terminating or non-terminating decimal is the denominator. If the denominator is, for instance, 4, it doesn't matter what the numerator is: it always terminates. If the denominator is 3, however, the decimal only terminates when the numerator is a multiple of three.

Thus, (1) is insufficient: it tells you nothing about the denominator. (2) is sufficient: if the denominator is 8, it always terminates. The decimal equivalent of the remainder must be one of the following: 0.0, 0.125, 0.25, 0.375, 0.5, 0.625, 0.75, or 0.875. Choice (B) is correct.

14.   B

EXPL: When converting a fraction to a decimal, the goal is to find an equivalent fraction with a denominator of 10, 100, 1000, or something similar. While you could use long division to answer this one, that's almost never the best way.

Instead, recognize that 125 is $\frac{1}{8}$ of 1,000. (If you don't yet have this memorized, spend more time with the decimal equivalents in this chapter.) Thus, we can convert the fraction to something easier to work with:

$\frac{32}{125}(\frac{8}{8}) = \frac{256}{1,000} = 0.256$, choice (B).

15.   A

EXPL: While the GMAT doesn't expect you to know your equivalencies of 11ths and 13ths, it's very handy to know 9ths. Thus, when you see 0.44, you should recognize that it's approximately $\frac{4}{9}$.

Statement (1) is sufficient: $\frac{4}{11}$ is less than $\frac{4}{9}$; a number gets smaller as the denominator gets bigger. Thus, if u is less than $\frac{4}{11}$, it must also be less than $\frac{4}{9}$, or 0.44. Statement (2) is insufficient: $\frac{4}{13}$ is also smaller than $\frac{4}{9}$, but knowing that u is greater than $\frac{4}{13}$ tells us that u could be less than $\frac{4}{9}$ (if it's between the two fractions), or greater than $\frac{4}{9}$. Choice (A) is correct.

16.   D

Explanation: This is one of the very rare problems that requires long division. However, you don't have to get close to the 24th digit to answer the question. It's handy to know that 11ths, in decimal form, are repeating, non-terminating decimals with a period of two. In other words, the same two digits keep repeating toward infinity.

In other words, to find the 24th digit of this fraction, you just need to find the 2nd digit. The first two digits are .72, so the 24th digit must be 2 as well, choice (D).

17.   E

Explanation: For a problem like this, you'll have to go through each of the answer choices. However, don't get bogged down in lengthy calculations; in many cases, you can simply approximate and eliminate choices.

(A)   0.5
(B)   0.25
(C)   0.05
(D)   0.25
(E) $\frac{1}{\frac{1}{2}} = 1 \times \frac{2}{1} = 2.$

(E) is the only choice larger than 1, so it must be correct.

160   Explanations: Simplifying Expressions: Drill

1. Evaluate each of the following expressions:
    a. $2 \times 3 + 4 \times 5 = (2 \times 3) + (4 \times 5) = 6 + 20 = 26$
    b. $4 - 6 \div 2 - 1 = 4 - (6 \div 2) - 1 = 4 - 3 - 1 = 0$
    c. $3(5 - 2^2) + 4^2 = 3(5 - 4) + 16 = 3(1) + 16 = 3 + 16 = 19$
    d. $\frac{5 \times 3^2}{4^2 - 1} = \frac{5 \times 9}{16 - 1} = \frac{45}{15} = 3$

2. Distribute each of the following:
    a. $3(x - y) = 3x - 3y$
    b. $-(a + b) = -a - b$
    c. $3m(n + 3m) = 3mn + 9m^2$
    d. $-2x(y - z) = -2xy - (-2xz) = -2xy + 2xz = 2xz - 2xy$
    e. $a^2(a - a^2) = a^3 - a^4$
    f. $n(n + 1) = n^2 + n$

3. Factor each of the following:
    a. $4m + 4n = 4(m + n)$
    b. $xy + 2xz = x(y + 2z)$
    c. $6a + 3b + 12c = 3(2a + b + 4c)$
    d. $a^3 - 2a^2 - 8a = a(a^2 - 2a - 8)$
    e. $8jkm - 12kmn = 4km(2j - 3n)$

4. Simplify each of the following expressions:
    a. $4x + 2(x - 1) - x = 4x + 2x - 2 - x = 5x - 2$
    b. $10 - 3(x - y) + x(1 - y) = 10 - 3x + 3y + x - xy = 10 - 2x + 3y - xy$
    c. $a^2 + a(2 + a) - 2 = a^2 + 2a + a^2 - 2 = 2a^2 + 2a - 2 = 2(a^2 + a - 1)$
    d. $m(n + p) - p(m - n) - n(m + p)$
          $mn + pm - pm + pn - nm - np = 0$
    e. $y^2 - 2y(y + 1) - 4y = y^2 - 2y^2 - 2y - 4y = -y^2 - 6y = -y(y + 6)$

161   Explanations: Simplifying Expressions: Practice

21.   A

EXPL: When the GMAT gives you a big number, as in $x > 1,000$, in a context like this, don't worry about the precise value: the point is that x is very big. Next to x, then, adding 3 (in the numerator) or 2 (in the denominator) doesn't change the value of the expression very much.

For instance, plug in $x = 1000$:

$\frac{2(1000)+3}{3(1000)+2} = \frac{2003}{3002} \approx \frac{2}{3}$

As x gets larger, the value–already very close to $\frac{2}{3}$, gets closer still, so the correct choice is (A).

22.   C

EXPL: Plug in the values for a and b:

$a - b + 2a^2 = (-6) - 6 + 2(6)^2 = -6 - 6 + 2(36) = -12 + 72 = 60$, choice (C).

23.   E

EXPL: Start by plugging in $-x$ for x:

$(\frac{(-x)}{(-x)-1})^2 = (\frac{-x}{-x-1})^2$

Split up the numerator and denominator:

$\frac{(-x)^2}{(-x-1)^2} = \frac{x^2}{x^2+2x+1} = \frac{x^2}{(x+1)^2}$

Now, since the numerator and denominator are both squared, put them back in parentheses and square the whole thing:

$(\frac{x}{x+1})^2$, choice (E).

24.   E

EXPL: Obviously, this question is going to involve some serious algebra. Start by distributing the left side; that'll make the left side look a bit more like the right:

$xp + \frac{x}{p}q^2 + \frac{x}{p}r^2 = xp + yq + zr$

$\frac{x}{p}q^2 + \frac{x}{p}r^2 = yq + zr$

Statement (1) is insufficient. It allows us to simplify the left side of the equation a little bit, eliminating either q or r. However, we can't do anything with the right side, since knowing that q^2 and r^2 are equal doesn't necessarily mean that q and r are equal as well.

Statement (2) is also insufficient. Again, it only applies to one side: we could simplify the right side of the equation with no effect on the left.

Taken together, the statements are still insufficient. To do the simplification described so far:

$\frac{x}{p}q^2 + \frac{x}{p}q^2 = yq + yq$

$2(\frac{x}{p}q^2) = 2(yq)$

$\frac{x}{p}q^2 = yq$

$\frac{x}{p}q = y$

We don't know the relationship between $\frac{x}{p}q$ and y, so we can't answer the question. Choice (E) is correct.

25.   A

EXPL: It's not strictly necessary, but it's a good habit to simplify Data Sufficiency questions whenever possible. For instance, the question here could be rewritten as:

Is $x(a + b) = 7$?

That makes it a bit easier to recognize that (1) is sufficient. Given the value of x and $a + b$, we can plug into the question:

$6(1) = 7$?

and get an answer. ("No.") Statement (2) is not sufficient. To confirm, you could substitute $24ab$ in for x:

$24ab(a + b) = 7$?

There's no way to answer that question without knowing more about a and b, so the correct choice is (A).

26.   B

Explanation: Whenever statements have the same variable on both sides of the equation, be sure to simplify it: the GMAT may be hiding something. Statement (1) is insufficient. Simplify:

$2x + 4 = 2(2 + x)$

$2x + 4 = 4 + 2x$

That's a tautology: it doesn't tell us anything, so it's insufficient.

Statement (2) is sufficient. Simplify:

$2x + 3 = 3(2 + x)$

$2x + 3 = 6 + 3x$

$-3 = x$

Choice (B) is correct.

162   Explanations: Linear Equations: Drill

1. True or False? For each of the following, is this is a linear equation?

    a. $y = 2x + 7$
        True
    b. $y^2 = 3 - 4x$
        False
    c. $y = x^2 + x - 12$
        False
    d. $y = x$
        True
    e. $y = 4$
        True

2. Solve for x:

    a. $9 = 2x + 5$
        $4 = 2x$
        $x = 2$
    b. $4 - x = x - 4$
        $8 - x = x$
        $8 = 2x$
        $x = 4$
    c. $\frac{x}{3} = \frac{2}{5}$
        $5x = 6$
        $x = \frac{6}{5}$
    d. $5 = \frac{x}{4} + \frac{1}{2}$
        $5 = \frac{x}{4} + \frac{2}{4} = \frac{x+2}{4}$
        $20 = x + 2$
        $x = 18$
    e. $\frac{1}{4} = \frac{18}{x}$
        $x = 18(4) = 72$
    f. $3(2 - x) = 2(x - 3)$
        $6 - 3x = 2x - 6$
        $12 - 3x = 2x$
        $12 = 5x$
        $x = \frac{12}{5}$
    g. $\frac{x+2}{3} = 5x$
        $x + 2 = 15x$
        $2 = 14x$
        $x = \frac{2}{14} = \frac{1}{7}$
    h. $\frac{6}{1-x} = \frac{2}{x+3}$
        $6(x + 3) = 2(1 - x)$
        $6x + 18 = 2 - 2x$
        $8x + 18 = 2$

$$8x = -16$$
$$x = -2$$

3.   Solve for k in terms of m:

a. $m = 2k$

$k = \frac{m}{2}$

b. $m - 3 = \frac{k}{4}$

$k = 4(m - 3) = 4m - 12$

c. $km = 12$

$k = \frac{12}{m}$

d. $k - 4 = km + 2$

$k - km - 4 = 2$

$k - km = 6$

$k(1 - m) = 6$

$k = \frac{6}{1-m}$

e. $m(2 + k) = k(5 - m)$

$2m + km = 5k - km$

$2m = 5k - 2km$

$2m = k(5 - 2m)$

$k = \frac{2m}{5-2m}$

f. $\frac{6}{11} = \frac{m}{2k}$

$6(2k) = 11m$

$12k = 11m$

$k = \frac{11m}{12}$

g. $\frac{3m}{2k} = \frac{3-m}{1-k}$

$3m(1 - k) = 2k(3 - m)$

$3m - 3km = 6k - 2km$

$3m = 6k + km$

$3m = k(6 + m)$

$k = \frac{3m}{6+m}$

163   Explanations: Linear Equations: Practice

31.   C

EXPL: First, convert the phrase into an equation:

$-2 = y + 4$

And solve for y by subtracting 4 from both sides:

$y = -6$

Finally, divide by two:

$\frac{y}{2} = \frac{-6}{2} = -3$, choice (C).

32.   B

EXPL: Any time you see an equation in the question of a Data Sufficiency problem, see if you can simplify it. In this case, it's begging for simplication, with x terms and y terms on both sides.

$x - y = y + 2x - 1$

$x = 2y + 2x - 1$

$-x = 2y - 1$

$x = 1 - 2y$

Statement (1) is insufficient: as we discovered by simplifying the question, the equation given is something that we already knew! Statement (2), however, is sufficient. The question gives us one linear equation with the variables x and y, and (2) offers another, distinct one. Put them together and you can solve for both variables. (B) is correct.

33.   B

EXPL: Simplify the equation by multiplying both sides by the denominator of the left side:

$5 = 8(0.125 + x)$

$5 = 1 + 8x$

$8x = 4$

$x = \frac{4}{8} = 0.5$, choice (B).

34.   A

EXPL: To combine all the x's, multiply both sides by the denominator, $1 - x$:

$3 + x = x(1 - x)$

$3 + x = x - x^2$

Move everything to one side of the equation:

$x^2 + 3 = 0$

$x^2 = -3$, choice (A).

35.   B

EXPL: Statement (1) is insufficient; the fact that y appears in that equation squared should be a strong hint to that effect. To simplify:

$1 = 4y^2$

$y^2 = \frac{1}{4}$

$y = \pm\frac{1}{2}$

Since there are two possible values for y, we need more information.

Statement (2) is enough information: it's a linear equation with only one variable. To simplify (though you don't need to in order to successfully answer the question):

$4 - y = y + 3$

$4 = 2y + 3$

$1 = 2y$

$y = \frac{1}{2}$

Choice (B) is correct.

36.   D

Explanation: Since we don't know the value of the denominator p, there are two possible ways in which the fraction could not equal 2: if $p = 0$ (in which case the value of the fraction is undetermined), or if $m - n = 0$ (in which case the value of the fraction is 0, regardless of the value of p).

Since the question is asking about possible values of m, we know the issue is the latter. If $n = 1$, then $m - 1$ can't be zero, so m can't be 1, choice (D).

37.   D

When we're told that a variable is a constant, that means we only have to solve for it once. Given a set of values for x and y, we can plug those in to find m:

$y = mx - 5$

$16 = 7m - 5$

$21 = 7m$

$m = 3$

Now we can always think of the equation as:

$y = 3x - 5$

Given $x = 16$, we can solve for y:

$y = 3(16) - 5 = 48 - 5 = 43$, choice (D).

164   Explanations: Systems: Drill

1.   Solve the following systems of equations using the combination method:

     a. $3x + 2y = 7$ and $x - 2y = 9$

         Add the equations:

$$3x + 2y = 7$$
$$+(x - 2y = 9)$$
$$4x = 16$$
$$x = 4$$

         Solve for y:

$$4 - 2y = 9$$
$$\text{-}2y = 5$$
$$y = -\frac{5}{2}$$

     b. $5a - b = 6$ and $b = 4$

         Add the equations:

$$5a - b = 6$$
$$+(b = 4)$$
$$5a = 10$$
$$a = 2$$

     c. $m + 2n = 13$ and $3m + 2n = 21$

         Subtract the equations:

$$3m + 2n = 21$$
$$-(m + 2n = 13)$$
$$2m = 8$$
$$m = 4$$

         Solve for n:

$$4 + 2n = 13$$
$$2n = 9$$
$$n = \frac{9}{2}$$

     d. $\frac{y}{3} + z = 17$ and $y - 3z = -3$

         Multiply the first equation by 3

$$3(\tfrac{y}{3} + z = 17)$$
$$y + 3z = 51$$

         Subtract the equations:

$$y + 3z = 51$$
$$-(y - 3z = -3)$$
$$6z = 54$$
$$z = 9$$

         Solve for y:

$$\tfrac{y}{3} + 9 = 17$$
$$\tfrac{y}{3} = 8$$
$$y = 3(8) = 24$$

2.   Solve the following systems of equations using the substitution method:

a. $x - 5y = 3$ and $3x - y = 37$

Solve the first equation for x:

$x = 3 + 5y$

Plug into the second equation:

$3(3 + 5y) - y = 37$

$9 + 15y - y = 37$

$9 + 14y = 37$

$14y = 28$

$y = 2$

Plug into the second equation:

$3x - 2 = 37$

$3x = 39$

$x = 13$

b. $4x + 4y = 12$ and $3x + 5y = 13$

First, simplify the first equation:

$x + y = 3$

Then solve for x:

$x = 3 - y$

Plug into the second equation;

$3(3 - y) + 5y = 13$

$9 - 3y + 5y = 13$

$9 + 2y = 13$

$2y = 4$

$y = 2$

Solve for x:

$x + 2 = 3$

$x = 1$

c. $\frac{x}{2} - \frac{y}{3} = 2$ and $\frac{x}{3} + y = 13$

Solve the second equation for x:

$x + 3y = 39$

$x = 39 - 3y$

Plug into the first equation:

$\frac{39 - 3y}{2} - \frac{y}{3} = 2$

$39 - 3y - \frac{2y}{3} = 4$

$3(39 - 3y) - 2y = 12$

$117 - 11y = 12$

$11y = 105$

$y = \frac{105}{11}$

Plug into the second equation:

$\frac{x}{3} + \frac{105}{11} = 13$

$\frac{x}{3} + \frac{105}{11} = \frac{143}{11}$

$\frac{x}{3} = \frac{38}{11}$

$x = \frac{114}{11}$

d. $3a + 4b = 5$ and $18 + b = 2a$

The second equation is equivalent to:

$$b = 2a - 18$$

Plug into the first:

$$3a + 4(2a - 18) = 5$$
$$3a + 8a - 72 = 5$$
$$11a - 72 = 5$$
$$11a = 77$$
$$a = 7$$

Plug back into the second equation for b:

$$18 + b = 2(7)$$
$$18 + b = 14$$
$$b = 14 - 18 = -4$$

3.   Solve the following systems of equations using whichever method you prefer:

a. $\frac{b}{4} = a + 1$ and $a = 1$

Plug the second equation in for the first:

$$\frac{b}{4} = 1 + 1 = 2$$
$$b = 8$$

b. $3(m + 2) = n$ and $2m + n = 6$

Simplify the first equation:

$$3m + 6 = n$$
$$3m - n = -6$$

Add the equations:

$$2m + n = 6$$
$$+(3m - n = -6)$$
$$5m = 0$$
$$m = 0$$

Plug into the second equation:

$$2(0) + n = 6$$
$$n = 6$$

c. $50x + 65y = 21,500$ and $x + y = 400$

Multiply the second equation by 50:

$$50x + 50y = 20,000$$

Subtract the equations:

$$50x + 65y = 21,500$$
$$-(50x + 50y = 20,000)$$
$$15y = 1,500$$
$$y = 100$$

Solve for x:

$$x + 100 = 400$$
$$x = 300$$

d. $\frac{x+y}{x-y} = -5$ and $\frac{5x}{2} = 3y - 4$

Simplify the first equation:

$$x + y = -5(x - y)$$
$$x + y = -5x + 5y$$
$$6x + y = 5y$$
$$6x = 4y$$

$y = \frac{3}{2}x$

Plug into the second equation:

$\frac{5x}{2} = 3(\frac{3}{2}x) - 4$

$5x = 3(3x) - 8$

$5x = 9x - 8$

$8 = 4x$

$x = 2$

Solve for y:

$y = \frac{3}{2}(2) = 3$

4.   Solve the following three-variable systems of equations:

a. $2x + y = 1$, $2y + z = 1$, and $z = -9$

Plug the third equation into the second:

$2y + (-9) = 1$

$2y = 10$

$y = 5$

Plug that into the first equation:

$2x + 5 = 1$

$2x = -4$

$x = -2$

b. $x - y = 1$, $y - z = 3$, and $x + z = 4$

Add the second and third equations:

$y - z = 3$

$+(x + z = 4)$

$x + y = 7$

Now add the resulting equation to the first equation:

$x + y = 7$

$+(x - y = 1)$

$2x = 8$

$x = 4$

Plug that back into the first equation:

$4 - y = 1$

$y = 3$

Plug that into the second equation:

$3 - z = 3$

$z = 0$

c. $3a = b + 4$, $b = 11 - c$, and $c = 2a$

Substitute the third equation into the second:

$b = 11 - 2a$

$b - 11 = -2a$

Subtract the resulting equation from the first:

$3a = b + 4$

$-(-2a = b - 11)$

$5a = 15$

$a = 3$

Plug that into the first equation:

$3(3) = b + 4$

$$9 = b + 4$$
$$b = 5$$

Plug the value of a into the third equation:

$$c = 2(3) = 6$$

d. $3q = m + p$, $\frac{m}{p} = \frac{q}{8}$, and $\frac{m}{2} = \frac{p}{3} + \frac{q}{4}$

First, simplify the third equation:

$$6m = 4p + 3q$$
$$3q = 6m - 4p$$

Substitute into the first equation:

$$6m - 4p = m + p$$
$$5m = 5p$$
$$m = p$$

If $m = p$, then $\frac{m}{p} = 1$, so the second equation is as follows:

$$1 = \frac{q}{8}$$
$$q = 8$$

Thus, from the first equation, $m + p = 3(8) = 24$

Since m and p are equal, $m = 12$ and $p = 12$.

5.   True or False: For each of the following, are the equations equivalent?

a. $x + y = 6$ and $y = 6 + x$

Rewrite the second equation with x and y on the left side:

$$y - x = 6$$

False

b. $7 - 2z = -y$ and $y - 2z = 7$

Rewrite the second equation with 7 and $-2x$ on the left side:

$$-7 - 2x = -y$$

False

c. $\frac{a+b}{4} = 9$ and $a = 36 - b$

Simplify the first equation:

$$a + b = 36$$
$$a = 36 - b$$

True

d. $m = 4 - n$ and $3(m - n) = 12$

Simplify the second equation:

$$m - n = 4$$
$$m = 4 + n$$

False

165 Explanations: Systems: Practice

41.   D

EXPL: Using the first equation, you can solve for y, which you can then plug into the second equation to solve for z. Starting with the first step:

$2y + 4 = 0$

$2y = -4$

$y = \frac{-4}{2} = -2$

Plugging in:

$3y + 4z = -2$

$3(-2) + 4z = -2$

$-6 + 4z = -2$

$4z = 4$

$z = 1$

Choice (D) is correct.

42.   A

EXPL: The question gives you two equations:

$l = 3w$

$2l + 2w = 12$

The second can be simplified:

$l + w = 6$

Plug the first into the second:

$3w + w = 6$

$4w = 6$

$w = \frac{6}{4} = \frac{3}{2}$

Without solving for the length, you can select (A), as it's the only choice with $\frac{3}{2}$ in it. If you had to solve for length, plug the value for w into the first equation:

$l = 3(\frac{3}{2}) = \frac{9}{2}$

43.   C

EXPL: Each of the two statements is insufficient on its own. In each case, it's impossible to isolate the term $r - s$, and each has two variables in a single linear equation.

Taken together, the statements are sufficient. Since each one is a linear equation with the variables r and s, and since they are distinct, you can solve for r and s, and then find $r - s$. Choice (C) is correct.

While you don't need to actually solve for $r - s$ to answer the question, you would do so as follows. Start by isolating r in the first equation:

$r - \frac{s}{3} = 13$

$r = 13 + \frac{s}{3}$

Then plug that value of r into the second equation:

$\frac{13 + \frac{s}{3}}{3} - s = -1$

$13 + \frac{s}{3} - 3s = -3$

$$\frac{s}{3} - 3s = -16$$
$$s - 9s = -48$$
$$-8s = -48$$
$$s = 6$$

Then plug s back into the first equation:
$$r - \frac{s}{3} = 13$$
$$r - \frac{6}{3} = 13$$
$$r - 2 = 13$$
$$r = 15$$

Thus, $r - s = 15 - 6 = 9$.

44.   B

EXPL: As usual, try to simplify the question. In this case, $\frac{x}{3} + \frac{y}{3} = \frac{x+y}{3}$. Dividing by three isn't all that important here: if we can find the value of $x + y$, we can divide it by three. So we'll look for the value of $x + y$.

Statement (1) is insufficient: multiply both sides by 2, and the result is $x - y = 12$. Close, but not close enough.

Statement (2) is sufficient: again, multiply both sides by 2. This time you get something more helpful: $x + y = 18$. That's what we're looking for, so choice (B) is correct. Usually, when the GMAT gives you two statements that look very similar, there's some crucial difference. That difference leads to one of the choices being sufficient and the other insufficient.

45.   E

EXPL: Statement (1) is insufficient: Walter's age (ψ) is given in terms of a second variable we have no other information about. We can write it as an equation for future reference:
$$z = 2(w - 5)$$

Statement (2) is also insufficient: not only does it relate Walter's age to that second variable again, but only as an inequality, which is much less useful than an equation. It can be expressed algebraically as follows:
$$|w - z| < 3$$

Taken together, the two statements are still insufficient. While two linear equations with the same two variables is enough to solve for the variables, the same thing doesn't apply when one of the equations is replaced with an inequality, as it is in (2). Choice (E) is correct.

46.   C

EXPL: The question sets up what could turn out to be a 3-variable system of equations. To solve one of those, you need three distinct equations. The question itself gives you one:
$$f + q + z = 28$$

Statement (1) is insufficient. It gives you an equation:
$$f = q - 3$$
and an inequality:
$$q > z$$

The inequality isn't very helpful, since we need exact relationships to determine the value of any of the individual variables.

Statement (2) is similar, and is also insufficient. First, there's an equation:

$q = z + 5$

and also an inequality:

$z < f$

Again, we need one more equation to solve for any of the variables.

Taken together, we have all we need. The question provided one equation, and each statement added another, giving us a total of 3 distinct equations with the same three variables. No need to solve for f; we can confidently select (C).

166   Explanations: Quadratics: Drill

1.   FOIL each of the following:
   a. $(x + 2)(x + 3) = x^2 + 3x + 2x + 6 = x^2 + 5x + 6$
   b. $(x - 4)(x - 1) = x^2 - x - 4x + 4 = x^2 - 5x + 4$
   c. $(x - 3)(x + 3) = x^2 + 3x - 3x - 9 = x^2 - 9$
   d. $(2x + 1)(x - 2) = 2x^2 - 4x + x - 2 = 2x^2 - 3x - 2$
   e. $(x + y)^2 = x^2 + xy + xy + y^2 = x^2 + 2xy + y^2$

2.   Factor each of the following:
   a. $x^2 - 2x - 8 = (x - 4)(x + 2)$
   b. $x^2 + x - 6 = (x + 3)(x - 2)$
   c. $x^2 - y^2 = (x + y)(x - y)$
   d. $a^2 + 6a + 9 = (a + 3)(a + 3)$
   e. $z^2 + 9z + 20 = (z + 5)(z + 4)$

3.   Solve for x:
   a. $(x - 1)(x + 3) = 0$
         $x = 1$ or $x = -3$
   b. $(3x + 2)(2x - 3) = 0$
         $3x + 2 = 0$
         $3x = -2$
         $x = -\frac{2}{3}$
         or $2x - 3 = 0$
         $2x = 3$
         $x = \frac{3}{2}$
   c. $x^2 - 3x + 2 = 0$
         $(x - 2)(x - 1) = 0$
         $x = 2$ or $x = 1$
   d. $x^2 - 6x = 7$
         $x^2 - 6x - 7 = 0$
         $(x - 7)(x + 1) = 0$
         $x = 7$ or $x = -1$
   e. $x^2 + 4x = -4$
         $x^2 + 4x + 4 = 0$
         $(x + 2)(x + 2) = 0$
         $x = -2$

4.   Factor each of the following:
   a. $y^2 - x^2 = (y + x)(y - x)$
   b. $n^2 - 8n + 16 = (n - 4)(n - 4)$
   c. $p^2 - 25 = (p - 5)(p + 5)$
   d. $x^2 + 2x + 1 = (x + 1)(x + 1)$
   e. $z^2 - 4z + 4 = (z - 2)(z - 2)$

167   Explanations: Quadratics: Practice

51.   A

EXPL One of the two terms must equal 0 for the product of the two to equal zero, and as $a \neq 2$, the second term cannot. Thus, $4 + \frac{a}{2}$ must equal 0. So, if $4 + \frac{a}{2} = 0$, $4 = -\frac{a}{2}$, $8 = -a$, $a = -8$, choice (A).

52.   C

EXPL First, find the roots of the equation in the question stem. It factors to $(x - 5)(x - 1) = 0$, so $x = 5$ or $x = 1$. To find the answer, you'll have to work through each choice:

(A) factors to $(x + 1)(x - 7)$, no match, eliminate it.
(B) factors to $(x + 5)(x + 1)$, no match, eliminate it.
(C) factors to $(x + 4)(x - 1)$, so there's a match: it's the correct answer.
(D) factors to $(x + 4)(x + 1)$, so no match, eliminate it.
(E) factors to $(x - 2)(x + 5)$, so no match, eliminate it.

53.   D

EXPL: There are a lot of variables floating around, but you can set this up as follows:

$r^2 - kr - 36 = (r - 4)(r + x)$

The product of the two constants (-4 and x) must be -36, so:

$-4x = -36$

$x = 9$

We can rewrite the equation as follows:

$r^2 - kr - 36 = (r - 4)(r + 9)$

If we FOIL the factors, we find the value of k:

$(r - 4)(r + 9) = r^2 - 4r + 9r - 36 = r^2 + 5r - 36$

Since the middle term in the original quadratic was $-kr$, set that equal to $5r$:

$-kr = 5r$

$-k = 5$

$k = -5$, choice (D).

54.   B

EXPL: Statement (1) is insufficient: if you factor the quadratic, you get two possible values for c, one of which is 4:

$c^2 - 2c - 8 = 0$

$(c - 4)(c + 2) = 0$

$c = 4$, $c = -2$

Statement (2) is sufficient: there are multiple values of c, but neither of them are 4. c could be either 2 or -2, so the answer must be "no." (B) is the correct choice.

55.   B

EXPL: As usual, look to simplify the question before examining the statements. Multiply both sides by y-1:

$\frac{x-1}{y-1} = 1$?

$x - 1 = y - 1$?

$x = y$?

Really, the question is asking whether x equals y. Statement (1) is insufficient: while x could be the same as y (if x and y equal 2), there are an infinite number of other possibilities.

Statement (2) is sufficient: it answers the question directly. Choice (B) is correct.

56.   C

Explanation: First, take the square root of both sides.   Two possible equations result:

$x - 3 = 15$

$x - 3 = -15$

In the first, $x = 18$. In the second, $x = -12$. Thus, the possible values of $x + 3$ are 21 and -9. The latter is the only one that appears among the answer choices, so (C) is correct.

57.   C

Explanation: To find the value of $a^2 - b^2$, you need the value of a and the value of b, or the value of $a - b$ and $a + b$, the product of which are equal to $a^2 - b^2$.

Statement (1) is insufficient: it's only one equation with the two variables. It can be rewritten as $a + b = 4$. Statement (2) is also insufficient: again, one equation with two variables. It can be rewritten as $a - b = 3$.

Taken together, we have enough information. $a^2 - b^2 = (a + b)(a - b) = (4)(3) = 12$. Choice (C) is correct.

58.   D

Explanation: Factoring quadratics with a coefficient in front of the squared term is tricky, but the GMAT usually gives you those when the constant is 1, as in this case. It turns out you don't need to factor the quadratic to solve the question, but if you did, it would turn out like this:

$(4x + 1)(x + 1)$

Statements (1) and (2) are both sufficient on their own, as each one gives you a one-variable linear equation.   In either case, you can solve for x, then plug in to the expression and solve. Choice (D) is correct.

59.   C

To simplify the equation, get rid of the fraction by multiplying both sides by x:

$x(\frac{3}{x} - 2) = x(x)$

$x(\frac{3}{x}) - 2x = x^2$

$3 - 2x = x^2$

This is starting to look like a quadratic, so move everything to one side:
$x^2 + 2x - 3 = 0$
Now factor:
$(x + 3)(x - 1) = 0$
That gives you two values for x. Choice (C) is correct.

168   Explanations: Inequalities: Drill

1. Simplify each of the following inequalities.

    a. $2y > 6 - y$
            $3y > 6$
            $y > 2$

    b. $2a + b + 1 < a - b + 2$
            $a + b + 1 < -b + 2$
            $a + 2b + 1 < +2$
            $a + 2b < 1$

    c. $n - 10 \leq 2 - n$
            $2n - 10 \leq 2$
            $2n \leq 12$
            $n \leq 6$

    d. $(x + 2)(x - 3) \geq x(x + 1)$
            $x^2 - x - 6 \geq x^2 + x$
            $-x - 6 \geq x$
            $-6 \geq 2x$
            $x \leq -3$

    e. $z^2 < 4$
            $-2 < z < 2$

    f. $-3c > -6$
            $-c > -2$
            $c < 2$

    g. $\frac{5}{2} - m > -\frac{m}{4}$
            $10 - 4m > -m$
            $10 > 3m$
            $m < \frac{10}{3}$

    h. $-2w - 3 \geq -3w - 2$
            $w - 3 \geq -2$
            $w \geq 1$

    i. $17 < 4x + 3 < 29$
            $14 < 4x < 26$
            $\frac{14}{4} < x < \frac{26}{4}$
            $\frac{7}{2} < x < \frac{13}{2}$

    j. $6 > -3y > -15$
            $-2 < y < 5$

169   Explanations: Inequalities: Practice

61.   C

EXPL: First, simplify the second inequality:

$2z > -4$

$z > -2$

Thus, we know that z must be less than 8 (that's given also) and that z must be greater than -2. To find which choice must be true, we have to go through the first four one by one:

(A) z could be as large as 7.99, so it could be greater than 4. Eliminate.

(B) z could be as small as -1.99, so it could be less than 2. Eliminate.

(C) z must be greater than -2, so it must be greater than -8. Looks good.

(D)   like (A), z could be larger than 4. Eliminate.

(E)   We have a possible answer, so this can't be right.

The correct choice is (C).

62.   C

EXPL: Statement (1) is insufficient, as it gives us no information about y. Statement (2) has a similar problem: nothing about x.

Taken together, the statements are sufficient. If x is less than b and y is greater than b, y must be greater than x:

$x < b < y$

So to answer the question, y is greater than x. Choice (C) is correct.

63.   E

EXPL: Statement (1) is insufficient. xy could be less than 9, as when $x = 4$ and $y = 2$. However, xy could be greater than 9, when $x = 4$ and $y = 4$. Statement (2) is similar: xy could be less than 9 when $x = 2$ and $y = 4$, but xy could be greater than 9 when $x = 4$ and $y = 4$.

Taken together, the statements are insufficient. For one thing, you may notice that I used the same counterexamples when explaining both statements. If xy could be 8 or 16 in both cases, combining them doesn't help any. More algebraically, you can combine the statements as follows:

$2 \leq x \leq 4$

$2 \leq y \leq 4$

So xy could be as small as 4 (if $x = 2$ and $y = 2$) and as large as 16 (if $x = 4$ and $y = 4$). Choice (E) is correct.

64.   C

EXPL: Statement (1) is insufficient. It's easiest to think of it after manipulating the inequality a bit:

$y - z > x$

$y > x + z$

Since z is positive, $x + z$ is greater than x. If y is greater than $x + z$, it must also be greater than x:

$y > x + z > x$

However, we don't know whether z is greater than x, just that y is.

Statement (2) is insufficient: while it's helpful to know that $z > x$, we don't know anything about y.

Taken together, the statements are sufficient. (1) tells us that y is greater than x, and (2) tells us that z is greater than x. Choice (C) is correct.

65.   C

Explanation: Combine the inequalities to make further deductions. $k < g < j$; $f < h < j$. No more deductions can be made: for instance, there is no stated relationship between h and either g or k; neither is there a relationship given between f and either g or k. I is not necessarily true for that reason: that relationship is unknown. Eliminate (A) and (E). II is also not necessarily true, again, the relationship between f and g is not provided. Eliminate (B) and (D). Thus (C) must be the answer: III must be true, as $k < g < j$.

66.   C

Explanation: The fraction on the left side of the inequality is only there to make you waste your time. $x - y$ and $y - x$ will never have the same sign, and $x - y$ will always have the same sign as its reciprocal, $\frac{1}{x-y}$. The point is that, if $x - y$ is positive, $\frac{1}{x-y}$ is greater than $y - x$ (which would be negative), while if its negative, the opposite is true. To answer the question, we need to know the sign of $x - y$.

Statement (1) is insufficient: without knowing anything about x, we can't determine the sign of $x - y$. Statement (2) is also insufficient, since it doesn't give us any information about y.

Taken together, the statements are sufficient. If y is positive and x is negative, $x - y$ is (negative - positive), which is always negative. If $x - y$ is negative, then $\frac{1}{x-y}$ is negative, and $y - x$ is positive. Choice (C) is correct.

67.   E

Explanation: To answer the question, we need to know whether m is greater than q, and whether n is greater than q.

Statement (1) is insufficient: it tells us nothing about relationships with q. Statement (2) is also insufficient: it neglects to mention n.

Taken together, the statements are insufficient. We know that m is the largest integer, so it must be greater than q. But while we know that n is smaller than m, we don't know its relationship with q. Choice (E) is correct.

170   Explanations: Inequalities: Challenge

68.   E

EXPL: For xy to be less than 4, keep in mind that while both numbers could be positive (such as 3 and 1–though they needn't be integers), one or both could be negative, as well.

Statement (1) is insufficient. If x is greater than y, x could be 3 and y could be 1, in which case x is greater than 2. However, x could be 1 and y could be -2 (or any negative number), in which case $xy < 4$ and x is less than 2.

Statement (2) is insufficient as well: we can consider $x = 3$ and $y = 1$ again, where x is greater than 2. But it's also possible that $x = 1$ and $y = 1$, now that we don't care if x is greater than y.

Taken together, the statements are still insufficient. If y is positive and x is greater than y, both numbers must be positive. Once more, we can use $x = 3$ and $y = 1$ as one example, one in which x is greater than 2. It's also possible that $x = 1$ and $y = 0.5$, in which case x is less than 2, but xy is still less than 4 and all the other parameters are met. Choice (E) is correct.

69.   E

Explanation: If both variables are negative, $\frac{m}{n}$ is less than one only if $m > n$, as in the case m=-2 and n=-3, making $\frac{m}{n} = \frac{-2}{-3} = \frac{2}{3}$. Thus, the question is equivalent to: Is $m > n$?

Statement (1) is insufficient; if the product is less than 1, one or both of the numbers must be less than one, but there's no way to determine which of the two is larger. Statement (2) can be simplified by adding n to both sides: $m > 2n$. That's also insufficient: if $m = 2$, n could be either 1.5 or 3, giving a "yes" and a "no" answer.

Taken together, the statements are still insufficient. Statement (2) will still be true if $m = \frac{1}{2}$ and n is $\frac{3}{8}$ or $\frac{3}{4}$; both of those scenarios will make (1) true, as well. Since you can generate a "yes" answer and a "no" answer within the constraints of both statements, the correct choice is (E).

70.   C

Explanation: Statement (1) is insufficient: first, solve the equation for x or y. Multiple both sides by 2, and the result is:
$x = 2y - 6$
If $y = 1$, $x = -4$, so y is greater. But if $y = 10$, $x = 14$, so x is greater.
Statement (2) is also insufficient, as it provides no information about x.

Taken together, the statements are sufficient. In the equation given above $(x = 2y - 6)$, $y = 6$ is the point at which $x = y$, since $6 = 2(6) - 6$. For any value of y greater than 6, x is greater than y. (To better establish this, you might want to plug in a couple of values for y to confirm.) Choice (C) is correct.

171   Explanations: Absolute Value: Drill

1.   Simplify:

    a. $|-5| = 5$

    b. $|-3| + 2 = 3 + 2 = 5$

    c. $|-3 + 2| = |-1| = 1$

    d. $|11.5 - 2.91| - |2.91 - 11.5| =$

The positive difference between two numbers will be the same. There's no need to solve for the difference between 11.5 and 2.91; each of the two absolute values is equal. If they are equal, subtracting one from the other results in 0.

    e. $-\frac{|6|}{|-2|} = -\frac{6}{2} = -3$

2.   For each of the following, find the possible values of x:

    a. $x = |y|$

        $x = y$ or $x = -y$

    b. $x = |a - b|$

        $x = a - b$ or $x = b - a$

    c. $x = |m^2 + n^2|$

Any squared number must be positive, and the sum of two positives must also be positive.

        $x = m^2 + n^2$

    d. $x > |z - 5|$

        $x > z - 5$ or $x > 5 - z$

    e. $x \leq |y| + 3$

        $x \leq y + 3$ or $x \leq 3 - y$

172 Explanations: Absolute Value: Practice

71. A

EXPL: Absolute value is distance from zero: when you're working with numbers (as opposed to variables), you can just strip the positive or negative sign. To estimate the values on the number line:

    (A)   -2.1
    (B)   -1.5
    (C)   0
    (D)   1
    (E)   1.8

The corresponding absolute values are:

    (A)   2.1
    (B)   1.5
    (C)   0
    (D)   1
    (E)   1.8

The largest is 2.1, (A).

72. E

EXPL: Statement (1) is insufficient. It means that either $x < 2$ or $-x < 2$, which we can simplify:

$-x < 2$

$x > -2$

Putting those two together, $-2 < x < 2$. That's not enough to determine whether x is negative.

Statement (2) is also insufficient. Again, simplify:

$3 - 2x > 0$

$3 > 2x$

$x < \frac{3}{2}$

If x is less than $\frac{3}{2}$, it could be greater or lesser than 0.

Taken together, the statements are still insufficient. The second statement slightly modifies the first; knowing that x is less than $\frac{3}{2}$ tells us it can't be between $\frac{3}{2}$ and 2, so the resulting inequality is:

$-2 < x < \frac{3}{2}$

Still, x could be greater or lesser than 0. Choice (E) is correct.

73. E

EXPL: The line segment indicated in the figure depicts $-4 \leq x \leq 2$, so one of the choices must be equivalent to that. The most efficient way for most people to find the matching answer is to go through each one:

    (A) $|x| \leq 2$ is equivalent to two inequalities: $x \leq 2$ and $x \geq -2$. Only one of the endpoints matches the diagram, so this is wrong.

    (B) $|x| \leq 4$ is equivalent to two inequalities: $x \leq 4$ and $x \geq -4$. Only one of the endpoints matches the diagram, so this is wrong.

(C) $|x - 2| \leq 2$ is equivalent to two inequalities: $x-2 \leq 2$ and $x-2 \geq -2$. The first is $x \leq 4$ and the second is $x \geq 0$. Neither of the endpoints are correct.

(D) $|x - 1| \leq 3$ is equivalent to two inequalities: $x-1 \leq 3$ and $x-1 \geq -3$. The first is $x \leq 4$ and the second is $x \geq -2$. Neither of the endpoints are correct.

(E) $|x + 1| \leq 3$ is equivalent to two inequalities: $x+1 \leq 3$ and $x+1 \geq -3$. The first is $x \leq 2$ and the second is $x \geq -4$. These match the diagram, so (E) is correct.

74.   B

Since the expression is inside absolute value signs, it will always be positive. We'll have to test some values for n, however, to see just how small it can get. As n gets larger, $31 - 4n$ will get smaller. Once $31 - 4n$ falls below zero, though, $|31 - 4n|$ starts to get bigger, since the absolute value signs turn negative values positive. Let's try a few values for n (chosen so that $4n$ is roughly equal to 31) to see exactly what the results are:

$n = 6$
$|31 - 4n| = |31 - 24| = 7$
$n = 7$
$|31 - 4n| = |31 - 28| = 3$
$n = 8$
$|31 - 4n| = |31 - 32| = |-1| = 1$
$n = 9$
$|31 - 4n| = |31 - 36| = |-5| = 5$

If n is less than 6 or greater than 9, the value of the expression is larger than the values shown. Thus, the smallest possible value is 1, which we found when $n = 8$. Choice (B) is correct.

173   Explanations: Absolute Value: Challenge

75.   C

EXPL: Absolute value signs imply two possible values. If $y - z$ is positive, the equation can be simplified as follows:

$x = y - z$

But if $y - z$ is negative, it looks like this:

$x = -1(y - z) = z - y$

To answer the question, then, we need to know two things: is $y - z$ positive, and is the resulting equation true? Statement (1) is insufficient: while it asserts the truth of the first of our two equations, we don't know whether that's the equation we care about. If $y - z$ is negative, that equation is irrelevant.

Statement (2) is insufficient as well: it has nothing about x.

Taken together, the statements are sufficient. $y > z$ means that $y - z > 0$, that $y - z$ is positive. Thus, we can eliminate the second of our two equations and focus solely on whether $x = y - z$. Since (1) tells us that $x = y - z$, we know that the answer is "yes," and (C) is the correct choice.

76.   A

Explanation: With two separate absolute value expressions, it's difficult to get much from the question itself. There are four possible ways that equation will be true, depending on whether the left and right side are each positive or negative, but that's too involved to do under timed circumstances.

Statement (1) is sufficient. Since $x = y$, we can substitute one in for the other in the original equation:

Is $|x - z| = |y - z|$?

Is $|y - z| = |y - z|$?

Since the two sides are the same, the answer is "yes."

Statement (2) is not sufficient. We can add z to both sides and end up with the following:

$|x| = |y|$

It's possible that $x = y$, in which case we could apply the same logic we used with (1); but it's also possible that $x = -y$, in which case the answer might be "no." Choice (A) is correct.

77.   E

Statement (1) is insufficient.   Distances can be expressed algebraically as absolute values, which means that:

$|s - 0| = \frac{1}{2} |n - 0|$

or:

$|s| = \frac{1}{2} |n|$

That's not enough; even without the absolute value signs, we would need the value of n to find s.

Statement (2) is also insufficient: again, we've got an equation with absolute values. If -4 is halfway between the variables, the difference between -4 and each of the variables is the same:

$|n - (-4)| = |s - (-4)|$

$|n + 4| = |s + 4|$

Taken together, the statements are still insufficient. It would take far too long under timed conditions to establish the exact values that s and n could be, but here's how to think about it. If n and s are both negative, they could be equally distant from -4, with s half as far from 0 as n. The values would be around, but not exactly 2.75 and 5.5.

If n is negative and s is positive, there's also a pair of values that would work. In this case it would be about -16 and 8. No need to know the exact numbers, only that such a pair exists. Choice (E) is correct.

78.   E

EXPL: Before solving a quadratic, you must set it equal to zero. In this question, that means evaluating both the positive and negative results of the absolute value expression. If $x - 1$ is positive, the right side evaluates to $3 - (x - 1)$. If it is negative, it is $3 - (-1)(x - 1)$. Take them one at a time:

Positive:

$x^2 - 4x + 6 = 3 - (x - 1)$

$x^2 - 4x + 6 = 3 - x + 1$

$x^2 - 4x + 6 = 4 - x$

$x^2 - 3x + 2 = 0$

$(x - 2)(x - 1) = 0$

$x = 2$ or $x = 1$

Negative:

$x^2 - 4x + 6 = 3 - (-1)(x - 1)$

$x^2 - 4x + 6 = 3 + (x - 1)$

$x^2 - 4x + 6 = 2 + x$

$x^2 - 5x + 4 = 0$

$(x - 4)(x - 1) = 0$

$x = 4$ or $x = 1$

The three possible solutions are 1, 2, and 4, the product of which is 8, choice (E).

74.   B

EXPL: Statement (1) is insufficient. It's equivalent to one of two equations:

$x + 3 = 4$

Or:

$x + 3 = -4$

In the first case, $x = 1$, and in the second $x = -7$.

Statement (2) is sufficient. Subtract 3 from both sides, and the result is $|x| = 1$, the answer to our question.

174   Explanations: Exponents: Drill

1.   Simplify each of the following:
    a. $a^5 a^3 = a^{5+3} = a^8$
    b.. $c^3 c^{-3} = c^{3+(-3)} = c^0 = 1$
    c. $j^{-2} j^3 = j^{-2+3} = j^1 = j$
    d. $k^2 \sqrt{k} = k^2 k^{\frac{1}{2}} = k^{2+\frac{1}{2}} = k^{2\frac{1}{2}}$
    e. $\frac{1}{\sqrt{m}} = \frac{1}{m^{\frac{1}{2}}} = m^{-\frac{1}{2}}$
    f. $\frac{n^3}{n^2} = n^{3-2} = n^1 = n$
    g. $\frac{p^5}{p^7} = p^{5-7} = p^{-2}$ or $\frac{1}{p^2}$
    h. $\left(t^3\right)^4 = t^{3(4)} = t^{12}$
    i. $\left(w^x\right)^x = w^{x(x)} = w^{x^2}$
    j. $\left(\frac{x^y}{x^z}\right)^{\frac{1}{z-y}} = \left(x^{y-z}\right)^{\frac{1}{z-y}} = x^{y-z\left(\frac{1}{z-y}\right)} = x^{y-z\left(\frac{-1}{y-z}\right)} = x^{-1} = \frac{1}{x}$

2.   Solve for x:
    a. $2^{2x+1} = 2^{4x-3}$
          $2x + 1 = 4x - 3$
          $4 = 2x$
          $x = 2$
    b. $2^{x+3} = 4^x$
          $2^{x+3} = (2^2)^x$
          $2^{x+3} = 2^{2x}$
          $x + 3 = 2x$
          $x = 3$
    c. $9^{x+\frac{3}{2}} = 27^{x-1}$
          $(3^2)^{x+\frac{3}{2}} = (3^3)^{x-1}$
          $3^{2(x+\frac{3}{2})} = 3^{3(x-1)}$
          $2(x + \frac{3}{2}) = 3(x - 1)$
          $2x + 3 = 3x - 3$
          $x = 6$

175   Explanations: Exponents: Practice

81.   B
    EXPL If $x = -\frac{1}{2}$, then $(x^4 + x^3 + x^3 + x) = \frac{1}{16} + (-\frac{1}{8}) + \frac{1}{4} + (-\frac{1}{2}) =$
$\frac{1}{16} - \frac{2}{16} + \frac{4}{16} - \frac{8}{16} = -\frac{5}{16}$, choice (B).

82.   C
EXPL: First, simplify each of the equations so that all the bases are the same:
$(4^x)(8^y) = 32$
$(2^{2x})(2^{3y}) = 2^5$
$2^{2x+3y} = 2^5$
$(5^x)(25^y) = 125$
$(5^x)(5^{2y}) = 5^3$
$5^{x+2y} = 5^3$
Drop the bases, and you have two equations with two variables:
$2x + 3y = 5$
$x + 2y = 3$
Double the second equation, then subtract the second from the first:
$2x + 3y = 5$
$2x + 4y = 6$
$-y = -1$
$y = 1$
If $y = 1$, then:
$x + 2y = 3$
$x + 2 = 3$
$x = 1$
Thus, the answer is (C), $(1, 1)$.

83.   A
EXPL: Statement (1) is sufficient: there's only one number that, when cubed, equals 64. (Given any number, there's only one number, when cubed, that equals that number.) Statement (2) is not sufficient: simplify, and the result is:
$a^2 = 16$
With squares, there are multiple possible answers. Namely, in this case, a could be 4 or -4. (A) is the correct choice.

84.   D
EXPL: Algebraically, the question is:
$x^2 > x$?
To simplify that, you'll need to consider two possibilities: one where x is positive, one where x is negative:
If $x > 0$: $x > 1$?
If $x < 0$: $x < 1$?

In the second case, if x is negative, x must be less than zero, so the inequality doesn't provide any additional information. Basically, the answer is "yes" any time except for when x is between 0 and 1. So, the question is really asking: "Is x between 0 and 1?"

Statement (1) is sufficient: if x is less than -1, it cannot be between 0 and 1. Statement (2) is also sufficient: if x is greater than 1, it cannot be between 0 and 1. Choice (D) is correct.

85.   E

Explanation: The question tells you that y is a perfect square between 2 and 100. There aren't very many possible values of y that fulfill those requirements, and you should have the possibilities memorized.

Statement (1) doesn't narrow things down much; the square of any integer is not a prime number. Not only is (1) not sufficient, we can eliminate (C), because (1) doesn't tell us anything at all.

Statement (2) is also insufficient: there are multiple squares in the given range that are divisible by 3: 9, 36, and 81. Thus, because combining (2) with (1) cannot help us, neither statement is sufficient, and the correct choice is (E).

86.   E

Explanation: If $s^t = 1$, there are two possibilities: either $s = 1$, in which case s^t would be 1 regardless of the value of t, or $t = 0$, in which case s^t is 1 regardless of the value of s. That offers an infinite number of results for $s - t$, so statement (1) is insufficient.

Statement (2) is also insufficient: there are several sets of numbers that sum to 5.

Taken together, the statements are still insufficient. If $s = 1$, then $t = 4$, in which case $s - t = 1 - 4 = -3$. If $t = 0$, then $s = 5$, in which case $s - t = 5 - 0 = 5$. Since both answers are possible, choice (E) is correct.

176   Explanations: Exponents: Challenge

87.   C

EXPL: It may not be immediately obvious, but you can simplify the expression in the question as follows:

$(\frac{x^m}{x^n})^5 = (x^{m-n})^5$

Statement (1) is insufficient, though it does give us a way to determine the value of the exponent $m - n$. If $n - m$ is 2, $m - n$ is -2, so we can reduce the expression to:

$(x^{-2})^5 = x^{-10}$

Statement (2) is also insufficient: without the values of m, n, or $m - n$, we can't evaluate the expression. Taken together, though, the statements are sufficient. Plugging in all the information we've been given:

$(x^{m-n})^5 = ((\frac{1}{4})^{-2})^5 = (\frac{1}{4})^{-10}$

It doesn't matter what exactly that's equal to, just that we could figure it out. Choice (C) is correct.

88.   E

EXPL: When two terms with the same base and different exponents are added, you can only combine them by factoring. To do so, you may need to simplify each term to see what they have in common:

$3^{x+1} = 3^x 3^1$

$3^{x-1} = 3^x 3^{-1}$

Since both contain a 3^x, you can factor it out:

$3^x(3 + \frac{1}{3}) = 3^x(\frac{10}{3})$

There's no answer that matches that expression, but since a 10 appears in the last two choices, you may be getting warmer. A 3 in the denominator is the same as a 3^{-1} in the numerator, so rewrite the expression:

$3^x(10)(3^{-1})$

Finally, combine the two 3's:

$3^{x-1}(10) = 10(3^{x-1})$, choice (E).

89.   E

Rather than delving into algebra, think about what the exponents n and $n + 4$ represent. Since the questions tells us the equation is true for any value of n, one important consideration is that the exponents are 4 apart. Whenever one is odd, the other is odd, and whenever one is even, the other is even. The only values of a that ensure that the equation is always true are:

0, because 0 raised to any power remains 0.

1, because 1 raised to any power remains 1

−1, because −1 raised to any power either remains −1 (if the power is odd) or becomes 1 (if the power is even). Since the powers are both either even or odd, −1 raised to the power has the same result on both sides.

Statement (1) is insufficient. Simplify to $a^2 = 1$, and recognize that a could be either 1 or -1. That rules out $a = 0$, but it doesn't give us a single value of a.

Statement (2) is also insufficient. In fact, it doesn't give us any information at all. The information in the question essentially says, "a raised to some power has the same result as a raised to a power that is 4 greater." This statement says the same thing, using $n-4$ and n instead of n and $n+4$. So not only is it insufficient on its own, it has no content that we can use to combine it with statement (1). Thus, choice (E) is correct.

90.   D

Explanation: To find the value of n, we'll need to find k. Oddly, though, neither of the statements mentions k.

Statement (1) is nonethless sufficient. Given the value of n^2, we can determine the positive and negative value of n. (No need to calculate it, working with such cumbersome numbers.) However, keep in mind that since n is equal to 1.7 raised to a power, n must be positive. Thus, while the statement gives us two possible values for n, only one is possible for this question.

Statement (2) is also sufficient. n must be 1.7 times some integer power of 10. Thus, n is going to be something like 17, 170, 1,700, 17,000, etc. There is only one such number in the given range: 170,000. Choice (D) is correct.

177 Explanations: Roots: Drill

1. Simplify each of the following:

a. $\sqrt{32} = \sqrt{16}\sqrt{2} = 4\sqrt{2}$

b. $\sqrt{48} = \sqrt{16}\sqrt{3} = 4\sqrt{3}$

c. $\sqrt{50} = \sqrt{25}\sqrt{2} = 5\sqrt{2}$

d. $\sqrt{6(12)} = \sqrt{6(6)(2)} = \sqrt{36}\sqrt{2} = 6\sqrt{2}$

e. $\sqrt{x^4} = (x^4)^{\frac{1}{2}} = x^2$

f. $\sqrt[3]{a^6} = (a^6)^{\frac{1}{3}} = a^2$

g. $\sqrt{12x^3} = \sqrt{4}\sqrt{3}\sqrt{x^2}\sqrt{x} = 2x\sqrt{3}\sqrt{x} = 2x\sqrt{3x}$

h. $\frac{1}{\sqrt{2}}(\frac{\sqrt{2}}{\sqrt{2}}) = \frac{\sqrt{2}}{2}$

i. $\sqrt{\frac{8}{12}} = \sqrt{\frac{2}{3}} = \frac{\sqrt{2}}{\sqrt{3}}(\frac{\sqrt{3}}{\sqrt{3}}) = \frac{\sqrt{6}}{3}$

j. $\frac{3}{\sqrt{z}}(\frac{\sqrt{z}}{\sqrt{z}}) = \frac{3\sqrt{z}}{z}$

178   Explanations: Roots: Practice

91.   B
EXPL: The fastest way to complete this problem is by strategically guessing and checking. Try one of the middle numbers in the answer choices, such as 23. It'll take a few moments to figure out, but $23^2 = 529$. Thus, we know that $\sqrt{499}$ is smaller than 23, and probably not by much. In fact, it'd be a safe bet at this point to assume that the answer is (B). However, you may want to check by finding 22^2, which works out to 484. 484 is less than 499, so $\sqrt{499}$ is greater than 22, which means (B) is correct.

By picking the middle number, you guarantee that you won't have to try every one of the possibilities: if 23 was much too small or much too large, you could eliminate all the answers in the opposite direction.

92.   A
EXPL: It would be a nightmare to solve for $\sqrt[3]{277}$ without the aid of a calculator, so you're better off estimating. You're best off estimating with the help of the answer choices. First off, eliminate (D) and (E): if $15^2 = 225$, 15^3 is going to be much, much greater.

Start with something in the middle of the remaining numbers, like 7. $7(7)(7) = 343$, a bit greater than 277. The only answer choice that accomodates a number less than 7, is (A), so that must be our answer.

93.   D
EXPL: Since you're looking for x, simplify the equation in the question to be equal to x:
$$\sqrt{\frac{x}{y}} = n$$
$$\frac{x}{y} = n^2$$
$$x = n^2 y$$
Statement (1), then, is sufficient: x is equal to $n^2 y$, so if you have the value of the latter, you know the former as well. Statement (2) is also sufficient: using those two values, you can solve for x, whether you use the original equation or the simplified form that helped us recognize that (1) was sufficient. Choice (D) is correct.

94.   A
Don't add the radicals–you can't do that! Instead, simplify each one:
$$\sqrt{75} = \sqrt{25(3)} = 5\sqrt{3}$$
$$\sqrt{108} = \sqrt{36(3)} = 6\sqrt{3}$$
These you can add, just as you can add $5x$ and $6x$.
$5\sqrt{3} + 6\sqrt{3} = 11\sqrt{3}$, choice (A).

179 Explanations: Roots: Challenge

95. E

EXPL: Another way of asking whether $\sqrt{z}$ is an integer is asking whether z itself is a perfect square. It's not always clear from the question which way of thinking about it will be more useful, but it's handy to be able to consider both.

Statement (1) is insufficient. Start by recognizing that $\sqrt{xz} = \sqrt{x}\sqrt{z}$. If $\sqrt{x}$ is an integer, then $\sqrt{z}$ is as well; that's the only way (integer)($\sqrt{z}$) could be an integer. However, if $\sqrt{x}$ is not an integer (let's say it's $\sqrt{2}$), $\sqrt{z}$ can't be an integer either (it would have to be $\sqrt{2}$ or some integer times $\sqrt{2}$, such as $3\sqrt{2}$).

Statement (2) is also insufficient: x could be anything, so the fact that it's equivalent to z^3 doesn't help us much. If $x = 27$ (a perfect cube), then $z = 3$, but if $x = 2$, $z = \sqrt[3]{2}$.

Taken together, the statements are still insufficient. Since (2) gives you x in terms of z, you can plug that into (1):

$\sqrt{(z^3)(z)} = $ integer
$\sqrt{z^4} = $ integer
$z^2 = $ integer

Knowing that z^2 is an integer is not enough to answer the question: we want to know whether z itself is a perfect square. As is, z needn't even be an integer, let alone a perfect square: it could be $\sqrt{2}$. It could be an integer, but for Data Sufficiency, "could" isn't good enough. (E) is the correct choice.

96. A

Recognize the expression as the difference of squares. $(x+y)(x-y) = x^2 - y^2$, so:

$(\sqrt{x} + \sqrt{y})(\sqrt{x} - \sqrt{y}) = (\sqrt{x})^2 - (\sqrt{y})^2 = x - y$
We're given the values of x and y:
$x - y = 7 - 5 = 2$, choice (A).

97. B

Explanation: It's possible to tinker with the question by squaring both sides, but since the inequalities in the statements correspond directly to terms in the question, it's best to jump into the statements and start substituting.

Statement (1) is insufficient. It tells us that the right side of the inequality in the question is greater than $\sqrt{8m}$. However, the left side of that inequality is equal to $\sqrt{9m}$. Something that is greater that $\sqrt{8m}$ may be greater than $\sqrt{9m}$, but we don't know.

Statement (2) is sufficient. If $n > 8m$, then $m + n$ is greater than $9m$, so $\sqrt{m + n}$ is greater than $\sqrt{9m}$. As we've already seen, the left side of the inequality in the question is equal to $\sqrt{9m}$, so this statement is sufficient. Choice (B) is correct.

98. E

To simplify the fraction, take advantage of the difference of squares to get rid of the radicals in the denominator:

$$\frac{1}{\sqrt{x}+\sqrt{x+y}} \times \left(\frac{\sqrt{x}-\sqrt{x+y}}{\sqrt{x}-\sqrt{x+y}}\right)$$
$$= \frac{\sqrt{x}-\sqrt{x+y}}{x-(x+y)} = \frac{\sqrt{x}-\sqrt{x+y}}{-y}$$

That doesn't match any of the choices, so multiply by -1:

$$\frac{\sqrt{x}-\sqrt{x+y}}{-y} \times \frac{-1}{-1} = \frac{\sqrt{x+y}-\sqrt{x}}{y}, \text{ choice (E)}.$$

99.   E

EXPL: It's far from clear at the outset how you'll find the value of $9x^2$, but it's usually the case that you have to get rid of the radical signs to accomplish anything. You can start down that path by squaring both sides of the equation:

$$\left(\sqrt{3-x}\right)^2 = \left(1-\sqrt{2x}\right)^2$$
$$3 - x = 1 + 2x - 2\sqrt{2x}$$
$$2\sqrt{2x} = 3x - 2$$

There's still a radical, so square both sides again:

$$\left(2\sqrt{2x}\right)^2 = (3x-2)^2$$
$$4(2x) = 9x^2 - 12x + 4$$
$$9x^2 = 20x - 4, \text{ choice (E)}.$$

Questions like this are fairly reliable in that, if they ask for something non-traditional, such as $9x^2$, a textbook-style solution will lead you to that expression, as it did in this case.

180   Explanations: Lines and Angles: Drill

1.   The following questions refer to the diagram above:
- a.   Which of the line segments are perpendicular?
   EC and AF
- b.   What is the degree measure of $\angle AFC$?
   90
- c.   If the degree measure of $\angle BFC$ is 35°, what is the degree measure of $\angle AFB$?
   $90 - 35 = 55$
- d.   If the degree measure of $\angle BFC$ is 30°, what is the degree measure of $\angle EFD$?
   30
- e.   If the degree measure of $\angle AFB$ is 65°, what is the degree measure of $\angle DFC$?
   If $\angle AFB = 65$, then $\angle EFA = 65 + 90 = 155$. $\angle DFC$ and $\angle EFA$ are vertical angles, so $\angle DFC = 155$.

2.   The following questions refer to the diagram above, in which lines l_1 and l_2 are parallel, and lines k_1 and k_2 are parallel:
- a.   If $a = 120$, what is the value of d?
   120
- b.   If $g = 70$, what is the value of h?
   110
- c.   If $m = 112$, what is the value of w?
   112
- d.   If $x = 75$, what is the value of h?
   105
- e.   If $y = 72$, what is the value of b?
   72

181   Explanations: Lines and Angles: Practice

101.   A

EXPL: The angles $4x$ and $5x$ compose a straight line, so they sum to 180:

$4x + 5x = 180$

$9x = 180$

$x = 20$

Thus, $4x = 80$. Since $4x$ and $y - 40$ are vertical angles, they are equal. Thus:

$y - 40 = 80$

$y = 120$, choice (A).

102.   D

EXPL: To see the relationships between the angles in the figure, call the angle just to the left of b angle a. a is related to every other named angle in the figure: $b + a = 180$; a and d are vertical angles, so $a = d$; because l_1 and l_2 are parallel, $a = c$. Since all of the angles are related, you only need the measure of any one angle to determine the measure of c.

Statement (1) is sufficient: from b, you can find a, which gives you c. Statement (2) is also sufficient: from d, you can find a, which gives you c. Choice (D) is correct.

103.   E

EXPL: There are three distinct variables in the diagram: the measures of $\angle ABX$, $\angle XBY$, and $\angle YBC$. The sum of the three is what we're seeking.

Statement (1) is insufficient. $\angle ABY$ is the sum of $\angle ABX$ and $\angle XBY$; to answer the question, we'd need to know the measure of $\angle YBC$. Statement (2) is insufficient for a similar reason: $\angle XBC$ is the sum of $\angle XBY$ and $\angle YBC$; to answer the question, we'd need the know the measure of $\angle ABX$.

Taken together, the statements are still insufficient. We have two equations with three variables:

$\angle ABX + \angle XBY = 85$

$\angle XBY + \angle YBC = 95$

There's no way to find the values of the individual angles, so no way to determine the measure of $\angle ABC$. (E) is the correct choice.

104.   A

EXPL: You should recognize that y, and z are all equal. x and y are complementary angles, and because lines k and m are parallel, $z = y$. Thus, to find x, you only need the measure of one of the angles.

Statement (1) is sufficient: since $y = z$ and $x + y = 180$, $x = 70$. Statement (2) is insufficient: we established that $y = z$ before we even looked at this statement. (A) is the correct choice.

105.   C

EXPL: Statement (1) gives you two equations:

$\angle ABX = \angle XBY$

$\angle ABY = \angle YBC$

That's insufficient, because we don't have any actual measures of angles yet. Statement (2) is also insufficient: we can't find $\angle ABC$ from the measure of one part of it.

Taken together, the statements are sufficient. If $\angle XBY = 35$, then $\angle ABX = 35$, and $\angle ABY = 70$. If $\angle ABY = 70$, $\angle YBC = 70$, so $\angle ABC = 140$. (C) is the correct choice.

182   Explanations: Triangles: Drill

1.   True or False:
   a.   An equilateral triangle must be an isoceles triangle.
       True
   b.   An isoceles triangle can be a right triangle.
       True
   c.   An equilateral triangle can be a right triangle.
       False

2.   area $= \frac{1}{2}bh = \frac{1}{2}(6)(\frac{5}{2}) = \frac{30}{4} = \frac{15}{2}$

3. $35 = \frac{1}{2}(14)h$
      $35 = 7h$
      $h = 5$

4.   The next two questions refer to the diagram above:
   a.   The base is 4 and the height is 5, so area $= \frac{1}{2}(4)(5) = 2(5) = 10$

   b.   While the height is not inside the triangle, the height is the same as the height of triangle BCD. So the area is the same. Base = 4 and height = 5, so area $= \frac{1}{2}(4)(5) = 2(5) = 10$

5.   No, the third side must be less than 10.

6.   Yes, the third side must be more than 6.

7.   The third side must be between the difference and the sum of the first two sides, 1 and 5.

183   Explanations: Triangles: Practice

111.   A

EXPL: The third side of a triangle must be greater than the difference between the lengths of the other two sides and less than the sum of the other two sides. Thus, the third side of this triangle must be greater than $7 - 4 = 3$, and less than $4 + 7 = 11$:

$3 < x < 11$

The only roman numeral that satisfies that inequality is II, so (A) is the correct choice.

112.   B

EXPL: The angles of a triangle sum to 180, so $\angle ABC + \angle BCA + \angle CAB = 180$. The second two of those angles are given: y and 65, respectively. The first is the sum of two angles: x and 42. So, we can set up an equation with the information given:

$(x + 42) + y + 65 = 180$
$107 + x + y = 180$
$x + y = 73$, choice (B).

113.   B

EXPL: To determine which angle is the largest, you need to figure out which side is the longest. The angle that corresponds to that longest side is the greatest of the three. However, there are two variables. While you could figure out that a side with length $2x$ is longer than one with length x, you have no way of comparing y to either x or $2x$.

Statement (1) is insufficient. The right angle must be the greatest of the three, but you don't know whether than corresponds to the side of y or the side of $2x$.

Statement (2) is sufficient: if $2x$ is greater than y, we know that $2x$ is the longest side, since $2x$ must be greater than x. Choice (B) is correct.

184   Explanations: Triangles: Challenge

114.   D

EXPL: Since $\angle BDC$ and $\angle ADB$ compose a straight line, $\angle ADB = 180 - 2x$. We can also determine that $\angle CBD = 180 - 2x - 2x = 180 - 4x$. Using the three angles of the triangle ABC, we can find that $\angle ABC = 180 - x - 2x = 180 - 3x$. Since $\angle ABC$ is the sum of $\angle CBD$ and $\angle DBA$:

$$\angle ABD = \angle ABC - \angle CBD = 180 - 3x - (180 - 4x) = -3x + 4x = x$$

After doing all that work, the conclusion is simple: we know every single angle in the figure in terms of x. Thus, to find x, all we need is the measure of any angle in the figure.

Statement (1) is sufficient: we know that $\angle ABD = x$, so it's the same as $\angle DAB$. Statement (2) is also sufficient: we know that $\angle DBC = 180 - 4x$, so we can solve for x, which will give us $\angle DAB$. The correct choice is (D).

115.   E

EXPL: Statement (1) is insufficient. It allows us to determine that $\angle DAC = \angle DCA = 20$, but that doesn't give us any information about $\triangle ABC$. Statement (2) is also insufficient: it may prove helpful, but in order to solve this problem, we need some number to start with.

Taken together, the statements are still insufficient. Since $\angle DCA = 20$, $\angle BCA = 40$. Since $\triangle ABC$ is isoceles, two of the angles in the triangle are equal, but we don't know which ones. It may be that $\angle BCA = \angle BAC$, in which case $x = 180 - 40 - 40 = 100$. However, it could also be the case that $\angle BAC = \angle ABC$, in which case $180 = 40 + x + x$, so $x = 70$. Choice (E) is correct.

116.   D

EXPL: In either a square or an equilateral triangle, you can find out just about any measurement from any other measurement. In a square, for instance, the length of a side can give you area, perimeter, or the length of the diagonal. In an equilateral triangle, the base and height are always related in the same ratio, so knowing the area gives you perimeter, the length of the height, or the length of any side.

Statement (1), then, is sufficient. If you know the ratio of the areas, you can determine the ratio of the perimeters. To do so, you'd have to find the ratio between the perimeter of a square and the area of a square, and also the perimeter of an equilateral triangle and the area of an equilateral triangle. While you won't spend the time to do so on this question, the fact that you could means that the given ratio is sufficient.

Statement (2) is also sufficient. Again, since sides of squares and equilateral triangles always have the same ratios to the perimeters of the same figures, knowing the ratio between the sides of these two figures is enough to determine the relationship between the perimeters of the figures. Choice (D) is correct.

185   Explanations: Right Triangles: Drill

1.   Each of the following refers to the diagram above:

  a.   If AB=3 and AC=4, BC=
        It's a pythagorean triplet: $BC = 5$

  b.   If AB=8 and BC=10, AC=
        This is also a triplet: $AC = 6$

  c.   If AB=2 and AC=5, BC=
        $$2^2 + 5^2 = c^2$$
        $$c^2 = 29$$
        $$c = \sqrt{29}$$

  d.   If AC=5 and AB=12, BC=
        This is a triplet: $BC = 13$

  e.   If $AC = 3$ and $BC = 3\sqrt{5}$, AB=
        $$3^2 + b^2 = (3\sqrt{5})^2$$
        $$9 + b^2 = 45$$
        $$b^2 = 36$$
        $$b = 6$$

2.   If each leg of isoceles right triangle XYZ has a length of 4, what is the perimeter of the XYZ?

  If the leg of an isoceles right triangle is 4, the hypotenuse is $4\sqrt{2}$. The perimeter, then, is $4 + 4 + 4\sqrt{2} = 8 + 4\sqrt{2}$.

3.   The shortest side of 30:60:90 triangle MNP is $2\sqrt{3}$.   What is the perimeter of MNP?

  The ratio of the side lengths in a 30:60:90 is $x : x\sqrt{3} : 2x$.   If $x = 2\sqrt{3}$, then $x\sqrt{3} = 2\sqrt{3}(\sqrt{3}) = 2(3) = 6$, and $2x = 4\sqrt{3}$.   The perimeter is $2\sqrt{3} + 6 + 4\sqrt{3} = 6 + 6\sqrt{3}$

4.   What is the length of the diagonal of a square with a side of 6?

  In other words: what is the hypotenuse of an isoceles right triangle with legs of 6? Using the ratio, $6\sqrt{2}$.

5.   What is the area of an equilateral triangle with a side length of 4?

  If you draw the height of an equilateral, each half of the triangle is a 30:60:90 triangle. If the base is 4, the base of either of the 30:60:90's is 2, the x in the side ratio. The height is the longer leg, $x\sqrt{3}$. If $x = 2$, the longer leg is $2\sqrt{3}$. That's the height, so the area $= \frac{1}{2}bh = \frac{1}{2}(4)(2\sqrt{3}) = 4\sqrt{3}$.

  [diagram]

6.   In the figure above, if $CD = 3\sqrt{6}$, what is the length of side BD?

  ACD is an isoceles right triangle, so if $AD = x$, then $CD = x\sqrt{2}$. To find AD, divide $3\sqrt{6}$ by $\sqrt{2}$:
  $$\frac{3\sqrt{2}\sqrt{3}}{\sqrt{2}} = 3\sqrt{3}$$

  AD is also the longer leg of a 30:60:90 for which BD is the hypotenuse. Thus, if $AD = x\sqrt{3}$, $BD = 2x$. If $AD = 3\sqrt{3}$, then $x = 3$, and $BD = 2(3) = 6$.

186   Explanations: Right Triangles: Practice

121.   A

EXPL: Any triangle for which $a^2 + b^2 = c^2$ is true is a right triangle: that equation is the pythagorean theorem. The question, then, is equivalent to: is the triangle above a right triangle? It looks like one, but on the GMAT, we need more proof than that.

Statement (1) is sufficient: if $b = c$ are equal, c cannot be the hypotenuse: the hypotenuse of a right triangle must be larger than either of the two legs. The answer to the question is "no."

Statement (2) is insufficient: knowing that y is greater than x doesn't tell us whether the triangle is right or not. It could be, if the values of x and y were 40 and 50, respectively; however, if x and y were 30 and 40, respectively, the third angle would be 110, and the triangle would not be right. (A) is the correct choice.

122.   C

EXPL: Statement (1) is insufficient: it tells us that $lw = 24$, but in order to find the length of the diagonal, we need the precise values of l and w. Statement (2) is also insufficient: a relationship between l and w isn't enough to find the actual length of the diagonal.

Taken together, the statements are sufficient. We have two equations with the variables l and w, so we can find each of their values. Once we have the length and width of the rectangle, we can use the pythagorean theorem to find the diagonal, which is the hypotenuse of a triangle with sides that are the length and width of the rectangle. Choice (C) is correct.

123.   C

EXPL: Statements (1) and (2) are both insufficient on their own. Knowing the length of one side of a triangle–even in a right triangle–is never enough to find the perimeter of the whole thing.

Taken together, the statements are sufficient. Since the two given sides are equal, those must be the legs. Thus, we can use the pythagorean theorem to find the hypotenuse; in fact, we don't even have to use the formula, because since the sides are equal, we know it's a $45 : 45 : 90$, with a side ratio of $x : x : x\sqrt{2}$, meaning that the hypotenuse is $11\sqrt{2}$. Knowing the length of all three sides, we can find the perimeter. (C) is the correct choice.

187   Explanations: Right Triangles: Challenge

124.   A

EXPL: Because the two triangles are a 45 : 45 : 90 and a 30 : 60 : 90, respectively, we know the ratio of one side to any other within each triangle. Further, since the two positions of the support beam (the hypotenuses of the two triangles) are of equal length, we know the ratio of any side in either of the triangles to any other side in either of the triangles. In other words, if the ratio of the 45 : 45 : 90 is $x : x : x\sqrt{2}$ and the ratio of the 30 : 60 : 90 is $x : x\sqrt{3} : 2x$, the $x\sqrt{2}$ in the first is the same as the $2x$ in the second.

Statement (1) is sufficient. We can rewrite the ratio of the 45 : 45 : 90 by multiplying each part by $\sqrt{2}$, making the ratio $x\sqrt{2} : x\sqrt{2} : 2x$, so that each of the two equal hypotenuses are $2x$. Thus, in terms of x:

$$SU = SV - UV$$
$$SU = x\sqrt{3} - x\sqrt{2} = x(\sqrt{3} - \sqrt{2})$$

Knowing the length of SU, we can find the value of x. From the value of x, we can find the length of any side (or difference between sides) in the figure.

Statement (2) is insufficient. We've established already that we know all of the side ratios, even across different triangles. Further, in order to find an actual length, we need some length; otherwise, we have no idea of the size of the figure. Choice (A) is correct.

125.   C

Statement (1) is insufficent. TU and UV must be the equal sides. However, we don't know anything about the third side: it could be very small, or as large as 35.9. (Just less than the sum of the other two sides.)

Statement (2) is also insufficient. If one angle is 90 degrees, the triangle is a right triangle. That doesn't tell us any lengths, though.

Taken together, the statements are sufficient. The side opposite the right angle is TV, the side that isn't specified by (1). Thus, we're dealing with an isoceles right triangle, and we should be familiar with the side ratio of such triangles. If the legs are each 9, the hypotenuse is $9\sqrt{2}$, so we can find the perimeter. Choice (C) is correct.

126.   D

Explanation: If two of the angles are 45, the other angle is 90. We're dealing, then, with an isoceles right triangle, one with angles of 45, 45, and 90. That means that the sides have a ratio of $x : x : x\sqrt{2}$.

Statement (1) is sufficient. The area of a triangle is $\frac{1}{2}bh$, and in a right triangle, the base and height are the legs. In this triangle, the legs are equal, so we can solve:

$$\frac{1}{2}x^2 = 18$$
$$x^2 = 36$$
$$x = 6$$

Since each leg is 6, the hypotenuse is $6\sqrt{2}$, so we can calculate the perimeter.

Statement (2) is also sufficient. Once we know the hypotenuse, we can use the side ratio to determine that the legs are each 6. Again, we can calculate the perimeter. Choice (D) is correct.

188   Explanations: Quadrilaterals: Drill

1.   True or False:
      a.   A rectangle is a square.
            False
      b.   A rectangle is a quadrilateral.
            True

3.   If a square has a side length of $5\sqrt{2}$, what is its area?
      $a = s^2 = (5\sqrt{2})^2 = 25(2) = 50$

4.   Rectangle MNPQ has sides measuring 9 inches and 16 inches. What is the perimeter of MNPQ?
      $p = 2l + 2w = 2(9) + 2(16) = 18 + 32 = 50$

5.   If square ABCD has a perimeter of 18, what is its area?
      $p = 4s = 18$
      $s = \frac{9}{2}$
      $a = s^2 = (\frac{9}{2})^2 = \frac{81}{4}$

6.   Find the perimeter and area of each of the following:
      a. $p = 2l + 2w = 2(3\sqrt{2}) + 2(6\sqrt{2}) = 6\sqrt{2} + 12\sqrt{2} = 18\sqrt{2}$
            $a = lw = (3\sqrt{2})(6\sqrt{2}) = 18(2) = 36$
      b. $p = 5 + 8 + 4 + 10 = 27$
            $a = (\frac{b_1 + b_2}{2})h = (\frac{8+10}{2})4 = 9(4) = 36$
      c. $p = 4 + 5 + 10 + 5 = 24$
            $a = (\frac{b_1 + b_2}{2})h = (\frac{4+10}{2})4 = 7(4) = 28$
      d.   Draw a dotted line from point X perpendicular to YZ, and call the intersection point A. It has a length of 6 (like WY) and creates a 45:45:90 triangle with hypotenuse XZ. If XA's length is 6, AZ's length is 6 as well. YA = 8, so YZ = 8 + 6 = 14.

            XZ is the hypotenuse of a 45:45:90 triangle with legs of length 6, so its length is $6\sqrt{2}$.
            $p = 6 + 8 + 6\sqrt{2} + 14 = 28 + 6\sqrt{2}$
            $a = (\frac{b_1 + b_2}{2})h = (\frac{8+14}{2})6 = 11(6) = 66$
      e.   Draw a dotted line from point A perpendicular to CD, and call the intersection point X. Do the same from point B, and call the intersection point Y. ACX and BDY are both $30 : 60 : 90$ triangles. In each case, the hypotenuse is 2, so using the side ratio, $2x = 2$, so the short sides (CX and DY) are 1. Since XY is 5, the length of CD is $1 + 5 + 1 = 7$. The height of the figure is equal to either of the lines you drew, which is equal to $x\sqrt{3} = \sqrt{3}$.
            $p = 2 + 5 + 2 + 7 = 16$
            $a = (\frac{b_1 + b_2}{2})h = (\frac{5+7}{2})\sqrt{3} = 6\sqrt{3}$

189   Explanations: Quadrilaterals: Practice

131.   **B**

EXPL: First, find the area of panel C. Area is length times width, so:

$a_c = lw = 9(8) = 72$

If that area is double the area of panel D, the area of panel D is $\frac{72}{2} = 36$. Since the area of D is 36 and D is a square, each side of D must be $\sqrt{36} = 6$, choice (B).

132.   **B**

EXPL: Statement (1) is insufficient: because RU is parallel to ST, we already know that any two lines that connect those two sides and are perpendicular to RU must be equal. So if $SV = 80$, as we are given, TW must be 80 as well. (1) is not only insufficient, it won't help us find the answer, so (C) can't be the answer.

Statement (2) is sufficient. To find the area, we need the length of both bases (ST, which we have, and RU, which we don't) and the height (which we have: SV). Since we know that TW is 80 (not because of (1), but because it must be equal to SV) and that $\triangle TWU$ is a right triangle, we can use the hypotenuse of $10\sqrt{17}$ to find the other leg, WU. Since $STVW$ is a rectangle, VW must be 50, so once we find WU, we can compute the length of base RU: $RV + VW + WU$. Choice (B) is correct.

133.   **B**

EXPL: Each rectangular area is given by length times width, so we can set up the equation as follows:

$area_A = area_B$
$l_A w_A = l_B w_B$
$9(16) = l_B(8)$
$l_B = \frac{9(16)}{8} = 9(2) = 18$, choice (B).

134.   **C**

EXPL: Start by finding the area of one side, then double it. The area of one side is given by length times width:

$a = lw = 5(3.5)$

Rather than multiplying that out, jump ahead to the next step and double that area:

$2(5)(3.5) = 10(3.5) = 35$, choice (C).

135.   **D**

Explanation: The area of the mirror is $42(42)$. The area of the wall is $56(x)$, where x is the length of the wall. Since the wall has twice the area of the mirror, we can set up an equation:

$56(x) = 2(42)(42)$
$4(x) = 2(42)(3)$

$x = 21(3) = 63$, choice (D).

Note that we never multipled $2(42)(42)$; the question allowed us to simplify by cancelling out common factors.

190   Explanations: Circles: Drill

1.   If Circle O has a radius of 3, find the following:
    a. $d = 2r = 2(3) = 6$
    b. $p = 2\pi r = 2\pi(3) = 6\pi$
    c. $a = \pi r^2 = \pi(3)^2 = 9\pi$

2.   If Circle O has an area of 9π, find the following:
    a. $9\pi = \pi r^2$
$$9 = r^2$$
$$r = 3$$
    b. $d = 2r = 2(3) = 6$
    c. $p = 2\pi r = 2\pi(3) = 6\pi$

3.   If Circle O has a perimeter of 6, find the following:
    a. $6 = 2\pi r$
$$r = \frac{6}{2\pi} = \frac{3}{\pi}$$
    b. $d = 2r = 2(\frac{3}{\pi}) = \frac{6}{\pi}$
    c. $a = \pi r^2 = \pi(\frac{3}{\pi})^2 = 9/\pi$

4.   The following questions refer to the figure above:
    a.   What fraction of the circle is shaded?
$$\frac{150}{360} = \frac{15}{36} = \frac{5}{12}$$
    b.   What is the area of the shaded region?
$$\frac{5}{12}(\pi r^2) = \frac{5}{12}(\pi 12^2) = \frac{5}{12}(144)\pi = 5(12)\pi = 60\pi$$
    c.   What is the length of minor arc AB?
$$\frac{5}{12}(2\pi r) = \frac{5}{12}(2\pi 12) = 10\pi$$

5.   The following questions refer to the figure above:
    a.   What is the diameter of circle O?

The diameter of circle O is the diagonal of square ABCD. Draw the diagonal, and triangle ABD is a 45 : 45 : 90 right triangle. Thus, if the side has length 8, the diagonal (and the diameter of the circle) has length $8\sqrt{2}$.

    b.   What is the area of circle O?

If the diameter is $8\sqrt{2}$, the radius is $4\sqrt{2}$. $a = \pi r^2 = \pi(4\sqrt{2})^2 = 32\pi$

    c.   What is the sum of the areas of the shaded regions?

The shaded regions represent the difference between the area of the circle and the area of the square. We've already figured out the area of the circle, and the area of the square is $8^2 = 64$. The difference is $32\pi - 64$.

191   Explanations: Circles: Practice

141.   E

EXPL: Almost always, chords are not helpful when trying to calculate the more common measures of circles. Statement (1) is insufficient: knowing that P is the midpoint of AB doesn't help us understand the relationships between the various line segments; it also doesn't give us any idea of the size of the circle, which we'd need to calculate the radius.

Statement (2) is also insufficient. We don't know how the length of PQ relates to the length of OQ, the radius, so it's not helpful.

Taken together, the statements are still sufficient. To answer the question, we'd need some indication of the ratio between OP and PQ, which we don't have. Choice (E) is correct.

142.   E

EXPL: Questions like this require some creativity on your part: if you're exploring a number of possibilities, especially in geometry, it's helpful to picture them on your scratch paper. The line segments could intersect a circle at one point if the lines met at a point of tangency with the circle:

If the lines met at a point of tangency, but one of the lines extended downward and intersected with the circle again, you'd have two points of intersection:

If you return to the first diagram, but move one of the lines downward, you'll get three points of intersection:

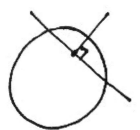

And finally, if you draw the line segments as a sort of "x" through the middle of the circle, there will be four points of intersection:

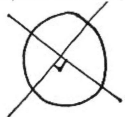

The correct choice is (E).

143. A

EXPL: Statement (1) is sufficient. If O is the center and the radius of the circle is 5, any point that lies less than 5 away from O must be inside the circle. So if $ON = 4$, that means N is 4 away from the center of the circle, so it must be inside the circle.

Statement (2) is insufficient. The statement tells us nothing whatsoever about the location of N.

Choice (A) is correct.

144. D

EXPL: If you're given one piece of information about a circle, you can usually find out everything else. Thus, given the relationship between the perimeters of T and W, you only need one piece of concrete information (a length, or an area) about either one to find the area of T.

Statement (1) gives you that: from the area of W, you could find the radius of W, which would give you the perimeter of W. The question tells you how to convert that into the perimeter of T, which would give you the radius of T, from which you could calculate the area of T.

Statement (2) is also sufficient. Skipping the first two steps of the process described for (1) above, you could use the perimeter of W to find the area of T. Choice (D) is correct.

145. B

EXPL: Statement (1) is insufficient: while the relationship between the larger and smaller region could come in handy combined with another piece of information, it doesn't give you any actual numbers. To find a radius, you need some number that represents the size of the smaller region, such as a perimeter or area.

Statement (2) is sufficient. The difference between the area and the circumference of the smaller region can be expressed as:

$\pi r^2 - 2\pi r = 24\pi$

And then you can solve for r:

$r^2 - 2r = 24$

$r^2 - 2r - 24 = 0$

$(r - 6)(r + 4) = 0$

$r = 6$ or $r = -4$

Since a radius can't be negative, the radius of the smaller region must be 6. Choice (B) is correct.

192   Explanations; Circles: Challenge

146.   C

Any time you're given a geometry question describing a figure, it's a good idea to draw it. In this case, the diagram shows a triangle formed by OA, OB, and AB, where OA and OB are radiuses of the circle and AB is a chord of the circle.

Statement (1) is insufficient: This tells us that OA and OB are equal to 5, but we don't know how those lengths relate to AB.

Statement (2) is also insufficient. Because OA = OB, triangle OAB is isoceles, meaning that angles OAB and OBA are equal. If AOB is 60, the sum of the other two is 120, which tells us that the triangle is equilateral. Without any lengths, though, we can't find the length of AB.

Taken together, the statements are sufficient. If we know the triangle is equilateral and the length of two of the sides is 5, we know the third side also has a length of 5. Choice (C) is correct.

147.   C

If a point is 12 inches from the center of a rim and it rotates in a circle, 12 inches represents the radius of a circle, and the distance traveled in one rotation is the circumference of the circle. To find the circumference:

$c = 2\pi r = 24\pi$

If the tire turns 250 times per minute, the distance traveled in one minute is:

$24\pi(250)$

We want to know how far the point travels in 10 seconds, which is one-sixth of a minute. So we'll divide the distance by 6:

$\frac{24\pi(250)}{6} = 4\pi(250) = 1,000\pi$, choice (C).

193   Explanations: Solids: Drill

1.   What is the volume of a cube with a side of 6?
$$v = s^3 = 6^3 = 216$$

2.   If one face of a cube has an area of 20, what is the volume of the cube?
The side has length $\sqrt{20} = 2\sqrt{5}$, so:
$$v = s^3 = (2\sqrt{5})^3 = 40\sqrt{5}$$

3.   What is the surface area of a cube with a side of $\sqrt{2}$?
$$sa = 6s^2 = 6(\sqrt{2})^2 = 12$$

4.   What is the volume of a rectangular solid with dimensions 3, 4, and 5?
$$v = lwh = 3(4)(5) = 60$$

5.   What is the volume of a rectangular solid that has a square base with an area of 12 and a height of 9?
Rather than using lwh, you can substitute the area of the base for lw.
$$v = area(h) = 12(9) = 108$$

6.   If a rectangular solid has a height of 5, a width of 6, and a length of 10, what is its surface area?
$$sa = 2lw + 2lh + 2wh = 2(10)(6) + 2(10)(5) + 2(6)(5) = 120 + 100 + 60 = 280$$

7.   If one rectangular solid has a volume of 60, what is the volume of another rectangular solid with twice the width, twice the length, and half the height of the first?
First solid: $lwh = 60$
Second solid: $(2l)(2w)(\frac{1}{2}h) = 2lwh = 2(60) = 120$

8.   What is the volume of a cylindrical solid with a radius of 4 and a height of 12?
$$v = \pi r^2 h = \pi(4^2)12 = \pi(16)(12) = 192\pi$$

9.   If the base of a cylinder has an area of 16π and the height of the cylinder is 9, what is the volume of the cylinder?
As with rectangular solids, you can replace πr^2 with the area of the base:
$$v = area(h) = (16\pi)(9) = 144\pi$$

10.   What is the surface area of a cylinder with a diameter of 6 and a height of 12?
First, be careful: if the diameter is 6, the radius is 3.
$$sa = 2(\pi r^2) + 2\pi rh = 2\pi(3^2) + 2\pi(3)(12) = 18\pi + 72\pi = 90\pi$$

194   Explanations: Solids: Practice

151.   E

EXPL: The volume of the Type A units is given as follows:

$$72 = lwh$$

The Type B units have double the length, width, and height, so their volume is:

$$v = (2l)(2w)(2h) = 8lwh$$

Since $lwh = 72$, we can substitute that back into the new volume equation:

$$v = 8lwh = 8(72) = 576,$$ choice (E).

152.   E

EXPL: The volume of the original solid is given as follows:

$$x = lwh$$

If the length and width are each increased by 50%, each is multiplied by 1.5. If the height is increased by 300%, that means it is now 4 times larger than before, so it is multiplied by 4. The new volume, then, is:

$$v = (1.5l)(1.5w)(4h) = (1.5)(1.5)(4)lwh = 9lwh$$

Since $lwh = x$, we can substitute x into that equation:

$$v = 9lwh = 9x,$$ choice (E).

153.   C

EXPL: To find the height of the box, you need to find either the length and the width of the box, or the area of the base of the box. (Of course, from the first, you can find the second.)

Statement (1) is insufficient: you would need to couple that information with the length of the box to find the height. Statement (2) is also insufficient: it provides no actual length for any side of the box.

Taken together, the statements are sufficient. If the box has a square base, the length and width are equal, meaning that if the width of the box is $2\sqrt{2}$, the length must be the same. From there, we can find the area of the base: $(2\sqrt{2})^2 = 8$, and find the height by dividing the volume by the area of the base: $\frac{32}{8} = 4$ feet. (C) is the correct choice.

195 Explanations: Solids: Challenge

154.   C

EXPL: Since each face of the container has an equal size (the dimensions are 8x8), it doesn't matter which face we use for the base of the canister. If the canister uses the entire width of the 8x8 face for it's base, the diameter is 8, so the radius is 4, and the area of the base is $\pi r^2 = \pi(4)^2 = 16\pi$. The maximum height is the third dimension: also 8. Thus, the volume of the largest possible canister is the product of the area of the canister's base and it's height:

$v = 16\pi(8) = 128\pi$, choice (C).

155.   C

To find the surface area of a cylindrical solid, you need two variables: the radius (or the diameter, or the area of the base of the container) and the height. Statement (1) is insufficient: it gives you an equation that contains those two variables:

$v = 45\pi = \pi r^2 h$

There are an infinite number of possible solutions for r and h, so there's no single answer for the surface area of the container.

Statement (2) is also insufficient: while we could find the radius from the diameter, we have no way of determining the height.

Taken together, the statements are sufficient. Since we know the volume:

$45\pi = \pi r^2 h$

We can use the radius (half of the diameter: $\frac{6}{2} = 3$) to find the height:

$45\pi = \pi(3)^2 h$

$45\pi = 9\pi h$

$h = 5$

Now that we have the height and the radius, we can solve for surface area. (C) is the correct choice.

156.   E

Explanation: The largest possible rectangular solid has the base overlapping the base of the cylinder, and the same height. (The entire height of the cylinder.)

The largest rectangular base is a square inscribed in the circular base. So, the diameter of the circular base is equal to the diagonal of that square. If the radius is 6 feet, the diameter, along with the diagonal, is 12 feet. The diagonal of a square forms a $45 : 45 : 90$ triangle with two of the sides, so the ratio of the sides of the the square to the length of the diagonal is $x : x\sqrt{2}$.

So, if $12 = x\sqrt{2}$, then x, the side of the square, is $\frac{12}{\sqrt{2}} = \frac{12\sqrt{2}}{2} = 6\sqrt{2}$. Now we know the three dimensions of the largest possible rectangular solid: $6\sqrt{2}$, $6\sqrt{2}$, and the height, 10. The volume is the product of those three numbers:

$(6\sqrt{2})(6\sqrt{2})(10) = 720$, choice (E).

157.   D

EXPL: The greatest distance between two points in a cube is between two points that diagonal to each other, both side to side and top to bottom. For instance, if one of the points is the bottom left front corner, the other point must be the top right back corner.

To find the distance of that diagonal diagonal line, first you need to find the diagonal of one face. For instance, if you wanted the diagonal of the base of the cube, you'd use the 45 : 45 : 90 triangle ratio to determine that the diagonal is $6\sqrt{2}$. Then, use that diagonal along with the height of the cube to form another right triangle, this time without a ratio to aid you. The legs have lengths of $6\sqrt{2}$ and 6, so the hypotenuse is given by the pythagorean theorem:

$(6\sqrt{2})^2 + 6^2 = c^2$

$72 + 36 = c^2$

$108 = c^2$

$c = \sqrt{108} = 6\sqrt{3}$, choice (D).

158.   E

To find the volume, we'll need all three dimensions.

Statement (1) is insufficient. Surface area is given by the following equation, and we can set it equal to 148:

$lw + lh + wh = 148$

That's three variables in one equation. We can't find the individual dimensions from that.

Statement (2) is also insufficient. We know that the product of two of the dimensions is 30, but without the third dimension, we can't find the volume.

Taken together, the statements are still insufficient. If we call the sides of the faces with area 30 l and w, we can rewrite the surface area equation like this:

$30 + lh + wh = 148$

That still isn't enough to answer the question. Choice (E) is correct.

196   Explanations: Coordinate Geometry: Drill

1.   For each of the following, find the slope of the line that runs through the two given points:

     a. $m = \frac{y_2 - y_1}{x_2 - x_1} = \frac{5-0}{5-0} = 1$

     b. $m = \frac{y_2 - y_1}{x_2 - x_1} = \frac{3-2}{2-3} = \frac{1}{-1} = -1$

     c. $m = \frac{y_2 - y_1}{x_2 - x_1} = \frac{1-(-7)}{-5-4} = \frac{8}{-9} = -\frac{8}{9}$

2.   For each of the following, find the equation of the line that runs through the two given points:

     a. $m = \frac{y_2 - y_1}{x_2 - x_1} = \frac{10-0}{0-(-4)} = \frac{10}{4} = \frac{5}{2}$

         The second point is the y-intercept, so $b = 10$:

         $y = \frac{5}{2}x + 10$

     b. $m = \frac{y_2 - y_1}{x_2 - x_1} = \frac{\frac{1}{2}-\frac{1}{2}}{\frac{3}{2}-(-\frac{3}{2})} = 0$

         $y = 0x + b$

         $y = \frac{1}{2}$

     c. $m = \frac{y_2 - y_1}{x_2 - x_1} = \frac{4-(-1)}{7-0} = \frac{5}{7}$

         $y = \frac{5}{7}x + b$

         $4 = \frac{5}{7}(7) + b$

         $4 = 5 + b$

         $b = -1$

         $y = \frac{5}{7}x - 1$

3. $y = \frac{1}{2}x + b$

     $-5 = \frac{1}{2}(-5) + b$

     $-5 + \frac{5}{2} = b$

     $-\frac{5}{2} = b$

     $y = \frac{1}{2}x - \frac{5}{2}$

4. $y = -\frac{4}{3}x + b$

     $2 = -\frac{4}{3}(-6) + b$

     $2 = 8 + b$

     $b = -6$

     $y = -\frac{4}{3}x - 6$

5.   Plug in $x = 10$ and see what the corresponding y-coordinate is:

     $y = \frac{2}{3}(10) - \frac{1}{2} = \frac{40}{6} - \frac{3}{6} = \frac{37}{6} = 6\frac{1}{6}$

     No.

6.   Even though the equation isn't in the traditional form, you can still test a point the way you did in (5).

     $x = 1 - \frac{\frac{1}{9}}{3} = 1 - \frac{1}{27} = \frac{26}{27}$

     No.

197 Explanations: Coordinate Geometry: Practice

161.   D
EXPL: If the graph is symmetric with respect to the y axis, the y-coordinate of the point where $x = 2$ must be the same as the y-coordinate of the point where $x = -2$, which is equidistant from $y = 0$ (the line of symmetry). Since $y = 1.25$ when $x = -2$, y must be 1.25 when $x = 2$. (D) is the correct choice.

162.   C
EXPL: To answer the question, you need to know whether x is positive or negative, and whether y is positive or negative. Statement (1) is insufficient: the sum of x and y could be negative if both are negative, or if one is negative and the absolute value of the negative variable is greater than the positive variable. Statement (2) is also insufficient: it tells us nothing about the value of x.

Taken together, the statements are sufficient. If $y = 7$, then:

$x + 7 < 0$

$x < -7$

x must be negative. If x is negative and y is positive, (x, y) is in quadrant II. The answer is (C).

163.   C
EXPL: To determine whether a given point lies on a certain line, you need the equation of the line. To find the equation, you need either two points, or one point and the slope. Both statements, on their own, are insufficient, as each provides only one point.

Taken together, they are sufficient: with two points, you can find the slope and then the equation of line k. With the equation of the line, you can figure out whether $(3, 9)$ lies on the line. Choice (C) is correct.

164.   A
Explanation: To find the distance of a line on the coordinate plane, you need the distance between the y coordinates of the two endpoints, and the distance between the x coordinates of the two endpoints. If you were to draw a right triangle where the line is the hypotenuse, the two differences would give you the length of a horizontal and vertical side of the triangle.

Thus, in this question, you need two things: the distance between m and n (the x-coordinates), and the distance between n and m (the y-coordinates). Of course, those are the same thing. so if you find one, you've found the other. Statement (1) is sufficient: it gives you both distances.

Statement (2) is insufficient: it doesn't give you either distance on its own. You don't need to look at both statements together. If you did, you could find the exact value of m and n, but that doesn't matter in calculating the distance between the two points.

198   Explanations: Coordinate Geometry: Challenge

165.   B

EXPL: This is an easier question to approximate than to work out precisely. We're aided in our approximation by the knowledge that the answer choices all contain round numbers. If the line bisects AB, we can draw in an approximation of AB that angles upward, perpendicular to the line $y = x$.

This puts B at approximately $(2, 3)$. If the y-axis bisects BC, that means that if the x-coordinate of point B is 2, the x-coordinate of point C must be -2 ($x = 0$ is right in the middle), so the approximate coordinates of point C are $(-2, 3)$, choice (B).

166.   D

EXPL: Statement (1) is sufficient: if the point is (0, -2) is the y-intercept, so we know it crosses the y-axis in negative territory.

Statement (2) is also sufficient. If a line goes down and to the right from a point to the left of the origin, it's not going to cross the y-axis above the origin no matter what the specific point or slope is. Choice (D) is correct.

167.   E

Explanation: To determine whether a point is on a given line (or line segment, as in this case), start by determining the equation of the line. To do that, find the slope. Given two points, find the difference in y and the difference in x:

$slope = \frac{4}{-8} = -\frac{1}{2}$

The equation of the line will look like this, then:

$y = -\frac{1}{2}x + b$

To find the value of b, plug in one of the points and solve:

$2 = -\frac{1}{2}(-3) + b$

$2 = \frac{3}{2} + b$

$b = \frac{1}{2}$

That's the y-intercept, which not only allows you to finish the equation of a line, but also eliminates one of the answer choices. $(0, \frac{1}{2})$ is on the line, so (B) cannot be correct. Our equation of the line is:

$y = -\frac{1}{2}x + \frac{1}{2}$

To find the answer, plug in the x value from each choice into that equation, and see if the resulting value of y matches the y value given in the choice:

(A) $y = -\frac{1}{2}(-1) + \frac{1}{2} = \frac{1}{2} + \frac{1}{2} = 1$ – on the line, so (A) is wrong.

(B)   Already established as on the line, this is the y-intercept.

(C) $y = -\frac{1}{2}(0) + \frac{1}{2} = \frac{1}{2}$ – on the line, so (C) is wrong.

(D) $y = -\frac{1}{2}(2) + \frac{1}{2} = -1 + \frac{1}{2} = -\frac{1}{2}$ – on the line, so (D) is wrong.

(E) $y = -\frac{1}{2}(4) + \frac{1}{2} = -2 + \frac{1}{2} = -\frac{3}{2}$.   If $(4, -\frac{3}{2})$ is on the line, then $(4, -1)$ cannot be. Choice (E) is correct.

168.   C

The question takes some time to understand, but it ultimately asks something rather straightforward. If a point is in the given region, its coordinates must fulfill the inequality $1 - x < 2y$. So, if the coordinates are (a, b), it must be true that $1 - a < 2b$. If that inequality is true, the point is in the region. If it is false, the point is not in the region. So the question boils down to: Is $1 - a < 2b$?

Statement (1) is insufficient. To get the variables on one side in the initial question, it's $1 < 2b + a$. To determine whether $2b + a$ is greater than 1, it doesn't matter which of a and $2b$ is greater. With the information in this statement, we don't know whether both are positive, both are negative, or anything else regarding their relationship to a concrete number such as 1.

Statement (2) is also insufficient. It does give us a number. We can simplify the question to: $1 - a < 2$? Or: Is $a > -1$? We don't know anything about a, however.

Taken together, the statements are sufficient. (2) tells us that we only need to know whether a is greater than -1. Since (1) tells us that a is greater than $2b$, and we know that $2b = 2$, a must be greater than 2. If it's greater than 2, it must be greater than -1, so we can answer the question. Choice (C) is correct.

169.   B

In the equation given, m is the slope, so we're looking for m.

Statement (1) is insufficient. Two parallel lines have the same slope, so we know that $m = m^2$. This is true if $m = 0$ or $m = 1$. Since we don't know which one, we can't answer the question. Note that if $m = 0$, the line is horizontal, parallel to the x-axis. The equation of the line would then be $y = 5$.

Statement (2) is sufficient. It tells us that the line we're interested in passes through the point $(-3, 2)$, which we can plug into the equation given:

$2 = m(-3) + 5$

$3m = 3$

$m = 1$

Choice (B) is correct.

199 Explanations: Polygons: Drill

1.   How many non-overlapping triangles can be created by drawing lines connecting the vertices of a(n)

      a.   pentagon?

           3

      b.   octagon?

           6

      c.   hexagon?

           4

      d.   quadrilateral?

           2

2.   What is the sum of the interior angles of a(n)

      a.   hexagon?

$$(6-2)(180) = 4(180) = 720$$

      b.   pentagon?

$$(5-2)(180) = 3(180) = 540$$

      c.   octagon?

$$(8-2)(180) = 6(180) = 1080$$

3.   What is the measure of a single interior angle in a regular

      a.   octagon?

$$\frac{(8-2)(180)}{8} = \frac{1080}{8} = 135$$

      b.   pentagon?

$$\frac{(5-2)(180)}{5} = \frac{540}{5} = 108$$

      c.   hexagon?

$$\frac{(6-2)(180)}{6} = \frac{720}{6} = 120$$

200   Explanations: Ratios: Drill

1.   Simplify each of the following ratios:

      a. $\frac{20}{8} = \frac{5}{2}$

      b. $\frac{54}{36} = \frac{3}{2}$

      c. $\frac{15}{25} = \frac{3}{5}$

2. $green : total = 5 : (5+3) = 5 : 8$

3. $women : total = 3 : (4+3) = 3 : 7$

4.   The ratio of under 21 to at least 21 is $1 : 3$

$$\frac{21+}{total} = \frac{3}{1+3} = \frac{3}{4} = 75\%$$

5.   If for every 5 ounces of solution there are two ounces of alcohol, that leaves three ounces of water. Thus, $water : alcohol = 3 : 2$.

6.   If $\frac{1}{4}$ are managers, $\frac{3}{4}$ are not managers. So, managers:non-managers $= \frac{1}{4} : \frac{3}{4} = 1 : 3$

7.   If 30% have blonde hair, 70% do not.

      $Notblonde : blonde = 70\% : 30\% = 7 : 3$

8. $A : total = 5 : (5+3+2) = 5 : 10 = 1 : 2$

9. $\frac{food}{total} = \frac{4}{3+4+9} = \frac{4}{16} = \frac{1}{4}$

10.   The given ratio of steak to chicken to fish is 1:2:5.

      $\frac{chicken}{total} = \frac{2}{1+2+5} = \frac{2}{8} = \frac{1}{4}$

11. $\frac{15}{1} = \frac{300}{x}$

      $15x = 300$

      $x = 20$

12.   You're given the number of total families and need to find the number who don't have children. First, find the ratio between those two quantities:

$$\frac{total}{no-children} = \frac{3+2}{2} = \frac{5}{2}$$

$$\frac{5}{2} = \frac{65}{x}$$

$$5x = 2(65)$$

$$x = 2(13) = 26$$

13.   The ratio of utilities stocks to total stocks is $1 : 5$. That means that, for every one utilities stock, there are four non-utilities stocks. The relevant fraction is $\frac{1}{4}$.

$$\frac{1}{4} = \frac{7}{x}$$

$$x = 28$$

14. $7(2) : 2 = 14 : 2 = 7 : 1$

15. $3(\frac{1}{2}) : 4 = \frac{3}{2} : 4 = 3 : 8$

16. $1(3) : 6 = 3 : 6 = 1 : 2$

17. $\frac{5x}{4x+2}$

18. $\frac{7x+10,000}{5x}$

201   Explanations: Ratios: Practice

181.   A

EXPL: When simplifying a ratio, treat it like a fraction. The ratio $\frac{3}{4}$ to $\frac{1}{8}$ is equal to this fraction:

$\frac{\frac{3}{4}}{\frac{1}{8}} = (\frac{3}{4})(\frac{8}{1}) = \frac{24}{4} = \frac{6}{1}$

The fraction $\frac{6}{1}$ is the same as the ratio 6 : 1, choice (A).

182.   E

EXPL: Statement (1) is insufficient. The rule of thumb here is that you can multiply and divide ratios and they behave in consistent ways, but if you add or subtract from them, they won't. If the statement said "x is half of y," it would be sufficient, but adding 3 means we can't determine the ratio of x to y.

Statement (2) is also insufficient: that the variables are integers doesn't tell us anything about their relationship.

Taken together, the statements are still insufficient. That the variables are integers doesn't change the explanation of insufficiency in (1); for proof, consider the following two possibilities:

$y = 10$, $x = 8$

$y = 4$, $x = 5$

Both of those pairs of variables satisfy both statements, but they result in very different ratios. (E) is the correct choice.

183.   E

EXPL: To find a three-part ratio, you'll need two distinct ratios; in this case, it would be sufficient to find the ratio of x to y and the ratio of y to z. (There are other possibilities, but the underlying rule is that two ratios are enough.)

Statement (1) is insufficient: not only does it not address z, but it doesn't give you a ratio at all. Statement (2) has the same problem: nothing about x, and no ratio.

Taken together, the statements are still insufficient. You could combine the statements to find the ratio of x and z, but you'd only have one ratio. To find the values of x, y, and z, you'd need three equations; to find the three-part ratio, you'd need two two-part ratios. The statements give you neither. (E) is the correct choice.

184.   C

EXPL: This is a ratio question. The rate given is $\frac{0.082}{1000}$, while we want to know how many children died out of a total of 2,000,000: $\frac{x}{2,000,000}$. To solve for x, set those equal to each other:

$\frac{0.082}{1000} = \frac{x}{2,000,000}$

Cross-multiply to isolate x:

$1000x = 2,000,000(0.082)$

$x = 2,000(0.082)$

$x = 2(82) = 164$, choice (C)

185.   D

Explanation: To find the number of students, find the fraction that the 9 seniors represent.   Seniors are the remaining fraction after subtracting the other three fractions from 1:

$$seniors = 1 - \frac{1}{6} - \frac{1}{4} - \frac{1}{3} = \frac{12}{12} - \frac{2}{12} - \frac{3}{12} - \frac{4}{12} = \frac{3}{12} = \frac{1}{4}$$

If 9 is one quarter of the total number of students:

$$9 = \frac{1}{4}s$$
$$s = 36, \text{ choice (D)}.$$

202   Explanations: Ratios: Challenge

186.   C

EXPL: If you modify a ratio by adding or subtracting from one of the numbers, you need introduce a variable into the mix. Instead of representing the original ratio as $\frac{5}{36}$, use $\frac{5x}{36x}$, which is equivalent, but represents the actual number of college graduates and non-college graduates. If 4 more non-college graduates were added, the new ratio would be $\frac{5x}{36x+4}$. Since the new ratio is $\frac{5}{38}$, we can set those equal to each other:

$$\frac{5x}{36x+4} = \frac{5}{38}$$
$$5x(38) = 5(36x + 4)$$
$$38x = 36x + 4$$
$$2x = 4$$
$$x = 2$$

Since x is a multiplier–it tells us what to do to the original ratio of 5 to 36 to get the actual original numbers, it's not yet the answer. We're looking for the original number of non-graduates, which was $36x = 36(2) = 72$, choice (C).

187.   D

Explanation: The initial ratio of salt to pepper is $3 : 30 = 1 : 10$. If that ratio is doubled, it becomes $2 : 10$, or $1 : 5$. The initial ratio of salt to oregano is $3 : 6 = 1 : 2$. If that ratio is halved, it comes $\frac{1}{2} : 2$, or $1 : 4$.

The ratio of salt to pepper is $1 : 5$, and ratio of salt to oregano is $1 : 4$, so the ratio of salt to pepper to oregono is $1 : 5 : 4$. We're given an amount of pepper and are looking for the corresponding amount of oregano, so we can set up an equation:

$$\frac{5}{4} = \frac{2.5}{x}$$
$$5x = 10$$
$$x = 2, \text{ choice (D)}.$$

188.   C

This one takes a lot of work. We'll need to combine the three ratios given to find the fourth ratio:

$$e : s = 5 : 2$$
$$p : s = 3 : 4$$
$$h : e = 5 : 3$$
$$p : h =?$$

First, combine the first two ratios by altering them so that they have an equal term. If we double the $e : s$ ratio, the s term in both of the first two ratios will be 4:

$$e : s = 10 : 4$$
$$p : s = 3 : 4$$
$$e : s : p = 10 : 4 : 3$$

Now we need to add in the h term. In the $e:s:p$ ratio, the e term is 10; in the $h:e$ ratio, the e term is 3. The easiest way to make them equal is to multiply every term in the first by 3 and every term in the second by 10:

$e:s:p = 30:12:9$

$h:e = 50:30$

$h:e:s:p = 50:30:12:9$

Finally, isolate the $p:h$ ratio:

$p:h = 9:50$, choice (C).

189.   E

It's best to think of this as a yes/no question. The student-teacher ratio in District 1 is:

$\frac{s_1}{t_1}$

The student-teacher ratio in District 2 is:

$\frac{s_2}{t_2}$

The question is equivalent to, "Is the student-teacher ratio in District 1 greater than that in District 2?"

$\frac{s_1}{t_1} > \frac{s_2}{t_2}$

Statements (1) and (2) are both insufficient on their own. To answer the question, we need to know about both the numbers of students and the numbers of teachers. Neither statement gives us both.

Taken together, the statements are still insufficient. Combined, we know that District 1 has more students and more teachers. That could mean that either district has the higher ratio. For instance:

$\frac{200}{10} > \frac{50}{5}$

By contrast:

$\frac{200}{10} < \frac{150}{3}$

Choice (E) is correct.

203   Explanations: Percents: Drill

1.   Convert each of the following to the equivalent percent:
   - a. $0.56 = 56\%$
   - b. $0.001 = 0.1\%$
   - c. $\frac{4}{5} = 80\%$
   - d. $\frac{3}{20}\left(\frac{5}{5}\right) = \frac{15}{100} = 15\%$
   - e. $\frac{16}{25}\left(\frac{4}{4}\right) = \frac{64}{100} = 64\%$

2.   Given the following values of x of y, what percent of x is y?
   - a. $x = 50$, $y = 32$
     $$\frac{32}{50}\left(\frac{2}{2}\right) = \frac{64}{100} = 64\%$$
   - b. $x = 6$, $y = 1$
     $$\frac{1}{6} = 16\tfrac{2}{3}\%$$
   - c. $x = 1.2$ million, $y = 30,000$
     $$\frac{30,000}{1,200,000} = \frac{30}{1,200} = \frac{3}{120} = \frac{1}{40}\left(\frac{2.5}{2.5}\right) = \frac{2.5}{100} = 2.5\%$$
   - d. $x = 25$, $y = 400$
     $$\frac{400}{25} = 16 = 1600\%$$
   - e. $x = 72$, $y = 90$
     $$\frac{90}{72} = \frac{5}{4} = 1.25 = 125\%$$

3.   What number is 25% greater than 40?
   $$40 + 40(.25) = 40 + 10 = 50$$

4.   What number is 6% greater than 200?
   $$200 + 200(0.06) = 200 + 12 = 212$$

5.   What number is 150% greater than 3?
   $$3 + 3(1.5) = 3 + 4.5 = 7.5$$

6.   What number is 15% less than 150?
   $$150 - 150(0.15) = 150 - 22.5 = 127.5$$

7.   What number is 90% less than 180?
   $$180 - 180(0.9) = 180(1 - 0.9) = 180(0.1) = 18$$

8.   What is the percent increase from 100 to 125?
   $$\frac{125-100}{100} = \frac{25}{100} = 25\%$$

9.   What is the percent decrease from 125 to 100?
   $$\frac{125-100}{125} = \frac{25}{125} = \frac{1}{5} = 20\%$$

10.   What is the percent increase from 24 to 30?
    $$\frac{30-24}{24} = \frac{6}{24} = \frac{1}{4} = 25\%$$

11.   What is the percent decrease from 144 to 36?
    $$\frac{144-36}{144} = \frac{108}{144} = \frac{3}{4} = 75\%$$

12.   What is the percent increase from 21 to 84?
    $$\frac{84-21}{21} = \frac{63}{21} = 3 = 300\%$$

204   Explanations: Percents: Practice

191.   E
   EXPL: Set up the equation as given by the question:
$150 = \frac{x}{100}(3)$
$15,000 = 3x$
$x = 5,000$, choice (E).

192.   B
   EXPL: Another way of phrasing this is: What percent of $100 is $5.20? Put
that way, it's a fraction:
$\frac{5.2}{100}$
Since a percent is just the numerator of a fraction over 100, you've already
got your answer: 5.2, choice (B).

193.   B
   EXPL: To determine what 70 percent of a number is, you need to know what
that number is. Statement (1) appears to provide an equation to find that, but
if you look closely, it's a tautology:
$0.25(2x) = 0.5x$
$0.5x = 0.5x$
   That doesn't give us any useful information: half of any number is equal to
half of itself.
   Statement (2) gives us another equation, and this one is actually useful:
$0.5x = x - 10$
$10 = 0.5x$
$x = 20$
Choice (B) is correct.

194.   B
   EXPL: Statement (1) is insufficient: we're interested in technology stocks,
not all stocks. Statement (2) is sufficient: it tells us the number of technology
stocks that increased, and the total number. Given that relationship, we can
determine the percent:
$\frac{27}{90} = \frac{3}{10} = 30\%$
Choice (B) is correct.

195.   B
   EXPL: If 20% of incoming freshman have taken a calculus course, 80% have
not. That 80% is represented by the 148 who have taken pre-calculus plus the
44 who have not, for a total of 192. Thus, we want to know: 80% of what
equals 192?
$0.8x = 192$
$\frac{4}{5}x = 192$
$x = 192(\frac{5}{4}) = 48(5) = 240$, choice (B).

196.   D

Explanation: First, simplify the question. $\frac{1}{10}(4000)$ is 400 and $\frac{1}{4}(1000)$ is 250. Thus, we want to know: what percent of 400 is 250? That's a fraction:

$\frac{250}{400} \times 100\%$

$\frac{250}{4} \times 1\%$

62.5%, choice (D).

Note that there are many ways of getting from the initial fraction to the answer; there's no need to set up a lengthy long-division problem.

197.   B

Explanation: To find the total estimate, find the estimate for cars, then for vans. If last year's cost for cars was \$49,000 and is expected to increase by 10%, the estimate is:

$\$49,000 + 0.1(\$49,000)$

$\$49,000 + \$4,900 = \$53,900$

Last year's cost for vans was \$27,000, which is expected to increase by 30%:

$\$27,000 + 0.3(\$27,000)$

$\$27,000 + \$8,100 = \$35,100$

The total estimate, then, is $\$53,900 + \$35,100 = \$89,000$.

198.   A

Explanation: Statement (1) is sufficient. If we know the average decrease in percent per year, we can figure out the decrease over the four-year period. If the mortality rate in 1972 was m, then it 1973 it was $0.9m$, then in 1974 it was $0.9(0.9m)$, in 1975 it was $0.9(0.9(0.9m))$, and in 1976 it was $0.9(0.9(0.9(0.9m)))$. We don't actually know that the intermediate mortality rates (in 1973, 1974, and 1975) are correct, but because the decrease is an average of 10%, the ending rate must be correct.

Statement (2) is insufficient. We're looking for the relationship between 1972 and 1976, not 1970 and 1980. If we knew the mortality rate decreased exactly 8% per year (instead of an average of 8%), we could answer the question, but it is an average. Choice (A) is correct.

205 Explanations: Percents: Challenge

199. C

Explanation: Start by translating the given equation to algebra. p percent is equivalent to $\frac{p}{100}$, so "x is p percent of y" is the same as

$x = \frac{p}{100}(y)$

To solve for p, isolate it:

$\frac{x}{y} = \frac{p}{100}$

$p = \frac{100x}{y}$, choice (C).

200. E

First, calculate the ratios for the two parts of the profits. $7 million in taxes on $50 million in profits is:

$\frac{7}{50} = \frac{14}{100} = 14\%$

$30 million in taxes on $150 million in profits is:

$\frac{30}{150} = \frac{10}{50} = \frac{20}{100} = 20\%$

Now we need the percent increase–the change divided by the original:

$\frac{20-14}{14} = \frac{6}{14}$

That's not an easy fraction to calculate, but we can recognize that it's a bit less than half. The only choice anywhere close to 50% is (E), which is correct.

206   Explanations: Rate: Drill

1. $\frac{176,000}{8} = 22,000\frac{wn}{h}$

2. $\frac{1200}{4} = 300\frac{m}{h}$

3. $\frac{900}{12} = 75\frac{f}{h}$

4. $\frac{1,800,000,000}{3,000,000} = \frac{1,800}{3} = 600\frac{\$}{person}$

5. $55 = \frac{275}{t}$

$55t = 275$

$t = 5$

6. $16 = \frac{960}{t}$

$16t = 960$

$t = \frac{960}{16} = 60$

7. $4 = \frac{27}{t}$

$4t = 27$

$t = \frac{27}{4} = 6\frac{3}{4}$

8. $24 = \frac{144}{t}$

$24t = 144$

$t = \frac{144}{24} = 6$

9. $35 = \frac{d}{2.5}$

$d = 35(2.5) = 87.5$

10. $120 = \frac{s}{8}$

$s = 120(8) = 960$

11. $600 = \frac{g}{1\frac{1}{4}}$

$g = 600(\frac{5}{4}) = 150(5) = 750$

12.   1 minute = 60 seconds

$18 = \frac{d}{60}$

$d = 18(60) = 1080$

13.   The distance for the first three hours is $3(50) = 150$, and the distance for the final two hours is $60(2) = 120$. Total distance over total time, then, is:

$\frac{150+120}{5} = \frac{270}{5} = 54$

14.   The first 180 miles take $\frac{180}{60} = 3$ hours, while the second 180 miles take $\frac{180}{45} = 4$ hours. Total distance over total time is:

$\frac{180+180}{4+3} = \frac{360}{7} = 51\frac{3}{7}$

15.   Total engines for the first six weeks is $220(6) = 1320$, and total engines for the last eight weeks is $8(320) = 2560$. Total engines divided by total weeks is:

$\frac{2560+1320}{6+8} = \frac{3880}{14} = 277\frac{1}{7}$

16.   The total time spent on the road is $\frac{770}{70} = 11$ hours, which means that, including the break, his total time is 12 hours. Average speed, then, is:

$$\frac{770}{12} = 64\frac{1}{6}$$

17.   Their combined rate is $4 + 5 = 9$ miles per hour. Thus, we want to find how long it takes to cover 12 miles at 9 miles per hour:

$$9 = \frac{12}{x}$$

$$9x = 12$$

$$x = \frac{12}{9} = \frac{4}{3} hours$$

18.   Their combined rate is 36 pages per hour. Thus, it takes them $\frac{144}{36} = 4$ hours to read the whole thing. Since Xavier is reading 20 pages per hour, he'll read a total of $4(20) = 80$ pages.

19.   Georgia is driving 6 miles per hour faster, so she's catching up at that rate. To cover 30 miles at 6 miles per hour, it will take $\frac{30}{6} = 5$ hours.

20.   Janelle sells $1,200 per day more. To catch up, she needs to sell $60,000 more than Karl, and to get $12,000 ahead, she needs to sell a total of $72,000 more. To sell $72,000 more at a rate of $1,200 more per day, it will require $\frac{72,000}{1,200} = \frac{720}{12} = 60$ days.

207 Explanations: Rate: Practice

201. C

EXPL: Statement (1) is insufficient: it tells us nothing about the final 60 miles of the trip. Statement (2) has a similar problem: it tells nothing about what preceded the final 60 miles.

Taken together, the statements are sufficient. From (1), we can find the total time for the first 180 miles. From (2), we can find the total time for the final 60 miles. Add those together, and you have the total time for the trip. Choice (C) is correct.

202. D

EXPL: To find train Y's time, we need train Y's speed. We have a relationship between X's and Y's speed, but to use that, we need train X's speed. That we can find, since we're given X's distance and time:

$r = \frac{d}{t} = \frac{100}{2.5} = 40$

25% faster than 40 miles per hour is:

$40(1.25) = 50$

Finally, we can solve for Y's time:

$50 = \frac{100}{t}$

$50t = 100$

$t = 2$, choice (D).

203. E

EXPL: To find the average speed, you need both distance and time. However, even average speed isn't enough to answer this question: if the average speed is, say, 300 miles per hour, that doesn't mean that the plane traveled at 500 miles an hour for a little while and 100 miles an hour for a little bit.

Statements (1) and (2) are both insufficient: neither gives us both pieces of information we need for average speed, let alone enough to determine whether the plane ever exceeded 400 miles per hour.

Taken together, the statements are still insufficient. We can calculate the average speed of 375 miles per hour, but we don't know whether the speed was always 375 miles per hour, or if it fluctuated enough throughout the flight that it surpassed 400 miles per hour at some point. (E) is the correct choice.

204. D

EXPL: Statement (1) is sufficient: if the pool is $\frac{5}{6}$ full after 40 minutes, that means $\frac{1}{6}$ of the water has been pumped out. If it takes 40 minutes to pump out $\frac{1}{6}$ of the water, it takes $40(6) = 240$ minutes to empty the entire pool.

Statement (2) is also sufficient: this time, we learn that $\frac{1}{2}$ the water has been pumped out (leaving $\frac{1}{2}$ the water remaining) in two hours. Thus, it takes $2(2) = 4$ hours to empty the pool. (D) is the correct choice.

205. C

EXPL: Factory B's rate is $\frac{100}{30}$ orders per minute. If A's rate is twice as fast, double the rate: $(\frac{100}{30})2 = \frac{100}{15}$. The number of orders fulfilled in 9 minutes is the product of the rate and the time:

$$orders = rt = (\tfrac{100}{15})(9) = \tfrac{100}{5}(3) = 20(3) = 60, \text{ choice (C)}.$$

206. E

Explanation: In order for the profit to be exactly zero, the selling price per unit would have to be \$65: just enough to cover costs.

To determine the price at this profit level, we need to figure out how much profit must come from each unit. Since there are 500 units sold, the desired profit per unit is $\frac{35,000}{500} = 70$.

Since it takes \$65 to cover costs and \$70 per unit is desired in profit, the minimum selling price to achieve that profit level is $65 + 70 = 135$, choice (E).

207. E

Explanation: To find time, you generally need distance and rate. Distance is given in the question, so you're looking for rate. Statement (1) is insufficient: it gives no clue as to how fast the bicycle wheel was going. Statement (2) is also insufficient: it provides information about the size of the wheel, but nothing about how fast it's going.

Taken together, the statements are insufficient. In fact, the two statements say the same thing: if you know the diameter of the wheel is 0.6, that means the circumference is 0.6π, which is the same as how long it takes for the wheel to make one full rotation. You don't need to get into that much detail to realize that you need the rate, and neither statement gives you that. Choice (E) is correct.

208. C

Explanation: To find what the phone company charged Victoria last month, you need to know how many minutes she used on days other than Sunday, how many minutes she used on Sundays, and what the regular per-minute rate is.

Statement (1) is insufficient: it provides a lot of information about how many minutes she used, but nothing about the per-minute rate.

Statement (2) is also insufficient: it gives you the per-minute rate, but nothing about how many minutes Victoria used.

Taken together, the statements are sufficient. We know that Victoria used 300 non-Sunday minutes in addition to the first 1,000, 200 Sunday minutes, and that the regular per-minute rate is \$0.10. From there, we can determine the various discounted rates and calculate her bill for last month. Choice (C) is correct.

208 Explanations: Rate: Challenge

209.   C

Explanation: Currently, a certain number of packages can be shipped at a certain price per package for a total of \$120:

$np = 120$

If the price were raised by 1, the number shipped for \$120 would decrease by 6:

$(n-6)(p+1) = 120$

$np - 6p + n - 6 = 120$

$np - 6p + n = 126$

Rewrite the first equation so that it can be substituted into the second:

$n = \frac{120}{p}$

Then plug in to the second:

$p(\frac{120}{p}) - 6p + \frac{120}{p} = 126$

$120 - 6p + \frac{120}{p} = 126$

$\frac{120}{p} - 6p = 6$

$120 - 6p^2 = 6p$

$20 - p^2 = p$

$p^2 + p - 20 = 0$

$(p+5)(p-4) = 0$

$p = 4$ or $p = -5$

Since the price of shipping a package can't be negative, it must be \$4, choice (C).

210.   D

EXPL: Since the rate is given in terms of seconds and the time is given in minutes, you'll have to convert one to the other. It's easier to convert a single number than a fraction, so convert m minutes to seconds: since there are 60 seconds in 1 minute, there are $60m$ seconds in m minutes.

Now, you can use the rate formula. $r = \frac{d}{t}$, and in this case, $r = \frac{f}{s}$ and $t = 60m$. To solve:

$\frac{f}{s} = \frac{d}{60m}$

$d = \frac{60fm}{s}$, choice (D).

209   Explanations: Work: Drill

1. $\frac{AB}{A+B} = \frac{12(8)}{12+8} = \frac{96}{20} = 4.8$

2. $= \frac{15(20)}{15+20} = \frac{300}{35} = \frac{60}{7}$

3. $2(\frac{AB}{A+B}) = 2(\frac{2(3)}{2+3}) = 2(\frac{6}{5}) = \frac{12}{5}$

4. $\frac{AB}{A+B} = \frac{40(60)}{40+60} = \frac{2400}{100} = 24$

5. $4(\frac{AB}{A+B}) = 4(\frac{3(3.5)}{3+3.5}) = \frac{4(3)(3.5)}{6.5} = \frac{42}{6.5} = \frac{42}{\frac{13}{2}} = 42(\frac{2}{13}) = \frac{84}{13}$

6. For 20 feet of fencing:

    $\frac{AB}{A+B} = \frac{6(8)}{6+8} = \frac{48}{14} = \frac{24}{7}$

    For 50 feet of fencing:

    $\frac{24}{7}(2.5) = \frac{60}{7}$

7. Combined, they can assemble 7 parts per hour. To assemble 105 parts, it would take $\frac{105}{7} = 15$ hours.

8. Combined, they can extract 350 gallons of oil per hour. To extract 70 gallons of oil, it would take $\frac{70}{350} = \frac{1}{5} hours$, or 12 minutes.

9. Twice as fast as one order in 20 hours is 2 orders in 20 hours, or 1 order in 10 hours. Combined, they fill 3 orders in 20 hours, so we can set up a ratio:

    $\frac{3}{20} = \frac{5}{x}$, where x is the number of hours it takes to fill 5 orders.

    $3x = 100$

    $x = \frac{100}{3} = 33\frac{1}{3}$

10. If Samir can paint 60 square feet in one-third of an hour, her rate is 180 square feet per hour. Combined, their rate is 240 square feet per hour. So, if they paint for 3 hours, they will cover $3(240) = 720$ square feet.

210   Explanations: Work: Practice

211.   C
EXPL: First, convert Lawrence's rate to a per-day number. If he repairs 15 components per half-day, he repairs 30 components per day. So, Krista and Lawrence working together repair 55 components per day. Thus, their number of days is $\frac{330}{55} = 6$, choice (C).

212.   C
EXPL This is a combined work question, so use the combined work formula: $\frac{AB}{A+B}$. A and B are times, so use 4 and 3: $\frac{4(3)}{4+3} = \frac{12}{7}$. That indicates how many hours it'll take to do the job, which is first defined as filling the entire pool. However, the question asks how long it takes for both pipes, working together, to fill $\frac{1}{2}$ the pool. Multiple $\frac{12}{7}$ by $\frac{1}{2}$, and the answer is $\frac{6}{7}$.

213.   A
EXPL: To answer the question, you need to know the individual rates for machines X and Y, respectively. The question gives us X's rate, so we only need Y's.

Statement (1) is sufficient: it gives us Y's rate in relation to X's rate, which we already have. X produces 120 boxtops in 30 minutes, so Y produces that many in 20 minutes, or 360 per hour.

Statement (2) is insufficient: the key phrase is "more than." If the statement gave us an equation instead of an inequality, it would be sufficient. As it is, the correct choice is (A).

214.   C
EXPL: To answer the question, we'll need the individual rates for hoses X and Y. Each statement alone is insufficient: both give us the time required for one of the hoses, but not both. Taken together, they are sufficient: if we know X's time and Y's time, we can use the combined work formula, $\frac{AB}{A+B}$, to find their time when working simultaneously.

215.   C
EXPL: To answer the question, we need to determine how long machine X takes to fill the order, then add that time to 9:30 a.m. Statement (1) is insufficient: it gives us information about machine Y, but nothing to connect the two machines.

Statement (2) is also insufficient: it provides a two-variable equation using the work formula. If the time for the two machines combined is 1:12 (or $1\frac{1}{5}$ hours), the combined work equation looks like this:
$$\frac{XY}{X+Y} = \frac{6}{5}$$
where X and Y are the times for each machine working independently.

Taken together, the statements are sufficient. (1) tells us that Y's time is 3 hours, so we can plug in one of the variables in the equation provided by (2):

$$\frac{3X}{X+3} = \frac{6}{5}$$

From there, we can solve for X to answer the question.   Choice (C) is correct.

211   Explanations: Work: Challenge

216.   D

We're given a rate in envelopes per minute, and we're looking for a rate in envelopes per minute, so let's convert the rate of envelopes per hour to envelopes per minute. One minute is $\frac{1}{60}$ of an hour, so a rate of envelopes per minute will be $\frac{1}{60}$ of the corresponding rate in envelopes per hour:

$$1,080\frac{e}{h}\left(\frac{1}{60}\right) = \frac{1,080}{60} = \frac{108}{6} = \frac{54}{3} = 18$$

Their combined rate is 18 envelopes per minute. Their combined rate is simply the sum of their individual rates, so if Carolina's rate is 8 envelopes per minute, David's rate must be 10 envelopes per minute, choice (D).

217.   D

Like many GMAT rate problems, this is not as much of a combined work problem as it first appears to be. While two rates are compared, the two machines never operate simultaneously. We can set up an equation to represent the question, where c is the number of chips produced per hour by C, and d is the number produced by D:

$$3c + 5d = 2100$$

To find the number of hours it would have taken D, we need to find d.

Statement (1) is sufficient. In terms of our variables, this says: $d = 1.5c$. Given a second equation with the same two variables, we can solve for c and d, determine how many chips each machine produce, and then figure out how long it would take D to produce 2,100 chips at that rate.

Statement (2) is also sufficient. Given that C produces 200 chips per hour, we know C produced 600 chips in its 3 hours. That leaves 1,500 chips for D to produce in 5 hours–or 300 per hour. That's enough information to solve the problem as well. (D) is the correct choice.

218.   C

When work problems appear to have more than two people (or machines, or hoses, or whatever), they can almost always be broken down into problems dealing with only two units. Here, to find Tara's time, it would be sufficient to know the time it would take Rhonda and Sam to complete the task together. Thus, instead of looking at the problem as containing three people (R, S, and T), we're looking at it as containing two units (R+S, and T).

Statement (1) is insufficient. Knowing Rhonda's time, we can calculate the time that S and T would take to complete the task together, but not their individual times.

Statement (2) is also insufficient. By the same reasoning, Sam's time is not enough to find Rhonda's or Tara's individual times.

Taken together, the statements are sufficient. Since know R's time and S's time, we can calculate their time together. Since we know R+S, we can find T's time. Given the numbers involved, it isn't a good idea to calculate on this Data Sufficiency question. Choice (C) is correct.

212   Explanations: Measurement: Drill

1.   288 inches is equal to how many feet?

$$288i \times \frac{1f}{12i} = \frac{288}{12} = 24$$

2.   27.5 kilometers is equal to how many meters?

$$27.5km \times \frac{1000m}{1km} = 27.5 \times 1000 = 27,500$$

3. $6\frac{1}{2}$ hours is equal to how many seconds?

$$6.5h \times \frac{60m}{1h} \times \frac{60s}{1m} = 6.5(60)(60) = 6.5(3600) = 23,400$$

4.   55 miles per hour is equal to how many miles per minute?

$$\frac{55m}{1h} \times \frac{1h}{60m} = \frac{55m}{60\,min} = \frac{11m}{12\,min}$$

5.   0.75 meters per second is equal to how many meters per minute?

$$\frac{0.75m}{1s} \times \frac{60s}{1\,min} = \frac{0.75(60)m}{1\,min} = 45$$

6.   0.5 miles per second is equal to how many miles per hour?

$$\frac{0.5m}{1s} \times \frac{60s}{1\,min} \times \frac{60\,min}{1h} = 0.5(60)(60) = 1800$$

7.   16 feet per second is equal to how many inches per second?

$$\frac{16f}{s} \times \frac{12i}{1f} = 16(12) = 192$$

8.   24 feet per second is equal to how many yards per minute?

$$\frac{24f}{s} \times \frac{1y}{3f} = \frac{24}{3} = \frac{8y}{s} \times \frac{60s}{1m} = \frac{8(60)y}{1m} = 480$$

9.   90 kilometers per hour is equal to how many meters per second?

$$\frac{90km}{1h} \times \frac{1h}{60\,min} \times \frac{1\,min}{60\,sec} = \frac{90}{3600} = \frac{1km}{40s} \times \frac{1000m}{1km} = \frac{1000}{40} = 25$$

10.   32 feet per second is equal to how many miles per hour?
(1 mile = 5,280 feet)

$$\frac{32f}{s} \times \frac{1mil}{5,280f} \times \frac{60s}{1\,min} \times \frac{60\,min}{1h} = \frac{32(60)(60)}{5280} = \frac{11520}{528} = 21\frac{9}{11}$$

213   Explanations: Measurement: Practice

221.   B

EXPL: Set it up as a ratio:

$\frac{1m}{1.61k} = \frac{xm}{5k}$

$1.61x = 5$

$x = \frac{5}{1.61}$

Since $1.6 \times 3 = 4.8$, $\frac{5}{1.61}$ is a little greater than 3. The only likely choice is (B), 3.1.

222.   E

EXPL: There are 60 minutes in an hour and 60 seconds in a minute, so you can convert from seconds to hours by multiplying by $(60)(60) = 3600$. To quickly multiply 1.86×10^5 by 3600, approximate. Say that the original speed is 2×10^5, and simplify 3600 to 36×10^2:

$(2 \times 10^5)(36 \times 10^2) = 72 \times 10^7 = 7.2 \times 10^8$

That number is higher than any of the answer choices, because we rounded 1.86 up quite a bit. It's sensible, then, to assume that the closest answer choice is correct: 6.7, choice (E), is not much less than 7.2, especially when compared to the other choices.

223.   C

EXPL: Statement (1) is insufficient. If a point in time 80 hours before the appointment was on Tuesday, it could be any time between 12:00 a.m. and 11:59 p.m. on Tuesday. 72 hours later than those times are 12:00 a.m. and 11:59 p.m. on Friday, while another 8 hours moves them to 8:00 a.m. Friday and 7:59 a.m. on Saturday. The appointment could be either Friday or Saturday.

Statement (2) is insufficient: it gives us no information to determine which day the appointment was on.

Taken together, the statements are sufficient: (1) told us that, if the appointment is 8 a.m. or later, it must be on Friday, so (C) is the correct choice.

224.   C

EXPL: This sounds like a question that will test your ability to convert from gallons to liters, but it turns out that it's irrelevant. Statement (1) is insufficient. It gives you one equation with two variables:

$10X + 6Y = 27$

Statement (2) is also insufficient, and also provides one equation with the same two variables:

$4X + 12Y = 25.20$

Taken together, the statements are sufficient. Combine the equations to solve for X and Y, which is enough to answer the question: what is the value of $X + Y$? Choice (C) is correct.

214   Explanations: Mixture: Drill

1.   The solution currently consists of 80 gallons of water and 20 gallons of alcohol. If 20 gallons of water evaporate, that leaves 60 gallons of water. The remaining solution consists of $\frac{20}{20+60} = \frac{20}{80} = \frac{1}{4} = 25\%$ alcohol.

2.   The solution consists of 45 ounces of water and 15 ounces of everything else. For water to be 50% of the solution, everything else must also be 50%, so 15 ounces must be half of the remaining solution. If 15 is half, the whole remaining solution must be 30 ounces, meaning that $60 - 30 = 30$ ounces of water must evaporate.

3.   Mixture A contains 80% water, while Mixture B contains 90% water. Since there are equal amounts of the two mixtures, the percentages can be averaged: the resulting solution is 85% water.

4.   Since there are equal amounts of the two mixtures, the percentages of ammonia from each solution can be averaged: the resulting solution is 35% ammonia.

5.   60% of 80 is 48 ounces of methanol in the original solution, meaning that there is 32 ounces of everything else. For a new solution to consist of 75% methanol, that 32 ounces of everything else must be 25%:

$$0.25x = 32$$
$$x = 128$$

128 is the number of ounces of the new solution; since we add only methanol to increase the percent of methanol in the solution, the amount of methanol added is $128 - 80 = 48$.

6. $200(0.35) = 70$
$100(0.2) = 20$
$70 + 20 = 90$ is the total amount of ethanol in the 300 gallon mixture, so the resulting percentage of ethanol is $\frac{90}{300} = \frac{3}{10} = 30\%$.

7.   You may find it useful to convert the ratios to percents. Solution R is 75% water, Solution S is 60% water, and the desired ratio is 70% water. You can set up an equation:

$$\frac{(0.75)(20)+(0.6)(x)}{20+x} = 0.7$$
$$15 + 0.6x = 0.7(20 + x)$$
$$15 + 0.6x = 14 + 0.7x$$
$$1 = 0.1x$$
$$x = 10$$

8.   The initial solution contains 72 gallons of water and 8 gallons of glycerol. The added 20 gallons is 10 gallons of each. Thus, the total solution is 100 gallons, consisting of 18 gallons of glycerol, 18%.

9.   The initial mixture consists of 72 gallons of water and 48 of chloride. If the resulting mixture of 200 gallons is 75% water, that's a total of 150 gallons. Thus, Y must contain $150 - 48 = 102$ gallons of water.

10.   If you convert the mixtures in each solution to decimals (or fractions), you can set up an equation. A contains 64% water. B contains 90% water. The equation is:

$$\frac{(0.64)(50)+(0.9)(x)}{50+x} = \frac{5}{7}$$

Note that x is the amount of B that must be added; once we find that, we'll have to convert that to a percent of 80.

$32 + 0.9x = (\frac{5}{7})(50 + x)$

$7(32 + 0.9x) = 250 + 5x$

$224 + 6.3x = 250 + 5x$

$1.3x = 26$

$x = 20$

Finally, 20 is 25% of 80, so that's our answer.

215   Explanations: Mixture: Practice

231.   C

EXPL: While the number of green marbles will change, the number of red marbles will stay the same. In other words, we want to determine what else must be true in order that the 13 red marbles represent 65 percent of the contents of the bag. Using those two pieces of information, we can find the desired number of marbles in the bag:

$0.65(total) = 13$

$\frac{13}{20}(total) = 13$

$total = 20$

If there are 20 marbles in the bag, that means that $20 - 13 = 7$ of them must be green. Since there are initially 22 green marbles, the number removed is $22 - 7 = 15$, choice (C).

232.   C

EXPL: The fraction of chlorine in the solution is $\frac{3}{20}$. We're looking for the amount of chlorine in a solution of 7 cubic centimeters; since the units are the same in both solutions, we don't have to worry about adjusting them. We can solve by setting up a ratio:

$\frac{3}{20} = \frac{x}{7}$

$x = (\frac{3}{20})(7) = \frac{21}{20} = 1.05$, choice (C).

233.   C

EXPL: If 1 percent of a 5,000 gallon solution is red dye, that's $5,000(0.01) = 50$ gallons. If 2,000 gallons of water evaporate, that leaves a total of 3,000 gallons of solution, 50 gallons of which is still red dye. The remaining percentage of red dye is:

$\frac{50}{3000} = \frac{5}{300} = \frac{1}{60}$

It's easier to convert that to a percent if you think of it as one-tenth of $\frac{1}{6}$. $\frac{1}{6} = 16.67\%$, so one-tenth of that is 1.67%, choice (C).

234.   C

EXPL: The question gives you two equations. First, the percents of the managers, where A and B stand for the total number of employees in each company's workforce:

$\frac{1}{10}(A) + \frac{3}{10}B = \frac{1}{4}(A + B)$

Since A and B are fractions (or percents) of the total resulting workforce:

$A + B = 1$

To combine the equations, first rewrite the second equation:

$A = 1 - B$

Then plug in to the first equation:

$\frac{1}{10}(1 - B) + \frac{3}{10}B = \frac{1}{4}(1)$

$\frac{1}{10} - \frac{1}{10}B + \frac{3}{10}B = \frac{1}{4}$

$\frac{2}{10}B = \frac{1}{4} - \frac{1}{10}$

$\frac{1}{5}B = \frac{3}{20}$

$B = (\frac{3}{20})5 = \frac{15}{20} = \frac{3}{4} = 75\%$

Thus, B represents 75% of the workforce. A, then, represents 25% percent of the workforce, choice (C).

235.   A

EXPL: To answer the question, we need to know the value of x (how many games the team played before its last 10, or total), or the weights of the first x and the last 10.

Statement (1) is sufficient. We can set up an equation to represent the two different ways of showing the number of games that A won:

$\frac{5}{8}(x + 10) = \frac{1}{2}x + 10$

$\frac{5}{8}x + 6\frac{1}{4} = \frac{1}{2}x + 10$

$\frac{1}{8}x = 3\frac{3}{4}$

$x = 3\frac{3}{4}(8) = 30$

(You don't need to actually solve for x once you recognize that you could solve for x.)

Statement (2) is insufficient. As suggested in the algebra above, the question already tells you the number of games A won is $\frac{x}{2} + 10$: half of x games $(\frac{x}{2})$ plus all of the final 10. Because it's redundant information, it can't be sufficient. Choice (A) is correct.

216   Explanations: Interest: Drill

1. $3(20,000)(0.06) = 3,600$

   2. $5,000 + 10(5,000)(0.08) = 5,000 + 4,000 = 9,000$

   3. $3000 = 5(12,000)(\frac{x}{100})$

          $3,000 = 5(120)(x)$

          $x = \frac{3,000}{5(120)} = \frac{600}{120} = 5$

   4. $50,000(1.08)(1.08) = 58,320$

   5. $6,000(1.2)(1.2)(1.2) = 10,368$

   6. $25,000(1.05)(1.05) = 27,562.50$

   7.   A: $10,000(1.1)(1.1)(1.1) = 13,310$

        B: $10,000 + 3(10,000)(0.1) = 13,000$

        $13,310 - 13,000 = 310$

   8. $20,000(1.05)(1.05) = 22,050$

   9. $40,000(1.02)(1.02) = 41,616$

   10. $100,000(1.005)(1.005) = 101,002.50$

217   Explanations: Interest: Practice

241.   D

EXPL: If 8 percent annual interest is compounded quarterly, that's 2 percent interest per quarter. For the first quarter, the interest is:

$20,000(0.02) = 400$

And the resulting sum is:

$20,000 + 400 = 20,400$

For the second quarter, the interest is:

$20,400(0.02) = 408$

And the resulting sum is:

$20,400 + 408 = 20,808$, choice (D).

242.   B

EXPL: The question gives you enough information to solve for y: if you have the initial amount and the resulting dollar amount of interest, you can calculate the interest rate (in this case, $y = 7$). Thus, statement (1) is insufficient: we already know that. Since (1) is redundant, (C) cannot be the correct choice either; (1) won't help, even in combination with the other statement.

Statement (2) is sufficient: to answer the question, we need the value of z. Since the question allows us to find the value of y, and (2) gives us the relationship between those two variables, (2) gives us the value of z. (B) is the correct choice.

243.   C

EXPL: If 4 percent interest is compounded semi-annually, that means that 2 percent interest is credited every six months. The amount of interest earned in the first six months is:

$5,000(0.02) = 100$

So the resulting sum, after the interest and the additional $1,000 deposit, is:

$5000 + 100 + 1000 = 6,100$

The amount of interest earned in the following six months is:

$6100(0.02) = 122$

So the amount in the account after one year is:

$6100 + 122 = 6222$, choice (C).

244.   E

Note, of course, that you don't have to find the actual value of the investment. That would be extremely cumbersome without a calculator.

Instead, think about what is happening mathematically when interest is compounding. After the first year, the total amount of money is:

$\$10,000 + 0.065(\$10,000) = 1.065(\$10,000)$

The next year results in more interest, because the interest is 6.5% on the sum at the end of the first year:

$1.065[1.065(\$10,000)] = \$10,000(1.065)^2$

For each successive year of compounding, multiply the result by another 1.065, for a final answer of:

$10,000(1.065)^4$, choice (E).

218 Explanations: Primes: Drill

True or False: Is the number prime?

1. 31

   True

2. 9

   False: 9 is divisible by 3

3. 23

   True

4. 71

   True

5. 27

   False: 27 is divisible by 3

6. 51

   False: 51 is divisible by 3 and 17

7. 111

   False: 111 is divisible by 3 and 37

8. 19

   True

9. 87

   False: 87 is divisible by 3 and 29

10. 2

    True: 2 is the only even prime.

219   Explanations: Primes: Practice

251.   B

EXPL: There are 9 numbers greater than 80 and less than 90, but many of them are not prime: you can start by ruling out even numbers, leaving the following:

$\{81, 83, 85, 87, 89\}$

81 is a multiple of 3, as is 87. 85 is a multiple of 5, leaving only

$\{83, 89\}$

83 isn't an answer choice, so 89 must be prime. But 89 is an answer choice, so you need to figure out whether 83 is prime. It isn't a multiple of 3 (its digits add up to 11), nor a multiple of 5, nor a multiple of 7 (84 is a multiple of 7), nor a multiple of 9 (its digits, again add up to 11). The square root is just a bit above 9, so we can stop there. 83 is prime, so the sum of all qualifying numbers is $83 + 89 = 172$, choice (B).

252.   D

EXPL: The question tells us that p is prime, which comes in handy in both statements. Statement (1) is sufficient: if p is 1 greater than another prime number, p must be 3. The only prime numbers that are one apart are 2 and 3, so $n = 2$ and $p = 3$.

Statement (2) is also sufficient: if p is prime, p must be 3: any other number that is divisible by 3 is not prime. Choice (D) is correct.

253.   C

EXPL: Statement (1) is insufficient. x could be anything from 2 to a very large number, while y could be as large as $\frac{1}{2}$ (the reciprocal of 2) or a very small number (the reciprocal of a very large prime.) $2(\frac{1}{2})$ is less than 5, but $17(\frac{1}{2})$ is not.

Statement (2) is also insufficient. If x and y are 6 and 5, respectively, the product is much larger than 5; but if x and y are 2 and 1, respectively, the product is smaller than 5.

Taken together, the statements are sufficient. The largest that x can be is 5, the largest prime less than 7. Since y cannot be greater than $\frac{1}{2}$, the largest possible product of x and y is the 2.5, the product of 5 and $\frac{1}{2}$, so xy must be less than 5. Choice (C) is correct.

254.   E

EXPL: The question, as worded, is really just a fancy way of asking whether p is not prime. The only positive integers that cannot be expressed as the product of two integers, each of which greater than 1, are primes.

Statement (1) is insufficient: an odd number can be prime (3, 5, 7, etc.) or non-prime (9, 15, 21, etc.). Statement (2) is also insufficient: there are several non-primes between 41 and 49, but 43 and 47 are both prime.

Taken together, the statements are still insufficient. If p is odd and between 41 and 49, p could be 43 (prime), 45 (non-prime) or 47 (prime). Because the answer to the question could be "yes" or "no," the correct choice is (E).

220   Explanations: Primes: Challenge

255.   B

EXPL: Go through the choices one by one, checking the numbers 4 less than and 4 greater than the choice for primeness:

(A)   cousins of 5 would be 1 or 9, but neither is prime.

(B)   cousins of 19 would be 15 and 23: 23 is prime, so this looks good.

(C)   cousins of 29 would be 25 and 33, but neither is prime.

(D)   cousins of 31 would be 27 and 35, but neither is prime.

(E)   cousins of 53 would be 49 and 57, but neither is prime.

(B) is the correct choice.

256.   C

Explanation: Statement (1) is insufficient: we're trying to determine the value of q, and this statement has nothing to do with q. Statement (2) is also insufficient: we don't find out anything out q, just the relationship between q and r.

Taken together, we can rephrase the question using the relationship between q and r in (2). If $q = 23$, then $r = 3(23) + 2 = 71$. In (1), if $r = 71$, then $71 = 2p + 1$, which means that $p = 35$. However, (1) states that p must be prime, so p cannot be 35. If p cannot be 35, r cannot be 71, which means that q cannot be 23. The answer is "no", so the correct choice is (C).

257.   C

Once you understand the meaning of the newly-defined term "prime total," work through each of the choices, finding the prime factors and prime total of each:

(A) $80 = 2 \times 2 \times 2 \times 2 \times 5$ - prime total of 2

(B) $82 = 2 \times 41$ - prime total of 2

(C) $84 = 2 \times 2 \times 3 \times 7$ – prime total of 3

(D) $86 = 2 \times 43$ – prime total of 2

(E) $88 = 2 \times 2 \times 2 \times 11$ – prime total of 2

(C) has the largest prime total, so it is correct.

221   Explanations: Factors: Drill

1.   For each of the following numbers, find all of its factors.
       Then, find the prime factorization:
       a.   110
             Factors: 1, 2, 5, 10, 11, 22, 55, 110
             Factorization: $(2)(5)(11)$
       b.   96
             Factors: 1, 2, 3, 4, 6, 8, 12, 16, 24, 32, 48, 96
             Factorization: $(2)^5(3)$
       c.   84
             Factors: 1, 2, 3, 4, 6, 7, 12, 14, 21, 28, 42, 84
             Factorization: $(2)^2(3)(7)$
       d.   60
             Factors: 1, 2, 3, 4, 5, 6, 10, 12, 15, 20, 30, 60
             Factorization: $(2)^2(3)(5)$
       e.   144
             Factors: 1, 2, 3, 4, 6, 8, 9, 12, 16, 18, 24, 36, 48,
                           72, 144
             Factorization: $(2)^4(3)^2$
       f.   147
             Factors: 1, 3, 7, 21, 49, 147
             Factorization: $(3)(7)^2$
       g.   180
             Factors: 1, 2, 3, 4, 5, 6, 9, 10, 12, 15, 18, 20,
                           30, 36, 45, 60, 90, 180
             Factorization: $(2)^2(3)^2(5)$
       h.   182
             Factors: 1,2,7,13,14,26,91,182
             Factorization: $(2)(7)(13)$
       i.   205
             Factors: 1, 5, 41, 205
             Factorization: $(5)(41)$
       j.   225
             Factors: 1, 3, 5, 9, 15, 25, 45, 75, 225
             Factorization: $(3)^2(5)^2$
2.   For each of the following, is x a factor of y ?
       a. $x = 15, y = 15$
             Yes
       b. $x = 9, y = 336$
             No
       c. $x = 3, y = 51$
             Yes
       d. $x = 8, y = 98$
             No

      e. $x = 4$, $y = 154$

           No

3.   Which of the following numbers are factors of 144?

      a.   24

      b.   9

      c.   16

           All three are factors.

4.   Which of the following numbers are factors of 96?

      a.   18

           Not a factor.

      b.   12

           Yes, a factor.

222   Explanations: Factors: Practice

261.   C

EXPL: The question suggests that the answer is the same regardless of which prime number you choose for p. (Otherwise no answer would be correct, or more than one answer would be correct, which is impossible.) So, choose a simple number for p, such as $p = 5$.

If $p = 5$, $n = 6p = 6(5) = 30$. The even factors of 30 are 2, 6, 10, and 30. That's 4 even factors. Choice (C) is correct.

262.   E

EXPL: Statement (1) is insufficient: If s is divisible by 16, s could be 16, 32, 48, etc. Some of those numbers are divisible by 32, but not all, such as 16, which is not divisible by 32. Statement (2) is also insufficient: in fact, we can go back to our thought process regarding (1). If s is divisible by 16, it must be divisible by 4. So if (1) is insufficient, (2) must be insufficient: (2) doesn't give us any information we didn't have in (1).

Taken together, the statements are still insufficient. As we've seen, (2) doesn't add anything that (1) didn't tell us, so if (1) is insufficient, the statements combined are insufficient as well. (E) is the correct answer.

263.   C

EXPL: Statement (1) is insufficient. A number that has exactly one prime factor is either a prime number or a prime number raised to an integer power. For instance, 7 has only one prime factor: itself. 9 also has only one prime factor: 3. So, among the members of this set, 25 (5^2) and 27 (3^3) both only have one prime factor. q could be either one.

Statement (2) is also insufficient: three numbers in the set (21, 24, and 27) are multiples of 3.

Taken together, the statements are sufficient. (1) tells us that q must be 25 or 27, and (2) indicates that q must be 21, 24, or 27. The only overlapping possibility for q is 27, so q must be 27. Choice (C) is correct.

264.   B

EXPL: First, simplify the question:
$$\frac{50-n}{n} = \frac{50}{n} - \frac{n}{n} = \frac{50}{n} - 1$$
$\frac{50}{n} - 1$ will only be an integer is $\frac{50}{n}$ is an integer, so we can disregard the 1 and focus on $\frac{50}{n}$. $\frac{50}{n}$ will only be an integer when n is a factor of 50. So, we can think of the question as asking, "is n a factor of 50?" It's the same thing.

Statement (1) is insufficient: if n is 1 or 2, n is a factor of 50. If $n = 3$, n is not a factor of 50.

Statement (2) is sufficient: 50 is divisible by the only possible values of n, 5 and -5. Choice (B) is correct.

265.   E

Explanation: Statement (1) is insufficient: if $x = 1$, then $n = 3$, which has exactly two factors. (Another way of saying it is divisible by two positive integers.) However, if $x = 3$, then $n = 9$, which is divisible by 3 positive integers (1, 3, and 9). Statement (2) is also insufficient: again, x could be 1 or 3, which generate different answers to the question.

Taken together, the statements are still insufficient. Even with both pieces of information, x could be 1 or x could be 3. Depending on which you choose, the answer to the question is different. (E) is the correct choice.

223   Explanations: Factors: Challenge

266.   B

EXPL: First, simplify the fraction $\frac{3p}{84}$ by cancelling out a 3: $\frac{p}{28}$. If $\frac{p}{28}$ is an integer, p must be a multiple of 28. Since p must be less than 75, p must be either 28 or 56. The question implies that regardless which value of p we choose, the number of different positive prime factors will be the same, so we can look at whichever of the two numbers we'd like. 28 is smaller, so focus on that.

This is a good time to do a prime factorization:

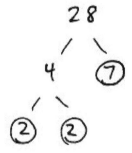

The only prime factors of 28 are 2 and 7, so the correct answer is (B).

267.   C

Explanation: Start with the factors you know. Most obviously, 1 and 625 are factors. Also obviously, 5 is a factor (since the last digit is a 5). 625 divided by 5 is 125, so 125 is also a factor. That means that anything divisible by 125 is a factor: thus, 25 is a factor. 625 divided by 25 is 25, so that doesn't generate another factor.

That's everything. To confirm that we didn't miss anything, you may want to find the prime factors. If you do that, you'll find that the only prime factor of 625 is 5, so all the factors must be 1 or multiples of 5. That confirms that the only factors are 1, 5, 25, 125, and 625, so the total number of factors is 5, choice (C).

268.   C

EXPL: Another way of stating the question's premise is that $k = 12!$. For 3^n to be a factor of k, it must be true that $\frac{k}{3^n}$ is an integer. To figure out how big n can be, we need to figure out how many 3's are contained in $12!$. Rather than writing out the entire expression, we can ignore all of the integers in $12!$ that are not divisible by 3. They are irrelevant to the question. Limiting ourselves to 3, 6, 9, and 12, we have:

$$\frac{3 \times 6 \times 9 \times 12}{3^n} = \text{integer}$$
$$\frac{3 \times (3 \times 2) \times (3 \times 3) \times (3 \times 4)}{3^n} = \text{integer}$$
$$\frac{3^5 \times 2 \times 4}{3^n} = \text{integer}$$

Since the numerator of the fraction contains 3^5, the denominator can have up to 5 3's. Any more, and the result isn't a fraction. There could be fewer, but the question is looking for the largest possible value of n. Choice (C) is correct.

269.   D

Start by finding the easiest factors. Since the last digit is a 0, the number is a multiple of 10, meaning that 2 and 5 are factors. To simplify:

$2730 = (2)(5)(273)$

Now we've found two prime factors, and we only need to worry about 273. Since the digits of 273 add up to 3, we know that it is a multiple of 3. Since 270 is 90×3, 273 must be 91×3. We've found another prime factor, 3, and now we can focus on 91.

You may know that $91 = 7 \times 13$; it comes up occasionally, in part because it is one of the few two-digit numbers that isn't obviously a multiple of 2, 3, or 5 but is not prime. If you don't know, 7 is the smallest remaining prime number, so check to see whether 7 is a factor of 91. One way to do this is to start with a number you know is a multiple of 7, like 70 or 77, and count by 7's: $77 + 7 = 84$; $84 + 7 = 91$. Now you know 7 is a factor, and you can divide to determine that $7 \times 13 = 91$.

Our prime factors, then, are 2, 3, 5, 7, and 13. Choice (D) is correct.

270.   D

In terms of factors, a square of an integer is defined by having an even number of all of its prime factors. For instance, 36 is a square because it's prime factorization is $2^2 3^2$–two of each. Presumably, 2,940 is not already a square; to find what k must be for $2,940k$ to be a square, we need to know 2,940's factorization.

$2,940 = 294(10) = (2)(147)(2)(5)$
$= (2)(3)(49)(2)(5)$
$= (2)(3)(7)(7)(2)(5)$
$= 2^2 \times 3 \times 5 \times 7^2$

There is already an even number of 2's and an even number of 7's. However, there are odd numbers of 3's and 5's. If we multiply this factorization by 15 (3×5), the result is all even powers:

$2^2 \times 3 \times 5 \times 7^2 \times (3 \times 5) = 2^2 \times 3^2 \times 5^2 \times 7^2$

Both the 3 and the 5 are necessary, so the smallest possible value for k is 15, choice (D).

224   Explanations: Multiples: Drill

1.   For each of the following, is x a multiple of y ?

     a. $x = 12$, $y = 1$
       Yes

     b. $x = 96$, $y = 3$
       Yes

     c. $x = 15$, $y = 30$
       No

     d. $x = 24$, $y = 8$
       Yes

     e. $x = 180$, $y = 8$
       No

     f. $x = 108$, $y = 9$
       Yes

     g. $x = 51$, $y = 17$
       Yes

     h. $x = 100$, $y = 16$
       No

     i. $x = 36$, $y = 36$
       Yes

     j. $x = 147$, $y = 7$
       Yes

2.   For each of the following, find the least common multiple (LCM) of x and y:

     a. $x = 6$, $y = 7$
       42

     b. $x = 3$, $y = 18$
       18

     c. $x = 8$, $y = 12$
       24

     d. $x = 70$, $y = 4$
       140

     e. $x = 56$, $y = 5$
       280

     f. $x = 12$, $y = 9$
       36

     g. $x = 48$, $y = 16$
       48

     h. $x = 18$, $y = 24$
       72

     i. $x = 6$, $y = 27$
       54

     j. $x = 37$, $y = 1$
       37

225   Explanations: Multiples: Practice

271.   C
EXPL: Essentially, the question asks for the least common multiple of 1, 3, 5, 7 and 9. We can ignore 1, since every integer is divisible by 1. We can also ignore 3, because any number that is divisible by 9 is also divisible by 3. That leaves us with 5, 7, and 9. Since those three numbers share no factors (5 and 7 are prime, and 9 is not divisible by either one), the LCM is easy to calculate: it's the product of the three numbers:
$(5)(7)(9) = 315$, choice (C).

272.   D
EXPL: Statement (1) is sufficient: the only way that y^2 could be divisible by 9 is if y itself is divisible by 3. Formally, if $y = 3(integer)$, $y^2 = 3(integer)(3)(integer) = 9(integer)$, a number divisible by 9. If y is divisible by 3, y^3 is divisible by 3^3, which is divisible by 9.
Statement (2) is also sufficient. Since y is an integer (as the question tells us), y again must be a multiple of 3. If it is not a multiple of 3, y^4 won't be a multiple of 3, let alone a multiple of 9. But if y is a multiple of 3, y^4 is a multiple of 3^4, which is divisible by 9. If y is a multiple of 3, as we saw in (1), y^3 must be a multiple of 9.

273.   A
EXPL: Divisibility rules come in handy here. Statement (1) is sufficient: if N is divisible by 9, the digits must add up to 9 or a multiple of 9. If $4 + 3 + G + 5 = 12 + G$ is a multiple of 9, G must be 6. Any other value of G that results in a multiple of 9 is not a positive digit.
Statement (2) is insufficient: the divisibility rule for 5 hinges on the last digit, which is already given. Any time the units digit is 5 or 0, the number is divisible by 5. So, regardless of the value of G, $4,3G5$ is divisible by 5. G could be any digit. Choice (A) is correct.

274.   A
EXPL: Statement (1) is sufficient. If r is divisible by 10, we can write:
$r = 10(integer)$
Taking that a step further, we know that s is an integer, so:
$rs = 10(integer)(integer)$
10 times any integer is a multiple of 10, and anything that is divisible by 10 is also divisible by 5.
Statement (2) is insufficient: the only factors of 5 are 5 and 1. If s is 5, then rs must be divisible by 5. But if s is 1, we don't know whether rs is divisible by 5: it could be any integer whatsoever. Choice (A) is correct.

275.   E

EXPL: If the digits in a two-digit number are given as variables, we can write the number as the sum of 10 times the tens digit plus the units digit. For instance, 51 is 10 times 5 (the tens digit) plus 1 (the units digit):

$51 = 5(10) + 1$

So, the integer PQ is $10P + Q$. When you reverse the digits, the integer QP is $10Q + P$. The difference between those two integers, then, is:

$10P + Q - (10Q + P) = 10P + Q - 10Q - P = 9P - 9Q = 9(P - Q)$

We don't know anything about the digits themselves, but we know that the difference is nine times the difference between them. The difference, then, must be a multiple of 9. There's only one of those among the answer choices: 27, choice (E).

276.   E

Explanation: If p is a multiple of 6, it can be written as $p = 6i$, where i is an integer. q can be written the same way, so $pq = 6i(6i) = 36i^2$. Since i^2 is still an integer, $pq = 36i$, which is the algebraic way of saying that pq is a multiple of 36. Since pq is a multiple of 36, it's also a multiple of any factor of 36.

6, 12, and 18 are all factors of 36, so pq is a multiple of I, II, and III, choice (E).

277.   B

Explanation: First, try to simplify the equation in the question stem. $\frac{1}{2} + \frac{1}{4} + \frac{1}{6} = \frac{6}{12} + \frac{3}{12} + \frac{2}{12} = \frac{11}{12}$

If $\frac{11}{12} = \frac{11}{x}$, $x = 12$. The only roman numeral that must be an integer is II, as $\frac{12}{12} = 1$, an integer. I is $\frac{12}{8} = 1.5$, and III is $\frac{12}{24} = 0.5$. (B) is correct.

278.   C

Explanation: To determine whether a number is a multiple of 18, you must know whether it contains factors of 3, 3, and 2. (Or 9 and 2, if you prefer.) Statement (1) isn't sufficient: if p is a multiple of 24, it must be a multiple of 2 and 3, but not necessarily of 9: the prime factorization of 24 contains only one 3.

Statement (2) is also insufficient: if p is a multiple of 27, it must be a multiple of 9, but there's no way to tell whether it's a multiple of 2.

Taken together, the statements are sufficient. (1) tells us that p is a multiple of 2, and (2) tells us p is a multiple of 9. If p is a multiple of both 2 and 9, it must be a multiple of 18.

226 Explanations: Multiples: Challenge

279. C

Explanation: The smallest possible LCM of two numbers is the greater of the two numbers, in this case x. That means that x, (C), could be the LCM of x and y. All of the other answers are less than x, so none of them could be the LCM of the two integers.

280. E

The "spin" of x is double the tens digit of x. For double the tens digit of x to be divisible by 4, the tens digit of x must itself be even; a multiple of 4 divided by 2 will always be even, though not necessarily itself a multiple of 4.

Statement (1) is insufficient. We don't know either of the digits, so we have two variables and one equation. If $x = 27$, the spin is 4, so the answer is "yes." If $x = 36$, the spin is 6, so the answer is "no."

Statement (2) is also insufficient. If $x > 50$, x could be any integer from 51 to 99. The spin of 51 is 10–not a multiple of 4–but the spin of 61 is 12–a multiple of 4.

Taken together, the statements are still insufficient. x could be 54, 63, 72, 81, or 90. The tens digit could be even or odd, so the spin could be a multiple of 4 or a non-multiple of 4. Choice (E) is correct.

227   Explanations: Evens/Odds: Drill

1.   If x is even and y is odd, determine whether each of the following is even, odd, or undetermined:

    a. $even(odd) + even = even + even = even$
    b. $even(odd) + odd = even + odd = odd$
    c. $odd - even = odd$
    d. $even - odd = odd$
    e. $(even)^2 - (odd)^2 = even - odd = odd$

2.   If both x and y are even, determine whether each of the following is even, odd, or undetermined:

    a. $even(even) - even = even - even = even$
    b. $(\frac{x}{2})y = (\frac{even}{2})(even) = \text{integer}(even) = even$
    c. $3(even) - even = even - even = even$
    d. $(even)^2 - 1 = even - 1 = odd$
    e. $(\frac{x}{2})(\frac{y}{2}) = (\frac{even}{2})(\frac{even}{2}) = (\text{integer})(\text{integer}) = \text{integer}$ (un-det.)

3.   If both x and y are odd, determine whether each of the following is even, odd, or undetermined:

    a. $odd(odd) - odd = odd - odd = even$
    b. $(odd)^2 + (odd)^2 = odd + odd = even$
    c. $2(odd - odd) = 2(even) = even$
    d. $3(odd) + 2(odd) = odd + even = odd$
    e. $odd + odd + odd(odd) = odd + odd + odd = odd$

4.   If x is even and y is an integer, determine whether each of the following is even, odd, or undetermined:

    a. $2(even + int) = 2(int) = even$
    b. $3(even - int) = 3(int) = int(undetermined)$
    c. $(even)^2 + 2(int)^2 = even + 2(int) = even + even = even$
    d. $3(even) - 2(int) = even - even = even$
    e. $2(even) - 3(int) = even - int = int(undetermined)$

228   Explanations: Evens/Odds: Practice

281.   D

EXPL: It's best to work through this question by elimination. There are 19 integers less than 20: the integers between 1 and 19, inclusive. 9 of those are multiples of 2: all the even numbers, from 2 to 18 inclusive. There is only one odd multiple of 7: 7 itself. That leaves us with 9 numbers not yet accounted for:

$\{1, 3, 5, 9, 11, 13, 15, 17, 19\}$

Some of those must be the sum of a positive multiple of 7 and a positive multiple of 2 (even number). Since the smallest positive multiple of 7 is 7, there's no way to get 1, 3, or 5 that way. However, we can get any of the larger numbers:

$7 + 2 = 9$

$7 + 4 = 11$

...

$7 + 12 = 19$

Thus, only 3 of the original 19 numbers don't fall into one of the three given categories. Thus, those categories encompass $19 - 3 = 16$ of the positive integers less than 20, choice (D).

282.   B

EXPL: Statement (1) is insufficient. If r is an integer, it would be sufficient: the only way an integer squared is even is if that integer is itself even. However, since we don't know that r is an integer, r could be, for instance, $\sqrt{2}$, the square of which is 2, an even integer.

Statement (2) is sufficient. Treat it like an equation:

$\sqrt{r} = even$

$r = (even)^2$

If you square an even integer, the result is an even integer. Therefore, r is even. Choice (B) is correct.

283.   B

EXPL: Any time you have consecutive integers, one must be even and one must be odd. If p is odd, then, q must be even. Statement (1) is insufficient: any time one of the numbers is even, the product of two integers is even. Thus, whether p is even and q is odd or p is odd and q is even, pq will be even.

Statement (2) is sufficient: if q is an integer (as we are told), the only way q^2 can be even is if q itself is even. If q is even, p must be odd, since the numbers are consecutive. (B) is the correct choice.

284.   A

EXPL: Even though we're working with number properties, treat the statements like algebraic equations. Statement (1) is sufficient. To write it algebraically:

$\frac{s}{2} = even$

$s = 2(even)$

Twice an even number is still an even number, so s cannot be odd. Statement (2) is insufficient:

$2s - 3 = odd$

$2s = odd + 3$

$2s = even$

If s is an integer, as we are told, $2s$ will always be even, whether s is even or odd. (A) is the correct choice.

285.   C

EXPL: Statement (1) is insufficient: if $r - 2$ is prime, $r - 2$ could be either an even number (2) or any number of odd primes. In the first case, $r = 4$, and in the latter cases, r is an odd number, such as 5, 7, or 9.

Statement (2) is also insufficient. If $r + 2$ is prime, $r + 2$ could, again, be either 2 or any number of odd primes. In the first case, $r = 0$; in the latter, r is an odd number, such as 1, 3, 5 ,or 9.

Taken together, the statements are sufficient. The possibilities that $r = 4$ and $r = 0$ do not satisfy both statements; the only possible values for r that work in both cases are odd, so r must be odd.

286.   C

Explanation: Statement (1) is insufficient. If m is a multiple of x, $\frac{m}{x}$ is an integer; for instance, it is an integer if $m = 4$ and $x = 2$; it is not an integer if $m = 3$ and $x = 4$.

Statement (2) is also insufficient. Again, $\frac{m}{x}$ is an integer if x is a factor of m; there are plenty of possible numbers that are factors of odd integers, and plenty that are not.

Taken together, the statements are sufficient. An odd integer has only odd factors, so if m is odd and x is even, m cannot be a multiple of x. The answer is "no," and the correct choice is (C).

287.   D

Explanation: Don't let the question fool you into working with probability or number properties just because it deals with dice and evens and odds. As it turns out, it's an algebra question. The question gives you one equation: $e = 6 + d$, where e is the number of even results and d is the number of odd results.

To solve for the variables, we need one more equation. Statement (1) gives us that: $e + d = 18$. Statement (2) also gives us a second equation with the same two variables: $2e + 1d = 30$, where each term represents a number of points. (D) is the correct choice.

288.   C

The inequality tells us that x is a three-digit integer. If the product of the digits is 70, the digits must each be one of 70's prime factors: 2, 5, and 7. There are other ways to multiply to 70 (for instance, $2 \times 5 \times 7 \times 1$, or 10×7), but the only way to do so with exactly three one-digit numbers is with 2, 5, and 7. Thus, the only question is in what order those three digits are to be arranged.

Statement (1) is insufficient. If x is larger than 600, the only possible hundreds digit is 7. x could be either 725 or 752, but we don't have a way of determining which one.

Statement (2) is also insufficient. If x is even, the units digit must be even, meaning in this case that the units digit must be 2. However, we don't know whether the number is 572 or 752.

Taken together, the statements are sufficient. If 7 must be the hundreds digit and 2 must be the units digit, the number must be 752. Choice (C) is correct.

289.   D

Consider each choice in turn:

(A)   These two integers are two apart. They are either both even or both odd. If they're both even, the result is even. If they're both odd, the result is odd.

(B)   These integers are four apart, meaning that they are either both even or both odd. By the same reasoning as (A), the result could be either even or odd.

(C)   Just like (B), the integers are 4 apart, so the result could be even or odd.

(D)   Either k or $k - 1$ must be even, and the other must be odd. Thus, the product of the two must be even. Regardless of whether $k + 4$ is even or odd, the product of the three must be even, since $(k)(k-1)$ must be even. This choice, then, must be even, so it is correct.

(E)   As with the first three choices, all of these terms must be the same—either even or odd. If they are all even, the result is even. If they are all odd, the result is odd.

Choice (D) is correct.

229   Explanations: Consecutive Numbers: Drill

1.   True or False: For each of the following, are the numbers in the sequence consecutive?

      a.   {1, 2, 4, 8, 16, 32, 64}
              False

      b.   {-25, -20, -15, -10, -5}
              True

      c.   {0, 1, 4, 9, 16, 25, 36}
              False

      d.   {101, 102, 103, 104, 105}
              True

      e. $\{x, x + 3, x + 6, x + 9, x + 12\}$
              True

2.   What is the average (arithmetic mean) of each of the following sets?

      a.   {60, 62, 64, 66, 68, 70, 72}
              66

      b.   {-12, -8, -4, 0, 4, 8}
              -2

      c. $\{y, y + 1, y + 2, y + 3, y + 4\}$
              $y + 2$

3.   Every other even number is a multiple of 4, so the fraction is $\frac{1}{2}$.

4.   Just as in the sequence of integers, every 7th multiple of 5 is a multiple of 7. Thus, the fraction is $\frac{1}{7}$.

230 Explanations: Consecutive Numbers: Practice

291.   D

EXPL: y is a little easier, so start with that one.   There are 21 integers between 50 and 70 inclusive, 10 odds and 11 evens.   (Since the endpoints are even, there are more evens than odds.)   To find the sum of a series of consecutive integers (or evens, in this case), find the midpoint and multiply by the number of terms.   Here, the midpoint is 60, and there are 11 evens, so the sum of the evens is:

$60(11) = 660$

If $x = 660$ and $y = 10$, $x + y = 670$, choice (D).

292.   D

EXPL: It takes a bit of experimentation to figure this out, but it turns out that the only set of consecutive integers that sums to 2 is $\{-1, 0, 1, 2\}$.   Thus, you don't need to consider a range of possible sets, just that one.

I is true: $n = 4$, so n is even.   Eliminate (B), (C), and (E).

II is false: $n = 4$.

III is true: in fact you don't have to figure out anything about this specific case to know that.   Whenever you have a set of consecutive integers, the median is equal to the mean.   The correct choice is (D).

293.   C

EXPL: Statement (1) is insufficient: there are an infinite number of possible values for the three variables, consecutive and not.   Statement (2) is also insufficient.   The variables are limited to five possible values: 20, 21, 22, 23, and 24, but that's not enough: they could be consecutive, like 20, 21, and 22, or non-consecutive, like 20, 21, and 24.

Taken together, the statements are sufficient.   If none of the numbers are multiples of 4, that eliminates 20 and 24 as possibilities, leaving only 21, 22, and 23.   Those three integers are consecutive, so the answer is "yes."   Choice (C) is correct.

294.   C

EXPL: Statement (1) is insufficient: if r and s are consecutive odds and prime, they must be 3 and 5 or 5 and 7, though we don't know which is which in either case.   Even if we knew that r and s must be 3 and 5, either variable could have either value.

Statement (2) is also insufficient: if r is odd, it could be 7 or 9.   We learn nothing here about s, so we don't know which is larger.

Taken together, the statements are sufficient.   If r is prime and between 5 and 11, it must be 7.   If the numbers are consecutive odds and primes and $r = 7$, s must be 5 – it can't be 9, since 9 isn't prime.   If $r = 7$ and $s = 5$, r is greater than s.   Choice (C) is correct.

295.   C

EXPL: To find the sum of the numbers, we need to find both the number of integers, and possibly the pattern that determines which numbers are included.

Statement (1) is insufficient: the list could be of any length, and we have no idea what the other numbers are.

Statement (2) is also insufficient: while this is helpful, we don't have any idea how large or small the numbers are.

Taken together, the statements are sufficient. Knowing that the list consists of 6 consecutive multiples of 4 and that the largest number is 12, the list must be:

$\{-8, -4, 0, 4, 8, 12\}$

Choice (C) is correct.

231   Explanations: Remainders: Drill

1.   What is the remainder when...

    a.   13 is divided by 2?

$$\frac{13}{2} = 6 + \frac{1}{2} = \text{the remainder is 1}$$

    b.   21 is divided by 4?

$$\frac{21}{4} = 5 + \frac{1}{4} = \text{the remainder is 1}$$

    c.   3 is divided by 7?

$$\frac{3}{7} = 0 + \frac{3}{7} = \text{the remainder is 3}$$

    d.   37 is divided by 10?

$$\frac{37}{10} = 3 + \frac{7}{10} = \text{the remainder is 7}$$

2.   If x is less than 40, what are the possible values of x if...

    a.   when x is divided by 5, the remainder is 2?

$$x = 5i + 2$$
$$2, 7, 12, 17, 22, 27, 32, 37$$

    b.   when x is divided by 9, the remainder is 8?

$$x = 9i + 8$$
$$8, 17, 26, 35$$

    c.   when x is divided by 7, the remainder is 1?

$$x = 7i + 1$$
$$1, 8, 15, 22, 29, 36$$

    d.   when x is divided by 17, the remainder is 3?

$$x = 17i + 3$$
$$3, 20, 37$$

3.   When 31 is divided by d, the remainder is 1. What are the possible values of d?

$$31 = d(\text{integer}) + 1$$
$$30 = d(\text{integer})$$

d could be any factor of 30: 1, 2, 3, 5, 6, 10, 15, or 30

4.   If $\frac{m}{n} = 7.12$ and m and n are integers, what are the three smallest possible remainders when m is divided by n?

$$0.12 = \frac{12}{100} = \frac{3}{25}$$

Thus, the remainder must be a multiple of 3. The three smallest multiples of 3 are 3, 6, and 9.

232   Explanations: Remainders: Practice

296.   E

Explanation: If n divided by 15 has a remainder of 4, that means n is four greater than some multiple of 15. Mathematically, we can express that as:

$n = 15i + 4$, where i is an integer.

Less technically, we can generate some possible values of n: 4, 19, 34, 49, 64, 79, etc.

Statement (1) is insufficient: there are several numbers on that list that have a remainder of 9 when divided by 10; any number ending with a 9 as the units digit will satisfy this statement. More specifically, n could be 19, 49, 79, or several others.

Statement (2) is also insufficient: if n is less than 50, it could be 4, 19, 34, or 49.

Taken together, the statements still aren't sufficient. Both 19 and 49 are less than 50 and have a remainder of 9 when divided by 10. Choice (E) is correct.

297.   B

EXPL: Statement (1) is insufficient. We can represent the statement algebraically as follows:

$z = 7i + odd$, where i is an integer. If i is even, $7i$ is even, and z is odd. If i is odd, $7i$ is odd and z is even.

Statement (2) is sufficient. Here's what it looks like algebraically:

$z = 8i + odd$

$8i$ will always be even, so z is always odd. Choice (B) is correct.

233   Explanations: Remainders: Challenge

298.   C
EXPL: Statement (1) is insufficient. The remainder of $\frac{m}{n}$ is equal to the quotient (an integer) plus the remainder divided by n. We know that 12 is the integer part, so:

$\frac{m}{n} = 12 + \frac{r}{n}$

We know that $\frac{r}{n} = \frac{64}{100} = \frac{32}{50} = \frac{16}{25}$

That doesn't tell us the value of r, though, it just gives us a ratio.

Statement (2) is also insufficient: there are 49 possible remainders that are less than 50.

Taken together, the statements are sufficient. A remainder must be a positive integer, and since n is an integer and the ratio of $\frac{r}{n} = \frac{16}{25}$ tells us that n must be a multiple of 25. There is only one multiple of 25 less than 50, so $n = 25$, which means that $r = 16$. Choice (C) is correct.

299.   E
EXPL: Given the information in the question, the value of a could be 8, 13, 18, etc.–3 greater than any multiple of 5.

Statement (1) is insufficient. a could be 7, 13, 19, 25, etc. There's one overlap so far between that list and the initial lists of possible a's–it could be 13. However, it could be 43 as well. To find that number quickly, realize that the patterns of multiples of 5 and 6 "restart" every 30 integers (30, because that's the least common multiple of 5 and 6). So a could be 13 greater than any multiple of 30.

Statement (2) is also insufficient. The logic in (1) suggests that, whatever the possible values of a, there will be more than 1. In this case, a again could be 13, and since the LCM of 5 and 4 is 20, the process will restart every 20 integers. So a could be 13 greater than any multiple of 20, meaning that a might be 13, 33, 53, etc.

Taken together, the statements are still insufficient. We've seen that a could be 13, and it could also be 13 greater than the LCM of the three numbers, which is 60, or any multiple thereof. So while a must be of the form $60i + 13$, that doesn't give us a single value. Choice (E) is correct.

300.   D
EXPL: The key concept here is that, if x, y, and z are consecutive integers, both the sum of the integers and the product of the integers will be divisible by 3. To see why, represent the integers in terms of one variable:

$a, a + 1, a + 2$

The sum of these is:

$a + (a + 1) + (a + 2) = 3a + 3 = 3(a + 1)$

Since a is an integer, $a + 1$ is an integer, so the sum is 3 times an integer, or a multiple of 3.

An easier way to see that the product is a multiple of 3 is to recognize that every third number is a multiple of 3. So whichever three consecutive numbers you choose, one of them will be a multiple of 3. Multiply that number by two other integers, and you still have a multiple of 3.

So, each statement can be evaluated in a similar manner. If $x + y + z$ has a remainder of 2 when divided by 3, it is not a multiple of 3, so the three integers are not consecutive. If xyz has a remainder of 1, it is also not divisible by 3, which means the numbers aren't consecutive. Choice (D) is correct.

234 Explanations: Average: Drill

1. Find the average (arithmetic mean) of each of the following sets:

  a. $\frac{200+208+234}{3} = \frac{642}{3} = 214$

  b. $\frac{4+6+10+11+14}{5} = \frac{45}{5} = 9$

  c. $\frac{96+82+86+90+86}{5} = \frac{440}{5} = 88$

  d. $\frac{3+5+7+9+11+13+15}{7} = \frac{63}{7} = 9$

  Also, you can use the method described in the consecutive numbers section: since the numbers are consecutive, the mean is the median, 9.

  e. $\frac{50+60+70+80}{4} = \frac{260}{4} = 65$

  Again, the terms in this set are consecutive, so the mean is the median.

2. Find the sum of the terms in each of the following sets:

  a. $sum = (\#)(avg) = 6(92) = 552$

  b. $sum = (\#)(avg) = 6.5(12) = 78$

  c. $sum = (\#)(avg) = 3(180) = 540$

  d. $sum = (\#)(avg) = 5(9.6) = 48$

  e. $sum = (\#)(avg) = 4(15\frac{3}{4}) = 63$

3. The sum of the terms is $3(140) = 420$. Take away 160, and the remaining terms sum to $420 - 160 = 260$.

4. The sum of the terms is $5(7.6) = 38$. Take away 8, and the remaining 4 terms sum to $38 - 8 = 30$, so the average is $\frac{30}{4} = 7.5$.

5. Note: The sum of the terms in the set is $6(32) = 192$.

  a. The sum of the remaining terms is $192 - 32 = 160$. $\frac{160}{5} = 32$

  b. The sum of the remaining terms is $192 - 22 = 170$. $\frac{170}{5} = 34$

  c. Those two terms sum to 72, meaning that the sum of the remaining terms is $192 - 72 = 120$. $\frac{120}{4} = 30$

  d. Those three terms sum to 63, meaning that the sum of the remaining terms is $192 - 63 = 129$. $\frac{129}{3} = 43$

  e. The remaining term is $192 - 165 = 27$

  f. The sum of those five terms is $5(30) = 150$, so the remaining term is $192 - 150 = 42$.

  g. The sum of the new set is $192 + 25 = 217$. $\frac{217}{7} = 31$

  h. If six terms average 39 and six terms average 32, you can just average the two averages. (This only works when they have the same weight–six apiece.) $\frac{39+32}{2} = \frac{71}{2} = 35.5$

235   Explanations: Average: Practice

301.   C

EXPL: Given an average of a certain number of terms, you can also find the sum of the terms; this isn't always helpful, but it's good to remember that they are one and the same. In this case, if the average of 6 numbers is 75, the sum of the 6 numbers is $6(75) = 450$.

Statement (1) is insufficient. If exactly four of the numbers are 75, then the other two numbers must sum to 150 (and also average 75) but cannot equal 75. In that case, one of the numbers is larger and one is smaller than 75. However, the question leaves a loophole: just because four of the numbers are 75 doesn't mean that the other two numbers can't be 75, as well.

Statement (2) is also insufficient: if one of the numbers is less than 75, there are a number of possibilities. One is a set like this:

$\{50, 75, 75, 75, 75, 100\}$, in which one number is greater than 75.

Another looks like this:

$\{50, 80, 80, 80, 80, 80\}$, in which five are greater than 75.

Taken together, the statements are sufficient. If four of the numbers are 75 and one of the numbers is less than 75, the other number must be greater than 75, as in the first set mentioned regarding (2) above. Choice (C) is correct.

302.   A

EXPL: To find Juan's highest score, we need to know his other two scores. Statement (1) is enough: with the sum of those two lower scores, we can set up an equation with the given average:

$57 = \frac{107+x}{3}$

The numerator represents the total of the three scores: the two lowest scores (107) and the one unknown, highest score. Solve for x to answer the question.

Statement (2) is insufficient. As a matter of fact, it doesn't give us any new information at all. When we learn the average of three terms, we also learn the sum of the terms: $(average)(3)$. In this case, the average of 57 gives us a sum of $57(3) = 171$, so (2) doesn't offer us any additional data. Choice (A) is correct.

303.   E

EXPL: To find the average of the two numbers, it's good enough to find the sum: with the sum, you could easily find the average. It's just a little simpler to look for the sum than the average.

Statement (1) is insufficient:

$\frac{3p+2q}{2} = 12$

$3p + 2q = 24$

There's no way to manipulate that equation to give us $p + q$.

Statement (2) is also insufficient:

$\frac{p^2+q^2}{2} = 26$

$p^2 + q^2 = 52$

Again, there's no way to manipulate that to find $p + q$.

Taken together, the statements are still insufficient. While we do have two distinct equations with two variables, the second equation is not linear. Thus, we can't solve these as a system; we would end up with multiple possible results for p and q, and thus multiple possible answers for $p + q$. (E) is the correct choice.

304.   C

EXPL: To find the average of three numbers, it's enough to find their sum, which you could then divide by 3. Statement (1) is insufficient: you're given two linear equations with three variables. You could tinker around the manipulate the equations, but you'll never find the value of $x + y + z$. Statement (2) is also insufficient: it offers no information about x or y.

Taken together, the statements are sufficient. They give you three distinct linear equations; more practically, you can use $z = 0$ to solve for x and y in the equations given in (1); with the values of x, y, and z, you can find the average of the numbers to solve the problem. Choice (C) is correct.

305.   B

EXPL: The question gives you two equations, each of which you can simplify:
$\frac{a+b}{2} = 40$
$a + b = 80$
$\frac{b+c}{2} = 56$
$b + c = 112$

Given those two equations, you don't have enough information to solve for any of the variables, but you may be able to calculate the difference between two of the variables. To do so, you need to find a way to combine the two equations and get rid of b, which has no part in the desired expression. Subtract the first equation from the second:
$b + c = 112$
$-(a + b = 80)$
$c - a = 112 - 80 = 32$, choice (B).

306.   A

In a set with five numbers, the median is the the middle term–half of the other terms are greater, half of the other terms are less. Thus, the median is $y + 4$.

To calculate the mean, sum the five terms:
$y + (y + 3) + (y + 4) + (y + 6) + (y + 7)$
$= 5y + 20$
Then divide by 5:
$\frac{5y+20}{5} = y + 4$
That's the same as the median, so choice (A) is correct.

236   Explanations: Weighted Average: Drill

1. $\frac{4(86)+2(92)}{6}$

   Subtract 86 from each term:

   $\frac{4(0)+2(6)}{6} = \frac{12}{6} = 2$

   Add 86: $2 + 86 = 88$

2. $\frac{3(14,000)+2(16,000)+2(19,000)}{7}$

   Subtract 14,000 from each term:

   $\frac{3(0)+2(2,000)+2(5,000)}{7} = \frac{4,000+10,000}{7} = \frac{14,000}{7} = 2,000$

   Add 14,000: $2,000 + 14,000 = 16,000$

3. $\frac{5(9.2)+3(8.4)}{8} =$

   Subtract 8.4 from each term:

   $\frac{5(0.8)+3(0)}{8} = \frac{4}{8} = 0.5$

   Add 8.4: $8.4 + 0.5 = 8.9$

4. $\frac{6(28)+4(x)}{10} = 31.20$

   Subtract 28 from each term:

   $\frac{6(0)+4x}{10} = 3.20$

   $4x = 32$

   $x = 8$

   Add 28 back to the answer: $8 + 28 = 36$

5. $\frac{3(7\frac{1}{4})+2(x)}{5} = 8\frac{1}{4}$

   Subtract $7\frac{1}{4}$ from each term:

   $\frac{3(0)+2x}{5} = 1$

   $2x = 5$

   $x = 2.5$

   Add $7\frac{1}{4}$ back to the answer: $2\frac{1}{2} + 7\frac{1}{4} = 9\frac{3}{4}$

6. $\frac{3(72)+5(52)+2(x)}{10} = 61$

   Subtract 52 from each of the terms:

   $\frac{3(20)+5(0)+2x}{10} = 9$

   $60 + 2x = 90$

   $2x = 30$

   $x = 15$

   Add 52 back to the answer: $15 + 52 = 67$

7. $\frac{5(480)+x(440)}{5+x} = 465$

   Subtract 440 from each term:

   $\frac{5(40)+x(0)}{5+x} = 25$

   $200 = 25(5 + x)$

   $200 = 125 + 25x$

$25x = 75$

$x = 3$

x represented the number of those who averaged 440 pounds, so the total number of participants is $5 + x = 5 + 3 = 8$.

8. $\quad \frac{2(18)+4(26)+x(30)}{6+x} = 26$

Subtract 18 from each term:

$\frac{1(0)+4(8)+x(12)}{6+x} = 8$

$0 + 32 + 12x = 48 + 8x$

$4x = 16$

$x = 4$

9. There are two equations here: the two weights sum to one:

$\frac{x(12)+y(15)}{1} = 13$

$x + y = 1$

$x(12) + (1 - x)(15) = 13$

$12x + 15 - 15x = 13$

$-3x = -2$

$x = \frac{2}{3}$

$y = \frac{1}{3}$

$y : x = \frac{1}{3} : \frac{2}{3} = 1 : 2$

10. There are two equations here, the second of which indicates that the weights sum to one:

$\frac{x(0.2)+y(0.56)}{1} = 0.4$

$x + y = 1$

$0.2x + (1 - x)(0.56) = 0.4$

$0.2x + 0.56 - 0.56x = 0.4$

$-0.36x = -0.16$

$36x = 16$

$x = \frac{16}{36} = \frac{4}{9}$

$y = \frac{5}{9}$

$x : y = \frac{4}{9} : \frac{5}{9} = 4 : 5$

237   Explanations: Weighted Average: Practice

311.   A
EXPL: This is a fairly straightforward example. Using the weighted average formula:

$\frac{(125)(200)+(25)(500)}{150} =$

As usual, this will be easier if you shrink the numbers involved. Subtract 200 from each of the quantities:

$\frac{(125)(0)+(25)(300)}{150} = \frac{25(300)}{150} = \frac{25(2)}{1} = 50$

To find the answer, add 200 back to the result:
$50 + 200 = 250$, choice (A).

312.   C
EXPL: Set up the weighted average formula, dropping the thousands for convenience:

$\frac{2(21)+1(22)+3(24)}{6} =$

To make things simpler still, subtract 21 from each of the salaries:

$\frac{2(0)+1(1)+3(3)}{6} = \frac{1+9}{6} = \frac{10}{6} = \frac{5}{3}$

Add 21 back to the result:
$21 + \frac{5}{3} = 22\frac{2}{3}$, which is closest to choice (C), \$22,700.

313.   B
EXPL: Set up the weighted average formula:

$\frac{10(10\frac{1}{4})+8(12\frac{1}{8})}{18} =$

Subtract $10\frac{1}{4}$ from each of the quantities:

$\frac{10(0)+8(1\frac{7}{8})}{18} = \frac{15}{18}$

Add $10\frac{1}{4}$ back to the result:
$\frac{15}{18} + 10\frac{1}{4} = \frac{30}{36} + 10\frac{9}{36} = 10 + \frac{39}{36} = 11 + \frac{3}{36} = 11\frac{1}{12}$, choice (B).

314.   C
EXPL: Statement (1) is insufficient: it provides an equation with three variables:

$\frac{a+b+c}{3} = 10$

or:

$a + b + c = 30$

Statement (2) is also insufficient. It doesn't tell us anything about c, though it does provide a second equation with some of the same variables mentioned in (1):

$\frac{a+b}{2} = 7.5$

or:

$a + b = 15$

Taken together, the statements are sufficient. If you plug in the equation from (2) into the equation from (1), the result is:

$a + b + c = 30$

$(15) + c = 30$

$c = 15$

Choice (C) is correct.

238 Explanations; Weighted Average: Challenge

315.   D

EXPL: All the variables may make this question look daunting, but it's exactly like any other weighted average question. The numerator contains the sum of the total numbers of points. If the team scored x points per game for m games, that's a total of xm points. Similarly, the next p games have a point total of py points.

As with any average, the answer is the sum $(xm + py)$ over the number, and the question almost gives you the denominator. Since you're dividing points per game, the denominator is the number of games, $m + p$:
$\frac{xm+py}{m+p}$, choice (D).

316.   C

Explanation: Statement (1) is insufficient. Knowing the average salaries of the two populations of employees doesn't tell us anything about which company had more employees.

Statement (2) is also insufficient. Again, knowing an average salary isn't enough to determine the number of people receiving any particular salary.

Taken together, the statements are sufficient. If there were an equal number of employees from each company, the overall average salary would be at the midpoint of the two company-average salaries. That midpoint would be $\frac{41,200+44,700}{2} = 42,950$. Since the average is higher than that midpoint, there must be more employees from Company B–Company B's employees have a greater "weight" in the overall average. Choice (C) is correct.

317.   D

This is a tricky question, and it would be even worse if you didn't know if was classified as a weighted average. First, reduce the number of variables in the equation by substituting $a + b$ for c:
$x = 8(\frac{a}{a+b}) + 16(\frac{b}{a+b})$
Combine the fractions:
$\frac{8a}{a+b} + \frac{16b}{a+b} = \frac{8a+16b}{a+b}$
This is easier to understand if you think of it as a word problem. Say a is the number of $8 tickets sold and b is the number of $16 tickets sold. Thus the numerator is the total price of the tickets and the denominator is the total number of tickets. The result is the weighted average. Since we know that a and b are both positive integers, the average must be between 8 and 16, eliminating (A) and (E).

Also note that b is greater than a. In terms of the hypothetical word problem, that means more $16 than $8 tickets were sold. If equal numbers were sold, the average price would be right in the middle, at $12. Since more $16s were sold, that means the average price is above $12. The only possible choice is 15, choice (D).

318.   B

The question tells us that Kelvin took six quizzes, his score on at least one of them was 70, and all of his other scores were no lower than 70.

Statement (1) is insufficient. We know that three of the scores are either 70, 72, 74 or something very close to that, but we don't know anything about the other three. If the other three scores are 75, 76, 77, the answer is "yes." If the other three scores are all 90, the answer is "no."

Statement (2) is sufficient. Three of his scores are 92, 92, 92, or something similar. While we don't know the specifics of the other scores, we do know they are each no less than 70. If they are as low as they can possibly be (70, 70, 70), the overall average is 81. If they are any higher, the average is higher than 81. Thus, the average score must be greater than 80. Choice (B) is correct.

239   Explanations: Statistics: Drill

1.   Find the median and range of each of the following sets. If any numbers appear more than once in a set, find the mode as well:

      a. $\{-4, 6, 3, 1, -7, 2, 3\}$
          median: 2
          range: 13
          mode: 3

      b. $\{12, 12, 18\}$
          median: 12
          range: 6
          mode: 12

      c. $\{1, 2, 3, 4, 5, 6, 7, 8, 9\}$
          median: 5
          range: 8

      d. $\{15, 16\}$
          median: 15.5
          range: 1

      e. $\{-10, 6, 11, -2, \frac{3}{2}, -15\}$
          median: $\frac{\frac{3}{2}+(-2)}{2} = \frac{-\frac{1}{2}}{2} = -\frac{1}{4}$
          range: 26

2.   e, c, a, b, d

3.   Find the value of x:

      a. $15 + 2(2.5) = 15 + 5 = 20$
      b. $12 - \frac{5}{3} = \frac{36}{3} - \frac{5}{3} = \frac{31}{3}$
      c. $-5 + 1.5(1.5) = -5 + 2.25 = -2.75$
      d. $m - 2(3.5) = m - 7$
      e. $m - sk$

240   Explanations: Statistics: Practice

321.   C
EXPL: To find the median of a list of numbers, first the numbers in order:
$\{54, 60, 65, 70, 72, 75\}$
Since there are an even number of terms in the list, the median is the average
of the middle two terms, in this case 65 and 70:
$\frac{65+70}{2} = \frac{135}{2} = 67.5$, choice (C).

322.   C
EXPL: If 1 standard deviation is 1.75, 3 standard deviations is 3 times that:
$3(1.75) = 5.25$. Thus, a number 3 standard deviations below the mean is 5.25
below the mean, which is this case is 13:
$13 - 5.25 = 7.75$, choice (C).

323.   E
EXPL: To find the mean of the numbers is S, add up the terms and divide
by the number of terms, which in this case is 6:
$\frac{18+7+11+3+15+0}{6} = \frac{54}{6} = 9$
To find the median, line up the numbers in ascending order:
$\{0, 3, 7, 11, 15, 18\}$
and, since there are an even number of terms, find the mean of the middle
two numbers, 7 and 11:
$\frac{7+11}{2} = \frac{18}{2} = 9$
The mean and median are equal, so the difference is 0.0, choice (E).

324.   D
EXPL: Statement (1) is sufficient. If the range of any subset of a set is
greater than 5, the range of the set must be greater than 5. For instance, if
x and y are 6 apart, it doesn't matter what w and z are; the range cannot be
smaller than 6, because x and y are that far apart. The range may be greater,
but the range of the subset (in this case, x and y) sets a lower bound for the
range.
Statement (2) is sufficient. If the range (positive difference) between any
two numbers must be greater than 3, the smallest the range of the entire set
could be would be something like this:
$\{0, 3.1, 6.2, 9.3\}$, in which the range is just a bit more than 9. Choice (D) is
correct.

325.   C
EXPL: Aside from the two variables, the range of the integers is 3, the
difference between 4 and 7. For the range of the six integers to be greater than
9, one of three things needs to be true:
     1. x or y is less than $7 - 9 = -2$
     2. x or y is greater than $4 + 9 = 13$

3.   The positive difference between x and y is greater than 9.

Statement (1) is insufficient. If x is large enough, the range could be greater than 9 (say $x = 5$ and $y > 25$), but if $x = 1$, y simply has to be greater than 1. That satisfies none of the possibilities set forth above.

Statement (2) is also insufficient: x and y could be 4 and 5, respectively (range is less than 9) or much larger numbers, in which case the range could be greater than 9.

Taken together, the statements are sufficient. If x must be an integer greater than 3, the smallest it can be is 4. If $y > x^2$ and $x = 4$, then y must be greater than 16, which satisfies the second of the possibilities described above. (C) is the correct choice.

326.   A

Explanation: In a set of numbers, the mean is equal to the median if the numbers are equally spaced, as in consecutive integers, consecutive evens, or consecutive multiples of 5.

Statement (1) is sufficient: it establishes that the numbers in the set are consecutive, so they are equally spaced, so the mean and the median are equal. Statement (2) is insufficient: it doesn't matter what the first number is; if the first number is odd, the numbers could be equally spaced, or they could not be. The correct choice is (A).

241   Explanations: Statistics: Challenge

327.   D

Explanation: To find a value one standard deviation below the mean,
subtract the standard deviation (d, in this case) from the mean (m). That
gives us the answer:

$m - d$, choice (D).

328.   C

Explanation: The question doesn't give us the order of the three numbers,
but we do know that the difference between the largest and smallest is 8. We
need to know the value of the smallest number in the set–at this point, we don't
even know which variable that is.

Statement (1) is insufficient. We can build an equation: $\frac{x+y+z+8}{4} = 12.5$,
which simplifies to $x + y + z + 8 = 50$, or $x + y + z = 42$. That might be
helpful when combined with the other statement, but it doesn't tell us how big
the smallest value is.

Statement (2) is also insufficient. What it does tell us is that, since the
mean and median are equal, the numbers in the set are equally spaced. Since
the largest and smallest numbers are 8 apart, the only way for the set to be
equally spaced is if the middle number is 4 away from each of the other two.
Thus, if x is the smaller number, $x+4$ is the middle number (median and mean),
and the largest number is $x + 8$. We know the differences between the terms,
but not exactly what those terms are.

Taken together, the statements are sufficient. If we call the smallest number
x (it doesn't matter what you call it – all we need is value of the smallest number,
regardless of which variable it is), we know that the sum of the three terms x,
$x + 4$, and $x + 8$ is 42. From there, we can solve for x (though we don't have
to, to answer the question):

$x + (x + 4) + (x + 8) = 42$
$3x + 12 = 42$
$3x = 30$
$x = 10$
Choice (C) is correct.

329.   E

Explanation: To find the median price, we're looking for the price at
which an equal number of automobiles are more and less expensive than that
price. One way to find the median is to find a complete list of all the prices.
Alternatively, if we knew that an equal number were more and less expensive
than a certain price, we'd also know the median.

Statement (1) is insufficient. While the average and median do sometimes
coincide, we don't know enough about the prices to know whether that is the
case here. While the average price reflects the total of the prices and the number
of automobiles, the median reflects the exact prices.

Statement (2) is also insufficient. The question establishes that, if we ranked the prices in ascending order, all the car prices would come first, followed by all of the truck prices. Since there are more trucks than cars, we know that the median is $27,500 or greater. However, without knowing the exact prices of some or all of the trucks, we can't find the exact median.

Taken together, the statements are still insufficient. Neither statement fills in the gaps of the other. We know that that the median price is at least $27,500 from (2), but the average of all the prices doesn't help us narrow things down. Choice (E) is correct.

242   Explanations: Overlapping Sets: Drill

1. $T = G_1 + G_2 - B + N$
         $T = 250 + 600 - 150 + 200 = 900$

2. $T = G_1 + G_2 - B + N$
         $T = 20 + 12 - 5 + 11 = 38$

3. $T = G_1 + G_2 - B + N$
         $180 = 35 + 50 - B + 125$
         $180 = 210 - B$
         $B = 30$

4. $T = G_1 + G_2 - B + N$
         $80 = 54 + 20 - B + 22$
         $80 = 96 - B$
         $B = 16$

5. $T = G_1 + G_2 - B + N$
         $36 = 21 + 25 - 15 + N$
         $36 = 31 + N$
         $N = 5$

6. $T = G_1 + G_2 - B + N$
         $96 = 65 + 40 - 18 + N$
         $96 = 87 + N$
         $N = 9$

7. $T = G_1 + G_2 - B + N$
         $32 = 20 + G_2 - 4 + 0$
         $32 = 16 + G_2$
         $G_2 = 16$

8. $T = G_1 + G_2 - B + N$
         $75 = 20 + G_2 - 15 + 13$
         $75 = 18 + G_2$
         $G_2 = 57$

9. $T = G_1 + G_2 + G_3 - (overlaps) + N$
         $45 = 22 + 20 + 15 - overlaps + 0$
         $45 = 57 - overlaps$
         $overlaps = 12$

10. $T = G_1 + G_2 + G_3 - (overlaps) + N$
          $T = 40 + 35 + 36 - (9 + 12 + 6) + 0$
          $T = 111 - (27) = 84$

243   Explanations: Overlapping Sets: Practice

331.   C

EXPL: If we use the overlapping sets formula and define the groups as follows:

Group 1: Women

Group 2: At least 40 years old

The first piece of information is "Both," while we're looking for "Neither." Since we're working with percents, the "Total" is 100:

$100 = G_1 + G_2 - 30 + N$

Statement (1) is insufficient. If 30 percent of the women are at least 40 and that represents half of the women, 60 percent of the club members are women. That gets us closer, but we still have too many variables:

$100 = 60 + G_2 - 30 + N$

Statement (2) is also insufficient. If 30 percent of the members are women who are at least 40, and that represents half of the 40+ population, 60 percent of the members must be 40 or older. That's Group 2:

$100 = G_1 + 60 - 30 + N$

Taken together, the statements are sufficient. (1) gives us Group 1, (2) gives us Group 2, and those leave us with only one variable, "Neither," which is what we're looking for. Choice (C) is correct.

332.   E

EXPL: The question gives us the total (100%) and "both" (30%). Don't be distracted by the fact that one of the characteristics is also a percent: that's irrelevant to our calculations.

Statement (1) is insufficient: we can call this Group 1, which leaves us with two remaining variables, Group 2 (the percent of stocks that increased at least 5%) and Neither (those that didn't return a dividend or increase at least 5%).

Statement (2) is also insufficient: in fact, it's worthless. We're interested in the stocks that increased at least 5% last year, and while we know that the number of stocks that increased 5% must be greater or equal to the number that increased 10%, we don't know by how much.

Taken together, the statements are still insufficient. (2) doesn't help at all, so we're still left looking for Group 2 and Neither. Choice (E) is correct.

333.   C

EXPL: The question gives us Group 1 (the percent of towels retailing for $9.99 or more), Group 2 (discounted), and Neither (less than $9.99, not discounted). Since the question uses percents, we know the total is 100, and we can solve:

$100 = 60 + 30 - B + 40$

$100 = 130 - B$

$B = 30$, choice (C).

334.   D

Explanation: If 25% speak Japanese, 75% do not. That 75% includes the 11 who speak Spanish and the 19 who do not, for a total of 30. We're looking for the number who speak Japanese. Since 25% is one-third of 75%, the number that speaks Japanese is one-third that of the number that doesn't speak Japanese, 30. One-third of 30 is 10, choice (D).

335.   72% of the total entrees were fish entrees, and 54% of the total entrees were salmon entrees. That means that 18% $(72 - 54)$ were fish entrees that were not salmon entrees.

We want to know what percent of the fish entrees were not salmon:

$\frac{not-salmon}{total-fish} = \frac{18\%}{72\%} = \frac{1}{4} = 25\%$, choice (B).

244   Explanations: Overlapping Sets: Challenge

336.   A

EXPL: Combining the first two clauses, $\frac{1}{3}N$ of the people received a degree in the applied sciences. $\frac{1}{4}$ of them graduated from a school in a northeastern state, so the number of people in both categories is:

$\frac{1}{4}(\frac{1}{3}N) = \frac{1}{12}N$

The question is asking for the opposite: all those who don't fit into both categories. The opposite of a fraction is 1 minus that fraction:

$N - \frac{1}{12}N = \frac{11}{12}N$, choice (A).

337.   C

EXPL: There are several subgroups in the 250 students:

mathematics, computer science, or biology only (though the question tells us that no student majors in mathematics only)

any overlap of two of the three subjects (though mathematics and biology only is impossible)

students who major in none of the three

So, 250 is the sum of five subgroups:

$250 = CS + B + (M\&CS) + (B\&CS) + None$

We're given one of those values:

$250 = CS + 90 + (M\&CS) + (B\&CS) + None$

We're looking for the sum of the two overlaps. To find that, we'll need both the number of CS only, and the number of None.

Statements (1) and (2) are both insufficient on their own, as they give us one of those categories, and not both.

Taken together, they are sufficient.   We know all of the subgroups except for the two overlaps:

$250 = 50 + 90 + (M\&CS) + (B\&CS) + 40$

$250 = 180 + overlaps$

$overlaps = 70$

Choice (C) is correct.

338.   B

If 116 of the shirts are long-sleeved and 75 percent of those are on sale, that means that $116(\frac{3}{4}) = \frac{116(3)}{4} = 29(3) = 87$ of the long-sleeved shirts are on sale. That leaves $116 - 87 = 29$ of the long-sleeved shirts that are not on sale. We're looking for the probability that a shirt is long-sleeved and not on sale; there are 29 of those shirts, and a total of 174, so the probability is $\frac{29}{174} = \frac{29}{6(29)} = \frac{1}{6}$, choice (B).

339.   C

Call the number who work part-time p and the number who have worked for at least five years f.

Statement (1) is insufficient. It introduces a third variable: The number of employees who fit into both categories. If 60 percent of p is not also part of f, that means 40 percent of p is part of f. Let's call that overlap x. Thus, $x = .4p$. 40 percent of those who work part-time have worked for the company for five years. That doesn't help us compare f and p.

Statement (2) is also insufficient. By the same reasoning, if 70 percent of those who have worked for five years do not work part-time, 30 percent do. Thus, $x = .3f$. This is a step forward, but not enough information to answer the question.

Taken together, the statements are sufficient. We know that $x = .4p = .3f$. More simply:

$$.4p = .3f$$
$$4p = 3f$$
$$\frac{4}{3} = \frac{f}{p}$$

If the ratio of five-year employees to part-time employees is 4 : 3, there are more five-year employees. We can answer the question, and the correct choice is (C).

340.   B

EXPL: The total number of students is given by the following:

$(basketball) + (soccer) + (tennis) - overlap =$

The overlap is the sum of all three of the specific overlaps, 6, 5, and 3:

$20 + 25 + 12 - (6 + 5 + 3) =$
$57 - 14 = 43$, choice (B).

245   Explanations: Probability: Drill

1. $(\frac{1}{2})(\frac{1}{2})(\frac{1}{2}) = \frac{1}{8}$

2. $(\frac{1}{2})(\frac{1}{2}) = \frac{1}{4}$

3. $p_{green} + p_{white} = \frac{4}{27} + \frac{8}{27} = \frac{12}{27} = \frac{4}{9}$

4. $p_{blonde} + p_{dark} = \frac{8}{20} + \frac{7}{20} = \frac{15}{20} = \frac{3}{4}$

5. $1 - p_{prime} = 1 - \frac{6}{24} = \frac{18}{24} = \frac{3}{4}$

6. $p_{budget} = 1 - p_{planning/acquisitions} = 1 - \frac{3}{4} = \frac{1}{4}$

7.   Find the opposite: the probability that neither number is odd:

$$p_{\text{neither is odd}} = (\tfrac{2}{3})(\tfrac{1}{2}) = \tfrac{1}{3}$$

$$p_{\text{at least one is odd}} = 1 - \tfrac{1}{3} = \tfrac{2}{3}$$

8.   Find the opposite: the probability that neither results in a prime number. Of the first six integers, three are prime, so the probability that a roll results in a non-prime is $\frac{1}{2}$.

$$p_{\text{neither is prime}} = (\tfrac{1}{2})(\tfrac{1}{2}) = \tfrac{1}{4}$$

$$p_{\text{at least one is prime}} = 1 - \tfrac{1}{4} = \tfrac{3}{4}$$

9.   The probability that the first selection is a boy is $\frac{6}{10}$. After one boy is removed, there are 5 boys and 9 total students remaining, so the probability that the second selection is a boy is $\frac{5}{9}$. Thus, the probability that both are boys is:

$$p = (\tfrac{6}{10})(\tfrac{5}{9}) = \tfrac{30}{90} = \tfrac{1}{3}$$

10.   The probability that Paula is selected as president is $\frac{1}{8}$. Once a president is selected, there are 7 possible secretaries, so the probability that Quentin is selected as secretary is $\frac{1}{7}$. The probability that both are selected is:

$$p = (\tfrac{1}{8})(\tfrac{1}{7}) = \tfrac{1}{56}$$

246   Explanations: Probability: Practice

341.   D

EXPL: When you see the phrase "at least," it's a clue that it will be easier to solve for the opposite of what the question is asking for. In this case, at least one head is the sum of a whole slew of probabilities: one head, two heads, or three heads. The opposite, however, is just one probability: the odds that three tosses results in no heads.

The probability of flipping a coin and not getting a head (that is, getting a tail) is $\frac{1}{2}$. So, the probability of not getting a head three consecutive times is:

$p = \left(\frac{1}{2}\right)\left(\frac{1}{2}\right)\left(\frac{1}{2}\right) = \frac{1}{8}$

But, recall, that's the opposite of what we're looking for. Thus, we need to subtract that number from 1:

$p = 1 - \frac{1}{8} = \frac{7}{8}$, choice (D).

342.   B

EXPL.   First, determine the total number of integers between 101 and 250, inclusive. The difference between 250 and 101 is 149, but because the endpoints are included, the total number of integers is one greater than that: 150.

Second, figure out how many of those 150 integers have a tens digit of 1. In the 100s (100 to 199, inclusive), there are 10 numbers with a tens digit of 1: the integers between 110 and 119, inclusive. The same goes for the 200s: we can include all the integers between 210 and 219, inclusive. That gives us a total of 20 desired outcomes.

The probability, then, is desired over possible:

$p = \frac{20}{150} = \frac{2}{15}$, choice (B).

343.   E

EXPL: While this looks like a probability question, it relies more on your fraction manipulation skill. If a random number is to be selected, it is most likely to occur in the range of numbers that is the largest. So, you must evaluate each of the five choices to determine which is the largest. To do that, it's important to make them easier to compare; rather than using an amalgam of different denominators, convert them all to one common denominator and find the difference using that denominator:

(A) $\frac{13}{20} - \frac{10}{20} = \frac{3}{20}$

(B) $\frac{14}{20} - \frac{13}{20} = \frac{1}{20}$

(C) $\frac{15}{20} - \frac{14}{20} = \frac{1}{20}$

(D) $\frac{16}{20} - \frac{15}{20} = \frac{1}{20}$

(E) $\frac{20}{20} - \frac{16}{20} = \frac{4}{20}$

Of these, (E) is the largest, so it is the correct choice.

344.   In this case, probability is the same as a fraction. If $\frac{1}{2}$ of the residents are men over the age of 60, the probability of selecting such a resident is $\frac{1}{2}$.

If the number of residents is r, the number of men is $0.4r$. If 15% of those are over 60, the number of men over 60 is:

$(0.15)(0.4)r$

It might be easier to work with fractions here:

$(\frac{3}{20})(\frac{2}{5})r = \frac{6}{100}r = 0.06$, choice (B).

247   Explanations: Probability: Challenge

345.   D

EXPL: For xy to be even, either x, y, or both must be even. The only way xy will not be even is if both x and y are odd. Since the latter is only one probability, while the former is three, it's most efficient to solve for the latter–the opposite of what the question is asking for. Just remember to subtract the result from 1 before selecting an answer.

The probability that both numbers are odd relies on the probabilities that each individual number is odd. In the set that x is chosen from, there are 3 numbers, 2 of which are odd. Thus, the probability that x is odd is $\frac{2}{3}$. In the set that y is chosen from, there are 4 numbers, 2 of which are odd. Thus, the probability that y is odd is $\frac{1}{2}$. The probability that both are odd, then, is:

$$p = \left(\tfrac{2}{3}\right)\left(\tfrac{1}{2}\right) = \tfrac{1}{3}$$

Remember that $\frac{1}{3}$ is the opposite of what we're solving for; subtract that from 1:

$$p = 1 - \tfrac{1}{3} = \tfrac{2}{3}, \text{ choice (D)}.$$

346.   D

Explanation: Take the first bag of 100 marbles.   10 of the numbers overlap, so there is a $\frac{10}{100}$ chance that there is a possibility of an overlap. (There's a 90% chance already that the numbers will not be the same; for instance, that's the case if the first marble drawn is numbered 72.)

Once the first marble is drawn, the only way the two marbles will have the same number is if the second marble has exactly the same number. In other words, if we drew 96 from the first bag, we're looking for the probability of drawing 96 from the second bag, as well.

The probability of drawing a specific number from the second bag is $\frac{1}{60}$. In order to draw the same marble from both bags, we need both of those events to happen, so we multiply the probabilities:

$$\tfrac{1}{10} \times \tfrac{1}{60} = \tfrac{1}{600}, \text{ choice (D)}.$$

347.   C

First, consider how students could be selected so that more juniors than sophomores are selected. It's impossible to have 4 juniors and 0 sophomores, because there are only 3 juniors to choose from. There could be 3 juniors and 1 sophomore. Any fewer juniors, and there are equal numbers of juniors and sophomores. So, to find the probability of selecting 3 juniors and 1 sophomore, figure out how many combinations of students consist of 3 juniors and 1 sophomore, then how many total combinations of students could be selected.

First, 3 juniors and 1 sophomore. There is only one way to select 3 juniors from a group of 3 juniors–by selecting them all. There are 3 ways to select one sophomore from a group of 3 – we can choose any of the individual sophomores. Thus, the number of combinations consisting of 3 juniors and 1 sophomore is $3(1) = 3$.

Now, for the total number of combinations. There are 6 total students, of which 4 will be chosen. For this, we can use the combinations formula:

$\frac{n!}{k!(n-k)!}$, where $n = 6$ and $k = 4$.

$\frac{6!}{4!(2)!} = \frac{6 \times 5 \times 4 \times 3 \times 2 \times 1}{4 \times 3 \times 2 \times 1 \times 2 \times 1} = 15$

The probability of selecting 3 juniors and 1 sophomore, then, is $\frac{3}{15} = \frac{1}{5}$, choice (C).

348.   A

EXPL: Say that the number of members older than 35 in the group is n. The probability that both selected members will be 35+ is $\frac{n}{8} \times \frac{n-1}{7}$—that is, the probability that one member selected is over 35+ times the probability that the other member selected (from a smaller pool, and a smaller number of 35+ members) is also 35+. Don't do too much work with that before proceeding to the statements, as you could easily spend 2 or 3 minutes working out the possibilities with various numbers of 35+ members.

Statement (1) is sufficient. The minimum number of 35+ members that would constitute more than half of the group is 5. To see if the minimum number generates a p greater than $\frac{1}{3}$, set $n = 5$. Thus, $p = \frac{5}{8} \times \frac{4}{7} = \frac{20}{56} = \frac{5}{14}$. That's a bit higher than $\frac{1}{3}$, since $\frac{1}{3} = \frac{5}{15}$, and the smaller the denominator, the bigger the number. So, if 5 members are 35+, $p > \frac{1}{3}$. If more members are 35+, the probability is even higher.

Statement (2) is not sufficient. We can be fairly confident from the work we did in (1) that the minimum number of 35+ members required so that p is greater than $\frac{1}{3}$ is 5. Let's see, when $n = 5$, what the probability is that both members will NOT be 35+. If the number of 35+ members is 5, the number of other members is 3. For both selections to be other members, the fractions look like: $\frac{3}{8} \times \frac{2}{7} = \frac{6}{56} = \frac{3}{28}$. That's a little bigger than $\frac{1}{10}$, since $\frac{1}{10} = \frac{3}{30}$. So, when (2) is true, it's possible that $n = 5$ and $p > \frac{1}{3}$. However, 3 is merely the minimum possible number of other members. It could be 4, 5, 6, 7, or 8, all of which would generate a different answer to the question. We don't have to do the math–we know that, if when $n = 5$, p is just barely big enough, any smaller number of 35+ members will make p less than $\frac{1}{3}$. Choice (A) is correct.

349.   B

EXPL: The probability we're looking for is actually two separate probabilities: one from Company X and one from Company Y. Start with Company X: the odds of randomly selecting one half of a married couple from Company X is $\frac{50}{800}$. The total number of possibilities is 800, the number of employees. The number of desired outcomes is 50, because there are 50 people in Company X who are married to an employee of Company Y. To simplify:

$p_x = \frac{50}{800} = \frac{1}{16}$

Once we've selected a person from Company X, we only have one chance of selecting that person's spouse from Company Y. While there are 50 employees of Company Y who have spouses in Company X, there's only 1 employee of Company Y who is the spouse of the person we randomly selected from Company X.

Thus, the probability of selecting that person is 1 over the number of employees of Company Y:

$p_y = \frac{1}{600}$

The probability of selecting a married couple, then, is the probability of selecting both a married person from Company X and that person's spouse from Company Y. That's given by the product of the two probabilities:

$p = (\frac{1}{16})(\frac{1}{600}) = \frac{1}{9600}$, choice (B).

350.   C

If she wins on the third day, that means she lost on the first and second day. The probability that she lost on each of the first two days is 1 minus the probability that she won, or 0.9. So, the probabilities that she lost the first day, lost the second day, and won the third day, are 0.9, 0.9, and 0.1. The probability that all three occurred is the product:

$(0.9)(0.9)(0.1) = 0.081$, choice (C).

248   Explanations: Combinations: Drill

1.   For each of the following, determine whether it is a combinations
problem or a permutations problem:
   a.   Permutations
   b.   Combinations
   c.   Combinations
   d.   Permutations

2.   For each of the following, find the number of combinations given
the size of the group n and the size of the subgroup k:

   a. $c = \frac{n!}{k!(n-k)!} = \frac{6!}{3!(6-3)!} = \frac{6!}{3!3!} = \frac{6\times5\times4\times3\times2\times1}{3\times2\times1\times3\times2\times1} = 5 \times 4 = 20$

   b. $c = \frac{n!}{k!(n-k)!} = \frac{8!}{5!(8-5)!} = \frac{8!}{5!3!} = \frac{8\times7\times6\times5\times4\times3\times2\times1}{5\times4\times3\times2\times1\times3\times2\times1} = \frac{8\times7\times6}{3\times2\times1} =$
$8 \times 7 = 56$

   c. $c = \frac{n!}{k!(n-k)!} = \frac{5!}{4!(5-4)!} = \frac{5!}{4!1!} = \frac{5\times4\times3\times2\times1}{4\times3\times2\times1\times1} = 5$

3. $n = 8$ and $k = 3$:
   $c = \frac{n!}{k!(n-k)!} = \frac{8!}{3!(8-3)!} = \frac{8!}{3!5!} = \frac{8\times7\times6\times5\times4\times3\times2\times1}{3\times2\times1\times5\times4\times3\times2\times1} = \frac{8\times7\times6}{3\times2\times1} = 56$

4. $n = 6$ and $k = 2$
   $c = \frac{n!}{k!(n-k)!} = \frac{6!}{2!(6-2)!} = \frac{6!}{2!4!} = \frac{6\times5\times4\times3\times2\times1}{2\times1\times4\times3\times2\times1} = 15$

5.   For the subset of three employees from Company X, $n = 5$ and $k = 3$:
   $c = \frac{n!}{k!(n-k)!} = \frac{5!}{3!(5-3)!} = \frac{5\times4\times3\times2\times1}{3\times2\times1\times2\times1} = 10$

   For the subset of 2 employees from Company Y, $n = 8$ and $k = 2$:
   $c = \frac{n!}{k!(n-k)!} = \frac{8!}{2!(8-2)!} = \frac{8\times7\times6\times5\times4\times3\times2\times1}{2\times1\times6\times5\times4\times3\times2\times1} = 28$

   The resulting number of combinations is the product of those two
numbers: $10(28) = 280$.

249   Explanations: Combinations: Practice

351. C

EXPL: This is a classic combinations question. You can use the formula, where $n = 5$ (the set of lions) and $k = 2$ (the subset selected for each performance):

$c = \frac{n!}{k!(n-k)!} = \frac{5!}{2!(5-2)!} = \frac{5 \times 4 \times 3 \times 2 \times 1}{2 \times 1 \times 3 \times 2 \times 1} = \frac{20}{2} = 10$, choice (C).

352. A

EXPL: While the problem refers to matches, it could just as easily say "pairs of players," which would make this example more obviously a combinations problem. The total number of players is 6, and we want to know how many possible pairs could be generated, so $k = 2$:

$c = \frac{n!}{k!(n-k)!} = \frac{6!}{2!(6-2)!} = \frac{6 \times 5 \times 4 \times 3 \times 2 \times 1}{2 \times 1 \times 4 \times 3 \times 2 \times 1} = 15$, choice (A).

353. D

EXPL: This question involves two separate combinations. First, how many pairs of non-fiction books could Mari select from a group of seven?

$c = \frac{n!}{k!(n-k)!} = \frac{7!}{2!(7-2)!} = 21$

Second, how many single books could she select from a group of ten? That's easier: there are ten individual books she could select. That's 10 "combinations" of one book.

To find the total number of combinations, multiply those numbers:

$21 \times 10 = 210$, choice (D).

354. D

Explanation: This is a combinations problem. There are 10 beads to choose from, and we're looking for of distinct 4-bead subsets. The order doesn't matter. Plug in $n = 10$ and $k = 4$ to the combinations formula:

$\frac{n!}{k!(n-k)!} = \frac{10!}{4!(10-4)!} = \frac{10!}{4!6!} = \frac{10 \times 9 \times 8 \times 7}{4 \times 3 \times 2 \times 1} = 10 \times 3 \times 7 = 210$, choice (D).

250   Explanations: Combinations: Challenge

355.   D

EXPL: This sounds tricky, especially if you try to draw it and work it out on paper. However, you can create a triangle from any three vertices in a hexagon. In fact, this is exactly like a more traditional combinations question: you're choosing three points (the vertices of a triangle) from a set of six (the vertices of the hexagon), and order doesn't matter. Solve it using the equation with $n = 6$ and $k = 3$:
$$c = \frac{n!}{k!(n-k)!} = \frac{6!}{3!(6-3)!} = \frac{6!}{3!3!} = \frac{6\times5\times4\times3\times2\times1}{3\times2\times1\times3\times2\times1} = 5 \times 4 = 20$$

356.   C

EXPL: This is essentially three combinations problems in one, though two of them are very easy. $n = 4$ in all cases, since there are four colors to choose from, but you have to consider the possibilities when $k = 1$, $k = 2$, and $k = 3$. When $k = 1$, there are four possibilities; she could use any of the four colors. When $k = 3$, there are also four possibilities: she could leave out any of the four colors.

For 2 colors, use the formula:
$$c = \frac{n!}{k!(n-k)!} = \frac{4!}{2!(4-2)!} = \frac{4\times3\times2\times1}{2\times1\times2\times1} = 6$$
Thus, the total number of color combinations is $4 + 4 + 6 = 14$, choice (C).

357.   A

EXPL: The team we're looking for will choose 1 person from a population of 10 with professional experience. There are 10 such choices. The team will also have 2 people from the remaining 8 who do not have professional experience. The number of such choices is determined by the combinations formula:
$$\frac{n!}{k!(n-k)!} = \frac{8!}{2!(8-2)!} = \frac{8!}{2!6!} = \frac{8\times7}{2} = 28$$
Since there are 10 choices for the one professional and 28 choices for the pairs of non-professionals, the total number of possible teams is the product:
$$28 \times 10 = 280, \text{ choice (A).}$$

358.   C

Since an equal number of violinists and cellists must play the piece, there are two possible total numbers of performers: there will either be one of each, or two of each.

If there are one of each, there are 6 possible violinists to choose from and 2 possible cellists. That's a total number of groups of $6(2) = 12$.

If there are two of each, there is only one possible group of cellists: the group formed by the two available cellists. To find the number of groups of 2 violinists that could be selected, use the combinations formula, where $n = 6$ and $k = 2$:
$$c = \frac{n!}{k!(n-k)!} = \frac{6!}{2!(6-2)!} = \frac{6\times5}{2} = 15$$
Since there is only one possible group of cellists, the number of 2 violinist/2 cellist groups is 15. Add that to the number of one violinist/one cellist groups, and the total number of possible groups is $15 + 12 = 27$, choice (C).

251   Explanations: Permutations: Drill

1.   There are three possible awardees of the gold, two of the silver, and one of the bronze, so the number of permutations is $3 \times 2 \times 1 = 6$

2.   6 difference companies could be placed in the first office, 5 in the second, etc., down to 1 in the final office:
$$6 \times 5 \times 4 \times 3 \times 2 \times 1 = 720$$

3.   5 different entrants could place first, four second, three third, and so on. The number of permutations is given by:
$$5 \times 4 \times 3 \times 2 \times 1 = 120$$

4.   12 cases could be chosen to go first, 11 second, and 10 third:
$$12 \times 11 \times 10 = 1320$$

5.   10 could be chosen for A, 9 for B, and 8 for C:
$$10 \times 9 \times 8 = 720$$

6.   Any of the 7 managers could work the first shift, leaving 6 possibilities for the second shift, 5 for the third shift, and 4 for the last shift. The resulting number of permutations is:
$$7 \times 6 \times 5 \times 4 = 840$$

7.   If X must be in the middle, only four dancers are being arranged. In the leftmost spot, there are four possibilities; in the next, 3, in the middle spot, only 1 (X), in the next, 2, and in the last, 1. The number of permutations is:
$$4 \times 3 \times 1 \times 2 \times 1 = 24$$

8.   To avoid back-to-back HR meetings, the HR meetings must be 1st, 3rd, and 5th. Thus, the 1st meeting could be any of the 3 HR meetings, the 2nd could be either of the 2 other meetings, the 3rd could be either of the remaining HR meetings, while the 4th is the remaining other meeting and the 5th is the remaining HR meeting. The number of permutations is:
$$3 \times 2 \times 2 \times 1 \times 1 = 12$$

9.   In the front row, any of the three women could be placed in the first seat, either of the remaining two in the next seat, and the last woman in the third seat. The same numbers apply for the men: any of the the three in the first seat of the back row, either of the remaining two in the next, and one in the last. The number of permutations, then, is:
$$3 \times 2 \times 1 \times 3 \times 2 \times 1 = 36$$

10.   Any of the six entrants in race A could be seeded 1st, leaving 5 possible 2nd seeds and 4 possible 3rd seeds. Starting over: any of the six entrants in race B could be seeded 4th, leaving 5 possible 5th seeds and 4 possible 6th seeds. Thus, the number of permutations is:
$$6 \times 5 \times 4 \times 6 \times 5 \times 4 = 14,400$$

252   Explanations: Permutations: Practice

361.   C

EXPL: Each leg of the trip contains a number of options: 2, 3, and 2, to be exact. For each one of the routes she could take from A to B, she could pair it with any of the routes from B to C, and any of the routes from C to D. Thus, the number of possible routes is the product of the three numbers of individual options:

$2 \times 3 \times 2 = 12$, choice (C).

253   Explanations: Permutations: Challenge

364.   C
EXPL: The word "arrangements" signals that this is a permutations question. Since there are seven seats in which to arrange seven children, draw seven lines.

First, deal with the girls. There are three possible girls to put in the second seat, so write a 3 there. That leaves 2 girls for the fourth seat and 1 for the sixth seat:.

Next, fill in the number of possible children for each remaining seat. There are four boys, so for the first seat a boy sits in, there are 4 possibilities. Working your way across the empty seats, there are 3, 2, and 1 possibilities:

Finally, multiply the numbers:

$4 \times 3 \times 3 \times 2 \times 2 \times 1 \times 1 = 144$, choice (C).

365.   B
EXPL: There are nine different possibilities for the first digit: anything between 1 and 9. The tricky part of this question is moving to the second digit. Again, there are nine possibilities for the second digit: any number between 0 and 9, not including the one using for the first digit. Remember, a three-digit number can have zero as a digit, just not as the first digit. Finally, the third digit has eight possibilities: anything between 0 and 9 except for the two digits used already. The number of possible integers, then, is:

$9 \times 9 \times 8 = 648$, choice (B).

366.   E
EXPL: While this looks like a probability question, the probability component isn't much of a challenge. There's only one matching code, so the number of desired outcomes (the numerator) must be one. The more difficult part of this question is determining how many different codes there are: the number of possible outcomes.

Since the letters may repeat, there are 6 possibilities for the first letter, 6 for the second, and 6 for the third. The total number of possible codes, then, is:

$6 \times 6 \times 6 = 216$

The probability is $\frac{1}{216}$, choice (E).

367.   C
EXPL: Usually with permutation questions, you can work through the various possibilities from left to right.   However, since the restriction on this question is that the numbers must be odd, we need to start with the last digit, the one that determines whether the number is even or odd.

There are 5 possibilities for the final digit: 1, 3, 5, 7, and 9.   The first digit has 8 possibilities: any number from 1 to 9 except for the number in the final digit. The tens' digit has 8 possibilities: any number between 0 and 9, except for the two already chosen. The hundreds' digit has 7 possibilities: any number between 0 and 9, except for the three already chosen. The number of possibilities is:

$5 \times 8 \times 8 \times 7 = 2240$, choice (C).

368.   C

EXPL: If there weren't repeated letters, this would be an easy question. To find the number of distinct sequenes, we take the factorial of the number of letters:

$6! = 6 \times 5 \times 4 \times 3 \times 2 \times 1 = 720$

However, there are repeated letters. So, those 720 sequences contain some duplicates. For instance, since there are 2 X's, we've counted each permutation twice. XXYYZZ is the same as XXYYZZ, even though the X's might be in a "different order." Since we've counted each of those X arrangements twice, we need to divide 720 by 2, leaving us with 360. But wait–we've counted all the Y arrangements twice, too. Divide by 2 again, and now our number is 180. Finally, we've double-counted each of the Z arrangements, so we need to divide by 2 one more time. $\frac{180}{2} = 90$, choice (C).

254   Explanations: Symbolism: Drill

All of the following exercises refer to one or more of the following:

a.   If $y \neq 0$, $x \Leftrightarrow y = \frac{x^2}{y}$

b. $a \spadesuit b = (a - b)(a + b)$

c. $p \oplus q = |2p - q|$

1. $4 \spadesuit 5$

   $a \spadesuit b = (a - b)(a + b)$
   $4 \spadesuit 5 = (4 - 5)(4 + 5) = (-1)(9) = -9$

2. $1 \oplus 3$

   $p \oplus q = |2p - q|$
   $1 \oplus 3 = |2(1) - 3| = |-1| = 1$

3. $2 \Leftrightarrow 6$

   If $y \neq 0$, $x \Leftrightarrow y = \frac{x^2}{y}$
   $2 \Leftrightarrow 6 = \frac{2^2}{6} = \frac{4}{6} = \frac{2}{3}$

4. $\left(-\frac{3}{2}\right) \oplus \frac{1}{2}$

   $p \oplus q = |2p - q|$
   $\left(-\frac{3}{2}\right) \oplus \frac{1}{2} = \left|2\left(-\frac{3}{2}\right) - \frac{1}{2}\right| = \left|-3 - \frac{1}{2}\right| = \left|-3\frac{1}{2}\right| = 3\frac{1}{2}$

5. $(-2) \spadesuit (-4)$

   $a \spadesuit b = (a - b)(a + b)$
   $(-2) \spadesuit (-4) = (-2 - (-4))(-2 + (-4)) = (2)(-6) = -12$

6. $(-3) \Leftrightarrow \frac{1}{3}$

   If $y \neq 0$, $x \Leftrightarrow y = \frac{x^2}{y}$
   $(-3) \Leftrightarrow \frac{1}{3} = \frac{(-3)^2}{\frac{1}{3}} = \frac{9}{\frac{1}{3}} = 27$

7. $(1 \oplus 2) \oplus 3$

   $p \oplus q = |2p - q|$
   $1 \oplus 2 = |2(1) - 2| = |0| = 0$
   $0 \oplus 3 = |2(0) - 3| = |-3| = 3$

8. $(\sqrt{2} \Leftrightarrow \sqrt{2}) \Leftrightarrow (2 \Leftrightarrow 2)$

   If $y \neq 0$, $x \Leftrightarrow y = \frac{x^2}{y}$
   $(\sqrt{2} \Leftrightarrow \sqrt{2}) = \frac{(\sqrt{2})^2}{\sqrt{2}} = \sqrt{2}$
   $(2 \Leftrightarrow 2) = \frac{2^2}{2} = 2$
   $(\sqrt{2} \Leftrightarrow 2) = \frac{(\sqrt{2})^2}{2} = \frac{2}{2} = 1$

9. $(-1) \spadesuit (3 \spadesuit 6)$

   $a \spadesuit b = (a - b)(a + b)$
   $3 \spadesuit 6 = (3 - 6)(3 + 6) = (-3)(9) = -27$
   $(-1) \spadesuit (-27) = (-1 - (-27))(-1 + (-27)) = (26)(-28) = -728$

10. $(0 \Leftrightarrow 0.5) \spadesuit (0.5 \oplus 0)$

   If $y \neq 0$, $x \Leftrightarrow y = \frac{x^2}{y}$
   $0 \Leftrightarrow 0.5 = \frac{0^2}{\frac{1}{2}} = 0$

$p \oplus q = |2p - q|$

$0.5 \oplus 0 = |2(0.5) - 0| = |1 - 0| = |1| = 1$

$a \spadesuit b = (a - b)(a + b)$

$0 \spadesuit 1 = (0 - 1)(0 + 1) = (-1)(1) = -1$

255   Explanations: Symbolism: Practice

371.   A
EXPL: The question gives you the rule for @, so plug in the given values:
$m = 2$ and $n = -4$.

$(m + n)(m - n)$

$(2 + (-4))(2 - (-4))$

$(2 - 4)(2 + 4) = (-2)(6) = -12$, choice (A).

372.   E
EXPL: When a symbol represents an operation, there's often no choice but to evaluate each statement by considering each possible operation. This gets faster with practice, but there's no great shortcut.

Statement (1) is insufficient: if $2 \blacktriangleright 3 = 3 \blacktriangleright 2$, the symbol could stand for addition or multiplication:

$2 + 3 = 3 + 2$

$2 \times 3 = 3 \times 2$

The equation does not hold true with subtraction or division. If the operation is addition, $2 \blacktriangleright 3 = 5$; if it is multiplication, $2 \blacktriangleright 3 = 6$.

Statement (2) is also insufficient: again, the symbol could be addition or multiplication, but not subtraction or division:

$2 + 3 > 4$

$2 \times 3 > 4$

As in the reasoning for (1), the two possible operations result in different answers to the question.

Taken together, the statements are still insufficient. Both statements fail to differentiate between addition and multiplication, so there are two possible operations that the symbol could represent. As we've seen, that gives two possible answers to the question. (E) is the correct choice.

373.   D
EXPL: Given the rule for $a * b$, plug in the values given: $a = 3$ and $b = -2$:

$ab + a(2 - b)$

$3(-2) + 3(2 - (-2))$

$-6 + 3(4) = -6 + 12 = 6$, choice (D).

256   Explanations: Symbolism: Challenge

374.   E

EXPL: The question gives you the rule for the symbol ˆˆ, so given the equation $x\,\hat{}\,\hat{}\,4 = 9$, plug in $p = x$ and $q = 4$, and set the result equal to 9:

$x\,\hat{}\,\hat{}\,4 = 9$

$(x + 4)(x - 4) = 9$

$x^2 - 16 = 9$

$x^2 - 25 = 0$

$x = \pm 5$

There are two possible values for x, as suggested by the question itself, which uses the phrasing "could be the value of x" instead of something more concrete. The only one of those two values among the answer choices is -5, choice (E).

375.   B

EXPL: As with any non-symbolism algebra problem, start with the expression inside the parentheses. If $m * n = \frac{m^2}{n}$, then $-3 * -2 = \frac{(-3)^2}{-2} = \frac{9}{-2} = -\frac{9}{2}$

Now, find the value of $6 * -\frac{9}{2}$:

$\frac{6^2}{-\frac{9}{2}} = 36(-\frac{2}{9}) = 4(-2) = -8$, choice (B).

376.   E

Explanation: Use order of operations and start with the expression inside the parentheses. For $5 \Diamond 2$, $y = 5$ and $t = 2$:

$\frac{y}{t^2} = \frac{5}{2^2} = \frac{5}{4}$

Now the question is:

$\frac{5}{4} \Diamond 5 =$

Here, $y = \frac{5}{4}$ and $t = 5$, so:

$\frac{y}{t^2} = \frac{\frac{5}{4}}{5^2} = \frac{\frac{5}{4}}{25} = \frac{5}{4} \times \frac{1}{25} = \frac{1}{20}$, choice (E).

257   Explanations: Functions: Drill

1.   Evaluate each of the following for the function $f(x) = \frac{x+1}{x-1}$:

    a. $f(3) = \frac{3+1}{3-1} = \frac{4}{2} = 2$

    b. $f(\frac{1}{2}) = \frac{\frac{1}{2}+1}{\frac{1}{2}-1} = \frac{\frac{3}{2}}{-\frac{1}{2}} = \frac{3}{2} \times -\frac{2}{1} = -3$

    c. $f(2) = \frac{2+1}{2-1} = \frac{3}{1} = 3$

           $f(3) = \frac{3+1}{3-1} = \frac{4}{2} = 2$

    d. $f(x+2) = \frac{(x+2)+1}{(x+2)-1} = \frac{x+3}{x+1}$

2.   Evaluate each of the following for the function $f(x) = 2^{-x}$:

    a. $f(4) = 2^{-4} = \frac{1}{2^4} = \frac{1}{16}$

    b. $f(-\frac{1}{2}) = 2^{-(-\frac{1}{2})} = 2^{\frac{1}{2}} = \sqrt{2}$

    c. $f(0) = 2^{-0} = 2^0 = 1$

           $f(1) = 2^{-1} = \frac{1}{2^1} = \frac{1}{2}$

3.   For which of the following functions is $f(0) = 1$?

    For each function, figure out what $f(0)$ equals:

    a. $f(0) = (0-1)^2 = (-1)^2 = 1$

           True

    b. $f(0) = 0^0 = 1$

           True

    c. $f(0) = 0(0-1)(0+1) = 0(-1)(1) = 0$

           False

258 Explanations: Functions: Challenge

381.   B

EXPL: For each choice, try both $f(0)$ and $f(1)$, seeing if they have the same value:

(A): $f(0) = 0 + 1 = 1$; $f(1) = 1 + 1 = 2$. Not equal.
(B): $f(0) = 0^0 = 1$; $f(1) = 1^1 = 1$. Equal–this is the correct choice.
(C): $f(0) = 0^2 - 1 = -1$; $f(1) = 1^2 - 1 = 0$. Not equal.
(D): $f(0) = \frac{0-1}{0+1} = -1$; $f(1) = \frac{1-1}{1+1} = 0$. Not equal.
(E): $f(0) = (0+1)^2 = 1$; $f(1) = (1+1)^2 = 4$. Not equal.

Choice (B) is correct.

382.   E

EXPL: First, evaluate $f(7)$ and $f(3)$ individually:
$f(7) = (7+1)(7-1) = 8(6) = 48$
$f(3) = (3+1)(3-1) = 4(2) = 8$
$f(7) - f(3)$, then, is $48 - 8 = 40$, choice (E).

383.   D

EXPL: Go through each of the choices to determine the value of $f(f(3))$:

(A): $f(3) = \frac{3+1}{3-1} = 2$; $f(2) = \frac{2+1}{2-1} = 3$
(B): $f(3) = -3$; $f(-3) = -(-3) = 3$
(C): $f(3) = \frac{1}{3}$; $f(\frac{1}{3}) = \frac{1}{\frac{1}{3}} = 3$
(D): $f(3) = 3 - 1 = 2$; $f(2) = 2 - 1 = 1$
(E): $f(3) = 3$; $f(3) = 3$

Choice (D) is the only one that doesn't evaluate to 3, so it must be the correct answer.

384.   D

As with many functions problems, the hardest part is understanding the given rule. In this case, the function "maxint" provides two numbers, and the value of the function is the largest integer between the two numbers. The value of $\text{maxint}(7, k)$ depends, of course, on the value of k. If k is less than 7, the function equals 7; if k is greater than 7, it gets more complicated.

Statement (1) is sufficient. As noted, if k is less than 7, the maximum integer between k and 7 is 7.

Statement (2) is also sufficient. This one is trickier. If k is less than 8, it could be greater than 7, but it cannot be greater than an integer that is larger than 7. For instance, if $k = 7.99$, the function is $\text{maxint}(7, 7.99)$. The largest integer between those two points is 7. Unless k could be equal or greater than 8 (which this statement tells us it is not), the value of the function must be 7. Choice (D) is correct.

385.   D

There are two ways to solve this problem.   The first way is easier but does not take advantage of the formula provided.   In any set of equally-spaced numbers, the mean and median are equal, and the mean and the median are equal to the midpoint of the two endpoints.   In this case, that means the mean is the midpoint of 250 and 350, or 300.   There are 101 numbers between 250 and 350 inclusive, so the sum of the numbers is the product of the mean and the number of terms:

$101(300) = 30,300$, choice (D).

The alternative is to use the formula.   The sum of the integers between 250 and 350 can be thought of as the difference between the sum of the integers up to 350 and the sum of the integers up to 249.   We can use the formula to figure out both of those:

$$\frac{350(351)}{2} - \frac{249(250)}{2}$$

That's more arithmetic than we want to do, so approximate:

$$\frac{350^2}{2} - \frac{250^2}{2}$$
$$= \frac{350^2 - 250^2}{2}$$

Now use the difference of squares to simplify:

$$= \frac{(350+250)(350-250)}{2}$$
$$= \frac{600(100)}{2} = 300(100) = 30,000$$

We've approximated, so it's no surprise that the answer doesn't match up exactly.   It's close, though, and (D) is correct.

259   Explanations: Sequences: Drill

1.   a. $S_1 = 2(1) - 1 = 2 - 1 = 1$
$S_2 = 2(2) - 1 = 4 - 1 = 3$
$S_3 = 2(3) - 1 = 6 - 1 = 5$
$S_4 = 2(4) - 1 = 8 - 1 = 7$
$S_5 = 2(5) - 1 = 10 - 1 = 9$

   b. $S_1 = 1 - \frac{1}{2^1} = 1 - \frac{1}{2} = \frac{1}{2}$
$S_2 = 1 - \frac{1}{2^2} = 1 - \frac{1}{4} = \frac{3}{4}$
$S_3 = 1 - \frac{1}{2^3} = 1 - \frac{1}{8} = \frac{7}{8}$
$S_4 = 1 - \frac{1}{2^4} = 1 - \frac{1}{16} = \frac{15}{16}$
$S_5 = 1 - \frac{1}{2^5} = 1 - \frac{1}{32} = \frac{31}{32}$

   c. $S_1 = \frac{1-1}{1+1} = \frac{0}{2} = 0$
$S_2 = \frac{1-2}{2+1} = -\frac{1}{3}$
$S_3 = \frac{1-3}{3+1} = \frac{2}{4} = -\frac{1}{2}$
$S_4 = \frac{1-4}{4+1} = -\frac{3}{5}$
$S_5 = \frac{1-5}{5+1} = \frac{4}{6} = -\frac{2}{3}$

   d. $S_1 = (-1)^1 - (-2)^1 = (-1) - (-2) = -1 + 2 = 1$
$S_2 = (-1)^2 - (-2)^2 = 1 - 4 = -3$
$S_3 = (-1)^3 - (-2)^3 = 1 - (-8) = 9$
$S_4 = (-1)^4 - (-2)^4 = 1 - 16 = -15$
$S_5 = (-1)^5 - (-2)^5 = 1 - (-32) = 33$

2.   a. $S_3 = S_2 - S_1 = 3 - 2 = 1$
$S_4 = S_3 - S_2 = 1 - 3 = -2$
$S_5 = S_4 - S_3 = -2 - 1 = -3$

   b. $S_3 = (S_2)(S_1) = 4(1) = 4$
$S_4 = (S_3)(S_2) = 4(4) = 16$
$S_5 = (S_4)(S_3) = 16(4) = 64$

   c. $S_3 = S_1 = 5$
$S_4 = S_2 = 10$
$S_5 = S_3 = 5$

3.   a. $S_k = \frac{144}{2^{k-1}}$

   b. $S_k = k^2 - 1$

   c. $S_k = 3k - 10$

260   Explanations: Sequences: Practice

391.   C

EXPL: Judging from the sequence given, each number is one-third of the number that precedes it. Thus, if we continue the sequence, it looks like this:

$$270, 90, 30, 10, \frac{10}{3}, \frac{10}{9}, \frac{10}{27}$$

$\frac{10}{9}$ is the last number that is greater than 1, giving us a total of 6 numbers in the sequence that are greater than 1. Choice (C) is correct.

392.   C

We don't need to find the complete 100-term sequence of S, we will need to find something about the rule governing the sequence.

Statement (1) is insufficient. It gives us the rule, but nothing to anchor it to. If we knew that the first term was 10, we could add 4 enough times and eventually find the 83rd term. However, without some term to help us find the concrete values of the rest, we can't find the 83rd term.

Statement (2) is also insufficient. It gives us a relationship between two terms, but again, no actual numbers. Also, there is no guarantee that a certain type of pattern governs the whole sequence unless we are directly told that it does. We don't know, for instance, that the 82nd term would be twice the 80th term.

Taken together, the statements are sufficient. If each term is 4 greater than the preceding term, the 84th term is 8 greater than the 82nd term. Call the 84th term x and the 82nd term y:

$x = y + 8$

$x = 2y$

With two variables and two linear equations, we can solve for those two terms. It turns out that $x = 16$ and $y = 8$, meaning that the 83rd term must be 12. Choice (C) is correct.

261   Explanations: Sequences: Challenge

394.   E
EXPL: To find the value of s_6, you'll need the value of both s_5 and s_4. You're given s_5, but not s_4. You can find that by setting up the following equation:

$s_5 = (s_4)(s_3)$
$8 = (s_4)(2)$
$s_4 = 4$

Now that you have s_4, you can solve for s_6:
$s_6 = (s_5)(s_4) = (8)(4) = 32$, choice (E).

395.   E
EXPL: The easiest way to tackle this problem is to use an example set for p, r, s, t, u. Since the only restriction is that the numbers are equally spaced, you can use $\{1, 2, 3, 4, 5\}$. The object is to look at each of the five sets in the answer choices and determine which of them is most widely spaced, using those five numbers for the corresponding variables:

(A) 1, 2, 3, 4, 5
(B) $\frac{1}{2}$, 1, $\frac{3}{2}$, 2, $\frac{5}{2}$
(C) 5, 6, 7, 8, 9
(D) 5, 7, 9, 11, 13
(E) 5, 8, 11, 14, 17

So, the differences between each term in the choices are as follows:

(A) 1
(B) $\frac{1}{2}$
(C) 1
(D) 2
(E) 3

So, the largest value of k (the space between terms) occurs in (E).

396.   D
EXPL: Statement (1) is sufficient. Recognize that all the subsets of three consecutive terms overlap: so in a set like $\{1, 3, 9, 27, 81\}$, not only are $\{1,3,9\}$ and $\{9,27,81\}$ subsets, $\{3,9,27\}$ is as well. So, if $\{1,3,9\}$ is a geometric progression, then the quotient between the second pair of terms (3 and 9) must be the same quotient between the next two terms in the series, or else $\{3,9,27\}$ wouldn't be a geometric progression.

Statement (2) is also sufficient. Not only does the statement tell you that each two successive numbers have the same quotient, it tells you what that quotient is. Choice (D) is correct.

397.   A
EXPL: First, get a grasp of the sequence. Since we're interested in the factors that every term shares, notice that every term is a multiple of 6. Since

the first term is 6, the largest factor that every term shares is itself 6; since we're interested in prime factors, we can limit ourselves to 2 and 3. While subsequent members of the series may have other prime factors (for instance, 66 is divisible by 11), 2 and 3 are the only primes that every term is divisible by.

Statement (1) is sufficient: if p is greater than 3, the answer to the question is "no:" every term in T is NOT divisible by p.

Statement (2) is not sufficient: if at least one term in T is divisible by p, p could be 2 or 3 (as we've seen–every term is divisible by those) or 11 (which is divisible by at least one term–66–but not all the others). Depending on which of those values p represents, a different answer results. (A) is the correct choice.

398.   B

EXPL: First, understand what the question is describing. We don't have any concrete numbers to work with, but let's say that, when $x = 0$, $p = 8$ and $q = 8$. Thus, when x is increased by 1, p decreases by a factor of 4 (is divided by 4) and becomes 2, while q decreases by a factor of 2 and becomes 4. If we know what the numbers are, we can work out the sequence.

Statement (1) is insufficient. If $p = q + 2$ when $x = 6$, each of the variables will have been decreased by their respective factors twice by the time that $x = 8$. p is divided by 16 and q is divided by 4:

$\frac{p}{16} = \frac{q}{4} + 2$

$p = 4q + 32$

Thus, when $x = 8$, $\frac{p}{q} = \frac{4q+32}{q}$. There's no way to simplify that without knowing the value of q, which we don't.

Statement (2) is sufficient. If $p = 3q$ when $x = 7$, each of the variables will have been decreased by their respective factors once by the time that $x = 8$. p is divided by 4 and q is divided by 2:

$\frac{p}{4} = 3\frac{q}{2}$

$p = 6q$

We can now simplify $\frac{p}{q} = \frac{6q}{q} = 6$. We have an answer, so choice (B) is correct.

399.   B

First note that as n gets larger, a_n, or $2^{10-n} - n$, gets smaller. Not only does the exponent decrease, but the amount (n) that is subtracted gets larger. Try the first couple of numbers:

$n = 1$: $2^9 - 1$. You might know that $2^9 = 512$, but even if you don't, it's a good bet that this term is greater than zero.

$n = 2$: $2^8 - 2$. Again, you don't have to calculate to know that this term is greater than zero.

Since the numbers are quite large at this point, skip a few to save time.

$n = 6$: $2^{10-6} - 6 = 2^4 - 6 = 10$. Still positive. Since all the preceding terms must be larger, we know that at least the first six terms are positive.

$n = 7$: $2^{10-7} - 7 = 2^3 - 7 = 1$. Still positive, but just barely. It should be clear that since the exponent will get smaller and the amount subtracted will get smaller, when $n = 8$, the term will definitely be negative. Thus, we've found all the positive terms, so there is a total of 7, choice (B).

Made in the USA
Charleston, SC
22 August 2010